THE LIFE AND ADVENTURES OF ELI WIGGILL

THE LIFE AND ADVENTURES OF ELI WIGGILL

SOUTH AFRICAN 1820 SETTLER, WESLEYAN MISSIONARY, AND LATTER-DAY SAINT

Edited by Fred E. Woods, Jay H. Buckley, and Hunter T. Hallows

GREG KOFFORD BOOKS
SALT LAKE CITY, 2024

Copyright © 2024 Fred E. Woods, Jay H. Buckley, and Hunter T. Hallows
Cover design copyright © 2024 Greg Kofford Books, Inc.
Cover design by Loyd Isao Ericson

Published in the USA.

All rights reserved. No part of this volume may be reproduced in any form without written permission from the publisher, Greg Kofford Books. The views expressed herein are the responsibility of the authors and do not necessarily represent the position of Greg Kofford Books.

ISBN 978-1-58958-804-2 (paperback)
Also available in ebook.

Greg Kofford Books
P. O. Box 1362
Draper, UT 84020
www.gregkofford.com
facebook.com/gkbooks
twitter.com/gkbooks

Library of Congress Control Number: 2024934005

Contents

Preface, vii

Acknowledgments, xiii

The Life and Adventures of Mr. Eli Wiggill, 1

Bibliography, 259

Index, 271

PREFACE

Written in 1883, Eli Wiggill's autobiography encapsulates his family's immigration from Gloucester, England, to South Africa and then to Salt Lake City, Utah Territory. His life epitomizes an inspiring example of the worldwide gathering of the Saints to Zion in the mid-nineteenth century. Eli and his wife, Susannah Bentley Wiggill, joined The Church of Jesus Christ of Latter-day Saints in South Africa while Eli served as a Methodist missionary. Both became stalwart members following their conversion. Eli and Susannah Wiggill's faithful dedication affected the lives of hundreds of South African Saints. His autobiography reveals the details about their immigration from England to South Africa, their conversion to the restored gospel, their missionary labors, their role in congregation formation and leadership, and their efforts to gather to Zion whilst building up and strengthening communities of South African Saints during the 1850s, 1860s, and 1870s.[1]

Wiggill's autobiography chronicles Eli and Susannah Wiggill's great faith and their missionary efforts after their conversion to form a community of South African Saints. Studying their lives and writings reveals how early missionaries like Elder William Walker preached basic gospel principles such as faith, repentance, and baptism. Their record chronicles the opposition and persecution missionaries and converts faced, and their lives provide insights into early church organization and the formation of branches. Finally, Wiggill's journal documents how his and Susannah's experiences represent one of the most well-documented accounts of South African Saints answering the call to immigrate to Zion.

On November 5, 1811, Isaac and Elizabeth Grimes Wiggill welcomed son Eli into their family living in Painswick, Gloucestershire, England. Eli became the oldest of eight children eventually born to Isaac and Elizabeth.

---

1. Eli Wiggill (November 5, 1810–April 13, 1884), also spelled Wiggall and Wiggell, was one of the earliest LDS converts in the Eastern Cape. He eventually served as the branch president in Port Elizabeth. He represents one of the few South African converts to keep an extensive journal, both before and after his conversion to the Church. We thank Nancy and Mike Wiggill for their assistance with finding additional information about Eli Wiggill and his family. This study of Wiggill's life is based upon research from his unpublished, handwritten autobiography: Eli Wiggill, "Autobiography," MSS 9137. For additional biographies see Jay H. Buckley and Joshua Rust, "Eli and Susannah Wiggill: South African Saints," 129–42; Kate B. Carter, "Eli Wiggill," 8:169–212; Michael T. Lowe, *African Eden II: The Lowes of South Africa*; Fred E. Woods, "From South Africa to Salt Lake City: Eli Wiggill, the Latter-day Saints, and the World of Religion," 1–22.

Isaac's profession as a millwright and carpenter served the family well. On January 10, 1820, Isaac, Elizabeth, Eli and his siblings George, Joseph, and Elizabeth decided to leave England and start a new life in South Africa. They embarked from Bristol, joining the Samuel Bradshaw Company of sixty-four emigrants aboard the *Kennersley Castle*, arriving in Cape Town, South Africa, on March 5, 1820, after a four-month voyage from England. These 1820 British Settlers, as they were known, then traveled east through the Indian Ocean to Algoa Bay and the harbor city of Port Elizabeth in the Eastern Cape. They trekked inland and settled in Lemon Valley, which they renamed New Gloucester. Additional siblings born in South Africa include Elijah, Jane, Mary Ann, and Jacob.

Eli apprenticed with his father, an industrious builder who crafted mills, wagons, and plows and did other carpentry work for a living. When his mother Elizabeth died in 1827, she left behind all eight children. As the oldest son, Eli recognized he needed to learn a trade to help care for his family. He chose wagon-making and became a wheelwright, spending about a year away from home. Meanwhile, his father Isaac married Mary Sears.

Twenty-two-year-old Eli continued in his wagon-making and carpentry profession and married nineteen-year-old Susannah Bentley on February 20, 1831, in Grahamstown, Cape Colony, South Africa. They lived in various locales—including Grahamstown, Bathurst, Thaba 'Nchu, Winterberg, Port Retief, Portugals Rivier, Bongolo, Queenstown, and Port Elizabeth [Algoa Bay]—and raised four sons and six daughters: John Wesley, Sarah Ann, Jemima Rosetta, Jeremiah Francis, Sarah Ann Susannah, Margaret Alice, Rosannah Maria, France Amelia, Joseph Elijah, and Abram.

Eli and Susannah moved to Grahamstown where they lived some of the most comfortable and happy years of their lives.[2] Wiggill was always a professed man of God; soon after moving to Grahamstown, he sold his property and became a Wesleyan Methodist assistant minister to Reverend John Edwards. He traveled to various places along the South African frontier. During his ministry in Umpukani [Umpukane] Station, he taught the gospel in English and learned a smattering of Dutch/Afrikaans. He was released from his mission in 1842 and settled in Queenstown.

At Queenstown, Wiggill met Elder William H. Walker and other Latter-day Saint missionaries, who baptized Eli's brother George and George's wife Mary Ann Wiggill. Eli purchased every available book or pamphlet on LDS doctrine and read them. He related that "on the road home my mind was so full of light and knowage [knowledge] of the scriptures and it seemed to me that I could see the meaning of every text in the Bible, so when I

---

2. Wiggill, "Autobiography," 111.

got home my Wife said she thought I had got completely converted to Mormonism."[3] Thereafter he dedicated his leisure time to studying his new library. This awoke the missionary spirit in him so much that he "had a great many arguments with religious people with whom I was surrounded and especially with my Wesleyan Brethren."[4] Unfortunately, Wiggill's zeal towards a peculiar American Christian religion brought harsh criticism, censure, and opprobrium from their acquaintances. Susannah asked Eli to stop investigating further, citing as evidence their friends had already distanced themselves and several potential business clients refused to engage in trade with Wiggill because of his favorable view of Mormonism.

After about a year of unofficial dedication to the Church, Eli, Susannah, and two daughters were baptized and confirmed members of the Church by Elder John Green, who traveled a hundred miles to Winterberg to perform the ordinance on March 1, 1858. Soon thereafter, Eli and Susannah sold their beloved Queenstown property and purchased a nearby farm in Bongolo, where he and his family held Sunday meetings attended by the Talbots and other converts.[5] Some Methodist friends tried to convince Wiggill of his supposed folly in being baptized. He rebuffed them. In one iconic instance he recorded the words of a confounded Methodist preacher who, in Eli's words, claimed "there was no use in talking or arguing with me for it seemed to him that I knew the Bible from end to end by heart."[6] Eli's dedication to the Church continued as he, Henry Talbot, and Talbot's son Henry James Talbot began their proselytizing in Bongolo and Queenstown to help establish the Church.

Eventually, many of the converted Saints decided to gather to Zion and travel to Utah Territory in the United States, a massive undertaking that carried them across the Atlantic Ocean and overland to Salt Lake City. To prepare for the exodus, Henry and Ruth Talbot sold their Bongolo property and moved their family to Port Elizabeth in 1860. Eli and Susannah Wiggill prepared to do the same, although they faced several setbacks when floods inundated their home and farm in Bongolo near Queenstown.[7]

After they sold their property and moved to Port Elizabeth, Latter-day Saint Church leaders called Eli Wiggill as the conference president and Henry Talbot as branch president of the forty Port Elizabeth Saints.[8] Over the next year they strengthened the Port Elizabeth branch and prepared for their overseas journey. Between 1855 and 1865, at least 270 Saints emigrated to the

---

3. Wiggill, 366–67.
4. Wiggill, 372.
5. Wiggill, 401.
6. Wiggill, 385.
7. Wiggill, 423.
8. Wiggill, 426.

United States from the Port Elizabeth seaport, the most populous city in the Eastern Cape province. Most of these early converts were of British descent, and many came from the 1820 British Settler groups since the early missionaries did not learn to speak Afrikaans. As the Saints in Port Elizabeth prepared for their oceanic voyage, Wiggill and Talbot went to Algoa Bay to build up the branch there. Then, they entrusted the Algoa Bay branch to Edward Slaughter so they could answer the call to gather to Zion. Susannah Wiggill went on a last-minute quest back to Bongolo to entice their son Jeremiah, who had initially declined to go to America, to rejoin the family before they embarked. She succeeded. The Wiggill-Talbot group of South African Saints departed on the bark *Race Horse*, a fast clipper ship, on February 20, 1861. Of the thirty-seven passengers, twenty-eight possessed the surname of Wiggill or Talbot while the Ellis and Wall families comprised the others.

Seasickness plagued Wiggill during the two-month ocean voyage. Luckily, they all arrived without incident in Boston on April 19, 1861, barely a week after the start of the American Civil War. The Saints stayed there while awaiting the arrival of the *Emigrant*, another ship carrying converts bound for Zion. Nine hundred converts from the two ships joined together and traveled by rail to Chicago and on to St. Joseph, Missouri. There they boarded a steamboat and traveled up the Missouri River to Florence (formerly Winter Quarters; now north Omaha). The company purchased supplies and wagons for the arduous overland journey ahead.

Eli and Susannah paid eighty dollars for their wagon and made it more comfortable by fitting it with ride boxes, carpets, and two covers. They purchased six oxen, two cows, and a calf at Florence. After securing their outfit, they departed with the Homer Duncan Company on June 25, 1861. The company included 264 individuals and forty-seven wagons. Eight of those wagons consisted of the South African Saints. Captain Duncan elected Henry Talbot as the chaplain, which the company sustained.[9]

Captain Duncan made use of Wiggill's skills repairing wagons and wheels, and Wiggill grumbled in his journal about having to guard the cattle during the night. Susannah's persistence in bringing their son Jeremiah helped unite the Wiggill and Talbot families further through intermarriage. Jeremiah Wiggill married Priscilla Talbot and Margaret Wiggill married Thomas Talbot.[10] Throughout the journey, Eli and Henry bought supplies and continued to help converts migrate to Salt Lake City.[11] While crossing the Nebraska plains, Henry Talbot reunited with his son John, who had emigrated previ-

---

9. Wiggill, 466.
10. Wiggill, 465–66.
11. Wiggill, 465.

PREFACE

ously and was returning to South Africa to serve a mission. They passed the familiar Mormon Trail sites of Ash Hollow, Chimney Rock, Independence Rock, Devil's Gate, Fort Bridger, Echo Canyon, the Devil's Slide, and Big and Little Mountains. The entire entourage arrived safely in Salt Lake City via Emigration Canyon on September 13, 1861.[12]

Eli and Susannah Wiggill settled initially in Salt Lake City but eventually moved twenty-five miles north to Kaysville and built a home adjacent Holmes Creek because Susannah claimed that the cold dampness in Salt Lake was bad for her health.[13] After a few years of living peacefully in Kaysville, fifty-six-year-old Susannah passed away on August 29, 1869. Following her death, Wiggill was set apart as a missionary by George Q. Cannon. Wiggill returned to South Africa where he blessed and named many children and baptized one man by the name of Cook. He preached in the Queenstown area to many diamond prospectors and converts. Having left Salt Lake City on December 12, 1869, Wiggill sailed for Boston from Cape Town on March 12, 1873, a voyage that took six weeks. Wiggill returned home to Salt Lake City on May 26, 1873, and was released, having completed his three-and-a-half-year South African sojourn.

Once back in Utah Territory, Wiggill entered the final stage of his life. His autobiography ends with his return to Salt Lake City; his granddaughter, Susannah (Susie) Margaret Lowe Dodge, helped him complete his account, recording the last ten years of Wiggill's life in six pages. On April 13, 1884, Eli Wiggill passed away in Salt Lake City at the age of seventy-three and was buried next to Susannah in the Kaysville City Cemetery.

Wiggill's autobiography highlights wide-ranging experiences in southern Africa, beginning with his arrival as a ten-year-old boy to the Eastern Cape in 1820 with his parents, siblings, and others among the first group of British settlers to the area. Wiggill vividly describes several decades including several years as a Wesleyan Methodist missionary in Bechuanaland, the emancipation of slavery in the British Cape Colony (1834), and the Xhosa frontier wars. On a personal and religious level, he documents his conversion to The Church of Jesus Christ of Latter-day Saints (1858) and his ecclesiastical service as an LDS Church leader in Port Elizabeth (1860). Following the details of his four decades in South Africa, Wiggill's narrative provides an account of his immigration to Utah (1861) as well as his experiences when he lived in Salt Lake City and Kaysville, Utah, during the 1860s. It further records his 1869 return to South Africa as a missionary "to see his friends" until his return to the United States in 1873.

Wiggill's autobiography provides an authentic voice that deserves to be heard—one that offers a vivid description of life among a mixture of Dutch,

---

12. Wiggill, 471, 485.
13. Wiggill, 490.

English, and native indigenous African peoples as well as the early beginnings of The Church of Jesus Christ of Latter-day Saints in southern Africa, some two decades after the Church was founded in New York.

The valuable handwritten, four-volume original manuscript of the "Autobiography of Eli Wiggill" is housed at the L. Tom Perry Special Collections, Harold B. Lee Library, Brigham Young University in Provo, Utah, USA. A copy of this manuscript also resides at the Church History Library, Salt Lake City, Utah, USA, which is the official library for The Church of Jesus Christ of Latter-day Saints.[14] The Church History Library also houses "The History of Eli Wiggill"—a typescript of the autobiography that was compiled by Mearl Kay Bair, a Wiggill descendant.[15] According to Bair, the autobiography was passed down through the Wiggill family, and in his typescript he "made minor corrections, changed some chapter headings and bolded names of people mentioned." Bair's work is hosted online at the 1820 British Settlers to South Africa website.[16]

Furthermore, in 2008, Vivienne Meston, another Wiggill descendant, completed "The Life and Adventures of Eli Wiggill: An 1820 Settler with Explanations, Commentary and Illustrations." This unpublished manuscript was later deposited at the Cory Library, Rhodes University, Eastern Cape, South Africa. This work was similar to what Bair had done but with more editorial additions. Both of these works are helpful in gleaning information for research, especially with names but, in both cases, these unpublished works do not follow the Eli Wiggill autobiography with exactness. Neither followed standard academic editorial procedures nor scholarly attribution practices, leaving their manuscripts unclear with precisely what Wiggill wrote and what the well-intended descendants had supplemented, added, or modified.

For this publication of Wiggill's autobiography, the editors have sought to rectify these shortcomings by providing an exact typescript of Wiggill's original manuscript and have augmented it with hundreds of additional footnotes to assist and inform the reader regarding flora, fauna, geographical locations, biographical information, historical background, etc. Unless necessary to decipher meaning, the precise grammar and original spelling has been preserved throughout to capture the integrity of the text. Through these efforts we hope to provide greater access to this riveting and important transnational story about crossing borderlands that contains themes as relevant at informing the present as they are at revealing the past.

---

14. "Eli Wiggill Autobiography," Church History Catalog.
15. "Typescript History of Eli Wiggill," Church History Catalog.
16. "Eli Wiggill History," British 1820 Settlers to South Africa.

ACKNOWLEDGMENTS

The editors wish to thank the following institutions and individuals who assisted them with their research: At Brigham Young University, the College of Religious Education and the Department of Church History and Doctrine for financial support; the Harold B. Lee Library Interlibrary Loan staff; Jennifer Schill, Harold B. Lee Library Director of Faculty Services; and Ryan Lee, L. Tom Perry Manuscript Collections Coordinator and Associate Librarian, for the opportunity to review the original Eli Wiggill manuscript. We are particularly grateful to the Religious Education Faculty Support Center staff Ally Bichsel, Kelsi Dynes and, especially, Beverly Yellowhorse, for their proof checking, standardization of bibliographic references, online research, and review of the manuscript. An additional thanks is expressed to Riley Moffat and Jena Lathen for their assistance with proofreading. We thank Marny Parkin for completing the index.

We thank the Albany Museum Grahamstown staff as well as Erika le Roux, Western Cape Archives and Records Service director, and her team for their excellent service provided during our research. We appreciate the assistance of Jan Whitton, archivist of the Cranham Gloucestershire Historical Society. Wiggill descendent Theo N. Wiggill gave permission for the editors to make a copy of his book, *The Cotswolds to the Cape: Isaac Wiggill, 1820 Settler*. Michael T. Lowe granted authorization to use Wiggill family images in his possession and generously shared additional documents. Diana and Russell Lindeman, Keith McPheeters, Jack and Bonnie Herron, Pam Ogden, Robin Petterson, Nancy and Mike Wiggill, as well as other Wiggill family members who also provided useful information. We thank Loyd Isao Ericson and his team for their editorial assistance and Greg Kofford Books for publishing our book. Finally, we thank our wives JoAnna, Becky, and Danielle for their support.

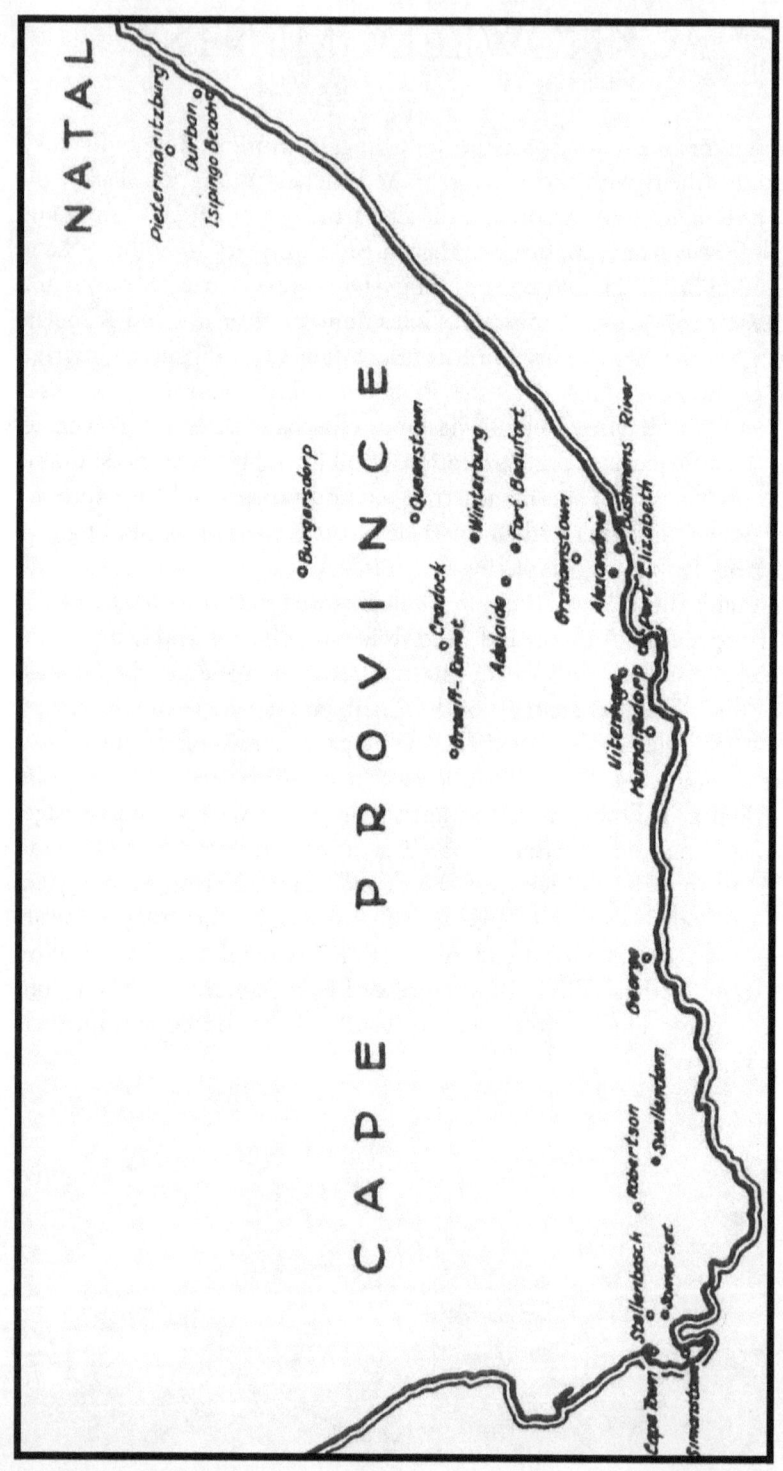

LDS Missionary Activity in South Africa, 1853–65. Adapted from Farrell R. Monson. Courtesy Jay H. Buckley.

The Life and Adventures of Mr. Eli Wiggill.

I was born in Glostershire [Gloucestershire] England[1] in the year of our lord one thousand eight hundred and eleven,[2] on the fifth day of November.

Been the eldest Son of Isica [Isaac] and Elizabath [Elizabeth] Wiggill.[3]

My Mothers maiden name was Grimes of whom I know but little nor do I know but very little on my Fathers side. My father was a Millwright and Carpenter by traid [trade] and in them days He was considered a first class work man.[4] And besides myself there were three other children George Joseph and my sister Elizabath [Elizabeth].

I know but very little of England only I remember going to School and learning the first rudiments of Education untill I was about eight years old.[5] At that time on the 12 day of July being the last day of the session. Mr

---

1. The Wiggill family lived in Gloucestershire, England, for three centuries, commencing in 1609. Eli and his parents lived in the village of Cranham, an English village located a mile or so east of the road between Stroud and Cheltenham. The Cotswold Way long-distance footpath—now recognized as a National Trail—runs nearby.

2. Eli Wiggill was born in 1810, not 1811. See "Eli Wiggill History," British 1820 Settlers to South Africa.

3. C. Pama, *British Families in South Africa: Their Surnames and Origins*, 152 asserts that the name Wiggill comes from Wighill, Yorkshire. For the genealogy of Isaac Wiggill and his posterity from 1789–1986, see the seven-page letter from Douwina M. Wiggill to Ms. Sandra Fold, dated October 25, 1986. For a full treatment on the life of the Isaac and Elizabeth Wiggill family, see Theo N. Wiggill, *The Cotswolds to the Cape: Isaac Wiggill, 1820 Settler*. Nancy Wiggill has spent two decades compiling a fourteen-generation Wiggill family tree which covers the past four hundred years. The editors express appreciation for her assistance in networking to find Wiggill descendants and for introducing us to the http://wiggall-wiggill-wiggle-family.com website.

4. The conclusion of the Napoleonic Wars in 1815 brought about a serious decline to the weaving industry, as military uniforms were no longer in demand. This had a significant economic impact in the region where the Wiggill family lived and contributed to Isaac, a skilled labourer, wanting to find economic opportunity elsewhere. See Wiggill, *The Cotswolds to the Cape*, 53–54.

5. A small school existed in the St. John Baptist Church, the Pitchcombe churchyard in the neighbourhood where the Isaac Wiggill family lived. It was the only school located in Stroud End during the period of 1815–1820, a tithing in Painswick parish, Gloucestershire, near Stroud. Wiggill, *The Cotswolds to the Cape*, 58.

Eli Wiggill, Salt Lake City, 1861. Courtesy Michael T. Lowe.

CHAPTER 1

[Nicholas] Vansittart,[6] Chancellor of the Exchequer, made that far famed speech which was the leading cause of the embarkation for the Cape of Good Hope[7] of more than four thousand Settlers of various descriptions.

Mr. Vansittart is reported to have said: The Cape is suited

[Page 3]

to most of the productions both of temperate and warm climates of the olive and the Mulberry and vine and persons emigrating to this Settlement would soon find themselves comfortable. But my father thought of emigrating to America long before the Africaean emigration was talked of but never made up his mind to untill the emigration to Africa was talked of so strong. It was then he made up his mind to be one of the number of the four thousand souls who left thire native land to find a home in

[Page 4]

South eastern Africa.[8] It was suggestive of little but waterless wilds, burning suns, the deathwinds of the desert, and the slave trade.

In many minds the distinctions of South, East, and West coasts were little recognised, and their differences—physical, climatic, or social hardly known. But despite the appalling, which is so often associated with the unknown, and despite the gloomy pictures drawn by those who would fain have detained them, there was courage enough in the breasts of those pioners, and of their life compani-

[Page 5]

ons, to brave the dangers, real or imaginary, of a voyage to, and a settlement on, the shores of South Africa, although that was the point remotest of all from the land of their birth,

---

6. For a biographical sketch of Nicholas Vansittart, see "The Right Hon. Nicholas Vansittart," 554–56.

7. In 1488 Bartolomeu Dias named the present-day Cape of Good Hope the "stormy cape." Portugal's King John II renamed it the Cape of Good Hope "because the doubling of the Cape gave hope of a sea route to India. [Yet] some authorities believe Dias himself bestowed the name. The term is often extended to include the entire Cape Province." Peter Raper, *Dictionary of Southern African Place Names*, 88.

8. "Eli Wiggill History," 1. For a copy of Vansittart's speech and the immediate reaction to it, see William Wilberforce Bird, *State of the Cape of Good Hope, in 1822*, 272–73. The British government devised the plan to have British emigrants depart from their mother country to ease its troubles of "unemployment and social unrest" and strengthen its trading position in Cape Town, South Africa, at the same time. The strategy included supplying funding for the transport of 4,000 British citizens (out of 80,000 applicants) with the limited resources (£50,000) authorised by the British Parliament. Leonard Thompson, *A History of South Africa*, 52–55. Isaac Wiggill was among the five percent of applicants whose pleas were heard and circumstances accepted. Isaac Wiggill, letter, October 24, 1819.

Algoa Bay. Painting by Charles Peers. Courtesy Western Cape Archives.

But the day came at last like all other days for to embark, which was in December one thousand eight hundred and nineteen and arrived at Cape Town in March one thousand eight hundred and twenty and in April anchored in Algo [Algoa] Bay[9] and safely disembarked on the following morning[10]
[Page 6]

---

9. Algoa Bay is a "large inlet on the Indian Ocean, between Cape Padrone and Cape Recife, on which Port Elizabeth is situated. Named Angra da Roca by Bartolomeu Dias in 1488, it was subsequently renamed *Bahia da Lagoa*, which was corrupted to Algoa Bay." Raper, *Dictionary of Southern African Place Names*, 27. For a first-person account of the voyage, see Thomas Phillips, *Phillips 1820 Settler: His Letters*.

10. The Bradshaw Party, which included the Wiggills, survived difficult spring storms aboard the *Kennersley Castle* before they arrived at Algoa Bay on April 29. Rev. William Shaw, who arrived the following month with the Sephton party at Algoa Bay aboard the *Aurora*, provides a helpful picture of the challenging nature of oceanic arrival at the coast during the spring of 1820. On May 16, 1820, Shaw wrote, "Algoa Bay. We find that many ships have arived before us. Some have landed their portions of the settlers, and are gone; others are waiting their turn in the order of disembarkation, and we of course must wait untill they are cleared before we can disembark. There is such a heavy surf on the beach that the landing of the people and the luggage is tedious and dangerous. The Government have however kindly provided surf boats." *The Journal of William Shaw*, 34.

CHAPTER 1

at its little fishing village. Upon landing, the Settlers were disappointed to find their locations distant full one hundred miles from the port.[11]

Wagons were, however, provided by the government in sufficient number, at the cost of the immigrants, a debt which was afterwards most considerately remitted, as was the charge also of rations issued for several months; in fact, the British government of that day behaved with the greatest liberality to the young Plantation.[12]

On the 18th of April, the

[Page 7]

first or "Chapman party"[13] commenced their inland progress in ninety six wagons from Algoa Bay, afterwards named Port Elizabath [Port Elizabeth], which at that time numbered thirtyfive souls, (including its small garoison [garrison]).

The name of the ship which my father embarked on is Kennersly [Kennersley] Castle[14] and Mr. Bradshow [Bradshaw] had command of the

---

11. The 1820 British settlers expressed disappointment and concern with what they saw after landing at Algoa Bay. Henry James Talbot, a convert to The Church of Jesus Christ of Latter-day Saints in the same year as Eli Wiggill (1858), and whose family was also part of the 1820 British settlers Sephton party, wrote of the bleak and dangerous place where they landed: "At that time the country was a wild and a deserted looking place, Algoa Bay is a bad looking place at best of times, nothing but sand and rocks. It was an awful sight to men and women coming from a city like London to such a barren place like Algoa Bay. No home, no house to shelter them from the storms that seacoast is subject to at all seasons of the year. I have seen the southeast wind blow in Algoa Bay. The sea become very ruf, and blows the fome of the sea all over the town. Many ships came ashore at one time. There were eleven ships wrecked in one of these southeast windstorms. Algoa Bay is a very dangerous port for ships." See "Short Sketch of the Life of Henry James Talbot Sr. in South Africa (An Unfinished Autobiography)," 1. We thank Diana and Russell Lindeman for sharing this document.

12. Not all emigrants approved of the British government's handling of the Eastern Cape, and some left the region within the next few decades. In 1837, P. Retief, a respected emigrant, gave ten reasons for disaffection that resulted in British citizens leaving the Cape region. These complaints included severe losses that occurred because of the emancipation of slaves, plunder by the local indigenous tribes, and dishonest persons. See George McCall Theal, *History of South Africa Since September 1795: The Cape Colony from 1828 to 1846, Natal from 1824 to 1845 and Proceedings of the Emigrant Farmers from 1836 to 1847*, 266–67. For a general history of the British connection between the Cape and South Africa, see A. Wyatt Tilby, *The English People Overseas, vol. 6, South Africa, 1486–1913*.

13. The "Chapman party" refers to the ship *Chapman*, which embarked on December 3, 1819, with British emigrants onboard belonging to the Bailie and Carlisle parties. M. D. Nash, *The Settler Handbook: A New List of the 1820 Settlers*, 35.

14. The *Kennersley Castle* embarked from Bristol, England, on January 10, 1820, transporting the British emigrants from the parties of Bradshaw, Greathead, Holder,

company, or the party that my father belonged too.[15] Mr. Samual [Samuel] Bradshaw was the head of that company and the name of the location was

[Page 8]

called Lemons [Lemon] Valley before it was settled by the new emmigrants, and then it was called New Gloster [Gloucester], after the City that my father came from, The names are as follows; Samual [Samuel] Bradshaw the head of the party. Richard Bradshaw, Isaca [Isaac] Wiggill, S. [Samuel] Burt [Birt],

---

Phillips, and Southey. Nash, *The Settler Handbook,* 35. Thomas Phillips, his wife, and their seven children journeyed with the Wiggill family aboard this ship. Among other things, Phillips recounted the challenges at sea, including the spread of measles and whooping cough and performing his "ministerial duties by committing the bodies of the Deceased Children to the deep." He also described the fierce storms the passengers encountered. After making it through a particularly strong storm, he optimistically noted, "Well done Kennersley Castle, you have behaved nobly, you rode out the tempest and sat like a duck in the water." Several months into the voyage, Phillips recorded, "Table Mountain is quite visible. . . . I am so often pored over Maps and prints, that the whole scene appears quite familiar to me." The passengers finally disembarked at Algoa Bay on April 30, 1820. For a complete account of the voyage, see *Phillips, 1820 Settler: His Letters,* 17–46, and especially his diary entries (later sent to his sister Catherine by letter) for the dates of January 11–13, 19; February 2, 8; March 26; April 30, 1820, which note the incidents mentioned above.

15. The Bradshaw Party is listed as "No 45 on the Colonial Department list, led by Samuel Bradshaw, a weaver and freeholder of Cam, near Dursley, Gloucestershire. Bradshaw was recommended by the Cam parish authorities and the Member of Parliament for Gloucester, Robert Bransby Cooper. This party was sponsored by the parish and organized on a joint-stock basis." Nash, *The Settler Handbook,* 49.

Here is the list of Bradshaw's party by family and occupation: "BAKER, Thomas 38. Weaver. w [wife] Esther 25 c [children] Elizabeth 13, Hannah 12, Thomas 11, Sarah 10, Ann 8; BENNETT, Samuel 35. Labourer. w [wife] Anne 40. c [children] Ann 5, Thomas (born at sea); BRADSHAW, Samuel 34. Weaver; BRENT, Thomas 36. Weaver and Royal Marines pensioner. w [wife] Grace 27. c [children] Thomas 6, Sarah 3; CARTER, Richard 36. c [children] Thomas 13, John 12; COOK, John 22. Labourer. w [wife] Jane 22. c [children] Harriet 3, Matilda 1; KING, Alfred 10 (in care of his brother Edward King); KING, Edward 18. Labourer; KING, Henry 32. Labourer. w [wife] Sarah 26. c [children] Samuel, 5, Hannah 3; KING, Henry 18. Labourer. w [wife] Mary Ann 18; KING, Joseph 37. Labourer. w [wife] Ann 25 c [children] Joseph 11, Philip 8, Charles 6, Ann 3; KING, Philip, 30. w [wife] Maria 30. c [children] Richard 8, Andrew 5, Elizabeth 3; KING, Sarah 17 (in the care of her brother Edward King); NEWTH, William 40. Labourer and RN pensioner. w [wife] Sarah 30. c [children] William 13, Benjamin 3, Thomas 2; WIGGILL, Isaac 30. Carpenter. w [wife] Elizabeth 29 c [children] Eli 9, George 7, Joseph 3, Elizabeth 1; WILCOCKS, John 25. Labourer (servant to Isaac Wiggill)." See "1820 Settler Party: Bradshaw," British 1820 Settlers to South Africa.

CHAPTER 1

A Voortrekker Wagon. Courtesy Western Cape Archives.

Thomas Brant [Brent], William Nuth [Newth], Joseph King, Henry King, Philiph [Philip] King, Samual Bennet [Samuel Bennett], Thomas Baker, Joshua Davis [Davies], John Giddens [Gittens], with their wives and children.

On the locations," it was a forlorn-looking plight in which we found ourselves, when

[Page 9]

the Ducth [Dutch][16] waggoners had emptied us and our luggage on the greensward [grass-covered ground], and left us sitting on our boxes and bundles "under the open firmament of heaven."[17]

Our roughly kind carriers seemed as they wished us goodbye, to wonder what would become of us There we were in the wilderness; and when they were gone we had no means of following, had we wished to do so.

---

16. For an overview of the Dutch settlement in South Africa, see "The Dutch Settlement," South African History Online.

17. Concerning the description of the Dutch wagon caravans bringing the British emigrants inland from Algoa Bay, Rev. Dugmore recalled the emigrants "braced themselves for action. And then began to arrive the strange looking conveyances . . . the light loosely-made wagons . . . the long-horned oxen,—the drivers with their monster whips and strange speech,—the little impish-looking leaders with dark skins and scanty clothing, and with stranger speech than their masters. . . . And so the trains of pilgrims began to wend their way . . . [with] as yet, no temples in the wilderness." Henry H. Dugmore, *The Reminiscences of an Albany Settler by Rev. Henry Hare Dugmore, Together with his Recollections of the Kaffir War of 1835*, 15–16.

A Native Village in the Eastern Cape. Originally titled "A Kaffer Village." 1804 Aquatint by Samuel Daniell.

We must take root and grow, or die where we stood. But we were standing on our own ground, and it was the first time many could say so.
[Page 10]
This thought roused to action, the tents were pitched the nightfires kindled around them to scare away the wild beasts, and the life of a settler was begun.

Thus was the land over spread by a new race of occupiers; sanguine in their hopes, and eager to develop its capabilities. Tribes of barbarians had dwelt in it But they had gone (driven out by the British tropes[18]) one year

---

18. The series of conflicts historically known as the Frontier Wars date back to 1779 when Xhosas, Boers, Khoikhoi, San, and the British clashed intermittently for nearly a hundred years. The fifth frontier war (1818–19)—the War of Nxele—resulted from an 1817 judgment by the Cape Colony government about stolen cattle and their restitution by the Xhosa. A Xhosa civil war between the Ngqika (royal clan of the Rharhabe Xhosa) and the Gcaleka required the British to provide military assistance to the Ngqika's 1818 request due to a Cape Colony–Ngqika defense alliance treaty. Xhosa prophet-chief Maqana Nxele (or Makana) supposedly promised to turn British bullets into water. Maqana led an army ten thousand strong and attacked Grahamstown, which was defended by 350 troopers, on April 22, 1819. The garrison repulsed the Xhosa attack with the aid of a Khoikhoi force led by Jan Boesak. The battle site is called "Egazini," the Place of Blood, since Maqana lost 1,000 men. He was eventually captured and imprisoned on Robben Island. The British pushed the Xhosa further east

CHAPTER 1

or two before Settlers came, and the new occupants had to dispute the possession of the soil with inhabitants of other kinds (Wild Beasts) such

[Page 11]

as Elephants Tigers and Wolves Jackalls and hyena were the nightly serenade of the new settlers, to which the little ons listened and trembled. By day even, the tigers deep voice sounded for hours togather amongst the rocks. And packs of wild dogs roved over the country, The country also abounded with game of various kinds such as Spring boks in thousands bounded playfully. As thire snowy backs shone in the sunlight, while the ostriches ruffled thire plumes, hartebeests and quaggas[19] and other

[Page 12]

antilopes of various kind ranged over the planes of Mount Donkin.[20] or as we Boys used to call it the round hill flats.

We "little ones" of those days felt none of the care that weighed on the hearts of our fathers and mothers the wild fruits and flowers so new to us banished both care and fear. And excited by the beautiful flowers and the differant kinds of fruits that myself with many others run head long into dangers both unknown to our parants and ourselves the fruit, were of the

turn to the 15 page[21]

[Page 13]

There is one little item which I forgot to mention and having missed those two pages I thought I would put it in here, My father bowred a Sled to do some work with having none of his own at that time so he got both Sled and Oxen which was six in nomber, and having finished the work for which they were bowred [He borrowed the sled and oxen from an Irishman] Myself and Brother

---

beyond the Fish River to the Keiskamma River. The British designated the resulting "Ceded Territories" as a buffer zone for loyal Africans' settlements. Cape authorities established the Albany district in 1820 on the Cape's side of the Fish River, and that is where the 5,000 Britons settled. Noël Mostert, *Frontiers: The Epic of South Africa's Creation and the Tragedy of the Xhosa People*, 426–93.

19. "(Equus quagga). Extinct animal, striped like the Zebra on head and neck, plain brown elsewhere, formerly widespread, especially in the Karroo and Orange Free State, and shot by Voortrekkers for their servants' food. Last Quagga believed to have died in the Orange Free State about 1878." Eric Rosenthal, *Encyclopedia of Southern Africa*, s.v. "Quagga."

20. This mount is named after Sir Rufane Shaw Donkin, the acting governor of the Cape.

21. The fruit referred to "the wild fig or secemoor [sycamore] and the myrtal Apple," mentioned on page 15 of the manuscript. This notation has been left to preserve the original manuscript, but the text simply continues on to page 13.

George was sent to take them home he was leading the Oxen and I was driving and flurshing the great whip has boys will do, Then I thought that I would take the Tow and lead the Oxen, and let my brother ride, But before I could get to the head of the Oxen they became frightened and started to run, and ran over

[Page 14]

me drawing Sled too which cut my leg and layed the bone bare, But it was done so quick that I did not know that I was hurt untill I found my shoe full of blood, the wound was about three inches in length, Then we turned round and went back home again, I could not walk when I found that I was hurt so bad, so my Brother lead the Oxen and I went home on the Sleigh, and was confined to the house for several weeks. which was a great trouble to me for in them days I wanted to be out for we Boys had so much to do what with playing and hunting wild hunny, wild fruits and flowers and many other things so it was a great punishment to me

[Page 15]

wild grapes of a very large kind and black when ripe and will run up and over trees in the forests fifty and an hundred feet high also the wild fig or secemoor [sycamore] and the myrtal Apple, a very nice fruit and a wild plum which grows on a specie of Mahogny[22] they are generaly found in clusters on the ends of the young branches and also the Cape gose berry which is a delisious fruit and grows in a pod and many other fruits too numerous

[Page 16]

to mention which us Boys used to rome about to gather never thinking of any danger. and also the gum from the mimosa[23] which we use to eat, in them days we used to call it the Kaffer thorn, of which the Dutch and English settlers used to draw together with oxon and make thare kraals [thorny brush livestock enclosure to help deter predators].

[Page 17]

---

22. "Several S.A. trees have received this name, although not belonging to the same genus as the real—(*Swietenia Mahagoni*)." Rudolf Marloth, "*The Flora of South Africa*": *Dictionary of the Common Names of Plants with List of Foreign Plants Cultivated in the Open*, 55.

23. Acacia Karoo (sweet thorn), the most common thorn tree of the veld, is a fast growing, drought-resistant Acacia with sparse foliage and dark green leaves. It bears quantities of sweetly scented, golden-yellow, and mimosa-like balls of flowers several times during summer and often grows to the height of twelve meters. Acacia species prosper in Mediterranean climates with cool, wet winters and hot, dry summers like those in the Eastern Cape. They can be cut and interwoven to create a livestock corral. Marloth, "*The Flora of South Africa*," 58.

Chapter II

I will now try to discribe the features of the Valley or Lemons Valley as it was caled, by being first occupied by Dutch people who left relics of Lemon Trees standing and grapevines were also thare and a water ditch was traised which had been used by them for watering thire gardens and cornfields. And also the ruens of a house which had been built of mud and distroyed by the Kaffers[1] by fire after driving the inhabetants away as also a tracking flore which had been use by the Dutch.

Well when my parents settled in that Valley I was about ten years old and I thought it was the prittyest place I had ever seen for the rising hills and mountains were so beautiful bedect [bedecked] with all the most beautiful fruits and flowers[2] and a beautiful Serpentine river runs through the center of the Valley and sckirted on its sides with the wild dates figs[3] and other beautiful trees and in the distance the rising hills were covered with beautiful grass and evergreens such as the Mimosa, and other spreading trees. Well my father and those of the company began to think that they could not live in Tents always. then they drew lots which should have this field and who should have that field

---

1. "Kaffer" or "Kaffir" represents a racial slur coined by the Dutch (Boer) settlers and mimicked by British settlers to describe African peoples in South Africa during the colonial and national periods. It is now considered a pejorative, derogatory, and offensive term. The origin of the word Kaffir stems from an Arabic word meaning "infidel" and continues to be an offensive racial slur pertaining to indigenous black African peoples. The term has also been specifically associated with the Xhosa Nation in the Eastern Cape. "Kaffir: Racial Slur Used in Africa to Describe Indigenous African People." We have kept Eli's usage of this term to be true to the manuscript, but personally find the term distasteful and offensive. Further, it appears that Eli did not mean for it to be offensive when it was used in his day. For an excellent treatment of the indigenous African people and their relationship with white settlers at the time, see Mostert, *Frontiers: The Epic of South Africa's Creation and the Tragedy of the Xhosa People*. See also J. B. Peires, *The House of Phalo: A History of the Xhosa People in the Days of Their Independence* and John Henderson Soga, *The Ama-Xosa: Life and Customs*.

2. For an excellent treatment of the flora, see David Shearing, *Karoo: South African Wild Flower Guide 6*.

3. "*Ficus capensis*. A large forest-tree. Caulifloral, i.e., the clusters of flowers (and fruit) appear on the old wood or even on the old roots near the trunk." Marloth, "*The Flora of South Africa,*" s.v. "Fig, Wild," 28.

and so they contunied untill all was sattisfide, then they begun to build thire houses, some with bushes others with reads and others with wattle and daub, neither of which were wind or water tight.

My father built

[Page 20]

His house upon one of the eigh rigeses, of strong material such as stoute posts from six to eight inches square these posts my father carried on his shoulders from the forests from two to four miles distant, these posts had then to be filed in with wattle which I well remember helping to carry and roofed in with sawed Lumber sawed in an old fashioned sawpit.

And when the house was plastered and finished it looked has well as a nice Brick house would look it was

[Page 21]

two stories high, and in this house my Bro Elijah was born,[4] After the they got thire houses built it was then that the ground had to be attende to such as gardens made and fields plowed and sowed which was commenced in good earnest for I have seen men with my own eyes digging by moonlight.

And after so much labour and toil to raise wheat just as it began to bloom and look promising it took the rust and was of no use for bread and so it contunied

[Page 22]

for several years, then they sowed Barley and other grain which was uesed for bread.

But vegetables of all kinds grew well such as Pumpkin Corn Beans Peas and vegetables of every discription.

But at this difficult time all, the Settlers still received the government Rashans [rations] which without them we must have suffered,

[Page 23]

---

4. Elijah Wiggill was born July 10, 1821.

Chapter III

The time soon came which brought three commissiners who apointed the Settlers thire Homesteads, then they spread out one in this place and another in another place four five and six miles apart, Then they began to live more comfortable and built better Houses, But at the same time they had to go some eighteen to twenty miles for thire Rashans which was very Laborious for a while but they soon began to get Cattle around them by saveing an ox now and then from thure Rashans

[Page 24]

and by so doing they very soon got every man a yoke of oxon, Then they made Sleds and worked with them for a while, and then blockwheeled Wagons were thought of and made which was more conveinant but they did not last long for they soon thought of a better plan than that which was to buy second hand Wagons from the Dutch settlers who had been in Africa for year before the British settlers came but in a different Locality. But the Country is so very level that it was not much trouble to make

[Page 25]

roads from one settlement to another which were many in that Locality.

But the princiable road which was made was the road to Bathurst[1] here the rashans was, perhaps I had better say what they were, Well we got flour Rice live Sheep oxon, rum. and when the rashons was brought to the Settlement to a surtain place where they had to be devided, haveing the rum I have seen many a drunken spree, and quarel too. Has [As][2] Bathurst and the Kowie [River][3] in them days where concidered places of note.

[Page 26]

Bathurst was appoinde by the British Govenerment to be the seite of Governement for the Abany [Albany] Settlers[4], They built a large Government

---

1. "Town on the Kowie River, 55 km south-east of Grahamstown and 15 km north-west of Port Alfred. Founded in 1820 and named after Lord Bathurst, Secretary of State for the Colonies, by Sir Rufane Donkin (1733–1841), Acting Governor of the Cape at that time." Raper, *Dictionary of Southern African Place Names*, s.v. "Bathurst," 45.

2. Wiggill uses "has" instead of "as" throughout his autobiography.

3. "River with a tidal mouth navigable for 35 km. It rises south of Grahamstown and flows 60 km in a southeasterly direction, entering the Indian Ocean at Port Alfred. The name is probably derived from Khoekhoen and means 'pipe river.'" Raper, *Dictionary of Southern African Place Names*, s.v. "Kowie," 274.

4. For more information on the Albany Settlers, see Destination Albany 1820.

Thomas Baines painting, 1849, "View of Bathurst showing ox-drawn covered wagon." Courtesy Western Cape Archives.

house for the chief magistrate which was caled in them days the Drausdy [Drostdy][5] House, but to my knowlage it was never occupide by a Magistrate.

But at the Kowie which was a Sea port town they built a large Custom House and several Government buildings for the differant Government officers to reside in. Under the directions of Sir Rufane Shaw Donkin,[6] who was

[Page 27]

acting Governor in absence of Lord Charles Sumerset [Somerset],[7] having gone to England on leave, and the building of these places gave employment to the

---

5. "Located in Graaff Reinet in the Eastern Cape, Drostdy House was built in 1806 by French architect Louis Michel Thibault to serve as the 'Drostdy' or magistrate's court of the region. The house is now a hotel with a small museum." See Rooms For Africa, s.v. "Drostdy House."

6. Donkin was the acting governor of the Cape of Good Hope while Lord Charles Somerset was temporarily gone in 1820. Eric Rosenthal, ed., *Encyclopedia of Southern Africa*, s.v. "Donkin, Sir Rufane Shaw," 160.

7. Somerset arrived at the Cape in 1814 and proved to be a problematic official due to his authoritarian disposition. He served as the governor of the Cape of Good Hope. Some considered him extravagant and lacking financial skills, yet he genuinely aided the agricultural endeavors of British settlers in the Eastern Cape. Rosenthal, *Encyclopedia of Southern Africa*, s.v. "Somerset, Lord, Charles, Henry," 532. For an overview of this period of Donkin's administration during the period of Lord

CHAPTER 3

Mechanics and other Labouring Men and by that means many of the Settlers left thire Homesteads and resided in those Villiges and built them very nice and good Houses and all went on well to the best of my knowlage for about two years, Then Lord Charles Sumerset [Somerset] came back and upset and disarrainged all that Sir Rufane Shaw Donkin had done to the great dissatis

[Page 28]

faction of the people, and moved the head quarters to Grahams Town [Grahamstown][8] and the Sea port to Algo [Algoa] Bay but now and then Vessels would come to the Kowie with thare Cargo, and was still a little buisness transcacked [transacted] thare but on account of so many accidents happening through drunkenness and bad management the Vessels quit coming there and went to Algo [Algoa] Bay which at the preasent time is a flurishing Seaport Town, both Bathurst and the Kowie are beautiful parklike country as anyone would wish to see. The Kowie in the

[Page 29]

year of 1872 by the perseverance of Mr. William Cock[9] the head of Cocks party one of the Settlers of 1.20 [1820][10] of all the heads of the partyes of 1820 this Mr. Cock is the only one living.

Somerset's absence and his subsequent return, see George McCall Theal, *History of South Africa Since 1795: The Cape Colony from 1795 to 1828, the Zulu Wars of Devastation and the Formation of New Bantu Communities*, vol. 5 of *History of South Africa*, 346–69.

8. Established in 1812 as a military headquarters, the town was named after Colonel John Graham. Later it became the principal gathering place for British settlers in the Eastern Cape. Raper, *Dictionary of Southern African Place Names*, s.v. "Grahamstown," 187. See Richard Marshall, "A Social and Cultural History of Grahamstown, 1812–c1845."

9. William Cock pioneered harbor developments in the Eastern Cape province. "Born in Oxfordshire, England, in 1794, came to the Cape with the 1820 settlers and recognized the possibilities of a harbor at the mouth of the Kowie River. To this scheme he devoted many years and much capital. A settlement sprang up, called Port Frances, later named Port Alfred. Cock was elected to the Cape Legislative Council from 1847 to 1853 and again from 1856 to 1868. With the establishment of the first Colonial Parliament, he entered the original House of Assembly. He died in 1876." Rosenthal, *Encyclopedia of Southern Africa*, s.v. "Cock, William," 119.

10. The party of William Cox is listed as number 31 on the Colonial Department list, and it was "a joint stock party of 40 men (including 11 servants)." Nash, *The Settler Handbook*, 61.

Chapter 4

Now I must return again to the days when I was only eleven years old which was about the year of 1822 and 3 in this time the Settlers had got lots of Cattle about them by traiding thar cloathes for which the Dutch were glad to get in return for what they had

[Page 30]

and then a great many of the Settlers turned thire attention to traiding, and many of them used to carry thire goods on pack Oxon but as they done well in traiding and kept makeing a little here and thare they soon got them selves Wagons, Then they would make a trip of five and Six Months at a time but before they done this the Dutch used to ware dresses made of skins but when those traiders begun to take to them dress goods and all sorts of what is dry caled [called dried] goods they was wiling

[Page 31]

to pay almost any price and by that means the Settlers soon began to get rich. They would pay a great deal in Soap which they made and it was very good. and also in Ostrich feathers[1] for they were great hunters.

But I must say, that is the traiders soon got rich both in goods and Cattle. The great Fishriver [Great Fish River][2] been the boundry line between the Settlers and the Kafirs [Kaffirs] it been such a bushy and wooded place that the Kafirs used to come under the cover of these bushes and steal our

[Page 32]

Cattle and be gone with them, and far away before anyone would know any thing about it, and many a time we suffered in this way through their treachery. They have many a time come into the Koroll and into the pasture and taken them almost before our eyes.

And very often they have murdred the herds, and then take the Irons of the plows to make assagais and spears with which they are very expert for they practice with them when very young, a Treaty was made that the Kafirs [Kaffirs] should not cross that river neither

---

1. "(Struthio calemus). Indigenous bird connected with an important industry. Of the five local varieties, the predominating one is the Southern Ostrich. From the earliest days of white settlement, ostriches were hunted for their plumes, for the European market." Rosenthal, *Encyclopedia of Southern Africa*, s.v. "Ostrich," 415.

2. The Great Fish River was well known in the Eastern Cape province as it marked the dividing line between the British colonists and the Xhosa Nation. Its headwaters flow from the Sneeuberg Mountains before emptying into the Indian Ocean north of Port Alfred. Rosenthal, *Encyclopedia of Southern Africa*, s.v. "Great Fish River," 228.

CHAPTER 4

[Page 33]

should the Settlers but they (the Kafiers [Kaffirs]) would brake it and did which was a great loss to the Settlers very often.

When the Children would be herding through the day the Kafirs [Kaffirs] would be laying in ambush and looking out for the best of either Cattle or sheep and the first thing they would know towards evening and many a time in midday they have pounsed upon them like Wolves and taken them off and would slaughter some of them right in the thickets, and if they thought they were persued

[Page 34]

they gorge what they could and leave the rest.

The Settlers were earnest and energetic in thire first attempts to make Albany an agricultural district and just as they had got thire Lands in good order and thire gardens planted then came the great flood of Oct 1823[3] which reached all the Settlements and sweeping all that came in its way even washing the plowed ground away as deep as the plow went.

There was one man had his house built with strong posts with an upstairs to it and himself

[Page 35]

and his family were in bed when the flood came he got up and thought to keep the water out of his house by making a small opening in the wall and instead of leting a little out he let the river in and when he seen what he had done he went back to bed again.

The early struggles and privations of the Settlers appealed to the hearts of British humanity never appealed to in vain Contributions generous and hearty came from east and west. India joined

[Page 36]

the Mother country in subscriptions which amounted to several thousands pounds "Boards of Relief" sat, and many cases of painful interest came before them, and by that means it enabled them to start again although some got more than thare share.

Poetry

>Wilderness lands of break and glen,
>The wolfs and the Leopard's gloomy den;
>Wilderness plains where the springbok bounds

---

3. The eastern districts suffered terribly from a flood that occurred in October 1823. Having never endured something like this before, the British settlers in Albany who had built in the floodplain saw their cottages, gardens, orchards, and cornfields ruined or washed away. Many settlers were left with nothing more than the clothes on their backs. Theal, *History of South Africa Since September 1795: The Cape Colony from 1795 to 1828, vol. 5*, 330.

And the Lion's voice from the hills resounds,
And the vulture circles in airy rounds
Are Africa's southern wilds."[4]

Coppyed from the lecture of the British Settlers Jubilee. May 1870.[5]
[Page 37]

---

4. Poem quoted in lecture by Rev. Henry H. Dugmore, "Past and Present," in *A Treasury of South African Poetry and Verse*, 44–45.

5. Rev. Henry Hare Dugmore spoke at the British settlers' jubilee celebration lecture in 1870, and his speech was later published as *The Reminiscences of an Albany Settler*.

Chapter 5

About the year eighteen hundred and twenty three there was a young man staying at my father's house whos name was Edward King, He was one of the same party of Settlers that my father was[1] and of corse was very intamate he was one of those traders and had made two or three trips up the Country amongest the Dutch community and returned.

Then he indused my father to let him take me with him to help him with his Wagon and Oxen that is, lead the oxen and herd them when unyoked,

[Page 38]

Well my father gave his consent for me to go with him and we started and remained in Graham's Town [Grahamstown] for some five or six weeks, working at differant kinds of work somtimes hauling firewood.

Then we started out with Government Military stores for the post at Fortwilshire [Fort Wiltshire][2] which was about fifty mils from Graham's Town [Grahamstown] right in the heart of Kafir [Kaffir] Land, we left Grahams Town [Grahamstown] and crossed Boata's hill [Botha's Hill] which at that time was very steep and rocky on the Kafir [Kaffir] land side, commenced almost one contunied low scruby bush

[Page 39]

of differant species intermixed with all kinds of beautiful runing vines and many of them in full bloom and beautifull blossoms all the year round also a beautiful tree which the Dutch calls Speckboom [Spekboom][3] known by the English as the Elephants food the trees leaves are very thick and sour about the size of an English sixpence but the flowers which it bares is a beautiful Liloc collor rather small. But the wood is very porous and is like spunge and is of no use for either

[Page 40]

---

1. Eighteen-year-old laborer Edward King embarked on the *Kennersley Castle* with the Bradshaw Party. Nash, *The Settler Handbook*, 49.

2. "Fort Wiltshire was erected by the British military during the frontier war of 1818–19, and was named in honour of Lt-Col Thomas Wiltshire of the 38th Regiment, who commanded the British troops during this campaign. Work on the stone tower, which stood on a hill overlooking the confluence of the Keiskamma and Ngqakayi rivers, was begun in November 1819." The British abandoned the post in 1836. South Africa History Online.

3. "*Portulacaria afra*. A shrub or small tree of the eastern Karoo, Addo bush, etc., possessing a very nutritious and succulent foliage. Drought resisting. Also called Elephant's food." Marloth, "*The Flora of South Africa*," s.v. "Spek'boom," 76.

to work or to burn. Through this dense bush, the government made the road some time before the Settlers went out, our first day out from Grahams Town [Grahamstown] was through this bush to what is caled Hermanus Kraal which was a military port.[4] and I remember it well for I was so tired with that days travel for my limbs aked [ached] and hurt me so bad that I could not sleep. and the next morning having to go out from our camp to herd the oxen and that among what is caled prickely pears[5] from

[Page 41]

eight to ten feet high, and Child like I began to eat the frute which they bear and not been acquainted with them I got the thorns into my hands and mouth and for several days I was in such a state, Well it learnt me a good lesson for I knew how to handle them after that, This fort is right on the banks of the great Fish river whos banks is lined with this kind of frute, why it is called the Great Fish river is becaus thare are two rivers of the same

[Page 42]

name, and one is not so large as the other. although they both run into one finely. When we left this fort Hermanus Kraal we jurnyed through a simmeler [similar] country covered with Bush and over hill and dail [dale] and as far as the eye could see it was a dence forest only now and then we would come to an openen in fact it is the dence Fish river Bush which is so well known in that part African wilds which gives shelter to Kafirs [Kaffirs] and Elephants and many other wild beasts. And as we went down the hill to the great Fish

[Page 43]

river thare I saw Elephants in thare wild state but they did not molest us there we crossed the great fish river what is called the double drift an iland devids the stream which gives it that name, It was there to the best of my knowlege we staid the second night and the Elephants came down to drink that night that we seen the day before, Elephants genarely drink at night.

After leaving the great Fish river or double drift we began to assend a very steep hill when on the top we had a splendid new

[Page 44]

view of the Country all around for Miles and Miles and the great Fish river lay on both sides of this eminiance [eminence] like a thread, And from thare

---

4. Hermanus Kraal is also referred to as Fort Brown. Linda Robson and Mark Oranje, "Strategic Military Colonization: The Cape Eastern Frontier 1806–1872," 57.

5. "*Opuntia decumana.* From Central America, now growing here in two forms, via., the real O. decumana of HAWORTH, which is our Kaalblad, and the spiny form, called Doornblad, which we now designate of O. decumana va. Spinosa; the former being obtained from the latter by selective cultivation." Marloth, "*The Flora of South Africa,*" s.v. "Prickly pear," 68.

CHAPTER 5

to Fort Wilshire [Wiltshire] we went through the most beautiful parklike Country for about twenty miles or more.

Fort Wilshire [Wiltshire] is named for Colonel Wilshire [Wiltshire], the Colonel of one of the British Regiments who helped to drive the Kafirs [Kaffirs] back from the tract of Country about the year eighteen hundred and eighteen or nineteen where the British Settled in the year of twenty. *The British Settlers of twenty.

[Page 45]

I cannot give a better discription of the Country than from the pen of the Rev Henry H. Dugmore although the discription that Mr. Dugmore gives is a few years later than when I was there but has it so graphic and to the point, I give it in his own words.[6]

He says, there was another oppertunity afforded for the exercise of the commercial talents of the new colonists. The government, yielding at length to representations that were made to it on the subject, permitted, under certain

[Page 46]

restrictions, the opening of traide with the Kaffers, A periodical "fair" was established at Fort Wilshire [Wiltshire], where the colonial traders by scores, and the Kaffers by hundreds or thousands, met to exchange wares. The old post, long ago deserted, was a place of note in those days as the chief defence of the frontier, It has been silent and desolate enough since. Many years have elapsed since its stables were occupied by troop horses since its officers' quarters were scenes of jollity, or the reveille and "tattoo" sounded in the square; but it was a place of some animation,

[Page 47]

and that of a stranger and wild character when "fair-day" arrived. The traders were there with thire beads, buttons, and brass wire; and the Kaffers were there from Mountain range and seacoast lowland, from the Kieskamma [Keiskamma River] to the Key. Long files of women, headed by thire lords and masters, and laden with oxhides, horns, and gum, and here and there the more precious merchandize of an Elephant's tusk among them, threaded the bush paths in single file. or convirged down the hill sides towards the center of attraction under

[Page 48]

the guns of the Fort. The trees that fringed the banks of the Kieskamma river [Keiskamma] below the post gave shelter to hundreds of swarthy groups

---

6. In Wiggill's manuscript, pp. 45–52, he draws upon Rev. Henry Hare Dugmore's lecture later published as *The Reminiscences of an Albany Settler*, 34–36. This evidence suggests Wiggill used some published sources to write his autobiographical account.

of eager barbarians, wondering at the newly acquired value of articles they had formerly deemed worthless. Kaffers have since gleefully told me what diligent search they used to make for the horns that had long been thrown away; and how the troops of children swarmed among the thorntree[7] thickets, gathering gum for the new market.

There were no photographers in those days, nor had Mr. Jons[8] begun his Kaffer

[Page 49]

sketches, or we might have had some amusing scenes from life fixed for us to contemplate.

The grim old fort, with its wild scenery around it. would have formed the center of a very characteristic picture.

The motley throng of black, and white, and brown, varied by the red, green, and blue uniforms of "Line", Rifles and Artillery; the groups of women with thire crushing loads gladly laid upon the ground before them; the men, seated on thire heels, kerrie in hand, jealously watching thire property, or choffering [chaffering] with the traders who were making

[Page 50]

them rival offers for the coveted merchandise; the greedy chiefs, headed by Gaika[9] himself, laying seignorial taxation on thire own people, or pestering the white man for bribes and brandy. Strange Kaffer was spoken on these occasions; and strange Dutch and English too. Interpreters were at a premium; and sadly perplexed were the traiders now and then by the changes in the Kaffer fashions. Beads that were worth seventy dollars the pound, and buttons that were in universal demand one month, might be worth almost nothing the next. Speculators even in the Fort Wilshire [Wiltshire]

[Page 51]

market sometimes burnt thire fingers. There was little to do in brocades or artificial flowers, and as little in thin steel; but the Kaffer men were as particular about their necklaces, and the women about their turban covers and kaross back stripes which is three or four rows of brassbell buttons on their skin

---

7. The thorn tree with Doornbloom may be the Acacia Karoo. Marloth, "*The Flora of South Africa,*" s.v. "Thorn tree," 81.

8. This probably refers to an F. Jones, who created lithograph prints of South African landscapes and people during the 1860s. His work is found in books compiled by Thomas Bowler; the prints in these books portray areas familiar to Eli Wiggill, such as Grahamstown and Port Elizabeth. Yale Center for British Art Collections Online.

9. Xhosa Chief Gaika was the son of Mlawu, born about 1779; he became chief in 1819 and died a decade later. Rosenthal, *Encyclopedia of Southern Africa*, s.v. "Gaika," 202.

mantles and they also ware in great profusion brass copper and Ivery rings on their arms and legs, and they are as peticular in their fashions as the leaders of the mode in London or Paris are about their bonnets and ball dresses

[Page 52]

The Fort Wilshire [Wiltshire] Fair gave a fresh impulse to the young commerce of Graham's Town [Grahamstown], and it formed the commencment of an international traid with the Kaffer tribes that acquired great importance in a short time; and, but for the ruinous wars which followed, the result of barbarian cupidity, stimulated by civilized smugglers of guns and gunpowder, would have aided more than it has done in promoting their civilization.[10]

---

10. Some opportunists sold guns and powder to the Indigenous peoples of the region. This proved to be a deadly decision in the decade that followed with the outbreak of the Xhosa Wars, now known as the Cape Frontier Wars. For an overview, see Thompson, *A History of South Africa*, 70–109. For an understanding of the issues surrounding the conflict, see M. Wilson, "Co-Operation and Conflict: The Eastern Cape Frontier," in *A History of South Africa to 1870*, 233–71. For eyewitness missionary accounts, see Rev. Henry Calderwood, *Caffres and Caffre Missions: With Preliminary Chapters on the Cape Colony as a Field for Emigration, and Basis of Missionary Operation*, 48–64.

Chapter 6

When I left Fort Wilshire [Wiltshire] I took the rout to Fort

[Page 53]

Beaufort[1] which was about twenty five or thirty miles through a beautiful parklike Country, at that time it was a small military station about the year eighteen twenty three it is on the Kat river which is a large and beautiful stream and fringed with Willows and other trees of very large growth and the scenery of the surrounding Country is very beautiful, Then I went from Fort Beaufort to Grahams Town [Grahamstown] and haveing to cross the Kanap [Konap/Koonap] river[2] which is a very dencely wooded especly on the margen and banks.

Elephants had been there

[Page 54]

a day or two before we arrived and broke the trees fearfuly but I did see any of them we went from there to Fish river and forded it at Fee Krall [Vyge Kraal] Drift[3] or Ford, And at this Kraall it is one mass of prickely Pears, but I took care not to be so free with them as I was at Harmanus Kraall [Hermanus Kraal]. which place I tuched on on my return to Grahams Town [Grahamstown] which is from Fort Beaufort 46 miles, and was at that time a wild but beautiful Country, from Harmanus Kraall [Hermanus Kraal] to Grahams Town [Grahamstown]. I have already discribed the road and the scenery,

We staid in Grahams Town [Grahamstown]

[Page 55]

for a few weeks at a black smiths shop the owner whos name was William Bear[4] and carried on an extenceive buisness at that both in the smithing and

---

1. The town of Fort Beaufort was laid out in 1837 around a fort of the same name built in 1822. The town lay 147 kilometers northwest of East London, 80 kilometers north of Grahamstown and 22 kilometers west of Alice. Raper, *Dictionary of Southern African Place Names*, 164.

2. Koonap (or Konap) River is a tributary of the Great Fish River that "rises in the Winterberg and flows south-west past Adelaide and then south-east to enter the mother stream 35 km north of Grahamstown. The name, of Khoekhoen origin, may mean 'murder hole.' The incident to which the name refers has been forgotten." Raper, *Dictionary of Southern African Place Names*, s.v. "Koonap River," 271.

3. The Nguni peoples settled as far south as the Great Fish River by 1500. The Khoekhoe called it the Oub or Fish River, which served as a contested borderland between settler colonists and the Xhosa Nations. Fay Jaff, *They Came to South Africa*.

4. William Bear, a member of the Dyason Party (no. 43 on the Colonial Department list) led by George Dyason. Bear, a blacksmith, was twenty-six years old at the time

CHAPTER 6

Wagon makeing during this stay, this Edward King[5] went to see my father and on his return he brought word to me (which was false) that he permition from my father that I should go with him on his traiding expedition or to use his own words said he I am going to take you up the country to see the Dutch Boors which means Dutch farmers.

We stayed a few weeks longer in Grahams Town [Grahamstown]. after he, King, had seen my father geting things in order for

[Page 56]

the journey and while staying there I had to go every day to herd the oxen. And one day which I never shall forget I was out with the oxen in Captain Sumerset's [Somerset's] cloff [kloof] when there came up one of the most terfice [terrific] thunder storms I have never seen one like it since then I was only about twelve or thirteen yeas old the thunder just roled on the ground and the lightening played around my feet while I took shelter under a very large spreading tree which I learned afterwards that it was the worst place I could have found. And the rain came down in torants and flooded the ground and filled all the streams and

[Page 57]

rivelets so that I had a great time to get the oxen and myself home, or to where I was staying such storms are frequuint in Africa and the leightening very often sets fire to Barns and dwelling Houses as well as destroying life of both Man and Beasts.

After a little further delay this Mr King was ready to start which we did in the middle of the night which I learnt afterwards on account of his been so much in dept. He also took with him three passingers a Mr and Mrs Mitten [Mitton][6] and a Mr Dail [Dale][7] who were going through the Dutch Settlements which would be about six hundred Miles

[Page 58]

---

he embarked from the British Isles to South Africa with his wife Sarah, age 22. Nash, *The Settler Handbook*, 69.

5. Edward King was a member of the Bradshaw Party which included the Wiggills. Nash, *The Settler Handbook*, 49.

6. John and Ellen Mitton were members of the George Smith Party (no. 23 on the Colonial Department list). John is listed as age 35, a joiner and builder along with his wife Ellen, age 39 and their child Elizabeth, age 15. Nash, *The Settler Handbook*, 119–20.

7. In Wiggill's manuscript, p. 76, Mr. Dail [Dale] is referred to as "Mr. Deal a Shoemaker." His occupation reveals that this individual is most probably John Dale, a twenty-four-year-old boot and shoemaker who, along with his wife Mary, age 17, were members of the Benjamin Osler Party (no. 47 of the Colonial Department list). Nash, *The Settler Handbook*, 97.

from Grahams Town [Grahamstown] to Cape Town our first stage out was at a Dutch farme. and I remember the mans name was Nell [Nel] and it must have being a very old place has the manure in the Sheep and Cattle karaal were from seven to eight feet deep. The Dutch seldom clears out their kraals but keeps bushing it up with Mimosa thorns so the Cattle is upon a great mound of dung, and sometimes those kraals takes fire and I have known them to burn for six and seven years, Well our next stage was at another Dutchmans farm whos name was Joseph Van Dick [Dyk], and there were

[Page 59]

simeler kraals like the one I have just discribed. This King genraly done a little traiding at each of these places, we still contunied traveling and passed many farms untill we came to another Dutchmans farm whos name was Geart Ficter,[8] which was quite a Villige in apperance as the Dutchmans Children marry and settle all around him which accounts for the appearance of a Villaige I think this place is on the little Fish river, And we stayed there for a few days and loaded up some goods which he had left thare on a former ocation and among the goods was

[Page 60]

a hand Organ with dolls in it to dance when the Organ was played. We still contunied our jurney and past many farms and localitys whos name I used to know in them days but I have forgotten them but it was in the district of Sumerset [Somerset], I remember going over a very ugly rugged hill, or rather Mountain which had been excavated and so narrow that the Wagon could but barley get over it and if the Wagon had gone a little too much on eather side it would have gone down several hundred feet before it would found rest, At the time I

[Page 61]

went through on that jurney the farmers were all very rich in Cattle Sheep and Horses, and lived in ease and luxury, for at that time the Dutch were all slave owners,

From this place we passd an, and passed many a Dutch farm with their snug houses and beautiful gardens with their rich fruits and Vineyards of the very best kind. from which they made excelant brandy and wines and also reasons [raisins] and a great many kinds of dryed fruits, On those farms they have very large cellers and have their brandy and wine for yeas they make it in such large quantitys

[Page 62]

---

8. This name may possibly refer to a Gerrit Victor, the name of which has been well established for centuries in South Africa. See WikiTree, s.v. "Gerrit Victor."

CHAPTER 6

so that they put it away in large barrels and have it all ages. We still traveled on and by and by we came to a farm house on the Foal [Vaal] River[9] we stayed with these people two or three days who's name was Peter Detioe[10] And here Mr. King made· a change in Wagons with Detioe, and got Six Oxen to boot. While here I was out with the Oxen to herd them which it was my duty to do. When I went out in the morning I crossd a deep dry gully or a periodical stream which is generaly full of water when it rains.

This day I stayed a little too late and it seemed to become dark all of a suddon so that I could not find

[Page 63]

the same place again that I crossed in the morning. And the Sun had only just gone out of sight when the Wolves and Jackals were howling and barking all around me but at a little distance so that I thought I was taken, Well I tried to keep up my curage knowing that the Wagon road lay below where I was, I kept on down and it just happened that one of the Farmers Cows had being left out so when I came up to her she took the lead and my Oxen followed and I followed them and finely [finally] she brought us all right home which made me feel very glad and thankful to the Cow.

[Page 64]

We left this place and got on to extensive plains known as karoo plains [The Great Karoo] which is covered with a great veriety of herds which is very good food for both Sheep and Cattle. But very little water is found in dry times, we travled for thirty and forty miles at a time and find no water but the roads were very good, At the time I am writing about, on those plains I have seen hundreds of Ostriches guinea fowls and wild turkeys and many others kinds of Birds, and a great variety of wild game such as quagas and Hartebeest. and Springboks by the thousands and also Lions were plentyful at that time

[Page 65]

in fact the Lion is always plentyful where so much game abounds, for it is on them he depends on for a living. After we had crossed several of those plains we came to a tributaries to the Sundays river and there we halted for the night but there was no house near it was a dessolate wild, The banks of the river were thickly wooded with Willows Mimosa Kerie [Kerrie] wood which is a

---

9. The Vaal River emanates near Klipstapel in the vicinity of Breyten and Lake Chrissie and flows to join the Orange River some thirteen kilometers west of Douglas. In the Afrikaans language, "vaal" refers to the drab, brown-grey color of the muddy water. Raper, *Dictionary of Southern African Place Names*, s.v. "Vaal River," 560.

10. Possibly Peter Du Toit. The spelling of Detioe is phonetically how it sounds. Peter Du Toit and Peter Andrew Du Toit were both 1820 British settlers in South Africa. British 1820 Settlers to South Africa.

very tuff kind of willow from which the wild Bushmen makes their Bows. This track of Country belongs to the District of Graaff Reinet. which was in them days a Dutch Town, one

[Page 66]

hundred and fifty two miles from Grahams Town [Grahamstown].

This distrct contains the highest mountain in Southern Africa, called the Spitskop or Compassberg,[11] its altitude being computed at 10.250 feet above the level of the sea.

---

11. This 2,540-meter-high peak is fifty-five kilometers north of Graaff-Reinet, on the watershed between the Orange and Sundays rivers. It was named by R. J. Gordon in 1778 because he could see streams flowing in all directions at the summit. Raper, *Dictionary of Southern African Place Names*, s.v. "Compassberg," 102.

Chapter 7

While passing through the District of Graaff Reinet[1] I thought I would give a Short sketch of the country and its establishment in early times by the Dutch government, The Division comprises the first tract of country occupied by the Dutch inhabitants in the Eastern Province. It was formed into a district in 1786, and named after the then governor of the Cape, Van De Graaf [Graaff], and his

[Page 67]

wife Reinet [Reynet]. For many years, however, anterior to this, it had been occupied by the white man the colonists, in their migratory excursions from the westward in search of water and pasturage, penetrating to this neighbourhood, where they established themselves with their flocks and herds.

At that time it was found very thinly inhabited by straggling tribes of Bushmen who sustained a wretched and precarious existence by game, killed with their poisoned arrows by feeding on the larvae of ants, and on locusts large flights of which, and especialy when drought prevails farther in the interior. occasionally spreading over this and the

[Page 68]

adjacent divisions. They possessed neither flocks nor herds. never cultivated the soil, built no houses but lived in the most savage state their habitations being the clefts of the rocks, and their only care that of appeasing for the moment the cravings of hunger.

The early colonists the pioneers of civilization found these people for a considerable time excessively troublesome. The most daring acts of robbery were committed by them; whole flocks of sheep and large numbers of cattle and horses were frequently driven off and distroyed not solely for food, but to gratify that sanguinary propensity inherent in man when living in a savage state.

[Page 69]

These acts of robbery were often attended with the murder of the farmer's herdsmen, and there are also numerous instances on record where whole families of the whites have paid for their intrusion into this country by forfeture of their lives.

The two classes thus meeting in mutual hostility, a struggle ensued, not merely for territory, but for existance. Plunder and violence on the one side were followed by retaliatory measures on the other, untill the weaker party

---

1. Kenneth Wyndham Smith, *From Frontier to Midlands: A History of the Graaff-Reinet District 1786–1910.*

gradually gave way, and the country became premanently settled by the whites, and was included within the limits of the

[Page 70]

Colony. The division of Graaff Reinet, when originally formed, was computed to contain 50.000 square Miles but it has been greatly reduced the division of Beaufort (in the Western Province) Colesberg.[2] Cradock.[3] Somerset.[4] and part of Uitenhage having being dismembered from it. Its entire area is now estimated at 8.600 square Mils, with a population of about 9,000 souls.

We left the Sundays River and contunied on our jurney across an extensive country passing a great many farms houses and stoping at some of them to do a little traiding with the people some would buy

[Page 71]

one thing and some another and the Country abounded with all kinds of game such as already been discribed by and by we came to a great ruged range of mountains which reached hundreds of miles but not as rugged in some places as in others called the Swartberg or in english the Black Mountain, they extended through the whole colony from Cape district to Grahams Town [Grahamstown], We halted for the night at a farmhouse which was in an opening in the mountain, it is what the Dutch calls a port and what the Americans calls Canions, Well we staied two or three days

[Page 72]

at this place for I remember well when a Boy I was very fond of strouling about and try to see all that was worth seeing so with these feeling I started out and went up the Mountain which was so preceptious that when I returned I had to be so careful, or if I had made on misstep and fallen I should have being dashed to peaces. When we left this place we went through the great opening in the Mountain called the Sweartberg [Swartberg] Port. a river

---

2. Initially named Toverberg in 1830 after a nearby hill, the town was subsequently renamed after Sir Galbraith Lowry Cole, governor of the Cape Colony from 1828 to 1833. Located some twenty-nine kilometers south of the Orange River, twenty-nine kilometers south-south-west of Philippolis, and fifty-one kilometers north of Noupoort, Colesberg received municipal status in 1840. Raper, *Dictionary of Southern African Place Names*, s.v. "Colesberg," 101–02.

3. This town on the Great Fish River began as a frontier outpost on the Buffelskloof farm in 1813, some 258 kilometers north of Port Elizabeth by road. It became a township in 1814 and was named after Sir John Francis Cradock (1762–1839), governor of the Cape from 1811 to 1814, before receiving municipal status in 1840. Raper, *Dictionary of Southern African Place Names*, s.v. "Cradock," 105.

4. "Town 6 km east of Ronaldsey and 12 km west-north-west of Sabie Park. Thought to be named after the county of Somerset or Somersetshire England." Raper, *Dictionary of Southern African Place Names*, s.v. "Somerset," 507.

CHAPTER 7

runs through this place which drains the Country for many miles. But it runs fauls sometimes you find a great river then you find in the same river

[Page 73]

a few miles further on it is a great bed of sand and so it contunies. The banks of this river is thickly wooded with beautiful Mamosa [mimosa] willows and many other kinds of trees, and on each side of this great pass the rocks are several hundred feet high well they are fearful, and I have seen hundreds of Baboons of the largest kind siting here and there on them and looking down on us and makeing an auful barking such a bark, And as well as the Baboon there is thousands yes I may say millions of conies or rockrabbits, for on every little projecting rock I could see one of those little rabbits sitting suning themselves and makeing

[Page 74]

such a noise. sometimes both night and day, The wild animals in this rugged country are Wolves Tigers Porcupines and wildcats and also the Antbear, now we come to a farmshouse whos name is Knotts, we stayed one day at his house and was treated very kindly, for he, Knotts, was a very ceivel [civil] man, on leaveing there we traveiled for days in and out threading through this way and that way and the river on one side and these rugged preceptious rocks on the other. and only just room for the Wagon to travil and I remember one place the rocks were overhanging and we had to travil under them with those Baboons and rabbits for our company. This river

[Page 75]

was fringed all along its banks with Mimosa. This wild and rugged Country is inhabeted here and there by Dutch Farmers, but not of the wealthiest. We still contunued our jurney and campted one night and no house in sight that night their came a great Snowstorm some six inchs and our cattle were turned out so that we could not move for two days and nighs then Mr King went on foot in sirch of help and found a farmhouse some distance from the Wagon, and got Oxen and brough the wagon to the house. then Mr King engaged a Hottentot[5] to hunt for our Oxen who found

[Page 76]

---

5. The term Hottentot is now considered an archaic and pejorative term. The Dutch settlers in South Africa used it with reference to the Indigenous non-Bantu, nomadic, and pastoralist Khoikhoi (also spelled Khoekhoe) and San peoples. The Khoikhoi thrived as cattle and goat pastoralists, while the San hunter-gatherers lived primarily in dry, remote areas such as the Namib and Kalahari deserts. The preferred names now include Khoi, Khoikhoi, Khoisan, and San. "The origin of the name is believed to be a corruption of their clicking sounds. A yellow race of Mongolian appearance, with high cheekbones, they were fond of cattle and were nomads by instinct. Pure Hottentots have now become extremely scarce, having been decimated

them very soon then we contunied on our jurney a day further on but the winter became so sevear and cold for that country and the Oxen became poor and weak that King made up his mind to stay there for two months. who there Mr Mitten [Mitton] being a Carpenter and Mr Deal [Dale] a Shoemaker they both worked for the Dutchman, whoes house being large and not much in it we occupied a part of it and boarded ourselves and was very comfortable sometimes riding around and visiting the neighbours and traiding with them.

[Page 77]

---

by outbreaks of smallpox in the 18th century and later by interbreeding with their neighbors." Rosenthal, *Encyclopedia of Southern Africa*, s.v. "Hottentot," 256.

Chapter 8

After staying about two months at this place Mr King and myself started off on foot in search of our Oxen which had strayed away We traveled for miles and seen no one untill night then we came up to a farm house and I was so glad for I was so hungery and thirsty The houses is so far apart in this seccion of the country on account of water being so scarce, but we were kindly treated at this place with plenty to eat and drink and a good bed, The Dutch people in that country are very Hospitable if a stranger stays for a week or two at

[Page 78]

a time they never charge any thing for board, Well we left those friends the next morning feeling very much refrished. On another dreary day jurney but not to find such a home at night for there were no house to be seen so we had to lay down when night came on the ground both hungery and thirsty and the Wolves barking and howling around us all night we layed down but not to sleep much, we had an English fowling peice with us but did not use it.

Then we started again, on another days jurney and so hungery, we found some old marrowbones and broke

[Page 79]

them in peaces to see if we could find some marrow in them but the Beasts had been dead too long for they were dry and empty but we found water this day, and some wild bitter Kafir [Kaffir] Mellons[1] so bitter that we could not eat them.

Well we contunied on and on by and by we came to a road, and followed it for a long distance and finely it brought us to a farmhouse in an isolated place up in the mountains where one would think it imposable for anyone to live but we found a place of reffuge for the next twenty four hours which I enjoyed emencely, In

[Page 80]

all this time we found no trace of the Oxen then we turned back again by a differant rout and found houses all the way back to our Wagon which saved us a great deal of suffering, But found no Oxen, after we had been back a little while Mr King sold his wagon and what few Oxen he had left to those passingers Mr Mitten [Mitton] and Mr Dail [Dale] what he got for them in all I dont know but I remember that he got two or three Watches,

---

1. "A variety of *Citrullus vulgaris*, cultivated as stock-food." Marloth, "*The Flora of South Africa*," s.v. "Kaffir melon," 44.

While we were staying at this place I saw a sight that I never can forget, This Dutch man had a slave boy about fourteen yeas old who had

[Page 81]

a sister living at the next farm and he would run away from his home to her, although he had a good home and a good Master, so one day they brought him home and to punish him he was tied to a wagon wheel and the wagon turned on its side so the wheel would turn and every time it turned and the boy came round a man with a large strap in hand and a buckel on the end would give him a cut and the blood would run at every stroak so that the wheel was covered with blood then after such a whiping they rubbed salt into his wounds then set him

[Page 82]

to leading the Oxen at plowing with his hands tied fast to the tow, so that he could not run a way.[2] After this had all happened we, Mr King, and myself started again on foot and traviled two or three days and passed several very good farms with beautiful surrounding, their Orchords were grand, with Orienges. Lemons. figs. and many other kinds of fruit, And when night came on we were kindly received by the people of some of these places after traveling for about three days we came to a farm where a lived a Widdow woman and from her Mr King baught a wagon and I think about fifteen

[Page 83]

head of Oxen and one Horse and some Cows and one Bull after makeing this purches he started off with the wagon drawn by eight Oxen, and left me behind to ride the horse and drive the lose Stock, the horse was so lazey I could not get him along so I got down to get a switch to help him along but when I was about to Mount him again he started off at full gallop and me after him for miles, but he out run me and I never saw him any more and when I returned to where I left the stock they were no where to be seen, Then I had them to hunt for and Mr King going on and

[Page 84]

leaveing me behind for Miles well I had to hunt for the Cattle and found them over a hill then I brought them back to the road and the only way

---

2. "From 1806, the British introduced laws (amelioration laws) that aimed to improve the welfare of slaves in the Cape. The slave guardian appointed by the British government was responsible for enforcing these laws. As a result, the lives of some slaves improved after 1807. Even though there were reforms and laws to protect slaves, some masters continued to ill-treat their slaves by administering cruel punishments and ignoring these reform laws. Slaves were expected to report any ill treatment to the slave protector appointed by the colonial government." South African History Online. For a more detailed treatment on enslavement, see Elizabeth A. Eldredge and Fred Morton, eds., *Slavery in South Africa: Captive Labor on the Dutch Frontier*.

CHAPTER 8

that I knew Mr King had gone was that I knew the track his wagon made by haveing the wheeltiers full of large nails. Well when I came up to him he had got the wagon into an auquord [awkward] possion [position] coming up to the side of a small river, and haveing no leader the Oxen took a wronge turn and brought both Cattle and Wagon on to a narrow bank between the river and a mountain so that it was imposable to get the wagon out again

[Page 85]

by unyokeing the Cattle and backing the wagon out, then we were within one mile of a Dutch farm and coming up to there we halted for the night. and this night the Bull run away and the dogs stole our Meat and the next day he started on with the wagon and left me to walk and drive the lose stock.

And as usal I had to follow the track of the wagon orels [or else] I would never have found my way There were many tracks on the road but his was a differant one by haveing great nails on the tiers [tires] and then I had another eveidence of his goin that road

[Page 86]

which was, I picked up his tar bucket he had lost of his wagon I carried it a little distance and found it so heavy so I hid it under a bush by the road side and left it. After about two days journey we arrived again at Geart Knots.[3] the same farm we had been at some time before, and I thought and understood him that he was takeing me home I think to the best of my knowlege we were traveling for day in the District of Swellendam,[4] This was in the year of eighteen twenty three, then I was about twelve years old.

We stayed at Knots's for some time and made arraingment with him to leave the lose

[Page 87]

Cattle at his place for him to take care of, then him and I started with the Wagon on a back trip to the Sweartberg [Swartberg][5] Mountains amongest the farms that were scattered here and there to buy up a load of Brandy

---

3. A family surnamed "Knoetze" lived in Grahamstown, which may be the correct spelling for "Knots." The first name could be "Gerrit" or "Gert" as evidenced in records available at FamilySearch.

4. "Town 225 km east of Cape Town and 53 km west of Heidelberg. It developed around the drostdy established in 1747, and attained municipal status in 1904. Named in October 1747 after the Governor, Hendrik Swellengrebel (1700–1760), and his wife, Helena ten Damme." Raper, *Dictionary of Southern Africa Place Names*, s.v. "Swellendam," 524.

5. The Swartberg (Afrikaans for "black mountain") range extends about two hundred kilometers from near Ladismith to Willowmore. They are situated between the Great and Little Karoo and run parallel to the Langeberg and Outeniqua mountains. Raper, *Dictionary of South African Place Names*, s.v. "Swartberg", 522.

Swartberg Mountain Pass. Courtesy Western Cape Archives.

and dried fruite to take back to Grahams Town [Grahamstown], our road lead through very stupendious mountains like those already discribed, we suffered fearfuly for want of water one day we outspaned at a disserted house. it was disserted by its inhabitants but they had left a great many things in it and among them their was a small barrel of viniger, and while

[Page 88]

CHAPTER 8

Mr King went off into the mountains in seirch of water I enjoyed the viniger by drawing it out of the barrel with a read, after leaving this place we travald on for several days passing a farm now and then who were not very rich neither in garden, or Cattle but at one of those places one of the men who was their took pitty on me seeing that I was barfoot ordered me a paire of Shoes made for which I were very thankful, As we were travelig along and not taking notice of a turn we were coming to the wagon struck a large tree which toer off the cover and bows with such

[Page 89]

force so that it scared him (King) so much he threw his Hat of on one side while he jumped of [off] the other, and then blamed me for it. Well we contunied on our journey yet for days through such a Mountainous country untill we came to some very rick farmers who had full and plenty of everything and the very best of water for which I have suffered so much. They had the most beautiful vineyards, so extensive, and their fruit trees, I am sure that I saw Peare trees[6] at that place fifty feet high, and it was a fine Country for growing wheat. and they had their own grist

[Page 90]

Mills right at home. Well instead of this King buying Brandy as he said he was going to do he sold the Wagon and Oxen, and baught Horses. he Mounted me on to one and himself on to another and started off to the differant farmhouses, and I not been use to riding on Horseback I became so sore and tired that I could ride no longer then I told King that I could not sit on the horse any longer and it was no use to try, Then he told me to go too a Dutch farm that we had passed on our way into that part which was about forty miles from where we where then

[Page 91]

but coming up to a place some fifteen miles from where he started me from, and having to go on foot and all alone I stopt at this place to rest and told the people how I was and where I had to go to get (some thirty miles) they would not let me go any farther for they said it was not safe for me to go and alone for the way I had to go there were Lions plenty so they kept me with them they washed and cleaned me gave me a comb to dress my head so that I soon began to feel more comfortable and at home more than I had for a long time, I dont know how long I stayed with

[Page 92]

---

6. "Several trees called so on account of some real or imaginary resemblance of the wood to that of the fruit tree. Hard - Olinia cymosa." Marloth, *The Flora of South Africa*, s.v. "Pear," 65.

those kind people it was some time in the Winter when I went there, and I know that the trees were all out in bloom when I left, But while I stayed there I remember I would make myself useful and help their Children to do whatever they were set to do, such as herd Stock or make gardens during my stay at this place I never heard anything of Mr King for about three months, Then he sent a messenger after me to come to a neighboring farmhouse where he was staying, but as he had deceived me so often before I would not go to him with the first message so after a little

[Page 93]

while he sent again to me with such fair promises to take me home to my parents that I went to him and I had to walk fifteen miles back to him, The messenger he sent for me was a Hottentot. The people were very sorry to part with me but when I started they gave me so much good food enough to last me two or three days, Those peoples name was, or the Jentlemans name was, Daniel Straidam[7] of the Sweartberg Devision [Swartberg Division] of South Africa.
Cape Colony.

---

7. This surname is probably either "Strydom" or "Strijdom" as noted at FamilySearch.

Chapter 9

[Page 94]

When I got to where he was I hardly knew him for he had been very sick. He told me he had been in a secsion of the country where the people were very poor and that he had to live on riceants and wild game. those riceants are about half an inch long. The nest when dug out of the ground it is like a Honey comb and as large as a bushel basket this nest is full of eggs which is about a quarter of an inch long and the natives use it has rice. they are caled the white Ant.

The white Ant, being a vegetable feeder, devours articles of

[Page 95]

vegetable origin only, and leather, which by tanning is imbued with a vegetable flavor, "A man may be rich to day and poor tomorrow from the ravages of white ants, Himself and another man were prepared for a long journey when I got to him with Horses and provisions has he said to go direct home to Grahams Town [Grahamstown]. so that my hopes were once more raised thinking to get home once more, so we three started and traviled for about a Fortnight towards Grahams Town [Grahamstown], then we turned off quite another direction, and came upon extensive prairie flats covered with kroo

[Page 96]

karoo bush, on those flats Ostrichs Springboks and many other kinds of game abounds, Well after got on to those flats we rode for miles, and from house to house buying Ostrichs Feathers[1] I have carried great bundles of those beautifill feathers, then the first opprtunity Mr King would sell them eather for money or goods just what the customer might have, then we would go again and buy more and so we traviled for months But I dont remember what became of the other man that started out with us, but I expect his buisness lay in some other direction, Those people of whom we baught the feathers from were independly rich farmers

[Page 97]

so one day Mr King heard of a trader being in the neighberhood whose name was Mr William Kittson [William Kidson] of Wilson's [Willson's] party of Settlers,[2] This jentleman had seen my father some time before and my father

---

1. On Ostrich farming as a business in South Africa, see Arthur Douglass, *Ostrich Farming in South Africa: Being an Account of its Origin and Rise; How to Set About it; the Profits to be Derived; How to Manage the Birds; the Capital Required; the Diseases and Difficulties to be met with &c. &c.*

2. The William Kidson family were members of the Thomas Willson Party (no. 17 on the Colonial Department list). At the time of their departure from the British Isles

William Kidson (1785-1869). Courtesy Western Cape Archives.

CHAPTER 9   41

told him if he should happen to find me in any of his travils that he should bring me home with him, Mr King did not want to part with me and tried every way to dodge this man one by wanting me to go with him to swim and tried in many ways to get me out of the way of Mr Kittson [Kidson] but it was no use Mr Kittson [Kidson] would not let me go out of his sight so finly King had to let me

[Page 98]

go and I have never seen Mr King since but I heard of him many yeas afterwards, Then he was makeing great broadbrimed hats for the Dutch people in the district of Swellendam, Where I engage to go with this Mr Kittson [Kidson] it was at the entrance of the great Swartberg Port, or the Black Mountain Pass, we was then about two or three hundreds miles from Grahams Town [Grahamstown], When leaveing this place we had to call at all the Dutch farms on our way back to gather up stock that he had baught in coming and baught as many more has he could both Sheep and Cattle and also Goats and Dutch Soap and fat and Sheepskins.[3]

[Page 100]

    While on my way back my eyes became very sore and I was blind for one week, But after traveling for some weeks we arrived in Grahams Town [Grahamstown] and as soon as my dear mother heard of my being there she came to meet me with one of my little Sisters in her arms, After I left home my father and family had moved into Grahams Town [Grahamstown]. And here my father had built a windmill and was living in it, in the lower story after I had been at home a little while my father and myself used to go to the Forest to cut timber for to make Plows princebly, so one very windy day while in the Forest a young man came up on

[Page 101]

the hill and caled to my father and told him that the mill was on fire so that when we came to it, it was all one mass of coals, My mother had gone to Grahams Town [Grahamstown] on buisness which was about one mile from the mill, The mill was on an eminence overlooking the Town. It was suposed to have taken fire from coales left and shaveings laying about my fathers workbench and the wind blowing the coals and shaveings togather set fire to the place and by that my father lost all he was worth his tools furniture and

---

for South Africa, William is listed as a thirty-four-year-old farmer, and his wife was Ann, age 32. They had five children: Mary Ann (12), Amelia (9), Frederick (4), Emma (2), and Thomas (1). Nash, *The Settler Handbook*, 138–41. The William Kittson that Eli Wiggill mentions is most likely William Kidson. Guy Butler, ed., *When Boys were Men*, 65.

  3. Page 99 is missing from the original manuscript.

all so after so many years of hard labour and toil he had to begin the world afresh.⁴ After being burnt out

[Page 102]

my father moved his family into Grahams Town [Grahamstown] and there he found friends who gave him a house to live in rent free untill he could help himself again.⁵ The house was an old Artillery Barracks, which was built before the Town was layed out for it staud in the middle of the street, my

---

4. "Isaac Wiggill, like most of the settlers, suffered many reverses, but since he was a wheelwright and wagon-maker by trade, he decided to seek his fortune at Grahamstown. . . . Isaac and his son Eli often spent their time in the woods some distance from the mill and about two miles away from the centre of the village felling timber and preparing it for the use of their trade. . . . One day, when father and son were in the woods, their mother decided to walk the mile into town to do some shopping, but on the family's return to their home they found the place a smouldering ruin. The fireplace which had served a multitude of purposes, had unfortunately been constructed too near the building and a sudden gust of wind had blown a shower of sparks on to the mill and in a few minutes the whole place was in flames. . . . Many years later a Mr. C. Webb . . . said, 'The sails, fanned by the wind flew round with frantic velocity like some great giant fighting with the fire until, becoming burnt at the bottom, they came down with a crash.' A tragedy it was for the Wiggills for they had lost everything they possessed, including most of the tools with which they had earned their livelihood." Eric W. Turpin, *Grahamstown: Hub of the Eastern Cape*, 1.

5. Isaac Wiggill sent a letter to William Hayward from Grahamstown seeking help after this unfortunate episode: "your Memorialist belongs Mr Samuel Bradshaw's party—That he paid his own deposit and remained at this Location upwards of Three years. When he left it and erected a Windmill on one of the Heights near this Town, which unfortunately was burnt down—That when he left his Location he placed another person thereon to cultivate it and keep possession thereof for your Memorialist. That he has carefully preserved the Timber which beloned to themselves and he has learnt wich much surprise that they now intend seizing on that which [your] Memorialist considers his own property, and therefore he humbly and earnestly prays for your protection. That your Memorialist also entreats that you will be pleased to order the Land to be family divided, and the Titles granted, That as there does not exist any Agreement between the party and its Head Memorialist prays for an equal proportion of the surplus Land and he will ever feel himself in duty bound to pray Isaac Wiggill." Letter of Isaac Wiggill to William Hayward, August 25, 1824, book 8541, Western Cape Archives. Wiggill sent a follow-up letter concerning the matter to Hayward on October 9, 1826. Samuel Bradshaw allotted Isaac Wiggill fifteen acres and said, "The Party will not admit Wiggill's claim for his servant who died." Further, their point was that Wiggill's servant was working in Bathurst and not on Wiggill's land. It is difficult to ascertain the timeline of these events. Bradshaw Party, 306, Western Cape Archives.

CHAPTER 9

father then went to work and workd hard for one year before he got things comfortable around him again, Then he got the grant of a plot of land with water rights to build a Grist Mill which he did for the accomadation of the people, but he found out in a little while that the water was too weak to carry on the mill without

[Page 103]

distressing those in the Town who depended on the same water family survesses. So he between times he built another wind mill up in the same Cluff, and between the two he done a very good buisness, and my self and my brothers used to go into the Forest and cut and saw Timber for my father who contunied working at his traid which was Makeing Wagons and Plows and Carpenter work in genarel, one day while the water wheel was being built I came near loseing my life by been jambed in it while working at the wheel the props gave way and began to swing around and to try to save myself I tryed to step the paddles and

[Page 104]

did as long as I could then I fell and by so doing that saved my life, about this time I was sixteen years old, and soon after the windmill were completed and we where begining to be comfortable once more my mother took sick and died, to the best of my recolection it was about the year eighteen twenty seven My mother left eight Children myself being the eldest of five sons and three Daughters,[6] some time after the Death of my Mother I left home for I was so determined to learn the Wagon makeing, and hearing of a good chance with men who understood the buisness living in longcluff, or Georges Town [Georgetown][7] I started with a

[Page 105]

full intention of which was about eighty miles from home But when I had traviled about thirty miles I met with a man whos name is John Rogers, And he persuaded me to stay with him, He was living in a Forest he indused me by offering me big wages to stay which I did and helped him to saw timber for six months at thirty five shillings per month, Then I left him and went to work for a Dutchman at the same kind of work and for the same pay. Well I worked for those two men for one year, and never got one months wages or the vallue of a month. The Forest at that time was known by the name of

[Page 106]

---

6. Elizabeth Grimes Wiggill died in 1827. British 1820 Settlers to South Africa records Elizabeth Grimes and lists her birth and death dates along with her surviving Wiggill children by age, eldest to the youngest: Eli (17), George (14), Joseph (11), Elizabeth (9), Elijah (6), Jane (2), Mary Ann (2), and Jacob (infant).

7. The city of George, South Africa, was once known as Georgetown.

Peter Retiff [Pieter Retief][8] Bush, on the Zuurberg mountain, Haveing compleated the year with those two men I went home again to my father caring with me three tanned sheepskins just enough to make me a pare of Lether Britches or as they are caled in Africa leather Crackers, And one blacksilk Handkerchief.

---

8. Pieter Retief is the name used in George E. Cory, *The Rise of South Africa: A History of the Origin of South African Colonization and of its Development towards the East from the Earliest Times to 1857*, 2:146.

Chapter 10

After returning home I remained with my father and was determined to learn my trade, Well the Timber, in them days was not so easy got as now my Brother and myself used to go into the Forests and cut down laerg trees then make a Sawpit and sawed out our Timber into such as

we would want to use for makeing Wagons, some times my father would be there with us and we would be there for weeks, but would come home every night and bring a load of Timber with us. The names of the Timber's we used is black ironwood White ironwood, white Pear, red Pear, Assagai [Assegai] wood, Sneezewood, Chestnut, Myrtle wood, Stinkwood, both black and white, and Olivewood, Redelce [Red els], Redmilk, and Whitemilk wood, then their is the yellow wood of two kinds the real yellow wood, and the other is what is called the Bastard Yellowood, and many other kinds too numerous to mention.

These are all Dutch names for the differ-

ant kinds of wood, and the English uses them for they can find no better, especley the Sneezewood, for when it is worked it make one Sneeze just like takeing Snuff, and it will keep in the ground as posts for fifty years, and then looks frish [fresh] and sound, While some of the others will not last more than a year before it begins to rot. Then their is the White elce [els] which is such beau tiful wood to work. the Dutch people in Africa have all their Tables and Chests and other articals of furniture genarly made of it, But the Stinkwood. is the most used it is more like mahogany and is uesed both for furniture of all kinds and for makeing

Wagons, it is a great deal stronger than mahogany, The old Dutch wagons were made of the Black stinkwood and it seemed that thare was no end to its wareing doors and window shashes [sashes] are made from it, And it is taken to England by Shiploads and is used there for makeing gunstocks The axeltrees of those wagons were genearly made of assagai [assegai][1] wood, As I have being so used to working ever since I was able to use tools with all those differant kinds of wood and cuting them both with the ax and the Saw, and then, with every other kind of tools, so that I know them all so well, that is the reason I have numerated them.

Well about the time that I

---

1. An *assegai* is a slender, iron-tipped hardwood spear used by southern African peoples.

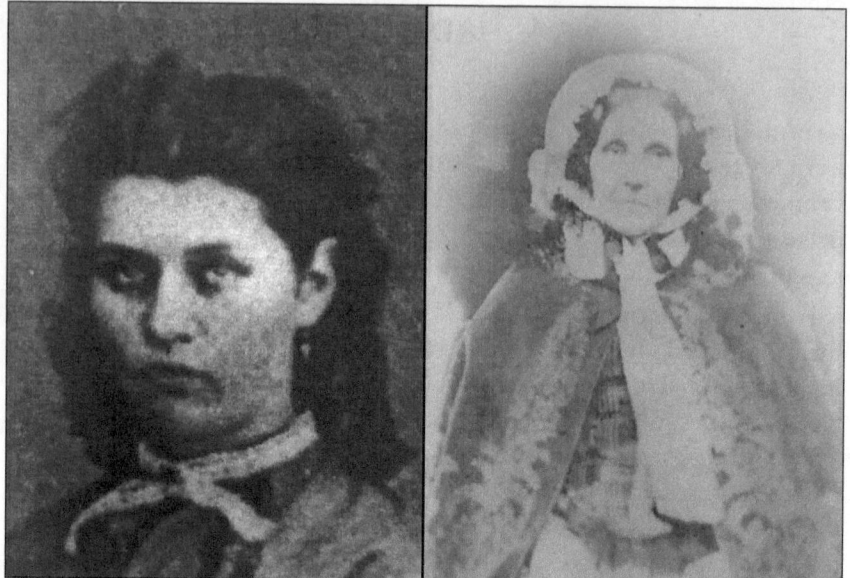

Susannah Bentley Wiggill as a young woman and later in life. Courtesy Michael T. Lowe.

[Page 110]

came home my father married his second wife, whos name was Miss Mary Seares [Sayers], by whom he had four Sons and one Daughter their are three of the Sons living married and in very good surcumstances whos names are James, Moses, and Aaron,[2] I contunied with my father and worked at my trade untill I was twenty two years old, then I got married to a Miss Susannah Bently [Susanna Bentley] the Daughter of one of the Settlers of eighteen twenty whoes names was Frances. Parrot. Bentley [Francis Parratt Bentley],[3] of Yorkshire England my Wife being their oldest Daughter, At this time I

---

2. "Isaac married his second wife Mary Sayers on January 5, 1829, at St. George's Church in Graham's Town. Mary, born about 1796 near Tottenham Court, London, was about 33 years of age in 1829 and had never married. She and her family were devout Baptists and deeply religious. . . . Isaac and Mary Sayers were to have four children together." Wiggill, *The Cotswolds to the Cape*, 146–47.

3. Francis, a farmer, age 37, and his wife Elizabeth Bentley, age 31, as well as their four children were members of the Wainwright Party, which embarked from Liverpool on the vessel *John*, arriving at Algoa Bay in May 1820. The names and ages of the children were listed as: "William 9, Susanna 8, John 4, George 3." Nash, *The Settler Handbook*, 131. Susannah was born September 8, 1812, in York, England. The Bentley family were employed as lace makers before they left for South Africa in December 1819. Zelda Jane Wall Shipley, "History of Susannah Bentley Wiggill Pioneer of 1861," typescript, 1. We thank Jack and Bonnie Herron for sharing a copy of this document with us.

CHAPTER 10

Rev. William Shaw (1798–1872). Courtesy Cory Library.

started a buisness for myself in Grahams Town [Grahamstown] and had two Apprenties's and had all the work at makeing

[Page 111]

new Wagons that myself and Boys could do and lived very comfortable and at that time Beef and very good too was only one English penny per pound and everything that was eatable was just as cheap accordenly,

And on the 7th day of December 1832 my first Child was born whoes name I called John[4] and was Baptized by the Rev Mr William Shaw who came from England as a minester with the Salem Party of Settlers of eighteen twenty, and belonging to the Wesleyans, to which I was a member,[5] And

---

4. Eli's son John Wesley Wiggill was born December 7, 1832. His name reveals the religious beliefs of Eli, who named his first-born son after the Methodism founder John Wesley.

5. Reverend William Shaw (1798–1872) no doubt influenced Wiggill's later decision to enter the ministry. Shaw had come to the Eastern Cape among the 1820 British settlers with the Sephton Party to Salem a dozen years earlier, yet he chose to reach beyond these boundaries and influence the entire Albany region. Therefore, young Eli would certainly have heard his sermons on many occasions. Wiggill, *The Cotswolds to the Cape*, 115. Reverend Dugmore noted "WILLIAM SHAW had an eye and a heart that embraced all Albany, and guided the elements of usefulness wherever he could find them." Dugmore, *The Reminiscences of an Albany Settler*, 45–46. When Rev. Shaw passed in 1872, the Wesleyan Missionary Society mourned the "loss of one

in October 14th 1834 my Wife gave birth to a Daughter whose name was Sarah. Ann, and she died November 5th 1835 in the Winterberg[6] in the distrect of Fortbeaufort [Fort Beaufort].

[Page 112]

I must now come back to Grahams Town [Grahamstown] things went on smoth and well with me untill 1835 up to this date the country were all at peace when the Kaafar War [Kaffir or Xhosa War] broke[7] out which I can not do better than coppy from the annals of Mr Chase's History of Cape colony[8] wherein he sketch the War of therty five of which I was an eye witness and also a sufferer. Mr Chase writes as follows. The reader is requested to take here a hasty glance at the aspect of the doomed British Settlement as it appeared but one week before this tremendous and unprovoked onslaught. The little Colony, so lately comenced, notwithstanding all its previous difficulties, had established a growing center of

[Page 113]

civilization, and fully recovered from the natural effects of transplantation from another soil. From innumerable happy hamlets the curling smoke-wreath ascended amid the forest trees surrounding the humble but comfortable dwellings. On the soft sward of the homesteads gambolled "legions" of blithesome little innocent Children, unsuspicious of danger, Sleek cattle

---

of the most servicable and valuable Missionaries ever sent for by this Society. . . . In the Eastern Districts of the Cape Colony he was the Society's first Missionary, being the spiritual guide for the original settlers. . . . By many of the colonists he came to be regarded as a father, and he held a high place in the esteem of the Community at large, and also of those who from time to time administered public affairs in that part of the British dominions. . . the Missions which he commenced, and for a long time directed, have been among the most satisfactory of all those he carried on under the Committee's care. By the blessing of God he lived to see the one station which he originally occupied grow into fifty-one, arranged in four Districts and a native Training Institution established and in full operation." W. B. Boyce, *Memoir of the Rev. William Shaw*, 393–94. See also W. D. Hammond-Tooke, ed., *The Journal of William Shaw*; Gerald H. Anderson, ed., *Biographical Dictionary of Christian Missions*, 615–16.

Henry James Talbot, converted to The Church of Jesus Christ of Latter-day Saints in the same year as Eli Wiggill, noted "The Rev. William Shaw was a great comfort to the colonists in their trubles [sic] in the early life of the settlers in Africa. . . . In Grahamstown, there was a chapel built, where Rev. Shaw preached to the people of that town." Talbot, "Short Sketch of the Life of Henry James Talbot," 1.

6. The Winterberg is an extensive mountain range running east to west just north of the towns of Adelaide, Bedford, and Fort Beaufort in the Eastern Cape of South Africa.

7. Robert Ross, *The Borders of Race in Colonial South Africa: The Kat River Settlement, 1829–1856*, 91–115.

8. Wiggill's autobiography, pp. 112–22, refers to Alexander Wilmot, *History of the Colony of the Cape of Good Hope. From Its Discovery to the Year 1819*, 308–12.

CHAPTER 10

and sheep by thousands grazed on the verdant hills and along the lovely valleys threaded by some bubbling stream. From the woods resounded the axe the hammer on its anvil beside the glowing forge. The plough quietly followed the steady going oxen, showing how busily engaged were the in-

[Page 114]

habitants in their industrious occupations, little dreading the "Damocles" weapon so suddenly to descend. From being an entirely consuming community, as at first, the Settlers had secured more than daily provisions, established a commerce with the home they had left in very many instances poor adventurers to the annual value of £125.000. and that despite obstacles enough to appal the most steadfast; but, as Lord Bacon says, "It was not with them as with other men whom small things would discourage, or small discontents cause to wish themselves home again."[9] They had at length set their feet on the high road to prosperity; but, alas! within

[Page 115]

less than fourteen days, the labours of fourteen years were at once annihilated. Forty-four persons were at once murdered, 369 dwellings consumed. 261 pillaged, and 172.000 head of livestock carried off by the savage, who had no cause of quarrel against the peaceful inhabitants. What aggravated this wicked inroad was the fact that during the great part of the year the Governor had commenced special negotiations for new, and to them (the Kafirs [Kaffirs]) a most advantageous system of relation, the details of which His Excellency had, through the Rev. Dr. [John] Philip, then on a tour in Kafirland [Kaffirland], entered into with the Chiefs, and all except Tyali had expressed

[Page 116]

satisfaction, The enemy, in over whelming force from 8.000 to 10.000, entered the Settlement in the night between the 21st and 22nd of December,[10] just before the looked for Christmas festival, and along a line of thirty miles of frontier, without even attracting the notice of the missionaries among them, so covert were the conspirators, boasting that now they would build their huts and villages at Algoa Bay; and by the 26th December their vanguard was already in the vicinity of Uitenhage, nearly one hundred miles westward of the great

---

9. This statement by Lord Bacon is noted in Wilmot, *History of the Colony of the Cape of Good Hope. From Its Discovery to the Year 1819*, 309.

10. Henry James Talbot reminisced, "The natives attected [attacked] the settlers; and the settlers not being used to the mode of their warfair, great losses and many lives were lost, which could have been avoided if the colonists had been aware of the Caffer mode of war. But as it was, the settlers had to learn their way of attacts, which allways begins through the night or at brake of day, and the settlers not being aware of that were taken by surprise." Talbot, "Short Sketch of the Life of Henry James Talbot," 1.

Fish river [Great Fish River], and only twenty from that of their threatened destination. So sudden and irresistible was the invasion that several extraord-

[Page 117]

inary, and, in any other circumstances, ludicrous hairbreadth escapes took place.[11] One in particular, among many others, came to the writers personal knowledge, where a lady was in the homely act of preparing the conventional and time honoured Advent pudding in fact, "welding" the ingredients, when her husband rushed in, caught her up, to her surpirse as she was then attired, thurst [thrust] her on a horse, and galloped off for "dear life," His houses one a very handsome and costly structure, just finished, with two others of lesser pretensions on neighbouring farms belonging to him were burnt to the ground, his large herds of cattle swept off from all three properties by the bloodstained

[Page 118]

and infuriated invaders, and this gentleman, like many others, who in the morning arose in the most prosperous circumstances, was that night little better than a beggar, without a change of apparel for himself and family.

Before the close of the year all that remained of the flurishing District of Albany was Grahams Town [Grahamstown], the village of Salem, and the Missionary Station of Theopolis [Theophilus],[12] into which places the inhabitants had fled for shelter. Within eight days from the time the savages burst into the Colony, a body of them, with their booty, returned into Kafirland [Kaffirland], as the Rev. Mr [Thomas] Chalmers[13] discribes, "exulting in their oun might and wisdom, because they have been able to

[Page 119]

obtain so much illgotton gain; and unless a check be given", wrote he. they will in a few days return to the Colony with redoubled fury. They are a wicked and ungodly race. They expect the Hottentots of Kat River[14] will not fire upon

---

11. This sudden invasion during the 1835 War caught the British settlers off-guard. Dugmore, *The Reminiscences of an Albany Settler*, 50–55.

12. Theophilus, "city of God," was a London Missionary Society station established in 1814 and located "near the mouth of the Kasouga River by the Reverend J G Ulbricht but razed to the ground in 1851." Raper, *Dictionary of Southern African Place Names*, s.v. "Theopolis," 534; Marion Rose Currie, "The History of Theopolis Mission, 1814–1851"; Jane Sales, *Mission Stations and the Coloured Communities of the Eastern Cape 1800–1852*, 79–100.

13. Thomas Chalmers was a Scottish, Presbyterian minister.

14. The Kat (Afrikaans for "cat"; Khoikhoi *hunca* for "wildcats") River rises in the Winterberg Mountains thirty kilometers north of Fort Beaufort and flows south before entering the Fish River northeast of Fort Brown. Its name is reflected in Katberg, Katberg Pass, and the Kat River Settlement. Raper, *Dictionary of Southern African Place Names*, s.v. "Kat River," 253.

CHAPTER 10

Khoikhoi or Griqua Warrior from Kat River Settlement, Eastern Cape, ca. 1820s.

them. but stand neutral, for they are their friends." This statement appears in a communication from the reverend gentleman, dated Chumi, 1st January, 1835, where a meeting was held, the missionaries forced to be present, trembling for their lives; for, as they wrote, "an angry look just now would be sufficient to send us all into eternity." Here the Rev. Mr Weir[15] was compelled to to pen a letter from the Chiefes with "overtures for peace," a proposal to abstain from farther

[Page 120]

hostility untill they could get an answer to a demand for compensation for wounding KloKlo. some charges against Colonel Somerset, all of which were without foundation, and this insolent document was dictated and dispatched only ten days after the invasion began, but after they had secured their emmence plunder were still reeking with the blood of the Colonists, and had laid waste a thriving and entire district of the Colony.

---

15. Mr. James Weir served as a lay missionary of the Glasgow society. Theal, *History of South Africa Since September 1795*, 2:95.

1835. —The news of the invasion reached Cape Town by express,[16] and took the authorities and public there as much by surprise as it did the borderers; but the most energetic measures were at once under-

[Page 121]

taken. Colonel Smith was instantly dispatched to the Frontier overland, and reached Graham's Town [Grahamstown], a distance of 600 miles, in six days, Martial law was immediately proclamed over the two border districts, Albany and Somerset, but meanwhile Fort Willshire [Fort Wiltshire], on the Keiskamma River, and Kafir's [Kaffir's] Drift Post, on the Great Fish river, were obliged to be evacuated, so fiery and rapid had been the savages' assault and they were burned by the enemy Of the condition of the country as it was found by the Colonel on his arrival we have his own words:- "Already are seven thousand persons dependent upon the government for

[Page 122]

the necessaries of life. The land is filled with the lamentations of the widow and the fatherless.

> "The war cry echoing wild and loud.
> The war of the savage, fierce and proud
> Would burst like the storm the thunder cloud
> Over Afric's southern wilds".[17]

---

16. The *Grahamstown Journal* (est. 1831) provided coverage. For an overview of early South African newspapers including the *Grahamstown Journal*, see Theo E. G. Cutten, *A History of the Press in South Africa*, 24–25.

17. Rev. Henry H. Dugmore quoted this poem in his 1870 jubilee address regarding the British 1820 settlers. Dugmore, *The Reminiscences of an Albany Settler*, 43.

Chapter 11

I now coppy a little from the pen the Rev. H. H Dugmores British Settlers of twenty, their jubilee in May 1870, held in Grahams Town [Grahamstown], South Africa.

I was not in the Colony, but in Kafferland, when the war of '35 broke out, All our first tidings, were from Kaffers. The plundering of the traders' stations was,

[Page 123]

to us, the first intimation of what was going forward. The arrival at the Mount Coke Mission[1] of such of the traders themselves as could effect their escape confirmed our worst fears. Some of them had barely saved their lives, and scarcely knew how they had done it. One of them (as he told me himself) had, while the Kaffers were discussing the subject of putting him to Death, given some of them lessions in shooting, that they might kill him with as little pain as possible. The climax of triumph seemed to have been reached when the news was spread far and near that Fort Wilshire [Wiltshire] (the impregnable, as the Kaffers had deemed it, was abandoned by the English

[Page 124]

garrison, and had fallen into the possession of Tyali and Macoma.[2] And then return parties of warriors, laden with the spoils of the Settlers' dwellings, passed through the station, taunting us with our helpless condition, and telling they could afford to let us alone for awhile, as they intended to finish us at leisure. The suspence, arisind [arisen] from the cuting off of all intelligence from the colony, was horrible. The burning homesteads of Lower Albany lighted up the horizon night after night. and imagination was left to paint its most fearful pictures. Where the end was to be we knew not. Days seemed to grow into weeks; and week after week elapsed without

[Page 125]

any sign of aggressive movement from the Colony; till old Letu, the chief who was protecting us, impatiently exclaimed "Akuseko 'Mlungu! inkomande ingavelinje, lapelile bonke!"[3]

---

1. Methodist Society Station established in 1825 by Reverend S. Kay and named after society founder Dr. Coke, located eighteen kilometers east of King William's Town. Raper, *Dictionary of Southern African Place Names*, s.v. "Mount Coke," 363.

2. Maqoma and Tyali were Xhosa chiefs and half-brothers. See Xhosa Royalty of Southern Africa on the Geni website.

3. "There are no white people left. Why doesn't the commander appear. They must be all finished!" Xhosa translation by Ayanda Ndaba.

Xhosa Chief Maqoma, in his regalia during the final period of his chieftaincy and before his imprisonment on Robben Island. Courtesy South African Library, Cape Town.

CHAPTER 11

Combatants of the 8th Xhosa War Defending Their Homeland in Water Kloof (1850–51).

The first gleam of relief appeared in an extraordinary commotion that surprised us one morning. Herds of cattle suddenly made their appearance, driven in eager hast past the station, and towards the Kye,[4] followed by troops of women and children, carrying loads of pots, mats, and baskets, and keeping company with the old packoxen that brought up the rear, laden with heavy milk sacks. A party of us at once mounted on horseback,

There are no white men left! No comando makes its appearance they must be all finished up!"

[Page 126]

and proceeded towards Wesleyville[5] to find out the cause of the movement. We saw that a sudden panic had seized the tribes which occupied the country

---

4. The Great Kei (Nciba) River in the Eastern Cape, formed by the confluence of the Black Kei and White Kei rivers, runs northeast of Cathcart before flowing into the Indian Ocean. The river formed the border between the Ciskei (the west side) and Transkei (across the Kei, pronounced Ki) regions. The River KyeKei is noted by James Edward Alexander, *Narrative of a Voyage of Observation among the Colonies of Western Africa in the Flag-ship Thalia; and of a Campaign in Kaffir-Land, on the Staff of the Commander in Chief in 1835*, 2:155.

5. Named after Methodism founder John Wesley. Wesleyville, or Wesley, was established sixty-nine kilometers south of King William's Town on the Twecu, a tributary of the Chalumna River, by Rev. William Shaw in 1823. Raper, *Dictionary of Southern African Place Names*, s.v. "Wesley," 583.

between us and the Fish River. The whole upper basin of the Chalumna[6] seemed alive with cattle, streaming down every bushpath from the ridges beyond, and all urged on in one direction Eastward oh! A night attack (as we learned afterwards), planned and carried out successfuly under the command of the rosey faced veteran, Major Cox, had surprised and destroyed the "Great Place" of the notorious old chief Eno, who himself narrowly and ignobly escaped disguised in the kaross of one of his wives. The frontier

[Page 127]

Kaffers, who securely revelling in the plunder of the colony, were confounded by the unlooked for exploit. My escort, armed, and looking like a cavalry patrol, might have captured the flying cattle by hundreds; for the few men in charge of them, mistaking us for a part of the invading force, abandoned them, and took shelter in the bush as we crossed the path of their flight. If that attack had been at once followed up, it would have confirmed on the side of peace the coast tribes who were then wavering, and it would have shortened the war. I will now relate an incident which happened to my wifes Brother John Bentley.[7] A young man whos name is Thomas

[Page 128]

Shone,[8] went out to his father's farm but started with government stores for Bathurst, and it was reported that he had gone to his father's farm in the Nottingham party eight or ten miles from Bathurst. So his parants became very uneasy about their Boy (for they had left their farm drove out and taken shelter in Grahams Town [Grahamstown] if he was there he would have been killed by some one of the stragling Kaffers, So they prevailed on my Brotherinlaw and a man whoes name was Chipperfield.[9] to go in surch of him they started with a Carte and six Oxen belonging to the young man's father, But when they arrived at a settlement

[Page 129]

---

6. The Chalumna River (Xhosa: *Tyolomnqa*) is approximately seventy-eight kilometers long, forming at the confluence of two small rivers: the Qugwala in the west and the Mtyolo in the east. The Chalumna empties into the Indian Ocean.

7. John Bentley came with his parents and siblings with the Wainwright Party in 1820. He was only four years old at the time and therefore would have been a mere youth at the time of this tragedy. Nash, *The Settler Handbook*, 131.

8. Thomas Shone was a member of the Scott party who came with his family and other 1820 British immigrants at the age of four to the Eastern Cape. Nash, *The Settler Handbook*, 113.

9. Twenty-year-old British immigrant John Chipperfield came without family to the Eastern Cape with the Rowles Party. Nash, *The Settler Handbook*, 111.

CHAPTER 11

Isaac Wiggill Cottage, Bathurst. Courtesy Fred E. Woods.

on the road called the Howard's Party.[10] There left the Cart and took the Cattle with them knowing that if they found the young man he would have a Wagon. in going through the Settlements which had been deserted by the Settlers, near to what is called the Waay Plaats[11] Wether they were waylayed by day or night it was never known as they had not been heard of for Several days and as the young man was safe in Bathurst a party went out in scurch of them I think the party consisted of about twenty men. about fifteen miles from Grahams Town [Grahamstown] they found the Yoks and rims but wether they had been unyoked by themselves or by the

[Page 130]

Kaffers it was never known from there they scirched further and about fifteen yards from the yoks they found my Brother John Bentley dead pearced with several assagai [assegai] wounds, He had crept away into a bush cluff his whip layed by his side but he was in a bad state of decomposition, but expecting to find them dead they took Coffens with them so they gathered my Brothers remains into a Coffen and buried him near by where they found him, But they

---

10. The Howard Party was number 21 on the Colonial Department list of British immigrants who arrived in Algoa Bay on April 15, 1820. Nash, *The Settler Handbook*, 82.

11. Waay Plaats is mentioned by George McCall Theal, *Records of the Cape Colony from January 1820 to June 1821*, 13:170.

Bradshaw Mill and water wheel, built by Samuel Bradshaw and Isaac Wiggill, Bathurst, 1821, burned down by Xhosa warriors in 1835, restored in 1981. Courtesy Fred E. Woods.

never found his companion, I stayed in Graham's Town [Grahamstown] untill peace was proclamed, in the mean time doing military duty, and working

[Page 131]

at my traid. Then I went from Graham's Town [Grahamstown] to Bathurst to occupy a property which I had baught before the war broke out and their I remained about two years working at my traid and it was about the year of eighteen thertyseven I left Bathurst to go with my father to fulfill a contract which, he my father had made with government to get five hundred posts of Sneezewodd twelve feet longe and eigh inches squear besides other Timber for rails and pallisadeing to Barrackade one side of Fort Beaufort, we had a great time to find the artical wanted we had to sirch the Forests far and near to get good sollid

[Page 132]

Timber in Sneezewood,[12] But before we had finished our contract, the order was countermanded by the government although they had commenced to put it up when the order came, so the Timber was used for military out posts for Veranda Posts.

---

12. *Ptaeroxylon* (pronounced '*teroxillo*'), a Greek translation meaning both "sneeze" and "wood," is an extremely durable hardwood highly sought after for wagon-making, furniture, and machine bearings.

CHAPTER 11

While I was engaged in this buisness my little Daughter Sarah Ann died who was ~~abou~~ about three years old, Then I left this place and went to Winterberg, where my Brother George had just got married and started the Blacksmith buisness, and I started ~~the~~ wagon makeing so we worked togather. but not as partners, for about one year.

[Page 133]

    Copyed

> "Our toilworn fathers have sunk to their rest,
> But their sons shall inherit their hope's bequest.
> Vallies are smiling in harvest pride;
> There are fleecy flocks on the mountain side;
> Cities are rising to stud the plains;
> The life blood of commerce is coursing the veins
> Of a new born Empire, that grows, and reigns
> O'er Afric's Southern Wilds."[13]

---

13. This poem is from the last stanza of a piece titled "Past and Present" by Dugmore in *A Treasury of South African Poetry and Verse*, 44–45.

Chapter 12

Some little time before I left Bathurst I had an engagement to go into the Buchanna [Bechuana] Country beyond the Oringe [Orange] river as an assistant to the Rev. John Edwards[1] of the ~~Meth~~ Wesleyans or Methodists Church.[2] I gave up my buisness in Bathurst and made preprations to go by making a new Wagon for the purpose which the Sociaty engaged to pay

---

1. John Edwards, born in 1804 at Bridford, Devonshire, converted to the Methodist faith in his youth and became a local preacher at age nineteen. He entered the ministry in 1828 and journeyed to South Africa in 1832 with his wife and several other ministers. Upon arrival, Rev. Barnabas Shaw greeted them and advised Edwards to "make your will and buy a gun." John complied with both suggestions. Edwards traveled northeast to Port Elizabeth, Grahamstown, and on to Buchnaap Station to commence his ministry among Indigenous peoples. He and his companions remained prepared against animal attack. Crop failure and the threat of starvation persuaded Edwards, his wife, and Rev. James Archbell, along with native followers made up of "Griquas, Barolongs, Korannas, and Newlanders," to the region of the Mantatees and the Basutos, where they secured land for themselves and their congregation through negotiations with local chiefs. Notwithstanding the constant threat of lions, poisonous snakes, and other obstacles, Edwards diligently worked among these tribes and spent time with his main body of congregants (the Barolongs) at Thaba 'Nchu. In 1839, he was assigned as the first minister in Port Elizabeth, in part so the coastal air might improve his wife's failing health. The couple served faithfully together before she passed away in 1871. Edwards continued to preach and settled in Grahamstown in 1876. He died there in 1887. John Edwards, *Reminiscences of the Early Life and Missionary Labours of the Rev. John Edwards, Fifty Years a Wesleyan Missionary in South Africa*, 89–118. Edwards recorded that the work at the Umpukani Wesleyan Mission Station increased and "these Koranas having to be attended to, Mr. Shaw sent up to my assistance from Grahamstown Mr. Eli Wiggel [Wiggill], who helped me much." Eli Wiggill served as Edwards' assistant at the Umpukani Mission Station in the Bechuana region of Thaba 'Nchu. Edwards, *Reminiscences of the Early Life*, 110. See also "Methodist Missionaries [Pamphlets] No. 4," in BP 4, vol. 43, Western Cape Archives and Records Service.

2. Although some British soldiers in the Eastern Cape professed Methodism, Reverend Barnabas Shaw established the Wesleyan Methodist Church in South Africa in 1816. Some of the 1820 British settlers were Methodists, and Shaw helped spread the denomination throughout the eastern province. Rosenthal, *Encyclopedia of Southern Africa*, 636. For a broad scope of Wesleyan missionary labours in South Africa, see volume four of G. G. Findlay and W. W. Holdsworth, *The History of the Wesleyan Methodist Missionary Society*; L. A. Hewson, *An Introduction to South African Methodists*, 1–9, for an overview of the Methodist ministry in the Western Cape and Eastern Cape; and J. Whiteside, *History of the Wesleyan Methodist Church of South Africa*, 109–15. For a detailed discussion of the Wesleyan mission to the Bechuana,

CHAPTER 12

Rev. John Edwards. From *Reminiscences of the Early Life and Missionary Labours of the Rev. John Edwards, Fifty Years a Wesleyan Missionary in South Africa*.

[Page 134]

me for and I also gave up an apprentise, Then I received a letter countermanding the whole affare from Mr Edwards, not on his personal authourity but the Socity to which he belonged Then I settled down again with my Brother in my buisness but did not feel right for, for a long time I had wanted to go on this mission I thought it would be so pleasant to be in that survies and Preach to the heathens. So. after receiveing that letter I sold the Wagon and made ready to go to work again, While at the Winterberg there came the Rev. G. [George] H. Green[3] at that time he was stationed at that time in Fort Beaufort. he had received a letter from Mr John Edwards requesting

[Page 135]

him to see me and to know my feelings in regard to going to the Buchanna [Bechuana] Country. just after seeing Mr Green myself and Brother George started to Graham's Town [Grahamstown] with two wagon's loaded with produce, at that time the roads was not very smoth for as we was going down the old Blinkwater Pass, my Brother Wagon upset and broak the top, or tent all to pecies I believe half the wagons that traviled that road upsets

---

including Rev. John Edwards, see, J. Du Plessis, *A History of Christian Missions in South Africa*, 176–81.

3. Rev. William Taylor, *Christian Adventures in South Africa*, 66–67, indicated that Rev. George H. Green supervised the Methodist Bathurst circuit during this era.

for the road was so bad and I have known wagons stick fast on that hill for days and could not move. But when we got to the bottom of the hill we went to work and repaired his Wagon, So when we got into Grahams Town [Grahamstown], I saw Mr Edwards and entered into an agreement
[Page 136]

with him to go into the Bechuana country for which I received a part of the first years Salary. After leaving him in Grahams Town [Grahamstown] myself and my Brother made a flying visit to Bathurst to see some of our old friends. And from there we went to the Kowie where my Brothers fatherinlaw lived whose name was Mr Joseph King Sr,[4] After visiting a few days with our friends we started back home to the Winterberg with our Wagons loaded with goods for our own use, we returned back through Grahams Town [Grahamstown]. takeing back a Mr Phillip King[5] as passenger an old friend of mine but we took another rout to escape that fearful hill, and when we got into what is called
[Page 137]

Bushneck being a very deep bushey valley while we were traviling through this valley, a comodation House was on the road so we thought we would have a little Wine and I sent one of our oxe leaders who was a Hottontott for the wine it was about Sunset. then we went on a little farther and outspaned, or unyoked for the night, has me and my friend King was takeing it easey on the road we lay down on our bed, and while laying there some money jalted out of my pocket afterwards my friend was looking for somthing and found it on the bed, and using a Scripture phrase let us gather up the fragments let nothing be lost so while gathring up those few pence I thought I would look for my pocketbook
[Page 138]

which I thought I put into the Wagon chest but it was not there and we shirched the wagon all over but it was no wheres to be found, Has we had not traviled more than a mile Mr King and myself made fiertorches by puting fat on sticks and we went back as far as I thought I had the pocketbook but did not find it there but before I had missed the book two persons had passed us and my friend King thought perhaps they might have picked it up. and he said let us go and see, so we went back to the Canteen or public house to enquire for it. but I told him that I thought it was a forlorn hope and would
[Page 139]

---

4. Joseph King, a thirty-seven-year-old laborer, immigrated with his family as part of the Bradshaw Party, which included the Wiggills, and arrived at Algoa Bay on April 29, 1820. Nash, *The Settler Handbook*, 49.

5. Phillip King is likely the eight-year-old son of Mr. Joseph King, Sr. Nash, *The Settler Handbook*, 49.

CHAPTER 12

not go, but he insisted. and been well acquainted with the propritory and had been for years I went back and enquired of him if their had any one being there haveing a pocketbook to spend any money, he answered no that he knew nothing about it. Then we asked him if their had been two persons their a man and woman who we had met on the road. He said yes that they were in another room and were both drunk. My friend said that he felt like shirching the man but Mr. Wilkie told him he could not do it without a Shirchwarrant notwithstanding all that was said. My friend rather insisted on shirching the man. I told them that if it was my book it had my name on it. and also a gold ring and several bank

[Page 140]

nots so then my friend rolled the man over just like rolling a log for he was dead drunk and put his hand into his pocket and said here it is I'll be bound and as soon as he puled the book out of his pocket I recognised it and said that it was my book the ring and nots were in the book but they had spent about one pound ten Shillings which was in silver, for drink and wareing apprel and some groceryes which the Shopkeeper gave to me then we went back to our Wagons and related to my Brother our adventure and camped their that night and the next day we reached home in the Winterberg.

When I got home I closed out my wagon buisness and made pre

[Page 141]

paration to go to the Buchanna [Bechuana] Country according to agreement with Mr Edwards which was the worst move that I ever made for at that time Wagon making was at its best it as never been as good since It was just then when the Dutch was emegrating farther into the interior towards Natal, They became dissattisfied because the government freed or emancipated their Slaves, but the English government payed them for them.

My Brother George contunied at the buisness and became immencely rich by the move of the Dutch for they, must have Wagons and would give any price for them eather old or new ones.

The last matter worthy notice, and closing this eventful year,

[Page 142]

was the final extinction of slavery at the Cape, which took place on the first of December, The abolition was proclaimed in 1834,[6] from which period the

---

6. "Slave-trading and slavery had been practiced in Africa from time immemorial, and the introduction of slaves to the Cape by the Europeans dates from the earliest days of the settlement. At first there were few in number, the return under [Jan] van Riebeeck in 1657 showing three males and eight females. . . . A slave rebellion in 1808 was suppressed with severity, but an easing of the position followed, and the 1820 settlers were forbidden to hold slaves. In 1833 the House of Commons passed an Act forbidding slavery throughout the King's possessions. . . . Of the 770,280

slaves were indentured for four years, thus exchanging the eternally odious name for that of apprentice. No greater credit has ever been assumed by the Philanthropists for England than for this act of humanity, but no greater injury was ever inflicted upon the inhabitants of the Cape than by the Manner in which it was effected. It is true that the munificent sum of twenty millions sterling was granted for a measure noble in itself and worthy all praise, but with it was a pledge that

[Page 143]

a just and equitable amount would be awarded to each proprietor. A fair and correct appraisement was made of the 35,745 slaves. for which £3.000.000 ought to have been forthcoming; but the average valuation of £85 per head was reduced in England to £33 12s; so that, instead of receiving £3.000.000, the Colony got only £1.2000.000. To add to the injustice of the act, the money, instead of being receivable in the Colony through the Colonial government, was made payable in London, by which a farther reduction was imposed by the necessity of employing agents. Many families were ruined by these deductions. Several sold their claims in

[Page 144]

the Colony at a discount of 25 to 30 per cent, and some rejected the paltry sum awarded to them altogather. Time, it is hoped, has blunted the sense of this manifest wrong, which with the insane native policy introduced to supersede that of Govenor D'Urban, drove its victims to migrate beyond the Trans Gariep [Transgariep] and to Natal. This I have copied from J.C. Chase's Cape Colony.

---

slaves liberated, the Cape possessed 39,021." Rosenthal, *Encyclopedia of Southern Africa*, s.v. "Slavery," 518–19.

Chapter 13

Having settled up all my buisness and affairs in the Winterberg I started on my journy to go into the interior with my own Wagon and Oxen eigh in number. with my wife

[Page 145]

and two Children whoes names were John and Jemima.[1] My first start was to Fort Beaufort to colect things together for the journy, My Brother Joseph acompanyed us that far, Then I left Fort Beaufort and started farely and travilled at the Base of the Cramey [Kroomie] Bush[2] on the road that leads to Cradock, we halted the first day out on the Kaga river the property of Sir. Andreas Stockenstrom who was at that time Lieutenant govenor of the frontiers. a traider who had a load of merchandice and on his way up into the Country among the Dutch campet [camped] with me that night. And nothing would do but he must have

[Page 146]

my Wagon and would not take no for an answar, well I thought perhaps I would not need it when I got to my journys end and as I had sold my Oxen to my Brother Joseph before I left the Winterberg on condicions that I would send them back to him by the first oppertunity and on the same terms I Sold my wagon to this traider Mr Bell,[3] for which he payed me in merchandice out of his Wagon, We journyed togather all the next day to Baviaan's [Baviaans] River and stopet at a Dutch mans farm there I left Mr Bell, Then we went past the Daggosboors Neck [Daggaboers Nek][4] which is a dreadful ruf rockey road

[Page 147]

then from there we crossed the Tarka river where their was a splended Dutch farm owned by a man whoes name is Lumbart [Lombard][5] and from there

---

1. Jemima is listed as "Daughter of Eli & Susannah Wiggill[,] Wheelwright of Bathurst in the District of Albany Cape of Good hope, was born on January 27th 1837." See South Africa Methodist Parrish Records (1822–1996) on FamilySearch.

2. The "Kroomie bush" is noted by G. E. Cory, *The Rise of South Africa: A History of the Origin of South African Colonization and of its Development towards the East from the Earliest Times to 1857*, 3:356.

3. James Bell is listed as a "(servant to Daniel Venables)" and a member of the Samuel Liversage Party. Nash, *The Settler Handbook*, 87.

4. The Daggaboers Nek is a pass south of Cradock located along the N-10. See Mountain Passes South Africa Online.

5. A family by the name of Lombard lived in the region at this time. See British 1820 Settlers to South Africa.

we passed many such farms for a fortnight and also passing what is called the Stormberg's [Stormberg] Spruit[6] a Division so called by a river which runs through it and thickly inhabeted by Dutch Farmers,

Then we crossed the great Oringe [Orange] river which was the first time I had ever seen it and looking down from the hights it was very beautiful all varigated with differant collers of rocks and the river was just as clear as posable and was about three hundred

[Page 148]

yards wide and fringed on both sides with beautiful willows at that time was just budding out, I crossed it at what is called Sand Drift, and another days travil brought us to another river called the Caledon[7] which is about half the size of the other one just mentioned, At the time I passed this place there was no inhabetance no wheres near neither Dutch or Natives but at this time it is thickly Settled by the Dutch farmers and abounds with game of many differant kinds also the Lordly Lion well we contunied our journy though a wild uninhabeted country with the exception of one missionery

[Page 149]

station which belonged to the Friench whoes name was Rev Mr Rowland and we stayed with them one night, and found them very agreable company, and the next night we stopt and Campt alongside of a very large Rock which had rolled down off the mountain of which their are many such in that secsion of the country, and that night our dog began to bark so I look out of the Wagon and it being very moonlight I could see everything around, and at a little distance perhaps fifty off I distinctly saw a Lion and was going to fier at him but my leader had wakened up and

[Page 150]

cracked his whip then the Lion just walked leasurely away without interfearing with us. And we rested well untill morning, when we got up, and eat our breakfast and started on our Journy again, over a beautiful road and now and then crossing such pritty streams and rivulets it was rather a flat country but abounded with Springboks Weldebeasts and quaggas also Ostrichs. We contunied on and on untill we came upon some men who belonged to the

---

6. The Stormberg Spruit country is mentioned in Cory, *The Rise of South Africa*, 2:345.

7. "Tributary of the Orange, it rises in the Drakensberg north-west of Lesotho and flows 500 km south-west through the districts of Clocolan, Ladybrand, Wepener, Smithfield, Rouxville and Bethulie, to enter the Orange east of the town of Bethulie. It was named by Colonel R Collins in 1809 after the Earl of Caledon, Governor of the Cape, 1807–1811." Raper, *Dictionary of Southern African Place Names*, s.v. "Caledon River," 84.

CHAPTER 13

Thaba Unchu ['Nchu]. Missionary Station.[8] I asked of those men how far it was to the Station and they told me that I could get there

[Page 151]

that night if I would drive hard so I agreed with one of them to drive for me. so he took the whip and from that moment his tongue and the whip were never still one minute, and we passed for miles and miles Kaffar gardens which we could see by moonlight for it got to be about midnight before we arrived at the Station where the Rev Mr, R. [Richard] Giddy,[9] was Stationed with a tribe of Barollongs [Barolongs] or Buchannas [Bechuanas] so we tied the Oxen fast and retired to rest untill morning it being Sunday When Mr Giddy got up and seeing the Wagon knowing that I was on the road he came to me

[Page 152]

and asked me why I did not call out and let him know that I had come I told him that I did not wish to disturb him then we were very soon invited into the house and took breakfast with them and was treated very kindly, That day I saw the first Congregation of Natives or Bechuanas, so called and Mr Giddy preached to them in their own Language, it was then I began to see what was before me and what I had to do myself when I arrived at the Station I was going too, The Thaba Unchu [Thaba 'Nchu] Station takes its name from a very large mountain in the vicinity which is a native

[Page 153]

name, and Moroca [Moroka][10] is the name of the Chief of that tribe, I knew him well, They build very good substansial round Huts or houses with good Verandas all around them under which they store away their grain in large earthen jars which will hold from four to five bushels each and when they want any for use they draw a plug at the bottom which lets the grain out, They also make baskets of grass which will hold from eight to ten bushels and put them away in the same manner, and outside of the Verand they build a Screen of reads some twelve feet high just leaving a

[Page 154]

gangway to go in and out, and at night that is shut up with a gate made of reads or saplings, Their dress and orniments are similar to the fronter tribes of Kaffers, After staying two or three days with Mr Giddy, I started for

---

8. Thaba 'Nchu was a Wesleyan Methodist mission station. R. L. Watson, "Missionary Influence at Thaba Nchu, 1833–1854: A Reassessment," 394–407.

9. Rev. Richard Giddy is mentioned in *The Missionary Register for 1842*, 73.

10. Chief Moroka I settled with the Barolong, a Tswana tribe in 1833. He died in 1880. Colin Murray, "Land, Power, and Class in the Thaba 'Nchu District, Orange Free State, 1884–1983," 30–32.

Umpukani [Umpukane][11] (Mantatees)[12] and when I started Mr Giddy, let me have a frish [fresh] span of Oxen and a man to drive for me who knew the road to where I was going, we was two days on the road before we arrived at Mr Edward's Station, through a country flat, and abounding with game which has already been discribed. On our first outspaning their were hundred

[Page 155]

of Kaffirs on a hunting exertion carring umberellas made of Ostrichs fethers to screen them from the sun, as well as to frighten the game, and if they are short of men they stick these screens into the ground to represent men, and generly have a large numbers of dogs of the grayhound breade to assist in the hunt, When they are pressed by the hunter they make for the water and plung right into it, While we were nooning their was one Weldebeast came and plunged into the water about two hundred yards from us, well sprinkled with assagais, so we went from the Wagon to see the

[Page 156]

sight and on our returning to the Wagon our little girl Jemima, had a bone in her hand which she was still picking from her dinner when a very large Eagle or Hawk, which of the two I dont know but it darted down and took the bone right out off her hand, which startled us all and frightened the Child, well we started on again and went a few miles farther on and then outspaned for the night, by the side of a very large rock. I am sure it was as big as a house which had rolled down of the mountain, and their were Lions in the vicinity, It was a pritty wild looking

[Page 157]

country with plenty of grass and water and would make splended farms if it had been taken up for the purpose, Next morning we contunied our Journy over and through the same pritty country and in and around such pritty hills which made the seenery very beautiful, We also passed a station on our left two or three miles distant from us called the Griqua station, Lishuani or green Cluffs [Groenkloof].[13] At that time it was presided over by the Rev.

---

11. Umpukane or Umpukani was a Methodist Wesleyan mission station in the Bechuana District, of the Manatee Country. Rev. William C. Holden, *History of the Colony of Natal South Africa*, 396; Du Plessis, *A History of Christian Missions in South Africa*, 433.

12. The Mantatee region was named after the Mantatee people who dwelt there. William F. Lye, "The Difaqane: The Mfecane in the Southern Sotho Area, 1822–24," 107-31.

13. "The Griqua-Bastaards under Barend Barends settled between Makwatling and New Platberg, on a place called Groenkkoof, near Mr. Daumas' mission station." George W. Stow, *The Native Races of South Africa*, 392.

CHAPTER 13

Umpukani Wesleyan Mission Station. From *Reminiscences of the Early Life and Missionary Labours of the Rev. John Edwards, Fifty Years a Wesleyan Missionary in South Africa.*

H. H. Garner.[14] a Wesleyan Station, This days travil brought us to our destination, which made both my Wife and myself feel very thankful. But was

[Page 158]

very much disappointed to find Mr and Mrs Edwards away from home, gone on a visit to another Station, but they left word with the people that was liveing there that if we should come to tell me what to do so they showed me the house that I was to occupy and I took possesion and went to work and unloaded the Wagon and soon made ourselves comfortable as we thought, but it was an old house and Thached with reads and when we put the Children to bed the Bugs was so many and so hungery that they just went to eating the poor little things up which woke them up with a scream, and

[Page 159]

when my wife went to see what was the matter she was frightened at the sight for the poor little creatures was pritty near covered, I never saw bedbugs so

---

14. W. H. Garner established a missionary station in 1839 "among the Bhaca tribe of Chief Ncaphayi." Gary Paul Van Heerden, "The Work of the Reverend James Cameron of the Wesleyan Methodist Missionary Society, 1829 to 1835," 10.

numerous in any place that I was ever in to eaquel that, Umpukani Station is high in the Mountain giving a beautiful and extensive vew over the country for miles and miles, and haveing a stream of beautiful water from the mountain runing past the door, Mr Edwards House was a very large dubble building with house and Chapel all under the same roof which was thached with reads, so all he had to do when he

[Page 160]

went to preach to his people was to go out of his dineing room into the Chapel,[15] The house being nicely whitewashed on the outside it could be seen for twenty miles or more on a bright day, soon after my arrival at this place, Mr Edwards came home after been on a tour of preaching, very tired, and the evening service had to be attended to so he said to me which do you think is the best man to night you or me and as I had not been away from home he pressed on me to preach that night I did which was my first attempt in the Dutch language which was quite an effert on my part for I had never

[Page 161]

attempted to speake before on Spiretual things neither in public, in the Language, but haveing a pritty good knowlage of the Language from a Boy I got along well and the people told me that they understood all I said which was more than they did[16] when Mr Edwards first came among them, I took for my text that night, from the 11th and 12th virses in the first chapter of St John Gospel which reads thus.

> 1 He came unto his own, and his own received him not.
> 2 But as many as received him, to them gave he power to become the sons of God, even to them that beleive on his name.

[Page 162]

---

15. Rev. John Edwards commented that Umpukani was a nice area to reside and preach to the Mantatee and Korana peoples, despite the lions, snakes, and occasional San visitors. "Umpukani . . . was pleasantly situated, and had a fruitful soil. Improvements had also been made, of which one would like to enjoy the benefits. Some of these consisted of a garden planted with fruit trees, and enclosed by a stone wall; a large piece of ground near the house fenced in for the purpose of a vegetable garden and tillage. . . . the pleasant site on which the Station was built; and its fruitful soil—our hearts very naturally clung to it and to the people." Wiggill assisted with the cultivation of both the site as well as the people. Edwards, *Reminiscences of the Early Life and Missionary Labours of the Rev. John Edwards,* 114.

16. Reverend Shaw sent Eli Wiggill from Grahamstown to the Umpukani Wesleyan Mission to assist Rev. Edwards, who recounted that Wiggill "helped me much." Edwards, *Reminiscences of the Early Life and Missionary Labours of the Rev. John Edwards,* 110.

CHAPTER 13

One of the first things which devolved upon me after I got settled, was to begin to teach School, And open it with singing and prayer in the Dutch Language, And between School hours, I was buissey at other employments such as makeing doors mantlepeaces and garden gate and many other things to fit up Mr Edwards house, And every other Sunday I had to go to the Korannas[17] [Korana] Station to preach to them, I had to start on Satuarday, which was twenty five miles and go on Hores back, The interpreter was a Griquas by the name of John Pinna [Pinnar],[18] he had being in the employ of the Socity for years as an interperter

[Page 163]

and School master to that tribe of Korannas [Koranas] and he could read the Dutch Language well, it was from this man that I learned to talk the Dutch Language much better than I had known it before I went into that part of the country He took a great likeing to me and the day that he would expect me he could see me comeing some five or six miles and when I would get there he would have the kettle boiling ready to make Tea for he knew that I was in the habbet of bringing some and he was extravegantly fond of a little, Well on sunday morning to draw the people togather he would

[Page 164]

crack a very large Whip under and along the mountain which would echo for miles and then we could see the natives coming from every direction to meeting, which we used to hold under a very large Olive Tree, and they would sit all around on rocks of all sises, Then I would speake in the Dutch tounge and this man would interpiret in the Korarna [Korana] Language, and when neither Mr Edwards or myself were their he would hold service himself, so it contunied for the first six months I was their, Well after service was over then I had to meet the members of the Church and hold classmeeting

[Page 165]

and when that was over then I would start for home which was a long distance and so lonely and it would be genarly after dark before I reached home I remember once when I was on the road I had such a dreadful fear of meeting a Lion, and I felt that their was one near by but I did not see it. Well when I

---

17. "Hottentot tribe living on the Northern Frontier of Cape Province, divided into a number of clans, including the Springbokke, the Towenaars (magicians) and Regshande (right hands). Believed to have originated near the Great Lakes in Central Africa, from which they were driven south by the Bantu. Many settled along the Orange River. Taller than other Hottentots, they were more aggressive and less honest." Rosenthal, *Encyclopedia of Southern Africa*, s.v. "Korana," 302. J. Henderson Soga, *The South-Eastern Bantu: Abe-Nguni, Aba-Mbo, Ama-Lala*.

18. This appears to be John Pienaar, who is evidenced on the 1820 Settlers list.

told my friend about it and how I felt, he said that their was one not very far away, which caused me to have such feelings. At the end of these six months I began to feel a little uncomfortable as though I did not want to be so confined so close to one place and I told Mr Edwards how I felt and he asked

[Page 166]

me how I would like to go and live at the Koranna [Korana] Station so I told him that I would like it very well so when the district meeting met they appointed me to that place, At this place their had never been a Mission House built untill I went there,

Chapter 14

After it was desided at the meeting that I should go to this place, my Wife left Umpukani [Umpukane] Station to go back to the colony in company with Mr H. H. Garner and a Frinch missionary whos name was La Meu [Lemue][1] who was also going to the colony, my wife also took two Children with her I accompanyed her as far

[Page 167]

as Mr Giddy Station which was Thaba Unchu [Thaba 'Nchu] and a few miles farther for I hated to part with my family for I did not know weather I should ever see my Wife again for she was going a distance of from five to six hundred miles from me to Bathurst. She tuched at Cradock, and the Winterberg where her father was living and went to see her people, But her reason for going away from me down to Bathurst was to be Confined. She felt timid to be among the natives at that time this was in the year 1839. And in May 12th she was delivered of a Son whoes name is Jerimia [Jeremiah] Francis. She was very weak and poorly for some time

[Page 168]

and while at Bathurst her driver and leader were both sick with the measels, And also a Native family and my little Children all had the measels in the Wagons while she was returning home to me the farmers on the road side was so affraid of them when they found that they had the measels they would not let them come near the house so they done the best they could, And all got home safe after an absence of from four to five months.

But I must go back again to where I parted with my Wife and two little Children to the new Station that I was to build up, But before

[Page 169]

I could begin to do anything in regard to building, I had to go to a place called sand river [Sand River] which the Korannas [Koranas] had baught some time preivous but had never occupied it. but it was occupied by the Dutch Emigrants who would not give it up. To see those Emigrants I went in company with the Koranna [Korana] Chief whos name was Isica Taibush

---

1. A French Methodist missionary named Jean Louis Prosper Lemue trained at the Paris Evangelical Mission Society and came to South Africa as a missionary in 1829 with two companies who labored in this region. Rodney Moffett, *A Biographical Dictionary of Contributors to the Natural History of the Free State and Lesotho*, 163.

[Taaibosch][2] and several of his followers and also a Bastard [Bastaard][3] man whos name was William Mottle who acted as an Interpereter for me as he understood the Koranna [Korana] Language, so we talked the matter over with the Dutch people, But as they were settled there they would not give it up

[Page 170]

on any turms what ever, Sand river was as handsome and parkelike Country as I ever saw, it was dotted all over with beautiful Mimosa and Koore[4] and other kinds of Trees, This part of the country at one time had been very thickly inhabeted by a tribe of people called the Mantatees who had been massecrede and driven back by a tribe of Zoolas [Zulus] a Warlike Nation, who gives no quarters, but slays both Men Women and Children, Their bones layed bleaching in the Sun at the time that I was there. So we returned back again to where the Korannas [Koranas] was staying a place called Mirametsu. Then I com-

[Page 171]

menced to build the Mission House as the buisness was settled in that way. I built a snug house with four rooms in it which was a siting room bedroom and kitchen, and also a smal room for a study which when done it was very comfortable. it was Thacthed with corse grass which is like the fine reads and sewed on with oxhide cut into stripes.

Well I had just got two rooms ready for leiving when one of my neighbors came to see me whos name was Rev. Mr. Domhas a French missionary[5] who brought two strange men with him to see me and my station and Mr. Domhas told me in

Well I had just got two rooms ready for liveing when one of my neighbours came to see me whos name was Rev. Mr [Dumas][6] a French missionary who brought two strange men with him to see me and my station and Mr Domhas told me in

---

2. The Korana tribes lived in the vicinity of Cape Town before the arrival of the first European settlers in 1652. By 1932 the Korana had nearly disappeared. The "Taaibosch," "Taaiboschse," or "Taaibosch Koranna" family served in leadership positions in the Koranna/Korana tribe. P. Erasmus, "The 'Lost' South African Tribe—Rebirth of the Koranna in the Free State," 77–91.

3. "Bastaard" was a derogatory term referring to mixed-race offspring of Dutch-speaking Boers (frontier farmers) and San or Khoikhoi women in the nineteenth century.

4. The word "Koore" here probably has reference to the karee tree.

5. Rev. Mr. Domhas is most probably referring to Rev. François Daumas, a French Protestant missionary who had helped establish Christian missions in South Africa for more than two decades. C. H. Bateman, ed., "The Children's Missionary Newspaper," 57.

6. *Encyclopedia Britannica or Dictionary*, s. v. "François Daumas."

CHAPTER 14

[Page 172]

his broken english who they were, He said they were two of the society of Friends who was Quakers whos names were Mrss Walker and Backhouse. they had being traviling and visiting all the Missionary Stations in the World as far as they posably could. and took Sketches of all the places and wrote a history on them, and wrote Tracks on the Quaker docterin and distributed them where ever they went,[7] I was very much surprised in my lonely situation to receive those strangers and talking so broad such as Thee and Thou for I had never heard Quakers talk before, and Mr Domhas

[Page 173]

was very thoughtful for he knew that I was alone (my wife had not returned yet) and he brought food along with him for fear that I might be out and we had dinner togather in my little study, and I found them intelegant and well informed men, They made it a practice to preach and talk to the people at every Station so my interpretor cracked his big Whip and very soon had the people togather under the Tree where I always held meeting so one of them commenced to speak in English and I to speak in Dutch to my Interpretor and then he

[Page 174]

spoke in the Koranna [Korana] Language so when I had interpretored for one I thought that I was through but the other one commenced and then I had to

---

7. "James Backhouse and George Washington Walker sailed from St. Katherine's Dock in London, England on 3 September 1831 bound for Australia. . . . Thus began a six year mission to Australia for these two Friends followed by a two year mission to Mauritius and South Africa. Though they were accredited by the Society of Friends in England their journey was self-funded." See Port Phillipp Pioneers Group. While in South Africa, "Backhouse even succeeded in learning enough Dutch to be able to preach in that language. He returned to England and arrived at London on 15 February 1841. . . . He kept up his religious work for the whole of his life, travelling and preaching much in England, Scotland and Ireland. He died at York on 20 January 1869." Percival Serle, *Dictionary of Australian Biography*, s.v. "Backhouse." Backhouse's South African memoir described the Marimetsu Wesleyan station where the Korana tribe dwelt and noted it "was under the charge of an intelligent, industrious, Wesleyan Catechist, named Eli Wiggil. We found him busily employed in building himself a house, in the absence of his wife and family in Albany. He had received no tidings from them for five months; in the course of this time, he expected his wife to be confined. Suspense of this kind is not unfrequent [sic] with Missionaries.—The Korannas are an original tribe of Hottentots who were formerly under a Chief named Kora; those at Mirametsu were descended from the people who inhabited the site of Cape Town, and the vicinity when the Dutch first took possession of the Colony." James Backhouse, *A Narrative of a Visit to the Mauritius and South Africa*, 393.

begin to interperate for him. My interpreter told me after we had got through that I was quite an Efficint Interpreter,

At this time Mr Edwards was from home with his family had gone to Graham's Town [Grahamstown] on buisness, so myself and Mr G Bingham[8] had to full the appointments at Mr Edwards Station and at the request of those Friends we had to be there to meet them on a cirtain day named to be there, so when I saw

[Page 175]

Mr Bingham the first thing he asked me, was. have you seen the Quakers, I told him I had, They both spoke at this station but would not occupy the Pulpit, so they spoke through Mr Binghams interpreter who was a Mantatee and could speake very good English and also understode the Basuto [Basotho] Language Mr Walke[r] was speaking and said in a mistake your teachers can tell you how to walk but they can not walk in the path themselves. So Mr Backhouse got up and corrected him by saying you mean to say that they can not walk in the path for you

[Page 176]

so after the service was over we made up a good fier for it was very cold at that time. so we sat and chatted untill a late hour, Their were two Sofas in the large sitting room, one of them was quite a good deal longer than the other. and Mr Backhouse being the shortest man of the two got possion [possession] of the longest sofa and would not give it up so Mr Walker had to take the short one and put a Chair at the foot to put his feet on. The next morning they took Sketches of the Station. Then we all left that Station and after riding a few miles togather we

[Page 177]

sepperated and I went to my home and never saw them any more. But after I had left that country for the colony these men sent a copy of their travils to all the Stations. from England. but I never got one, Then after a while I heard that Mr Backhouse had died, Just about this time my Wife arrived, I did not know that she was so near home, when I had to go away some twenty five miles away (when she came) at a Station called the Lishuani Station, and my wife sent a man after me on Horseback to let me know that she had come. In a jokei[n]g way Mr Bingham said to me

[Page 178]

you dont believe that she has come you are not going are you so I told him that I beleived it was true enough and I must go so I returned with the man

---

8. George Bingham chronicled Wesleyan missionaries and their assigned missionary stations in 1839. Bingham was in the Bechuana District, Mantatee Country, working with "The Griquas (Barend)," meaning the Khoi (now Griqua) leader named Barend. Du Plessis, *A History of Christian Missions in South Africa*, 433.

CHAPTER 14

whom she sent, and when I got home I found my wife and Children all well and happy to meet again after so long an absence, Then I went to work and finished the House, for she brought some materials back with her which I needed in building, and also a man who had being my servant when living in the colony. he was a good man then and I found him very useful and a great help to me about the Station The Koranna [Korana] Station is quite

[Page 179]

a Picturesquetic and romantic place the side of the mountain is strewed with Huge rocks which from time to time has roled down some of them is twenty and thirty feet high and so they run for miles and in between those rocks we could go in with a Wagon and cut down Timber with very little trouble But the Cluffs and revens[ravines] are perfectly grand dotted all over with beautiful Trees Shrubes and flowers, And in between these rocks the Korannas [Koranas] build their Huts Thare huts are built of what we call Mountain Bamboo,[9] which is very strong and grows from ten to fifteen feet in length

[Page 180]

these are stuck in the ground about six inches apart which bring them very thick at the top then they are covered in with mats made of rushes which grows from five to six feet high, so they can easy move their huts and carry them away on pack oxen they are a people who are always on the move from one locality to another and they are very rich in Cattle and Horses and live cheifly on milk and the Chace [cheese] they seldom every cultivate the soil, now and then to grow a little Tobacco,[10] While I was there with them their lived in a naighbouring Cluff a

[Page 181]

their was a mixed class of people of differant tribes who lived in this Cluff or Valley, and cultivated the soil. And the Korannas [Koranas] had lost Cattle and accused those people of stealing them so unkown to me they actacted them and plundered and drove them with fierarm, they took shelter where ever they could find it and many were wounded, so one day a man came to me and wanted me to go with him away up into the mountain and into a cave where I found wounded men, I rode my horse as far as I could and all the way I could where the bullets had struck and grazed the

[Page 182]

rocks so while I was up there with them I washed and dressed their wounds and prayed with them and left them while I was gone my wife felt dreadful uneasy for I was the only white man their. Well I contunied on at my work

---

9. "The indigenous bamboo (*Arundinaria tesselata*) is frequent on the mountains of the eastern parts." Marloth, "*The Flora of South Africa*," s.v. "Bamboo," 8.

10. "*Nicotiana glauca* . . . now a frequent shrubby weed throughout the country." Marloth, "*The Flora of South Africa*," s.v. "Tobacco, Wild," 82.

fixing building and beautifing my home untill the next district meeting when Mr Shaw came who was the general Superintendent of the Wesleyan Missions in South Eastern Africa He came to the station himself in company with others. So he wished to see me about erecting a water mill for grinding grain for the stations and he wanted it built at

[Page 183]

the Plattberg [Platberg] Station,[11] on account of its being a wheat growing country and also haveing plenty of water, So has the meeting had come to that conclusion it was not for me to say no, So Mr Shaw to reconsile me to do so he told that I should have a yearly remuneration over and above my Salary, after I had got things middlin comfortable and began to feel at home and the people attacthed to me, Then I was to be superseded by a Mr J. [Jeremiah] Hartley[12] a man I had known for years in Graham's Town [Grahamstown] so then I had to prepare to leave and could not do so until Mr Hartley came to take charge, so after a few weeks he arrived and

[Page 184]

we stayed togather for a week untill he became acquainted with the place and he would have me preach so he could see how I managed, Before I leave the Station I want to say a few words in regard to the Koranna [Korana] Cheifes. Isica Taibush [Taaibosch] who died of Consumption after lingering for a few weeks while I was on the Station, and he was superseded by his Brother Geart [Gert] Taibush [Taaibosch].[13] Their Uncle John Taibush [Taaibosch] was Cheif of the Korannas [Koranas] a few before my time with them this John went out with his followers on a great hunt for wild game as was their custom at times so one night after they had campted

---

11. For the excavation plans of the Platberg Mission Station, see South African Heritage Resources Information System online.

12. Jeremiah Hartley was seven years old when he embarked on the *Albury* with his family as members of the Calton Party, arriving at Algoa Bay on May 15, 1820. Nash, *The Settler Handbook*, 52–53. Hartley became a Wesleyan missionary and later died at age 35. "DEATH OF A MISSIONARY. The painful tidings of the death of Rev. Jeremiah Hartley, one of our Missionaries in the Bechuana Country, South Africa, have just reached us. Mr. Hartley finished his earthly course at Imparani, on the 22d of November 1848, after an illness of short duration." *The Wesleyan Missionary Notices Relating Principally to the Foreign Missions. Methodist Conference vol. 7 for the Year 1849*, 80.

13. The Taaibosch family was "the 'largest and most important' of the various Koranna families and they are thus known as the Kei (Big) Koranna, or the 'Bolanders.'" He also identifies Gert Taaibosch as one of the four sons of Jan Taaibosch. P. Erasmus, citing L. F. Maingard, "The 'Lost' South African Tribe—Rebirth of the Koranna in the Free State," 82.

CHAPTER 14

[Page 185]

and settled for the night they seen a Lion in the vicinity of the camp so John said that we must eather kill the Lion or move the camp so they saddled up their Horses to give chace to the Lion, so on coming up to the Lion they fired and wounded him and John being a brave man he rode up to the Lion. when the Lion turned and chaced him and sprung upon the Horse and laserated and tore him fearfully and John received such fearfull wounds that he died in a day or two afterwards and so ended the life of this brave Koranna [Korana] Chief. they have had none like him for bravery since.

[Page 186]

I left Mirametsu and went to Plaatberg where the Rev James Cameron[14] Chairman of the district where he resided. I went their to see about the water mill which as been spoken of I remained there for several weeks doing work for Mr Cameron then it was perposed that I should go to Graham's Town [Grahamstown] to get Iron and other things ready for building the Mill and Mr Cameron proposed to lend me his traveling Wagon to go down with as I had none of my own.

Book No. 2

[Page 187]

---

14. Gary Paul Van Heerden overviews Rev. Cameron's life, via an examination of his missionary journal from 1829–1835. Van Heerden cites W. G. Boyce, "In my day, as a preacher and as a theologian, he was unequalled in South Africa; and I do not think that he was second in these respects to any of his brethren in England." Van Heerden, "The Work of the Reverend James Cameron of the Wesley Methodist Missionary Society from 1829 to 1835," abstract.

Chapter 15

When I got everything ready and made all arrangements, I had to go to Taba Unchu [Thaba 'Nchu] to Mr Giddy to get a Span of Oxen before I could start, so I left Plaatberg on Horseback which was about twenty or thirty miles partly over a flat country and I started alone. although it is customery in that country to have eather a Man or a big Boy to ride with us which the Dutch calls an afterrider,) When I was about half way between the two places, I offsadled, at what is called (Low river) or Lion, river [Lions River] so when I thought that my horse had eat and rested long enough, I went to catch him but his being a spirited animal I went up to him to catch him when he got frightened and I mised catching the rim so he got away from me and kept doging around for more than a half an hour so I found there was no other Alterntive only to shoulder the saddle and drive the Horse on ahead of me, which I did untill night over took me. But still tryed to catch him at intervils but could not succeed. and not a soul on the road to help me. I never met a traveler all the distance but I contunied to travel untill some time in the night when I came up to a Wagon, that had broke a wheel, the wagon belonged to a Bastard Man who was trying to mend it and as I knew the man I proposed to stay with him untill morning. And has I was very hungery and faint I asked him if he would make some tea if he had any so he made the last drawing he had and I told him that I would bring him more in lue of it on my return which I did. Well it was Winter time and of corse I had to stay the rest of the night with this Man and haveing no bedcloaths with me he lent me an old wagonsail which was black with age and full of holes. and I had such a job to keep the frost from niping my back, I was so glad when it was morning, and I was up by times caught my Horse and started for Mr Giddy's which was about six miles a way but I soon arrived and got warmed up and a good Breakfast which made me feel so much better. So I arranged with Mr Giddy for the Oxen which he sent in due time. Then after I got the Oxen myself with my family started towards the Caladon [Caledon] river through a country that I had never traviled before but it was a beautiful undulated country dotted over with the wild Olive Trees and in what is called the Bottoms was the beautiful Mimosa Trees, Sometimes we where on one side of the river and sometimes on the other so

CHAPTER 15

we contunied traviling for eigh or ten day when we came to the great Orange river to what was known in that day Buffels flaydrift[1] and when we got there we could not cross for the river was flooded and their was no float or Port at that time so we had to go up the stream about four miles to a Dutch mans place who took us over by takeing our Wagon to

[Page 192]

all to peaces and takeing it over a peices at a time and then we put the Wagon togather again on a large flat rock in the Bed of the river but before we had got it compleated their came up a dreadful thunder storm and while it lasted it was fearful. We crossed the Orange just where the Kraai or Crow emptys itself into the Oringe river so the Dutchman left me right in the bed of the river, and I had to get out the best way that I could Then I put the Oxen to the Wagon and made a start and as the Bank was very steep and had become so soft by the Storm it was

[Page 193]

just as much as my Oxen could do, but to help them I had to dig a ditch some eighteen inches deep on the upper side of the Wagon to keep it from upsetting, and I had to hold on to a rope as well. But haveing a good driver and also knowing the theory of Wagons myself we got out all safe, and roled on untill we came to Buffels Vallie and Hot Springs which was near boiling. They were Sulpher Springs. When this place was first discovered it was about the year 1805 it was at that time occasionnally visited by Hunting Parties being the resort of immense herds of

[Page 194]

game and sometimes resorted to for the purpose of pasturage in very dry seasons but it was at this period too perilous a locality for permanent occupation, being inhabited by a few tribes of dangerous Bushmen, and the great lurking place of the Sovereign of the Forest the Lordly Lion and Buffolos and other game In 1809 we have the first written account of this remote territory. It was from the pen of amiable Colonel Collins who was ordered to visit and report upon the Lands in the vicinity of the Northern boundary of the Colony which at that time was circumscribed on the Northeast by the Zuurberg's

[Page 195]

river. This officer was accompanyed by Sir Andreas [Andries][2] Stockenstrom and Lieut Cowderoy of the 21st Light Dragoons, and on the 3rd of February 1809 this party discovered a stream recently become celebrated of about two

---

1. Buffels Vlei Drift, in *Basutoland Records: Copies of Official Documents of Various Kinds, Accounts of Traveller, &c" 1833–1852*, 1:489.
2. The officer's first name here is Andries not Andreas. British 1820 Settlers to South Africa.

thirds the volume of the great or Orange river coming from the North, to which they gave the name of the Caledon. in honor of the then Governor of the colony. They also discovered another fine stream and as no colonist had been here before says the colonel and the country was destitute of inhabitants from whom we could learn the name of the river if it had any. we honored it with that of

[Page 196]

Grays river a mark of respect to the honorable H. G. Gray. Lieuten[a]nt Governor of the colony, This name was after wards corrupted into that of Kraai or Crow river. The p[i]oneer Coloniest who first dared to commence a permanent establishment in this far east is said to have been one G. F. Bezuidemhout [Bezuidenhout].[3] This was in the year 1823 and he squatted on the place called Groene Vallei on the Kraamberg [Kramberg], other parties soon followed. Stephanus Erasmus, about the same time Petrus de Wet an emigrant from the neighbourhood of Drakenstein near Cape Town planted his household at Boffels [Buffels] Vallei [Valley].

[Page 197]

This man I was acquainted with and he told me the history of this Boffels [Buffels] Vallei [Valley] he told me that when he first came to this place it was a swamp of tall reeds about a mile in length and about a quarter of a mile in wedth and that his Cattle used to get swampted in it. Mr de Wet on examining the place he found two Conical shaped mounds which he turned too and opened and brought the water down to his homestead in a large furrow or secte and watered his garden and Cornfields and also used it in his house for domestic use when it was cold. When the water was brought into the furrow it was from

[Page 198]

eight to nine inches square enough to turn a large waterwheel. And when Mr de Wet had opened these mounds they sunk down to a level with with the Bog, And as the water dryed up the Cattle feed on and eat the reed all away so it is now a bed of Turf and to walk on it, It is like walking on Spunge. Boffels [Buffels] Vallei [Valley] is a fine open space containing some fourteen thousand acres of fertile grounds. A large portion can be irrigated from the Sulpher Springs which issue from two eyes or fountains both are about 78 feet in diameter and one measured 22 feet in depth the quanty of water thrown

[Page 199]

out has been measured by Mr Surveyer Ford and declared to be 1,497,600 gallons in 24 hours. This place of Mr de Wets is about two miles from the Great Orange river and there is no better water anywheres than that river

---

3. Casper Nicolaas Bezuidenhout. British 1820 Settlers to South Africa.

CHAPTER 15

a Villiage as been erected on the bank of the Orange river just at this place which is called Aliwal North. Having given quite a detail of Aliwal North, And the Sulpher Springs. I contunied on my journy to Grahamstown. we traviled on about ten miles and halted for the night where I thought that I would travil through an uninhabited country which was unknown to me I had

[Page 200]

heard about it but had never traviled it. It being Satuarday night and in them days we did not make it a practis of traviling on Sunday so I remained there and while their two Dutchmen came riding up to me on Horseback so Dutchmanlike they asked me where I had come from and where I was going too, So I told them where I was going and they told me that it was not safe for me to go that road alone as I was with my family for they said that it was infested with Lions, so I took their advice and went another road. which led through what is called the Stormberg's Spruit, through a rough

[Page 201]

rugged country inhabited for miles by Dutch farms who was very comfortable in rich Orchards Gardens Cornfields and Cattle and Sheep in abundance, We traviled through this country for three or four days till we came to a Scotchmans farm whos name was John Kurgon their we were weatherbound for two days on account of rain. They were very sivel and obligeing. Well we contunied on untill we came to a very steep hill which we had to descend which was called Donkerhoek or Dark Vallie. it was a terable rough Stoney pass but I got down all safe with but little trouble, to a beautiful

[Page 202]

flat country dotted over with the Mimosa thorntrees and along the Triberotry to the Class Smiths [Klaas Smits] river[4] which we crossed. their we came to a Station called Haslope Hills and who resided at that time the Rev. John Ayliff.[5] with whome we stayed over Sunday, and then it took us two days and

---

4. The Klaas Smits River is part of the Great Kei river system in the Eastern Cape. Originating south of Molteno, it flows through Sterkstroom, descending south and southeast toward its confluence with the Black Kei River.

5. John Ayliff, born in London in 1797, was one of the 1820 British settlers. He became an assistant Wesleyan missionary in 1827 and commenced his labors under the direction of Rev. William Shaw. Ayliff received his first missionary assignment in 1830 to work among the Hintza tribe at Butterworth, where he became well acquainted with the Fingo people. In 1839 he was sent to take charge of the Haslope Hills mission station. In 1845 he moved to Bathurst, then to Fort Beaufort (1848), and established a mission among the Fingos at the Birklands. He later became the founder of Healdtown and passed away in 1862. Rev. John Ayliff, *The Journal of "Harry Hastings" Albany Settler*, 14–15. For an extended view of his life and ministry, see John Ayliff, *The Journal of John Ayliff 1821–1830*.

a half before we reached the Winterberg, where my Wifes parents lived and also my Brother George. But before we reached them we had a rough road to travil. then we stayed about a week with them and had a good visit. and has I expected two Wagons down to get goods for

[Page 203]

the stations They did not intend going any farther than the Winterberg, I had to hire a wagon and my Brotherinlaw Thomas Bentley went with me to Grahamstown which was about fifty five miles passed Fortbeaufort [Fort Beaufort] and Fortbrown [Fort Brown] and so I arrived in Grahamstown.

Chapter 16

On my arrival in Grahams Town [Grahamstown] I found the arrangements for the gristmill at the Station was all countermanded, and all I had to do then was to gather up the Merchandise for the Stations and buy my own supplyes which

[Page 204]

kept me in Grahamstown a fortnight or three weeks attending to buisness and visiting friends for I had a great many there, and in the mean time my Brotherinlaw went to Algo Bay [Algoa Bay]. or Port Elizabath [Port Elizabeth], to get a load of fright to Grahamstown. My driver Cornelious went with him so that he could see the sea for he had never seen it. So on their return I was ready to start on my homeward journey which we did in a day or two. When we got to the Blinkwater[1] Hill it was so hard to get up that I had to send to my Brother Joseph for

[Page 205]

a Span of Oxen to help me up the Hill. So when I got back to the Winterberg I found the Wagons there, one of them was the Rev. G. [George] Bingham's[2] privet Wagon, which I loaded with sawed Timber a neat Plow and a wheel barrow which I got my Father to make while I stayed there, and had some repairs done to the Wagons. My Brother George carried on the wheelwright and Blacksmith buiness. Well in about a week I started back for my home at the Plaatberg Station. and my Father went with me as far as the Orange

[Page 206]

river as he had never seen it, he had a great dissire to see it and the surrounding country and my Brotherinlaw George Bentley went all the way with me to Plaatberg and also a young lady went with us as a companion for Mrs Wiggill, her name was Harriot Pote.[3] Before I left my Brother George I conclued to leave my Son John with him to go to School but instead of his going

---

1. Blinkwater (Afrikaans for "shining water") was a settlement at the junction of the Blinkwater and Kat rivers, about thirteen kilometers northwest of Fort Beaufort. Raper, *Dictionary of Southern African Place Names*, s.v. "Blinkwater," 57.

2. Rev. George Bingham was stationed in the Mantatee Country of the Bechuana District in 1839 and labored among the Griquas. J. Du Plessis, *A History of Christian Missions in South Africa*, 433.

3. Five-year-old Harriet Pote and her family were members of the William Parker Party, which sailed on the *East Indian* to South Africa in 1820. Nash, *The Settler Handbook*, 99–103.

to school he was sent out to herd Sheep and treated very differant to what I expected him to be by my Brother and his Uncle.

Having made an arraing-

[Page 207]

ment with my friends and acquaintances I bid them goodby and started with three Wagons on starting I had to encounter a steep grassey ridge of some three miles long which made it very hard to get up with Loaded Wagons, But when on the top we had a splended view of my Brother's Georges Farm and the country around for miles. This farm that I call Winterberg proper only in the vecinity of the great Winterberg Mountain but that farm and the one joining it is nown by the name of Cale Hock [Kaal Hoek].[4] And the farm in question was owned at that time by my Father Isaac Wiggill. And he called it

[Page 208]

Pinket Vail after a place lived at in England. Well arriving on the top of this ridge we had to decend a long rugged Hill down to the Konap [Koonap] river which we crossed, The Konap river takes its rise from the big Winterberg Mountain whos tops in the winter is covered with Snow. The top of this mountain can be seen in the distance from ninty to a hundred miles in clear weather. Four rivers takes their rise from this mountain First the Konap river then the Kat river then the Swart KeyKei river and the Tarka river.[5] After crossing the Konap river and traveling about six miles we came to

[Page 209]

one of the Spoor's [spurs] of the big Winterberg mountain which is very steep in places and is from four to five miles in length. But when on the top on looking back the scenery or view is perfectly grand the valley is dotted over with the Mimosa thorne and other kinds of Trees. besides large Forests of beautiful Timbers and the farms looking rich and gay. Well after leaveing the top of this mountain, we traveled on for a few miles on a beautiful level road with grass very corse and sour and it often rains on that hight from misty clouds so that the water runs in streams, while in the Konap

[Page 210]

and Tarka Valleys the Sun often is shining. We begin to decende down long grassey Valleys leading down to the Tarka river which river we cross half dozen times through a very stoney rugged country and surrounded by eigh rugged Stoney Mountains. But inhabited all the way by Dutch and English farmers whoes princiable fuel is dung taken from the Sheep carroll [corral] and when

---

4. Kaal Hoek is a farm location in the Eastern Cape.

5. The Tarka (Khoikhoi: "place of many women"; Xhosa: *Umncumuba*, "willow tree") tributary joins the Great Fish River nineteen kilometers southeast of Cradock. Raper, *Dictionary of Southern African Place Names*, s.v. "Tarka," 528.

CHAPTER 16

dryed makes a very hot fier. The farms through that section of country is a good wheat growing country and also good for Sheep. and Cattle. Having traveling through this Valley for about fifteen miles

[Page 211]

we turned off to the right leaving the Tarka river behind and went over what is called Tafelberg's neck.[6] which is a very ruff and difficult road for about eigh miles distance and in this vecinity their is an Institution for collord persons which was some time ago established by the Wesleyan Society.[7] in the Tarka district named Haslope Hills Two remarkable hills which stand nearly in the center of this property derive their names from their flattened summits being called the two table mountains. Those mountains are so high and rugged that only one of them is accessible and

[Page 212]

only at one point. being surrounded on all sides by preceptious hard granite rocks standing perpendiclar and to look at some of them they look as though the wind would blow them over. To apperance they seem detacthed from the mountain in perpendiclar masses, two or three hundred feet in hight and on the top of them are level and table shaped and game is found on these mountains. Having a little buisness with Mr Ayliff so my father and myself rode over to the Station to see him he being the missionary stationed there at that time. Well I attended to my buisness with him

[Page 213]

and we returned to the Wagons and found them outspaned on a nice flatt surrounded with beautiful Mimosa thorns known as goldons thorns. Here we was weather bound for two days it rained so hard that we could not move, and my father began to be very impatiant and was sorry that he had started on the journy with me. But he was all right when the rain was over and the sun was shining. So we traviled on from there for several days passing Dutch farms now and then and also crossing that Kassmits [Klaas Smits] river, and coming

---

6. Tafelberg (the Dutch name for Table Mountain) is a "flat-topped mountain 1,113 m high at the foot of which Cape Town is situated, between Devil's Peak in the south-east and Lion's Head in the north-west. It was named Taboa do Cabo by the Portugese admiral Antonio de Saldanha in 1503. The name appears as *Ye Table* about 1613." Raper, *Dictionary of Southern African Place names*, s.v. "Table Mountain," 526.

7. Such educational efforts to Christianize Africans proved very difficult for the early missionaries. Africans viewed them with great suspicion, and for good reason. Settler colonialists stole their land and resources and threatened to abolish their culture or at least change their conceptions of deity and spirituality. Hildegarde H. Fast, "'In at One Ear and out at the Other': African Response to the Wesleyan Message in Xhosaland 1825–35," 147–74.

[Page 214]

to a pass known as Pennhock [Penhoek] which is a steep romantic and elevated pass and very difficult to get up. And when on the top of this emenance I just enter upon the track of Country where the Dutchmen told me I had better not go for he said that it was infested with Lions. But haveing three Wagons and pritty strong handed we ventered to go. and found it a very beautiful country with plenty of grass and water and never seen a Lion all the way and it took us three days to travel over it well nothing very peticlur happened

[Page 215]

only one of the wagons got stuck fast in a swampy place and in geting it out we broke the Disselbome [Disselboom][8] or the Tongue. but we soon replaced it with a new one next morning. After been very near devoured the night before by Mosquitos, so we soon got through to Buffalo Vallei [Valley], on the Orang river. and when we got there we found it impassable, it was flooded. and their being no pont and no means by which we could cross we turned and went down the river some ten miles to Mr Holden and goldon who had a Pont on the river

[Page 216]

Well when we arrived at Messrs Holdon and Goldon's Pont the curant was so strong and the rops reaching from one side of the river to the other they had been broken by the rafts of Timber which was brought down by the flood, While I wated we tried several times to get the rops across and failed to do so. The way we tried to get the rope across the river was we tied a small rope to the big one, and then started to cross in a small Boat but the stream was so strong that it took the rope down in bow shape. well they could not draw it in. then they attacthed a span of ten or twelve Oxen to it and they failed to

[Page 217]

draw it in. and seeing that failed my Father Mr Holden and myself commenced to repeare a large Boat that was there and just as we got it ready for use the flood was about over so we got the rope over and did not use the Boat that we repaired. Well we got over at last after being detained four weeks their I left my father with Mr Holden they been well acquainted both being Settlers of eighteen twenty. Two or three weeks after I left the river their was a greater flood than had been that season, and they had just taken a Wagon over and was returning and when about the middle of

[Page 218]

the river, my father and Mr Holden both pulling on the same rope, The pont was taken by the current and reversed which caused Holden and my father to be under the front and in the water but holding on to the rope and going

---

8. A disselboom is a support pole for a horse-drawn wagon.

CHAPTER 16

Rev. John Ayliff (1797–1862). Courtesy Western Cape Archives.

hand over hand, and when my father got to the cross rope he soon got to the shore. it was a merical that any of them got out alive but to the best of my recolection their were one or two men drounded. After leaveing father I journeyed on to the Caladon [Caledon] river and when we got there the river was flooded and full up to its banks so we was detained

[Page 219]

there one week or more. while waiting at this river to cross and my money having run out and wanting meat. and I did not know how I was going to get any so while standing in front of my Wagon I seen a Shilling on the ground I picked it up and scratching around in the sand untill I found seven Shillings in Silver with which I went and bought a Sheep then we had plenty of Meat for our use. Then in the mean time a Dutchman came with a small Boat and we took our Wagons all to peaces and took them over, which was a dangerous undertakeing as the Willows which was

[Page 220]

thirty feet high we could just see the tops of them now and then so has we got the things over we landed them on an eminance on the opposite side as we thought out of danger, But we did not get the Wagons all over in one day. But my own Wagon was all over so we put that togather and my Wife and Children was over so we slept their that night, and just as we got the last wagon over the river rose some two or three feet heigher so that we had to move away off this eminence and in a hurry too or our Wagons and all our effects would have been washed away

[Page 221]

and after we got away off the bank and out of danger. I had to go to work and repair one of the Wagons which got broke it cost me three Pounds to get them Wagons over that river. This was in the year of eighteen forty one.

Well haveing got all things in order ready for moveing on we started, and those heavy Summer rains contunied with a great deal of Thunder and Lighening, and the roads that we had to travel was so soaked by the rain that it was like going through a Swamp and many times we would be as much as a mile out of the road to get on to rocks to keep from sticking fast which we did

[Page 222]

many a time, and would have to dig the wheels out when they would be sunk in up to the Axeltree. And if the Oxen stoad a few minits or tramped by trying to pull the Wagon out it would be perfect slush a foot or more deep all around them. We contunied this kind of traveling for three or four days from the Caladon [Caledon] river When we was within a day and a half's travel to Thaba Unchu [Thaba 'Nchu] and toiling so hard and sticking fast every now and then still working with the three Wagons, so just before Sunset we saw the black Clouds gathering which seemed to roll and rest upon the

[Page 223]

earth just then we had to cross a small rivelet which on the opsit [opposite] side was a rockey emeniance which we wanted to reach before dark to camp on thinking we would [be] safe thire, and with great difficulty we manigged to get two of the Wagons over by dubling the Teams, and by this time it began to rain in torants and got so dark that we could not see what to do, so I gave orders to the driver not to attempt to cross that night but to stay where he was till morning But contrary to my orders and unknown to me he made the attempt and got the Wagon into

[Page 224]

the middle of the stream with the fore wheels up on the bank and could get no further for it was pitch dark and raining in torants so the Wagon was left, and the earth was so full of water that it could hold no more, so the rain that fell that night flooded the small river and some time in the night it took the Wagon and all its contents down the Stream. Our servant girl wanted to sleep in that Wagon that night but my Wife would not lett her. And that night so has to have a cup of coffee I took a very large Umbrella and made a fier under

[Page 225]

it on a flat rock and boiled the kettle and made coffee had our supper and then went to bed but not to sleep much for the roreing of the storm and the

CHAPTER 16

rushing of the Waters was fearful, so when daylight came, the Wagon was gone it was no wheres to be seen, but the storm had abated and the stream had lowred some three feet so we went down the stream to see if we could see any thing of the Wagon. Well about a quarter of a mile down, we found the under stell or runing gears caught by a chain to a rock which had been left on the diselbom [disselboom] then we went on a little

[Page 226]

further and found the Plow sunk in a hole in the bed of the river. But as my Wife was so poorley, I left my Wife's Brother George Bentley in charge to surch up and down the river and gather up what he could find and follow me to Thaba Unchu ['Nchu], but before I got there I had to dig my Wagon out of the Mud several times, and in about two days my Brother came along with the two Wagons. Having searched the river for seven or eight miles up and down and after all, about eight Poudnds would have payed for all that was lost. Has the Wagon was mostly

[Page 227]

loaded with Timber. so about a month afterwards a Dutch man who lived on the river some miles below. seeing something in the rubbish that the water had driven up in a heap, has he had heard of Coffins having feet, he thought that he had found one, But after diging it out he found it to be Mr Binghams Wheelbarrow, which was washed down with the Wagon. So when I got to Mr. Giddy's[9] I learned from him that arrangements had been made while I was away that I was to come and live or reside with Mr Giddy at the Thaba Uncha ['Nchu] Station mostly to finish and put in

[Page 228]

order for living in a large barn of a place that had been built by a Mr [James] Archable [Archbell][10] who resided some years on that place he being the first to organize this Station and had this house built but never finished untill I went there and finished it and made a comfortable house of it. But after staying a day or two at Mr Giddy's I started with my family and went to Plaatberg and was there about two weeks, and gathered up my effects and returned again to Mr Giddys Station to assist in Preaching and do what every I was asked to do. This was in the year of eighteen forty one. The first thing

[Page 229]

---

9. Mr. Giddy is mentioned as a missionary working at the Wesleyan Methodist Station in Platberg by Rev. Wm. Shaw in a letter dated November 22, 1851. *Wesleyan-Methodist Magazine for 1852*, 205.

10. A Wesleyan missionary named James Archbell arrived in South Africa in 1819 and lived in the Thaba 'Nchu region at Platberg during the 1830s. D. J. Kotzé, *Letters of the American Missionaries, 1835–1838*, 171.

Missionaries of the Wesleyan Methodist Church, 1863. First row (left to right): J. Richards, P. Smailes, F. Creswell, R. Briggs, J. Smith, R. Lamplogh, S. D. Hepburn, Bertram, J. Holford, W. Impey, J. Fish, W. Sargeant, J. Start, G. Schreiner, G. Chapman, J. Daniel, H. H. Dugmore, J. Wilson, W. Maskary, E. Gedye, J. Scott, W. Hunter, J. R. Sawtell, John Thorn, J. G. Morrow and J. Hughes. Second row: William Clifford Holden, W. Shepstone, W. J. Davis, R. Giddy, J. Edwards, H. Garner and F. Guard. On step: J. Hillier, F. Robinson, G. H. Green, P. Hargreaves and D. M. Ludorf. Courtesy Western Cape Archives.

was to start on the eight day of August for my old station the Konanna's [Koranas] to get a load of cirtain kinds of hard Timber to use for repeairing Wagons or anything that might be wanted about the Station, I started on Horse back leaveing my Wifes Brother George Bentley to come after me with the Wagon I reached the Station about eight Oclock at night after riding forty miles. Mr Bentley did not arrive untill the next day on account of his Cattle been unruly which was the tenth. And on Thursday August tenth and Friday 11th I was in the mountains with Mr Hartley cuting wood, and Satuarday 13th in the mountain in surch of wood.

[Page 230]

Sunday the 14th in the morning I preached to the Korannas [Koranas] through an Interpreter. Monday August 15th I wrode to Mr W. [Wm.] Shepstone[11] Station called Umpukani a Mantatees Station and it had been actacted that morning by a Chief of the name of Sacuekanyale, but he was repulced by the people of the Station although he took them by surprize at the breake of day, two men of the Station was killed, and five of the enemy. and eight Horses taken by the men of the Station. Tuesday August 16th I left

---

11. Rev. Wm. Shepstone is mentioned in *The Missionary Register for 1842*, 73.

Tausi Soga, an example of a Xhosa Christian convert. She saved the Nivens party on their agonizing march from Keiskamma Hoek to the Tyumie mission on the first day of the war of 1850. She is wearing an aristocratic Xhosa dress, with missionary pride, as a lovely young Victorian lady; a reflection of changing times. Courtesy South African Library, Cape Town.

Umpukani for Lishuani Mr Bingham's Station and stayed there part of two days. Thursday 18th left Lishuani

[Page 231]

for Mr. Hartley Station, with Mr. G. Paxton and although our Horses was very weak we got their in good time and all safe. Friday 19th I went with Mr Hartley into a Cluff where he had Plowed a peace of Land and sowed wheat which had began to show a beautiful shade of green. Satuarday 20th I started from Mr Hartleys to go home on Horseback and arrived there about four Oclock in the afternoon all right and in good health. Sunday August 21st I had to take the sirvice for the day as Mr Giddy and Mr Allison been called to Umpukani, on account of the

[Page 232]

late disturbance in that part and on Monday 22nd and Tuesday 23rd and 24th I wrote several letters for Moracko [Moroka] the Chief of the Barolongs, on account of the disturbance with the Mantatees and other Tribes. Sunday August 29th I rode to a Bastard Villiage back of the Thaba Unchu ['Nchu] Mountain and held Preaching sirvices with them, September 17 my Brotherinlaw left Thaba Uncha ['Nchu] for the Winterberg in company with Mr Bingham for to fetch up a load of Timber on his own account, Sunday 20th preached to the Bastards at Thaba Uncha ['Nchu] in the morning, Monday 21st

[Page 233]

came a letter from the Plaatberg station from the Rev. J. [James] Camoren [Cameron][12] stating that things were very unsettled still in that quarter Thursday 23rd I sent for Mrs Deneson the midwife, to who was at the Umpukani Station, which was fifty miles to attend to my Wife, and she stayed with us about a month and on the 13th of Oct eighteen forty one my Wife gave Birth to a Daughter whos name is Sarah Ann Susannah. and was Baptized by the Rev. R. Giddy. Sunday Sep 26th I preached in the morning in the Bechuana Town to about sixty souls from the gospel of St Mark

[Page 234]

and in the afternoon I preached to a goodly number of Basterds, and Griquas, and I hope not in vain, and in the Evening of the same day Mr Giddy preached and administred the Sacrament to the members. Monday 27th Mr Giddy commited to the grave the remains of a Griqua, Peter Links. who died on the Station. Thursday Sep 30th my little Son Jeremiah Francis was taken very sick with a fever and as soon as he got a little better. Our little Daughter Jemima was taken down with the same fever which lasted

[Page 235]

---

12. Rev. James Cameron is mentioned in *The Missionary Register for 1842*, 73.

CHAPTER 16

five weeks before they got about again, Sunday Oct 3rd I preached from Revelations, to the people at the Station. From Oct 3rd eighteen fortyone up to Oct 30th eighteen fortytwo I was on the Station with Mr Giddy. employed as before mentioned,

Chapter 17

Copy of a letter from the Chairman of the District.

May 1st 1842 Rev J Camoren [Cameron]

Dear Brother
I have placed you at the disposal of the Rev. W. Shaw general Superindent of the Wesleyan Missions in South Easteran

[Page 236]

Africa, but should he decline employing you in the Albany District, I now write with the concurrence of my Bretheren, to inform you that your engagements with the Bechuana District, will terminate at the end of the preasent year.

I remain dear Brother yours truly

J. Camoren [Cameron],
Mr. Eli Wiggill
Thaba Uncha ['Nchu] Station.

After receiving this letter I contunied working on the Station untill the end of the year. When Mr Giddy and myself went down to the muder [Modder] river[1] and bought a span of Blue Oxen ten in number

[Page 237]

from a Dutchman whos name was William Pertouers[2] for the sum of 3.00 and fifty six dollars which is about 27 pounds in English money. and from that time I began to repair my Wagon and get things ready to leave Thaba Uncha ['Nchu] Station for the Winterberg. Our first days journey brought me to the muder [Modder] river to the residence of William Pertouers[3] who was an old friend of mine. So I stayed a day or two with him and put an Axeltree in a Wagon for him. And on leaveing there we traviled for three or four days through a country inhabeted by Dutch farmers. Mostly a flat country and abounding with game of various kinds.

---

1. The Modder River (Afrikaans: "modder" or "mud"), a tributary of the Riet River, originates near Dewetsdorp, then "flows westwards to join the main stream at the station Modder River in the Kimberley district." Raper, *Dictionary of Southern African Place Names*, s.v. "Modder River," 352.

2. This may be Andries Wilhelmus Jacobus Pretorius (1798–1853). See South African History Online, s.v. Andries Wilhelmus Jacobus Pretorius.

3. This name is not associated with any British immigrant party in the available lists. Nash, *The Settler Handbook*.

CHAPTER 17

Rev. Dr. John Philip, superintendent of the London missionary Stations of South Eastern Africa. From Jane Sales, *Mission Stations and the Coloured Communities of the Eastern Cape 1800–1852.*

[Page 238]

When we touched on Philippolis a London mission Station, which is a splendid farming and Cattle country and at that time inhabited by Bastards and Griquas and a few scattered Bushmen, This Station was named after the renowned Rev. Doc. [John] Philip, who was the Superintendent of the London missionary Stations of South eastern Africa,[4] and a man who was always in hot water with the Colonyest by advocating the Hottentotes and Kaffers [Kaffirs] Nations and depreciateing the White inhabitance. and accuseing them of makeing disturbance between themselves and the Colored poplation For which he gained the ill will of the greatest bulk of the

[Page 239]

---

4. John Philip was born in 1775, and he died in 1851. He was the "Scottish superintendent of the London Mission Society (LMS) in southern Africa. Philip was converted in the Haldane revival and in 1805 began a very successful ministry in Belmont Congregational Church, Aberdeen. There he married, in 1809, Jane Ross who bore four sons and three daughters. In 1819 the LMS work in South Africa was threatened with closure by the British authorities. John Campbell and John Philip were sent down as directors of the LMS to investigate fully and suggest reforms, and Philip was appointed to stay on as superintendent." Gerald H. Anderson, ed., *Biographical Dictionary of Christian Missions,* s.v. "Philip, John," 533–34. Andrew C. Ross, *John Philip (1775–1851): Missions, Race, and Politics in South Africa.*

View of Colesberg. Courtesy Western Cape Archives.

white population. And eventily was Drownded at the Mission Station called Hankey,[5] not many miles from Algo [Algoa] Bay, While he and his Soninlaw was passing through a Tunnel for a Cannal which the Doctor had superintended to bring the water through to water the Villiage of Hankey. Such was the end of this great man who had spent over forty years in the London Mission work and was the head of all the Stateons. And from Philipolis [Philippolis][6] we came to the Orange river. which we Forded. but came in contact with a large bolder in the middle of the river, but having good Oxen and also a good driver we got over all right and safe and stayed that night on its banks

[Page 240]

where we found a Company of Soldiers campted their wating orders to go to the free states. and was amusing themselves by Fishing. And the next day we proceided on our way and arrived at the Village of Colesberg, and stayed

---

5. "Town in the Gamtoos Valley, 27 km north-east of Humansdorp and 64 km west-north-west of Port Elizabeth. It was established in 1825 as a station of the London Missionary Society and named after the treasurer of this society, William Alers Hankey." Raper, *Dictionary of Southern African Place Names*, s.v. "Hankey," 199.

6. "Town 58 km south-west of Trompsburg and 56 km north-north-east of Colesberg. It was founded in 1823 as a station of the London Missionary Society and became a municipality in 1862. Named after Dr John Philip (1775–1851), Superintendent of the London Missionary Society, who selected the site." Raper, *Dictionary of Southern African Place Names*, s.v. "Philippolis," 440.

CHAPTER 17

there over Sunday. And attended service at the Dutch reformed Church. So on the Monday we started on our journey and came up to another large Company of Soldiers who was on their way to the free states and we campted with them, And while stoping there we had one of Africas terific thunder storms break over us, which blew down one half of the tents and the camp was one sheet of water.

[Page 241]

After leaveing Colesberg we contunied on and passed several Dutch farms untill we came to the farm of Mr Montgomery who was an Irish Settler. Their I had to stop two or three days on account of my Wife been very sick. But Mrs Montgomery being a Dutchwoman and clever with Medcian she soon got my wife all right again. And from there we traviled on passing Dutch and English Farmers, and while passing I heard that my Father was in the neighbourhood repearing a Waterwheel for a Mr W. Wright and when I called to see him I was informed that he had finished his work and had gone home to the Winterberg.

[Page 242]

Then about two days journey brought me to the Winterberg Farm where I started from, and arrived there all safe.

Chapter 18

When I came to the Winterberg I found my father there. But has he had Landed property in the Village of Bathurst. So he had rented his place in Winterberg to a man by the name of Cloake Bear. Then when I came down my father prevailed on this man to give up his lease to me which he did Providing I would devide the Crops which he had put in which I agreed too. for that one year. So I settled

[Page 243]

there and finished the house that my Father had partley built and on the place was a Watermill and also a wind mill, Then I built a snug workshop and went right into buisness at Wagon makeing. and Blacksmithing and also attended to my Farm. This was in the year of 1843. Well I lived at this place about two years and was real happy and comfortable. Still belonging to the Wesleyan society, And now and then preached in the neighborhood and some times I was called to preach at Fort Beaufort and at Kat river. And while here going to the Blinkwater

[Page 244]

after Timber for my Wagon buisness. and in returning we had come up a very steep bushey path in the upper Blinkwater Hill. I had just come to the Wagon on Horseback to see how the Wagon had got up the Hill and standing on the upper side of the road looking at the Oxen coming up the Hill. and my Son John who was walking behind the Wagon and on seeing me he turned to look. and while looking at me. a log rolled of the Wagon and struck him on back and bend of the Leg and tore the flesh of leaveing the bone and the Sinews

[Page 245]

all bare, This happened on the 5th of December 1843. So I had to put him on my Horse after tieing my handkercheife around his leg. and leave the Wagon with the Driver. And lead the horse home which was from four to five miles. But by good care and attention his leg soon got well so that in two or three weeks he was able to get around. And on Monday January 9th myself and my Wife and our Children started to the Bush or Forest. on a little picnic. and while their I cut a load of Timber for my shop, While still residing at this place, an accident happened to me

[Page 246]

while working at the bottom Plank of a Wagon and haveing it up on its edge takeing a little of one side to make it fit in between the sides of the Wagon, so just as I had got off the Wagon on to the ground, and turning around to do something to the Bolster a little wind sprong up and blew it over struck me just over the left eye and knocked me senceless to the ground And a

CHAPTER 18

neighbour came and bleed me as quick as posable whos name was William Bear, so in a few days with good attention I got around again, but I feel the effects of it to this day,

[Page 247]

This happened July 2nd 1844 and while residing at this place my Daughter Margret Alice was born, Oct. 11. 1843 and was Baptized by the Rev. C. Holdon.[1]

The yars of 1844 and 45 things went well with me and I was very comfortable and happy and had all the work that I could do, When things took a turn and about the month of Jan 1846 The rumers of War run through the Frontier Settlements which made the farmers very uneasy for we had those rumers to contend with for several weeks, and orders came at last from the Magestrate of Fort Baufort [Beaufort] by Circulars to the farmers to get into Camps and Forts

[Page 248]

for protection, and myself with many others went to a strong Fort called Post Retieff [Retief]. to where I moved my family and effects, and we were put under Marshel Law and received our rashens and done Soldiers duty, for the government and to protect ourselves. But the War was not so severe in the part where I was stationed as it was in the Lower districts. which were Fort Beaufort Grahamstown Bathurst and Lower Albany. Their were no houses burnt in the Winterberg district but in the Albany district, they suffered fearfuly by fier and Pillige,

[Page 249]

and a great many people were killed and hundreds of Cattle Horses and Sheep drove off by the Kaffirs. At a place called Burns Hill on the upper part of the Keiskamma river.[2] which place was reached on the 15th of April 1846 The next day some smart fighting took place when the mission station was attacked by the savages who succeeded in Captoring, Pundaring and distroying 63 baggage wagons out of 123 with which the force was incumbered, The expedition was then obliged to fall back upon Block Drift This was the

[Page 250]

---

1. Rev. William C. Holden who wrote *History of the Colony of Natal, South Africa*.
2. The Keiskamma (Khoikhoi: "puff adder," a venomous snake) flows in a southeasterly direction from the Amatole Mountains in the Middledrift and Victoria East districts before it empties into the Indian Ocean at Hamburg, fifty kilometers southwest of East London. "The Portugese name for this river was Rio de Sâo Christovâo." Raper, *Dictionary of Southern African Place Names*, s.v. "Keiskamma River," 255.

commencement of disasters soon followed up by others, The new post of Victoria[3] was obliged to be abandoned and burnt, And all connnunications with the Colony was thus cut off, 41 more Wagons fell into the enemy's hands at Trumpeter's Drift on the great Fish River. Fort Peddie[4] was attacked and the Cattle some 4,000 in number, taken, and in those affairs several lives were sacrificed, This War of 1846 is known by the Kafirs [Kaffirs] and Colonyet as the War of the Axe[5], from a Kafier [Kaffir] haveing stolen an Axe or hatchet, This Kafir [Kaffir] was sent to

[Page 251]

Grahamstown been handcuffed with a Hottentot for security and when within a few miles of Fort Beaufort, they were attacted in a bushy pass on the Kat River, by a strong Body of Kafirs [Kaffirs] who as they found it difficult to liberate their country man from the unfortenate Hottentot they deliberately severed the handcuff at his wrist and then pierced him to Death. While detained at this Post my Wife gave Birth to a Daughter, whom we named Roseanna Maria born Aug 31st 1846. And Baptized by the Rev. G. Smith.[6] Well I remained in the Camp while the War lasted, and I think

[Page 252]

that was about one year, and while there I done some work with my Wagon, and worked some at my traid, and also attended to Military dutys. My Brother George formed a Camp about 8 miles from Post Retieff [Retief], they were about forty men in that Camp and among them was my father who was in Winterberg on buisness. His home was at Bathurst so he was detained in Winterberg about 8 months on account of the War and away from his family, And while he was there he acted as Miller for my Brother George in a Windmill. And as the Kaffirs did not come with

[Page 253]

---

3. Alice is the principal town of the Victoria District, named after Queen Victoria, and is bounded by the Amatole Mountains and the Tyume, Great Fish, and Kat rivers. Raper, *Dictionary of Southern African Place Names*, s.v. "Victoria East," 567.

4. Fort Peddie was named after Lt. Col. John Peddie (died in 1840) who led the 72nd Highlanders against the Xhosa in the Sixth Frontier War. The modern town is situated some fifty-five kilometers southwest of King William's Town and sixty-seven kilometers east of Grahamstown. Raper, *Dictionary of Southern African Place Names*, s.v. "Peddie," 436.

5. For an overview of the War of the Axe, see Ross, *The Borders of Race in Colonial South Africa*, 144–63.

6. Rev. John Smith was a Methodist Wesleyan missionary stationed in the Albany District at Fort Beaufort in 1839. However, there is no mention of a Rev. G. Smith. Perhaps Wiggill was mistaken with regards to his first name. Du Plessis, *A History of Christian Missions in South Africa*, 433.

CHAPTER 18

any force to Winterberg, so there were nothing of any note transpired in their Camp. Neither did anything secariously happen at Post Reteiff [Retief]. But it was not safe for people to go and settle on their Farms untill Peace was proclamed, Then I returned to my farm again and settled down and comenced my buisness, This was in the year of 1847. Well I stayed on this farm about one year, Then I thought I would get a place of my own has I got tired of paying rent so I went to the Stormberg. and bought the right of a place (that had never been occuped) of a Dutchman under Teodores

[Page 254]

Rant, and has I left the place where I was my father rented to a man whos name was Mr. John Hoston. and he opened an accomodation house on it, Then I moved my family and my effects from the Winterberg to Teodores Rant. And when I got up there not one of the Dutchmen came to occupy their farms so I was entirely alone in the wilderness and the grass had all been burnt for miles as far as the eye could see, so I only stayed there about three weeks. just long enough to partly build a reed house and open a fountain and the wind blowing a huricane pritty

[Page 255]

near all the time that I was there. Game was plentyful and my Brotherinlaw Francis Bentley was unmarried and he went to live with me and I also took a Blacksmith with me with an intention to start the Wagon makeing buisness. But I found myself so alone and so far from anybody some 18 or 20 miles away. So I left it and went to my Brother Joseph on the top of the Stormberg Mountain. And the next day after I arrived a heavy Snowstorm fell which was about a foot deep all over the Stormberg Country, Then I sold the right of that place

[Page 256]

to Francis Bentley and he stayed there with my Brother Joseph, And as soon as the roads was fit to travil, I started for the Winterberg again, and stayed there a few weeks and I started and went to Bathurst to where my father was liveing, and my Daughter Jemima was there, so I thought that I would have a visit to the sea and have a look at the old Location where my father lived. he would have given this farm to me but I did not like the place so I would not take it to be forced to live on it, so I left there and came to Fort Beaufort.

[Page 257]

Here I hired a house from an old Frinch Lady who name was Mrs Salt and it was said that she was at the Battle of Watterloo and would go and search the Bodys and take what she could get from them. So when I returned to occupy the house has I thought she had rented it to some one els. Then I rented a house in an other part of the Town of one Mr Roorke, It was in very bad condition but I moved into it and went to work and made it comfortable, and stayed there only a few weeks, and neither myself nor my wife could stay in it and feel comfortable in it for it was troubled with sombody or somthing

[Page 258]

we did not know what. Then I started for the Winterberg which was about twenty miles and walked for my Horses were there and I went to see my Wife's father Mr Francis P Bentley who had a Lease on a peice of Land that I wanted to build on, Having made arrangements to that purpose I went back to Fort Beaufort and gave up the house, giving all that I had done to it into the Bargon and was glad to get rid of it. Then I moved back again to the Winterberg, having my own Wagon and Team so that I was under no expence of hireing, And I went on to a pritty Parklike place where thare had never been

[Page 259]

any improvements made only by nature, Their I lived in my Wagon and started and built a house, What the Dutch calls a hartebeest house they are made by planting the polls into the ground and then bending the tops in bow shape and then Tacthing from the ground to the top they are made squair and I lived in this house and my Wagon untill I built a large House which was seventy feet front, and contained two bedrooms a large kitchen and a sitting room which was in size twenty feet by twelve, and a large conveiant Shop which was attached to the

[Page 260]

and formed the letter L as well as conveiant out buildings, And then I cleared the Bushes away and planted trees of various kinds and made a good garden. I had a good faithful man whom I hired to help me do all this work whos name was Thomas Duff. a native of Scotland. Well while I lived at this place I was just has happy and comfortable as I had ever been in my life up to that time. Which was over two years, and in that time on the 6th of May 1849 my wife gave Birth to a Daughter whom we called Frances Amelia being our eight child. And Baptized by the Rev J Ayliff.

[Page 261]

and in this time I had several new Wagons making them to order. And I had from eight to ten Cows in milk. and also kept my own Wagon and a Span of Oxen ten in number, and my riding Horses so if myself or my Wife wanted to visit with a naighbour or take a ride for pleasure, my Horses were always ready. And I also built a nice room in addission to my house for the accomadation of my Father who payed me a visit now and then so that he could be privet and quite and not be troubled with the Children. Well just has I had got all fixed and was liveing so comfortable. rumers of the third

[Page 262]

Kaffir War came upon us, and I was makeing a Wagon for a Mr. Stanton but I had not finished it when he sent for it on account of the rumers of war been

CHAPTER 18

so threting from all quarters. So on the first day of December 1850 he took it away to Fort Beaufort unfinished, so the rumers still came day after day which caused us to feel very unsettled. Then all would be quite again for a few days. But in the mean time I sent material and half finished Wagons to Post Retieff [Retief] and had them put away under the care of a friend Mrs Edwards who resieded there, so I had to break up my buisness so soon after geting it started

[Page 263]

so nicely and doing so well. It was just about Christmas time when I received a circular from the magistarte to inform me to get into Camp has soon as posable that their was no time to lose, so we loaded two Wagons with as much as we could take. leaving Cupbords Bedsteads and many other things in the house, and that day we went as far as my Fatherinlaws place and would have gone further but they were going too so they presuaded me to wait untill morning which I did then we all started togather. But for all their was so much danger the folks was determined to have a merry time before

[Page 264]

starting, and haveing a fiddler in the company they had a dance and all seemed to enjoy themselves well, But I could not mix in with them for my feelings was dreadful I cannot discribe them, One of the Wagons which carried some of my things away belonged to a Bastard Man whos name was Jacub de Pree, He was a man who I had hired of and on for years and placed all confidance in him, And at this time I had rented him a farm which he cultivated on the half. And that night he stayed at his farm. And in the morning they de Pree and his Son was ready to

[Page 265]

start with the Wagons for the Camp. But before we had got away the Kaffirs had began to steal Horses that was on the Farm, Well we made a start in the morning. And after been on the road a little and still traveling we met hundreds of Fingos with their Cattle fleeing from the Kaffirs and going among the Dutch where they thought they would be safe. The Kaffirs and Hottontotts did not think that the Dutch would interfear that they would lay nutrial. and that they would War against the English and Fingo's (that is the Kaffirs) so we traveled on untill we reached Post Reteiff [Retief]. Where we found

[Page 266]

the people flocking in from all directions for protection.

Chapter 19

The Hottentot whos name was Jacub de Pree that helped me to move my effects to the Post also helped me unload the same and then went back to the Farm, and brought me my share of Potatoes that he had raised on shares. which he did the next day and seemed to be and feel all right when he left me. But instead of going back to the farm has I expected he went to the Upper Blink water [Upper Blinkwater] which was a Hottentot Settlement. and belonged to the Kat river, which was wholey a Hottentot with the exception of a few whites. In the year of 1850. and on Christmas day the work of Death and Blood commenced.[1] In the military Village of Johannesberg Woburn and Auckland were pillaged and burnt, and many of their male inhabitants cruelly butchered. And when the rumer of this attack had reached the weake camps and also that the Hottentots had jointed the Kaffirs, And the Kaffirs were in overwhelming force, and the small camps did not feel themselves safe so Mr Bear did not feel safe in his small Camp so he sent to Post Reteiff [Retief] for an escort to guard them to the Post. and there was about twenty men sent and among them was my Son John although he was only a boy. So when they got there the escort found the people already to move and started in the morning part of the day and came about half way to the Post when a Wheel broke of one of the Wagons so they had to make a full stop for a little while untill they could replace the Wheel. Then they started on without been molested and reached the Post sometime in the night. And we heard afterwards that it was a luckey thing for them that the Wheel broke. for a few miles further on the enemy was lieing in ambush in a Bushcluff on the road where they had to pass, just at the foot of a steep Hill where they had to clime. And as the enemy seen them Camped they left their place of concelement and went to Blinkwater to their own Camp concluding that the party would not come on that night. So that the breaking of the Wheel was the means likely of saveing the lives of the whole party, This was learned afterwards from some of the enemy. So the enemy that intended to attact this company, never disbanded themselves, but on New Years day 1851 they

---

1. The Eighth Frontier War (1850–1853), was perhaps the "longest, hardest and ugliest war ever fought over one hundred years of bloodshed on the Cape Colony's eastern frontier." Peires, *The House of Phalo: A History of the Xhosa People in the Days of Their Independence*, 12.

CHAPTER 19

[Page 270]

came and made an attack in the night and between 12 and 1 they shot the first gun on the Post Reteiff [Retief], and shot some shots through some of the Portholes. It was then that we knew for cirtain that the Hottentots had joined the Kaffirs. on finding one of them dead next morning at one of the corners of the Fort, who had been shot from an hastley built Blockade on the outside of one of the gates. And that night they took off thousands of Sheep which was outside the walls, not having rome inside on account of so many Cattle been inside. And about this time a Wagon was sent to Fort Beaufort for Ammunition with an escort of

[Page 271]

four men whos names are John Edwards. James Holt. John Hoston. George Gibbins. and on their return on the lower Blinkwater near to a petty Kaffir Chief's korll [corral] whos name is Hermanus. There the Wagon was actacted and plundered and two of the escort was killed. John Hoston and George Gibbins and James Holt was wounded but managed to make his escape to Fort Beaufort. and John Edwards made his escape and reached his home which was at Post Reteiff [Retief], and leaving the Wagon and all its contents in the possion [possession] of the Kaffirs and on the 7th of January 1851 the Kaffir Chief Harmanus

[Page 272]

made an unusually bold and desperate attempt to surprise the strong military Post of Fort Beaufort but after a short and sharp struggle were defeated in which they lost fifty men including the arch-trater Harmanus himself. Well our Cattle were herded in the vecinity of the Post, for a week or two after the Sheep was taken so one morning after they were turned out to graize and several of our men perhaps ten had rode off to look after their farms in about half an hour after they had gone. the Kafirs [Kaffirs] came down in devisions from differant dere-

[Page 273]

ctions from the Cluffs and Pounced on the Cattle and a company from the Post rode out to try to hinder them when a scrimage took place. and sometimes our little company would partly turn the Cattle towards the Post, When the Kafirs [Kaffirs] would gain on them again But the Kafirs [Kaffirs] proved the strongest and took them all away, There was a great deal of shoting done, but none of the people of the Post neither wounded or killed, and but one Kafir [Kaffir] killed, who was a giant in size and right in the midest of the firing and fighting my Son John

[Page 274]

was one of the formost and his Uncle Francis Bentley had a great time to keep him back. This all happened in sight of the Post, and in this scrimage I lost ten milk Cows, and a span of ten or twelve Oxen. And when our Patrols would be out to Reconnoiter around the vecinity of the Post. the enemy was also on the look out and on several accations the Kafirs [Kaffirs] tryed to cut our men off from coming to the Post. A Friend of mine whos name is Joseph Allison[2] he resided in what is called Bauta's [Botha's] Bush[3] and a part of the Kat rivers Settlement

[Page 275]

and hearing of the rumer of War, He thought he would move himself and his effects to the Post, and when he was on the Blinkwater hights. The Kafirs [Kaffirs] came upon him and releived him of his Wagon and Oxen, and he just barely made his escape to the Post, and about the same time their came over that rugged mountain six men in the dead of the night on foot to seek protection at Post Reteiff [Retief] and found it thare one of them was an old Man about 80 years old then, and I understoad that he lived to be over 100. His name was Cloake Bear. In the corse of two or three weeks after this an overwhelming host of Kafirs [Kaffirs]

[Page 276]

Hottentots combined surrounded the Post and they thought that they draw us out of the Post by turning the water out of the Furrow or Scect. They had stoleon a small Cannon from some other Camp and brought it and placed it on a hight and fired down on to the Post and all the damage they done they wounded some Cattle, they kept up a firing for a half a day. The bullets whistled over the Fort and bounded on to the zinc roof and while one party was fireing at the Fort, another party was Thrashing out the farmers wheat with sticks both men and women and hauling it away in Wagons

[Page 277]

and plundered farm after farm and took everything that they could lay their hands on, and the friuts of maney kinds were ripe so they just helpt themselves to all they could get besides burning and distroying everything in their way. Well they contunied around the Post untill a heavy Thunder Storm came over and we caught a great deal of Water from the roofes and our enemys said that they might as well leave as we had plenty of water they thought they

---

2. A three-year-old boy named Joseph Allison whose family voyaged aboard the *East Indian* with the Parker Party to the Eastern Cape in 1820. Nash, *The Settler Handbook*, 99–101.

3. Botha's bush was located near the confluence of the Blinkwater and Kat rivers. Ross, *The Borders of Race in Colonial South Africa: The Kat River Settlement, 1829–1856*, 198.

CHAPTER 19

would starve us out. Well after this attact a week or two, small parties would start out on Horse back to look after their

[Page 278]

farms, and parties would come to see how we were geting along at Post Retieff [Retief]. And all this time reportes was going back and forth what the enemy was doing, who was stealing and plundring all around from fifty to a hundred miles around and runing off all the Cattle that they could find eather with a herd or without one, and when followed by our men there would always be trouble and generaly lose of life on both sides, And sometimes our people would retake the Cattle, and at another time the enemy would take them entirely. In those scrimages there was always more Kafirs [Kaffirs] and Hottentots bit the ground than the white people.

[Page 279]

It was about the 8th of Febuary 1851 a large body of the enemy was seen on the mountain side near the Post, both Horse and foot men, we could see them by looking through our spyglasses. They had been and attacted a Camp a few miles from us, It was composed of a few farmers who had formed a Camp to protect themselves with a farmer who had a large family of grown up Sons and also Soninlaws which made a large family of themselves so they all joined togather with their naighbours and it was called Smiths Camp, Well the enemy took all the large stock such as Horses Oxen and Cows from this Camp, As there had been no communication from Smiths

[Page 280]

Camp after seeing the enemy passing a long the mountain we felt anxious to know what had been done, so seven men in our Camp volunteered to go and see, and among them was Francis Bentley my Broinlaw and my Son John who was but a Boy, but was always ready if there was anything to be done, Soon after our men had left the Post we seen the enemy returning again to Smiths Camp and for two days we heard nothing of what was going on so we were at a loss to know what had taken place at Smiths Camp, untill we seen a large body of the enemy on the mountain side about half mile away from our Post

[Page 281]

bearing a white flag. And on seeing him coming a Mr James Sweetnum [Sweetnam][4] a Fieldcornet, and who had charge of the Post, started out also with a flag of Truce, who met halfway between our Post and the enemy, and it was then that we learned that the enemy had four of our men Prisnoers and one of them was my Son John, Well after while Mr Sweetnum and the Hottentot rebel was parlying the one beging for Tobaco, and the other for the Prisnoers we

---

4. "Sweetnam, James," British 1820 Settlers to South Africa.

saw a large Body of men coming towards the Post, and at the first sight of them we did not know whether they were friends or foes, untill the Captain of the

[Page 282]

Company rode up to the Post in advance, whos name is Mr Pringle It was then that we knew that they was friends comeing to Post Reteiff Retief] for our protection, As they had heard through a message that we were Hemed in so they came to our assistance. After this company arrived my Wife my Sister Elizabeth and A Bastard man went up the hill to where the flag of Truce was, Then they all went to where the prisnoers was, for my wife was so ancious about her Boy, and when the Hottentots seen my Wife coming towards them some of them knew

[Page 283]

her and called to her to come along that they would not hurt her. And when she got up to where her Boy was it made her feel so bad to see him looking so distressed for the enemy had striped him of the most of his cloaths he had been in their hands two days. And this Bastard man explained to them that he was not held as a prisnoer but that he stayed at the Post of his own freewill, and he talked very sharp to them has though he was very angrey, And then he told the Prisnoers who was sitting on the rocks to get up and lets be going, so John asked if he might go

[Page 284]

and was answered that he could, when one of the enemy asked him if he would fight and shoot at them again, and he told them that he would if he was called upon to do so, When they answered and told him that was right that he could do no other, they had taken his Horse from him that he rode, which was his mothers, and when she was leaveing the Hottentots, She beged of them to take good care of her Horse and use him well for she had, Had him a long while and was very sorry to lose him So they told her not to say a word about your Horse

[Page 285]

Mrs for you have got your Boy, Yes said she. I know, but I must talk about my Horse too, and just has they was turning to leave one of the Hottentot men gave John a fine leg of mutton to give to his grand mother to whom he at one time had been her Servant, and he was the one who was the cause of saveing my Son's life. And in regard to those Prisnoers I will relate it here has my Son told it to me after he was released, These seven men was on their return from Smiths Camp, about half way when they saw one man in a hollow place who was a Hottentot and he called to them

[Page 286]

and said that he wanted to talk to them His name was Spellman Quivt, he was known by some of them men so they stopted and talked with him and

CHAPTER 19 111

he spoke has a friend, and four of the seven went to him to hear what he had to say, and as soon as they got up to him a hole party of Hottentots rushed out upon them, and unarmed and dismounted them and took them Prisnoers and by some of the Hottentots knowing my son and to whom he belonged, they did not kill them as it was their intention to do so, so the Kafirs [Kaffirs] and the Hottentots had quite a time about it the Kafirs [Kaffirs] wanted to kill them but the Hotten-

[Page 287]

tots would not let them, and to save and protect them from the Kafirs [Kaffirs], the Hottentots clung around these four men so thick to save them that the Kafirs [Kaffirs] could not get near them to hurt them, Then the Kafirs [Kaffirs] told the Hottentots that they would tell their Chief Sandilli [Sandili][5] that they were takeing Prisnoers and would not kill them, and the Hottentots told them that they did not care for Sandilli that he was not their Chief, and the Kafirs [Kaffirs] at the same time would grin over the Hottentots shoulders and call the Prisnoers <u>Sattons</u>. and for safer protection the Hottentots took the Prisnoers to a emty house which belonged to a

[Page 288]

Dutchman, They told my Son that they did not want to kill or hurt him for they said that they knew his father well and that he (his father was a good man and that he had never done them any harm, But that his father had Preached to them many a time, and they wanted to save his father to make Wagons for them. So the enemy made this house their place of Rendezvous, and while some watched the Prisnoers others was determined to take Smiths Camp and so a body of men went to make the attact and Fired at the Camp for hours, But the people had made themselves so secure that the enemy could not get them

[Page 289]

out, Well they contunied to fire untill they got tired, Then they succeeded in capturing their sheep which amounted to several hundreds haveing taken the Cattle before, so they took the Sheep to this house and commenced killing the Sheep just like a parscle of Wolves my Son said that the poor Sheep would run about with Assagais and spears sticking in them perfectly tortured. And as the Grapes were ripe just at the time they feed the Prisnoers on Grapes and Mutton. And when the rebels had filled themselves with Mutton they started again for Smiths Camp and felt determined to have them out they tryed to set

[Page 290]

---

5. Sandili was the son of Ngquika (Gaika) and the chief of the Ngquikas (Gaikas) at this time. See *Encyclopedia Britannica or Dictionary*, 8:33.

fire to the place but could not succeed, and John said that he felt safer in this house than he would at Smiths Camp, and that he felt so glad that his mother did not know he was a prisnoer, When the Enemy found that they could do no more damage at the Camp only to kill one man, They left. And started for their Headquarters which was the upper Blinkwater. And it was then that the prisnoers were set at Liberty which as been related. Then the Smiths Camp came to Post Reteiff [Retief] and joined our company for safer protection but had lost all their Stock,

[Page 291]

Chapter 20

The next thing of note which happened was the attact on my Brother George's Camp. Near the Konap river on what was called the Brambush Spruit,[1] where he had got everything in order both in the way of buisness such as Wagon makeing and Blacksmithing, and he had his good home with its extenceive vineyards orange and Lemon Orchards with gardons in great veriety, and also his gristmills and Distillerys where he made a great deal of differant kinds of Liquors, and he had large quantitys stored away in his cellars. And haveing a large threestory building unfinished which he intended

for another Mill, But hearing of the comeing War he loopholed it and put it in a steate for defence and its been built of solld rock in the two first storeys and the third storey was Brick and Loopholed, This stoad about thirty or Forty yards from his dwelling House, and he also built one or two Block houses of rock with loopholes so as to fire on the Enemy, so he got everything ready for an atact, A week or two before he had just got in his years Proviscions such as groceries and many other things, and at this time there came his tennants and several of his neighbours who was farmers and formed a Camp with him, But it

was not a good place for a Camp for the enemy could come within a hundred yards of them before they could be seen, The rebel Hottentots and Kafirs [Kaffirs] belonging to the upper Blinkwater which was thousands strong had marched in the night into the vinicity of my Brother's Camp and lay in ambush untill Sunday morning at the break of day when they attacted the Camp. But they came upon them so sudden and so early that they just barely escaped in their night cloaths and all that my Brother saved from his House was a Box with his money and Papers in it, and his Wifes mother was lieing sick at the time so they just picked her up like a Child

and carried her into the Fort and those Block houses was used by the Enemy, has well as the mills and other places to shelter themselves from the Shoots from the Tower, and his own Hottentots Servants joined the enemy and helped to Plunder the house, and when they had taken all they wanted they set fire to the House, which was a Thacthed roof and was easely fired, and while the enemy was Plundering the house there was only one door that

---

1. Brambush Spruit, a Native location. *Returns from Inspectors of Native Locations Under Acts Nos. 6 of 1876 and 8 of 1878, Detailing the Number of Huts, Natives, Stock, &c on the Several Locations, up to the 30th April 1880,* 72.

the folkes in the Tower could shoot at with any sattisfaction, so the enemy was perfectly secure in the house, They kepted up a continual fireing all that

[Page 295]

day, and two of the men in the Camp was wounded one in the neck whos name was William Wittle who was just makeing his escape into the Tower, and the other one who was shoot in the leg was Charles Roper. He was shot from one of the Loopholes, and when the House was burning the people in the Tower were almost sufficated with the heat and smoke, and the next morning the enemy had decamped and gone, and not one of the people in the Tower had any Tea or Coffee so my Brother went down to the burnt house to see if he could find some, and by hunting among the rubbish he found a little Coffee which was very

[Page 296]

exceptable, and the Cattle was Corrolled between the house and the Tower which was protected from the enemy untill the heat and smoke set them frantic and they broak out, when the enemy drove them all away with them, and on hearing the shoting a party started out from Post Retieff [Retief] to Reconnoiter and when on the Hights they could see the enemy both going and comeing to my Brother's Camp loaded with Plunder and going to the Upper Blinkwater which was a distance of 7 miles to their Camp, And of corse it made me feel very uneasey for I did not know how things was with them untill a party was dispacthed from our Post

[Page 297]

to find out how matters was with them. After this had passed a party came to there rescus from the Tarka District with Wagons and Oxen to move them away, This district is mostly Dutch with a few English people, And while my Brother was away from his own place the enemy came there with Wagons and gathered up all they could move, such as barrels of differant kinds of Liquor, and left their old Wheels and took the new ones that was in the Shop and also took new Wagons, and fired one of the water mills which burnt down But saved the large Barn which was built over the Cellar where the Liquor were

[Page 298]

and after the trouble was over, and were scurching around they found the dead body of a Mr Curtus, who appeared to be coming to my Brothers house, he was a labouring man who lived in the neighborhood who had fell into the hands of the enemy and killed Well, my Brother stayed a few weeks at the Tarka Camp and then returned again with a party of friends to his own place and formed a Camp and held his ground untill the War was over, But occasionly loseing a few head of Stock taken by stragling Kafirs [Kaffirs] and Hottentots. And myself and family was all this time hemed in at Post

CHAPTER 20

Xhosa Travelers near Grahamstown in 1848. Painting by Thomas Baines.

[Page 299]

Retieff [Retief], another incident of the war was the attack of the rebel Camp of Fort Armstrong,[2] of which last named place they had taken possession but were "shelled" out on the 22nd of February by Major general Somerset, with a sever loss of life on the part of the Hottentots. And from the 1st of January up to the 22nd of February they had no check of any note, But they contunied

---

2. "Fort Armstrong was constructed in 1836 to protect the Kat rivers valuable source of water. It was named after Captain Armstrong who fought in the area alongside the Cape Mounted Rifles during the 6th war of land dispossession. Because of its relative isolation, the fort was designed to operate independently if need be. It had wattle and daub barracks that could accommodate up to 30 mounted men with ordnance stores, a powder magazine, officers quarters, kitchen stables and cells. A few meters away was a cattle kraal. The forts first test came when forces led by Maqoma and Kona took possession of it for about a month. On 22 February 1851, Major-General Henry Somerset, son of the Governor of the Cape, Charles Somerset, reclaimed it—killing 46 people and taking 560 prisoners including 400 women and children. Six male settlers were killed and 25 sustained injuries. During the 8th war of land dispossession of 1853, William Uithaalder a Khoi who had served in the Cape Corps, led an attack on and took over control of the Fort. Colonial forces consisting of 200 British soldiers, 400 Burghers, 200 Fingoes and volunteers from Grahamstown under Commandant Currie regrouped and launched two howitzer attacks against the fort, partially destroying what they built to protect themselves in order to oust Uithaalder." See the Geocaching website, s.v. "Fort Armstrong."

their robbing and Plundering the farmers for miles from fifty to one hundred, They would take the peoples Wagons and Oxen and just load them with stolen goods and take them to Fort Armstrong which is almost Fortifyed by nature

[Page 300]

with Precipitous Rocks in the shape of a horseshoe on an ellevated emeneniance on the Kat river itseff, all the farmers or Berger force, from the diffrant districts was assembled at Post Retieff [Retief] several hundred strong as they was to meet genaral Somerset on the 22nd of February to atack the rebels. the Kafirs [Kaffirs] and Hottentots. These people started before daylight and left Post Reteiff [Retief] to meet the general. And althoughmy Son John had so receantly been a Prisnoer he soon made himself ready again, and equipted himself with a Horse a gun and other cutriments and was one with them, and they started

[Page 301]

the nearest way which was over the mountain to meet the general. So when they got down into the valleys in the vinicety of a place called Balfore, and they was atacked by an overwhelming force of the enemy Hottentots and Kafirs [Kaffirs], who surrounded them on every side and not seeing nor hearing of the general's approach, so they had to stand a scrimage for quite a while and lost two or three men, and several wounded, and also some Horses killed, and while thus situated they at length heard the report of Cannon at Fort Armstrong, and by that they knew

[Page 302]

that the general was on the ground, although he was two or three hours behind the time appointed to meet those men. But the cause was that he had been attacked by another party of the enemy, so this part of the men made a great rush through the enemy and joined the General, at Fort Armstrong,

Fort Armstrong is what may be called a small village where there are two or three trading Stores for the accomodation of Hottentots and Kafirs [Kaffirs] in the vecinity and their princible work was sawing Timber in the surrounding Forests and the Hottentots would bring

[Page 303]

their Timber to the Stores and trade it for what they wanted such as Tea and Coffee and many other things, Others would bring produce such as grain of differant kinds and many other things that they raised, so those storekeepers carried on a good profitable buisness with the Settlement which extended for ten and fifteen mils in differant directions from the Fort, Has it had been a Government Fort and with the Government building and also a large Tower built of cut rocks and a Battery built stareshape with angles and Loopholed, and with the privet Buildings there was altogather about twenty deacent

[Page 304]

looking houses, It was here that the enemy brought in all their Plunder from the surrounding Country and occupied these buildings has well as the Tower and Battery and ceaseing all the merchantdice in the Stores, so when the place was besieged the General found it nessery to demolish the buildings by Shell and shot and burn them out by burning the buildings, the Tower was also full of the enemy and to get them out they reared Timber against it and set fire to it to get the enemy out. it was then that they surrenderd and they took hundreds of Prisnoers. And hundreds more made their escape both men

[Page 305]

Women and Children, and fled to the strong hold of the Amatola mountains, and those that was take Prisnores was marched to Fort Hare, and tryed by Court marshal, and those that were found guilty was sent to the Cape District to work on the Public works. When my Son John returned from the attack at Fort Armstrong I learned from him and others what transpired there. That they went to work and ransacked the Wagonloads of Plunder, for there were lots of goods both wearing apparel and Household goods and a great number of Books with the owners names in them, And when the People had gathered from the pile what they could

[Page 306]

carry away on horseback they set fire to the rest and distroyed them, And among this company was my Son John, and he gathered a few things to bring away, and among them he had my Brother's George's Spyglass which he owned after he returned to his home, And my Son also got his Horse that the enemy took from him when he was a Prisnoer [prisoner] but it was in poor condition, And after they had attended to all this buisness they were all hungery and tyered so the company which consisted of Solders farmers and citizens so they made their Camp Fires and made their Tea and Coffee and

[Page 307]

eat and drank all they wanted, and dead Hottentots and Kafirs [Kaffirs] laying all around , For the Wolves and vulturs to feast on, and the enemy's Wagons all that was not burnt was besides some others that belonged to other people was taken to Fort Hare, and many of the owners came and took them away, Well after all this was over we had quite a Lull in affairs for some six or seven weeks, and the people began to feel free so myself has many others did visited our Farms, and gathered our vegtables and brought them to the Post And the Pumpkins layed in the feilds so thick that a

[Page 308]

person could hardly step for them, and no Cattle to eat them, But I went and gathered a Wagonload of them and hauled them to my house and put them in the Cellar, and I also took out a Bees nest which had not been molested in my gardon, at this time my house had not been burnt, I was still at the Post, and I had Wagons there unfinished so I went to work and finished them, By makeing a tempery Shop and Forge, The first Wagon that I finished I Sold it to get a Span of Oxen for I hated to be without them even in War, Well I had

[Page 309]

them but a little while when the Kafirs [Kaffirs] stole them, But before I lost them, myself my two Sons and a man that I hired went a mile or two from the Fort to get a load of Wood but before we had time to get a stick on the Wagon the Kafirs [Kaffirs] came and took my Cattle but left the Wagon and of corse I expected that we should all be killed but they did not molest us but when we saw them coming we run off towards a Farmhouse which was about two miles away But they was so intent on haveing the Oxen so they turned from us

[Page 310]

and went off with them. This was the first and also the last time that I ever run away from eather Hottentots or Kafirs [Kaffirs], so the next day I got a Span of Oxen from one of my naighbors and some three or four men went after the Wagon which they found all right even to the Axes. The reason that we escaped so easey, there was a party of men after them and for the sake of haveing the Cattle they turned and run with them and they took them into the Watercluff. And this Wagon I had to sell to get another Span of

[Page 311]

Oxen. And about this time a company of Highlanders under the charge of Captain Bruce took comand of Post Retieff [Retief] they belonged to the 74th regiment, He stayed quite while at the Post and according to his notions put things in order, And some of the people moved out to give room for the Soldiers, Mr Sweetnum [Sweetnam][3] with several other familys went to his Farm and formed a Camp, But I still remained at the Post, And haveing Oxen again I sometimes went to the Bush or Forest to get wood for the Soldiers haveing an escort with me. And

[Page 312]

Captain Bruce also built a lookout up on an emminence, back of the Post, which some called Bruce's folly, At this time I also worked at my trade and done what I was asked to do with my Wagon, And at this time I repaired a

---

3. The Thomas Sweetnam family joined the Menezes Party, which left Portsmouth in late January on the ship *Weymouth*, arriving in Algoa Bay on May 15, 1820. The Mr. Sweetnam referred to above is probably James Sweetnam, who was listed as age seven at the time of the voyage. He would have been nearly forty years old at this time. Or, it could have been his father Thomas, who was thirty-six years old at the time of embarkation and would have been in his late sixties by this time. Nash, *The Settler Handbook*, 91.

burnt House which was in the vicinity of the Post, and went and lived in it, and on the 3rd of November 1852 my Wife gave birth to a Son whom we called Joseph Elijah, and was Baptized by the Rev, Mr Shepstone, at Kamus Town, which is in the District of Queens Town [Queenstown]. Soon after the Birth of my Son the War Settled down and things became quite

[Page 313]

and as the Tambookie Tribes had forfited a part of their territory hitherto occupied by mapassa [Maphasa],[4] And at the suggestion of Mr Thomas, Holden, Bowker,[5] One of the Settlers of twenty, to the then governor Sir George Cathcart, sent out a notis[6] to the Farmers to make out an estimate of their losses sustained by the late War, And also to be singd by their Fieldcornets as a witness to their losses to persons that were not Landholders. Those doccuments had to be brought before a landborad survey which was held at Whittlesea. Whittlesea was established during the government of Sir. Harry Smith. And named by him after his Brithplace in England.[7]

[Page 314]

---

4. During the early 1830s, Maphasa "was intensely disliked by white frontier officials. The Commissioner General of the Eastern Districts, Andries Stockenstrom, denounced him as an 'apathetic barbarian,' while Capt. Henry Somerset wrote derogatorily of the 'ill disposed, ignorant, grasping savage.' Sihele painted a very different picture and . . . described him as a great warrior 'who dared situations that were usually avoided by others,' an eloquent speaker, and a capable leader." Elise J. C. Wagenaar, "A History of the Thembu and Their Relationship with the Cape, 1850–1900," 10.

5. Thomas Holden Bowker, nicknamed Holden, was a member of the Cape Parliament and the founder of Queenstown. Holden was the son of Miles Bowker, who led a party of colonists to the Cape. Thomas Holden Bowker was listed as being twelve years old at the time of departure from Portsmouth on the vessel *Weymouth*, January 7, 1820. His older brother, John Mitford Bowker, was killed in the Xhosa War of 1847. Nash, *The Settler Handbook*, 41. For a vivid description of the challenges the Cape government faced during this tumultuous time in South Africa, see Bowker, *Speeches, Letters, and Selections from Important Papers of the late John Mitford Bowker, Some Years Resident and Diplomatic Agent with Certain Kafir and Fingo Tribes*.

6. Earl Grey was displeased with Governor Harry Smith's inept handling of the Eighth Xhosa War (1850–1853). Therefore, he appointed Cathcart to take his place on January 14, 1852. George McCall Theal, *History of South Africa Since September 1795: The Cape Colony from 1846 to 1860*, 7:107. Regarding Cathcart's correspondence during this period, see Sir George Cathcart, *Correspondence of Lieut.-General the Hon. Sir George Cathcart, K.C.B., Relative to his Military Operations in Kaffraria, Until the Termination of the Kafir War, and to His Measures for the Future Maintenance of Peace on that Frontier, and the Protection and Welfare of the People of South Africa*.

7. Whittlesea is a "village near Queenstown, C.P. named after the birthplace of Governor Sir Harry Smith (q.v.). It was founded in 1849 and became an important

Then it was preposed to form a new town in the forfited Territory which was to be named Queens Town [Queenstown], In honnor of the Queen,[8] Has a Nucleus and ralling point of the new contemplated Terrytory to be settled by the garentees that would receive grants of Land. This District, named after its chief town, situated on the Komani River, exceedingly fertile and well watered, was parcelled out in free grant to numerous applicants, chiefly those who had distinguished themselves, in the late struggle, on the tenure of payment of a moderate quitrent, and that the occupant should, independant of himself, find two

[Page 315]

others armed white men, fully equipped with horse saddle, and weapons for every three thousand acres all liable to be called out by government whenever their services should be wanted, and to muster in full force, properly provided, on the Sovereign's Birthday, to be inspected by the authorities. No farm was to exceed 3,000 acres, and such extent only to be granted where the country could not sustain a large population; and on these terms Sir George Cathcart says, in his dispatch announcing the adoption of his judicious plan, he had applications from all directions from men admirably adapted

[Page 316]

for the purpose.

---

defense outpost in the native war of 1850–1853. Some of the old fortifications are still in existence." Rosenthal, *Encyclopedia of Southern Africa*, s.v. "Whittlesea," 640.

8. Queenstown, named after Queen Victoria, was founded in 1850 in the Eastern Cape province near the Katberg Mountains. "Because of the risk of native attack, [it] was laid out in an unusual hexagon pattern to allow the approaches to be commanded by artillery. The main open space lies in the centre of the hexagon." Rosenthal, *Encyclopedia of Southern Africa*, s.v. "Queenstown," 453. For a recent history, see Megan Voss, "Urbanizing the North-eastern Frontier: The Frontier Intelligentsia and the Making of the Colonial Queenstown, c. 1859–1877."

Chapter 21

Haveing no land of my own and had been paying rent for years and hearing of this new territory I thought that I would make a move for this new contemplated town and haveing a good Wagon and Oxen of my own, and after been two years at Post Reteiff [Retief] and the War been over, In the begining of the year of 1853 I started with my family then to begin the world again as it were, and this new place where I intended to locate was some fifty or Sixty miles from Post Reteiff [Retief] which was on the other side of the

[Page 317]

Big Winterberg Mountain and calling on my way at Kamas Town to visit with a friend for a few days whos name is Stephen Trollip, after staying at this place a few days I became acquainted with Mr J. [Joseph] C. [Cox] Waner [Warner],[1] who had lived in the Tambookie Country as a Missionary for years. but at this time he had quit the Missionry Station and was the Tambookie Agent under Government. Himself and family had taken shelter at Kmaus Town with a small Tribe of friendly Tambookies under a petty chief by the name of Bombana [Bonvana][2] so he was just ready to start to where the new Town was to be layed

[Page 318]

out so I started with him and traviled about two days and a half, when we came to the place where the supposed Town would be layed out which had been the Farms of two of Mr Warner Sons where they had built a good farm house which was burnt down by the enemy in time of the War they had plowed the Land and made waterfurrows. when I got there I found in waiting Mr. John Staples and two or three of his Sons and a Mr Ever and his Son, and Mr. Ridgway and Mr James Jennings and others. And also a company of Police Mounted. who was

[Page 319]

stationed there to patroll the country, We were there two or three weeks waiting for the Township to be survayed, Well at length Mr Robison came, a Survayer sent by the Government from Cape Town, Then he commenced to lay out the Town with the assistance of those that were there, and I had the honor of helping to turn the first Sod, as also my Sons John and Jerimiah The town was layed out in Hexagon shape for the purpose of better protection in case of an invasion by the enemy on account of its been on the extream Fronters. And has I had

---

1. Warner served as the colony's Tambookie agent. Lindsay Frederick Braun, *Colonial Survey and Native Landscapes in Rural South Africa, 1850–1913*, 80.

2. Bombana appears to be a misspelling for Bonvana. Wagenaar, "A History of the Thembu and Their Relationship with the Cape, 1850–1900," 7.

[Page 320]

been on the ground so long I had a good oppertunity of riding around to make a good selection for a Farm, It was then I heard from the survayer that my pertition was granted, and that I might seclect a place just where I chosed in the district of Queen's Town, through the influance of a friend who was acquainted with the Board and also with my losses and spoke a good word for me who was the Rev. Mr Shepstone with whom I had been acquainted for many years, So I chose a Farm at the head of the Komami river in what is called the Bongolo

[Page 321]

Basin in which place there are eight beautiful farms and the one that I chose was granted to me, been a Missionary Station before the War. But the Mission House was burnt down in time of the War, But the walls stoud firm and I rebuilt it, And the place was well supplyed with wood and water in abundance and while I was there, and my Brother Elijah had also a farm granted to him, I selected a farm for him joining mine, with which he was well pleased when he seen it, At the time (he my Brother) was away in the country with Stock. To take

[Page 322]

care of them in time of the War. Well when Queen's Town [Queenstown] was layed out I got a good City Lot in the center of the town on the cornor of a street by paying five pounds to the Government which was some three pounds cheaper than they sold other Lots on account of been on the ground early and haveing to wait so long, Then I commenced to build on my City Lot for I began to feel very ancious to get settled and see my family comfortable once more, and I then began to do Carpenter work for I could turn my hand to all kinds of wood work and I had all the work

[Page 323]

that I could do besides what I done for myself for every body was ancious to get a home over their heads again, and Queen's Town [Queenstown] very soon looked like buisness, For there were Stores established in a little while. I never saw any town or village grow so fast, for the people flocked to it from every direction from the surrounding districts looking for farms and City Lots, as there had been so many applycants for places and their names had been published in the Papers, that they made a grand rush for what they could get, That is they came to select farms and buisness men came from

[Page 324]

many differant places to buy Lots of ground to build Stores Houses and for buisness's of all kinds, And there were hundreds of farms given out to men who met with such great losses in the War, even merchants came from Whittlessa and started buisness thare, And ministers of various denominations came and built Churches and Chapels. Well has soon as I had my farm granted I remained

CHAPTER 21

in Queens town [Queenstown] and I sent my two Sons on to it John and Jeremiah who worked a little. they Plowed some and cut and hauled firewood and by this time my Brother Elijah had moved on to his farm so he was com-

[Page 325]

pany for them, and while my Boys were up there, Thare came one of the heavyest Snowstorms that ever was known in that district, it fell from twelve to eighteen inches, But the Snow does not lye long it melted so quick that it caused quite a flood but done no serious damage, Well I contunied to work at the Carpenter work untill the next Spring in Queenstown Then I was Obliged to go to my farm and according to the law that was. I had to build one Fireproof room and occupie the place myself Personly with my family, Then I went to work and plowed and sowed and raised good

[Page 326]

Crops and had plenty both for myself and also plenty to sell. And then I rebuilt one wing of the burnt house and made two rooms very comfortable, and as there was a good stream of water runing past the House I built a small gristmill, for my own convenience, and it also became very conveniant for my naighbours, for I done a great deal of Grinding for them, And it made no differance where I moved to I had all the work that I could do at both makeing new Wagons and mending old ones, I was so well known and also my work that the people would follow me if it was for mils, and I had

[Page 327]

plenty of time to attend to my buisness for my Boys could do the plowing and the most of my farming and attended to the Cattle, and about this time a man by the name of William Davis who had no plowed Land on the farm that was granted to him so he came to me and I rented him a peice of mine on which he had a splendid Crop, and he cut it and stacked on my farm and was not in any hurry to trash it, And one windy day the grass had been sat on fire on another farme so that it came with all fury and burnt his Crop up, He did not happen to be there at the time, But if he had it would have made no differance he

[Page 328]

could not have stoped it. Well after living about one year on my farm my Brotherinlaw Francis Bently came to me and wanted to exchange Town property with me for a part of my farm, It was a good house with four rooms in it, so I exchanged with him and then I left my Boys on the other part of the farm and I moved back to Queenstown and contunied working at my Trade. And by this time I think thare were not less than one hundred Houses been built in that little time, It was astonishing how fast Queens Town [Queenstown] growed and was improved, Well I worked and lived in Queens Town [Queenstown] about

[Page 329]

two years when word came to me as well as to others who owned farms that it was Personal and that every man must live on his farm, (But before I left Queens Town [Queenstown] my eldest Daughter Jemima was married to a man whos name is George Ellis[3] a Carpenter by Trade,) Then I sold my place and moved back on to my farm and finished my house and had four good large rooms with the fireproof one, Then I built a good storeroom, and contunied makeing and repairing Wagons and had just has much, as ever I could do, my Brother also having a farm granted to him. so he had to leave my

[Page 330]

farm and go and occupy his own farm. so myself and my Son John bought that part of the farm back again, and as my Son was about to be married so he settled right down in his uncle's house that he had built on the place. I mentioned further back in my narritive, that we all those that had farms granted to them. Had to muster on the Queens Birthday all mounted equipted, which took place on the 24th of May, and we had to be inspected muster, every Fieldconnet had to bring his men to the general muster and then had to be inspected by the civil Commissioner or Resident Magistrate, On

[Page 331]

that day it was always considered a Holladay, It was in the district of Queens Town [Queenstown] where I had to meet, all those farmes that were granted the owner of each farm had to pay a moderate quit rent to the Government which was perpetual that is to say unredemable, and we had to occupy those farms for three years before we could get our Title deeds of sell, and if a man did not stay on his farm three years, and left it altogather inside of that time, he forfited it, But very few left their farms for they was too valuable in that district. I concider Queens Town [Queenstown] District almost unsurpassed by any district on the

[Page 332]

Fronteres both for Cattle sheep and Horses, and also as for Agricultural purposes it abounds with good grass and plenty of good water. And at the date I am writing it is dotted all over with good Farms and good substantial Houses with their beautiful vineyards and Rich Orchards. I would also say that those farmers are all rich and in good sircumstances having no had Kafir [Kaffir] invation for the last twenty years, and many of the Kafirs [Kaffirs] are also very well in middling good sircumstances at this time.

[Page 333]

---

3. George Ellis was born January 1, 1829, in Lincolnshire, England, and he married Jemima Rosetta Wiggill, born January 27, 1837, on August 16, 1855. British 1820 Settlers to South Africa.

Chapter 22

But I must say, That some time before the conclusion of the last chapter there is one thing I want to speak of that the fronteres tribes of Kafirs [Kaffirs] tryed to agitate anarother disturbance by rasing up a Prophet whom they caled Umlangeni, in the first place he councled his people to kill all their Cattle with the exception of two Oxen one white and the other black which was to represent the white people and the black people, which they tortured to death and which lived the longest eather the white one or the black one that

[Page 334]

would prove which would be the strongest party. And their Prophet also advised the people to distroy all their Crops as well as to distroy all their animals, and he made them beleive that new Cattle would come up out of the ground and that they must make new Kraals to receive them when they rose up out of the ground. He also told them that he could hear their horns rattle under the ground, and they beleived him.[1]

The influence of the prophet rapidly increased, and the number of his adherents included the greater part of the people of Kreli and the

[Page 335]

gaikas. Slaughtering cattle, which had begun in the past July, continued to be carried on in almost every Kraal, and there was high feastings in all Kafirland [Kaffirland]. Emissaries were dispatched from Kreli with the behests of the wonderful seer to Moshesh, to the remote Faku, east of St John's River, to the Tambookies, and Her Majesty's sable, but not loyal, subjects in British Kaffraria. Faku, however, did not see the wizard's directions with a friendly aspect; Moshesh waited for "something to turn up" the Tambookies were malingerers, but most of the Kafir [Kaffir] lieges trembled and obeyed.

[Page 336]

The Governor, watching the progress of this extraordinary delusion, continued to prepare all the munitions necessary in the event of war, but calmly, imperceptibly, and without any outward show to alarm the Kafirs [Kaffirs] and precipitate hostilities. With the prescience belonging to his character he foresaw that the wild sacrifices making by the Natives would soon render them more and more unfit to cope with the Colony, even under the pressure of that hunger, the desperate nature of which the Chiefs had reckoned upon to impel the inroad; and he was made

---

1. For an excellent treatment of this topic, see John Zarwan, "The Xhosa Cattle Killings, 1856–57," 519–39.

Nongqawuse (left) and Nonkosi (right), two Xhosa prophetesses prominent during the cattle-killing prophecies. Photograph by M. H. Durney in Grahamstown, 1858. Courtesy South African Library, Cape Town.

CHAPTER 22

[Page 337]

acquainted with the fact that already a schism had arisen among the people, who had ranged themselves into two parties, the beleivers and unbeleivers.

A Mr. A Kennedy, an eye witness of the events referred to, gives the following graphic statement: "Whether the Chiefs had communicated the secret of the intended war to their subjects I am unable to say, but their demeanour at this time evidently showed that they were acquainted with it. Always proud and haughty in their bearing towards the white man, their pride and hauteur were now much increased. With their karosses folded round them, they stalked majestically

[Page 338]

along, scowling at you, if you happened to meet them, with magligant hatred in their eyes. Fat and saucy from his unusual feasting, in high state of excitement with the thought of the impending struggle, and of the fine fat herds of cattle which he beleived were soon to gladden his longing gaze, it was at this time you might see the Kafir [Kaffir] in his glory.

"The cottage in which I was then residing was only a stone's throw from the 'winkel' to which the gaikas mostly brought their cattle for sale, and I had, therefore, an excellent opportunity of witnessing their proceedings. The place at this time was like a fair. Kafirs [Kaffirs], cattle,

[Page 339]

and goats were in crowds. The cattle were sold for about 5s. each, but the trader there obtained by barter one hundred head for ls. a piece. He gave 6d. for hides, of which he used to send off several wagon loads dayly, and I heard that he cleared £40,000 by this buisness Goats were sold from 9d. to ls 6d. at first, but at last beccame unsaleable, and the place was literally over run with them most of the Kafirs [Kaffirs] bought new blankets with the produce of the sale of their cattle, and it was an amusing sight to watch these fine fellows trying on their purchases. Models for a statuary, with muscles fully developed, such as would

[Page 340]

excite the admiration of the anatomist, they threw themselves unconsciously into the most graceful attitudes; holding the blanket on their hands by two corners, and throwing back their extended arms, they stood for a moment like bronzed statues, displaying their powerful and athletic frames to the greatest advantage; then folded it tightly around them, repeating this operation several times, untill apparently satisfied with the fit, After all this excitement came the reaction. A Kafir's [Kaffir's] food consistes of mealies, i. e. Kafirs [Kaffirs] corn, pumkin, and sour milk, with an occasional feast of beef or goat's meat on special occasions, such as a sacrifice or

[Page 341]

a wedding, &c. The Kafirs [Kaffirs] had not only destroyed their cows, which supplied them with one of their principal articles of food, their oxen and goats, but also, in accordance with Umlakazi's command, they had not cultivated the ground, and starvation now stared them in the face. I shudder still when I call to mind the dreadful scenes of misery I witnessed during this sad time. Such edible roots and bulbs as they could find in the 'veld' served them for food for a time. The favourite of these was the tap root of very young mimosa trees, such as were from one to two feet high. The veld in many parts where the mimosa fluris

[Page 342]

hed became so full of holes, where these had been dug up, that it was quite dangerous to ride over it. A tuber, belonging, I beleive, to the convolvulus tribe, about as large as a small potato, and not unpalatable, was also eaten by them. It is known to them by the name of Tgoutsi. This kind of food. however rather hastened their fate, for it brought on dessentery, and they became living skeletons; numbers of them died, and Kafirs [Kaffirs] skulls and bones were strewn over the fields. They would doubtless nearly all have perished thus miserably had not the government interfered and saved a great many of them. They were told to come to the commissioners

[Page 343]

and they would be fed, and when strong enough to travel, be sent into the colony to work. The Gaikas came to Brownlee in great numbers; many, however, perished by the way, too weak to proceed further. Some I have seen drop down dead before my door, when almost at their journey's end. Many died after they arrived, too far gone for the nourishment then given to be of any service; but the greater number recovered, and were dispatched in parties into the colony. A Kafir [Kaffir] is naturally generous; give one piece of bread or tobacco, he divides it with his companion; but hunger makes him selfish. I have seen mothers snatch bread out of

[Page 344]

their starving children's mouths and it has been said, but I cannot vouch for the truth of this, that one or two instances occurred of mothers devouring their infant children. This is too horrible to dwell upon." A statement was made at the time that the number of hides sold to traders, no less than 130.300 cattle had perished, the greater portion having been killed by orders of the imposter. Why all this suffering, had the Kauffars [Kaffirs] any thing in veiw, yes they had and it was this, Umlangeni had been raised up by some of the Kafir [Kaffir] Chiefs who made their followers believe he (Umlangeni) was a profit

[Page 345]

CHAPTER 22

and by listening to him the Kafirs [Kaffirs] thought it was all right and that they was on the way to whelth and prosperity. but where were they to obtain the proparty promised them the Cheifs though by geting their people to distroy all their living by their secret and deep layed plan, That they would come down on the British Colonys and make war with them drive them away and take all their Stock and provisions

But the Governor Sir George Cathcart, then Governor, of Cape Colony fearing that there was a secret combineation against the Colony

[Page 346]

from all that he could learn from agents and missionerys and Kafirs [Kaffirs] traiders and others, and fearing a fourth Kafir [Kaffir] invasion, took the precausion to strenthen all the Out Milltary Posts on the border and also in Kafirland [Kaffirland], and at the same time supplied all the Military Posts with plenty of Commissary supplyes, and by so doing their plans were all frusterated, and hence their missery and starvation which as been spoaken of followed.

[Page 347]

Chapter 23

It was about the year 1857 that I heard there was a strange people had come to Africa from America preaching a strange doctrin and was makeing a great stire in Cape Town, and Baptizing a few of the people and one person was considered so wicked by the Cape papers that the Water was so leadened or heavy with His sins that when it reached the Waterwheel it broke several of the Cogs, and also a young Lady that was Baptized, died soon after and I think was buried, then her friends was so ancious to have her likeness that they had her exumed,

[Page 347]

for the perpus.

These strange reports went through all the papers from Cape Town to Grahams Town [Grahamstown]. And has I belonged to the Wesleyan denomonation at that time and had been a member for at least thirty years, and has I said to a friend that they must have been sent of the Devil to try to deceive the very elect, if it was posable, and I believe they were called Mormons which I thought was a very strange name.[1]

And the next thing I heard of them been in Grahamtown and makeing a great stire there, that as far as talking and rangling and mobing was con-

[Page 349]

cirneded but I did not hear that they made any converts there, Then the next thing I heard they had got up into Fortbeaufort [Fort Beaufort] and

---

1. "Mormons" is a nickname for members of The Church of Jesus Christ of Latter-day Saints. The Church prefers "members of The Church of Jesus Christ of Latter-day Saints" or "Latter-day Saints." In 1852 missionary Joseph Richards, en route to India, stopped at Cape Town for one month, "distributed pamphlets, and talked with a number of people, who were glad to hear the truth." After arriving in Calcutta, Joseph wrote a letter to his brother S. W. Richards, the president of the LDS British Mission in Liverpool. Joseph noted that South Africa "would be a good place for a mission." "The Work in Hindustan: Extracts of Letters from Elders William Willes and Joseph Richards," 541–42.

At a Church conference held in Salt Lake City in August 1852, leaders named Jesse Haven, Leonard I. Smith, and William Walker as the first Latter-day Saint missionaries called to serve in South Africa. The trio arrived in Cape Town in 1853. Jay H. Buckley, "'Good News' at the Cape of Good Hope: Early LDS Missionary Activities in South Africa," in *Go Ye into All the World: The Growth and Development of Mormon Missionary Work*, 471–502; E. P. Wright, *A History of the South African Mission, 1852–1970*; F. R. Monson, "History of the South African Mission of The Church of Jesus Christ of Latter-day Saints."

CHAPTER 23   131

there I heard that these Mormons had Baptized several familys[2] that I was well acquainted with, One a Mr Clark and his Wife and Mr William Loyde and his Wife and also a Mr Thomas Parker[3] and his Wife which made me feel very strange, And there they met with great opposition by been mobed and having brickbats stones and rotton Eggs thrown at them from every direction,[4] and storming the House of Mr Thomas Parker where they held

---

2. William Walker and LDS convert John Wesley traveled from Cape Town to Grahamstown, arriving December 27, 1853. The next day, Walker met with Reverend Shaw and tried to secure a school room to hold a meeting for preaching, but he was denied. Wesley stayed in Grahamstown to teach the gospel, yet Walker journeyed to Fort Beaufort. Once there, Walker baptized nine people and established a branch of the Church (February 23, 1854). He returned to Grahamstown at Wesley's encouragement but found that although many were willing to listen to him preach, (even three hundred on March 17, 1854), he faced stiff opposition and intense persecution. William Holmes Walker, *Missionary Journals of William Holmes Walker: Cape of Good Hope South Africa Mission, 1852–1855*], 73–93. In a letter sent from Fort Beaufort dated September 15, 1854, to European Mission President Franklin D. Richards, Walker summarized his Eastern Cape province experiences: "I have been labouring on the frontiers of Africa, the borders of Kaffir land. I first laboured two months in this place, and baptized nine, after which I spent some three or four months in Graham's Town. I procured a house, and held meetings three months of the time, which were well attended at first, but some seemed fully determined to break up the meetings. The excitement was so great, it caused many to stay away. I continued until none attended, except those who were disposed to make disturbance; and when they ascertained that no one else came, they were satisfied to stay away. I received much insult and abuse; not only that, but two months of the time, I had no home, no place to get my regular meals, but I used to sleep in the room where I held meetings, and now and then had an invitation to dine or to tea. Although quite a number said that they believed that it was truth, that it was the work of God, yet none would repent." *Latter-day Saints' Millennial Star*, cited in *Missionary Journals of William Holmes Walker*, Appendix A, 190.

3. Walker met Thomas Parker, a resident of Fort Beaufort who was visiting Grahamstown, on December 27, 1853. Walker carried a letter for Parker from his brother Paul who lived in Cape Town. Walker described Thomas Parker as "a very respectable influencial Wholesale Merchant who said I was wellcome to remain at his House." Walker traveled with Thomas to his home, arriving January 1, 1854. A week later he preached at the local Wesleyan Chapel in Fort Beaufort to over one hundred people. The following evening, he preached again to a group of about fifty and, after the meeting ended, Walker baptized Mr. and Mrs. Thomas Parker on January 9, 1854. On January 11 he baptized Mr. William Lloyd, and on January 26 Walker baptized George Clark and his wife. *Missionary Journals of William Holmes Walker*, 76–80.

4. Walker recorded the opposition he faced in a June 6, 1854, journal entry: "I received much abusive Language and many threats of being thrown into the River,

William H. Walker (1820–1908), ca. 1860s. Courtesy Church History Library, The Church of Jesus Christ of Latter-day Saints.

[Page 350]

their meetings. And breaking the windows and tried to break open the door. Then the mob ran the Mormon Preacher's Carrage down into the river which is called Kat river where I beleive it stayed for I never heard of its been got out, The Carrage belonged to a Mr William Walker who had come on a Mission in company with two others, whos names are Jessie Haven and Lenord. I. Smith. from Salt Lake City.[5]

---

whiped &c. and said that I ought to be Tared & Feathered." Walker, *Missionary Journals of William Holmes Walker*, 110. Some of the opposition may have resulted from advertisements early missionaries had created themselves. Walker created an advertisement in the newspapers to stir up curiosity but instead stirred up opposition. On December 28, 1854, Walker recorded, "The People throughout the Colony are allmost daily being Advertized both from the Press & the Pulpit! to beware of Mormonism." Walker, *Missionary Journals of William Holmes Walker: Cape of Good Hope South Africa, 1852–1855*, 146–47. South African papers were numerous from the mid- to late nineteenth century. Cutten, *A History of the Press in South Africa*, 30.

5. Walker recorded information about his mission call: "Aug 28/1852 I William Walker was appointed on a mission to the Cape of Good Hope. I settled my business and started Sept 15th in company with Jesse Haven and Lenard I Smith which were appointed to the same Mission as myself and also about one hundred Elders to different nations of the earth." Walker noted the missionaries' sea voyage ended on "Tuesday Apr the 19 1853 Landed in Cape Town Cape of Good Hope South

CHAPTER 23

And they had tracks published in Cape Town and distribueted them in every place has they traviled along and preached the tracks were in two

[Page 351]

languages Dutch and English. Then the next thing I heard of them they had made their way up into the Winterberg to My Brother George who received them kindly and listened to their teachings and read their tracks.[6]

And he been a very steady schrude thinking man and compareing their tracks with the Scriptures, He found that their tracks and preaching coresponded so well with the New Testament that he came to the conclusion that there must a great deal of truth in their Doctrin.

One of his naighbours said to him (My Brother) I hear you have got a new

[Page 352]

religon come among you but my Brother made answer and said that he thought otherwise he thought it was the old religon revived that Christ and his Apostles taught when they were on the earth.

So one of these Mormons[7] Preachers stayed and made his home with my Brother for several weeks preaching around in differant places and explaining this new doctrin as the people called it. Such was the news that was brought to me by people who had been at my Brother House.

And I thought it very strange especily for him

[Page 353]

who had never at any time investgated religon any in peticular. Well some time after these reports I was in Queenstown on buisness. when I heard that

---

Africa." Walker, *Missionary Journals of William Holmes Walker*, 2; 19. Reid L. Neilson and R. Mark Melville, eds., *The Saints Abroad: Missionaries Who Answered Brigham Young's 1852 Call to the Nations of the World*. Jeffrey G. Cannon, "Mormonism's Jesse Haven and the Early Focus on Proselytizing the Afrikaner at the Cape of Good Hope, 1853–1855," 446–56.

6. Walker noted that while in the Fort Beaufort area on February 11, 1855, he "preached at of mr. [George] Wiggills, very good attendance & the Lord blest me ... as mr. Wiggill & wife had offered themselves as Candidates for Baptism." Nine days later, Walker wrote, "Tuesday 20th . . . I Baptized Elizabeth and Mary Ann Wiggill daughters of Geo Wiggill also Charles Williams aged 24 years." Walker, *Missionary Journals of William Holmes Walker*, 158, 160.

7. One unusual reference to the name "Mormon" occurs in a death notice of a thirty-year-old African miner named Mormon from Basutoland. His father is listed as Bamaswam, and his mother is named Selini. Mormon died August 15, 1895. Mormon "left no property at Hospital" and had no will, suggesting there may have been some degree of contact between the Latter-day Saint missionaries with natives as well as settlers in this region. Western Cape Archives, MOK vol. 59 1/1/62, no. 6132.

my Brother and one Mr William Walker was in Queenstown who had come from Winterberg some sixty or seventy miles on Horseback princeably to see me, and has I had always been a great Wesleyan and a preacher among them my Brother thought he would like to hear what my opinion was and what I thought of the Doctrin.[8] So I had them ride home with me which was about 8

[Page 354]

miles to my farm in Bongolo. And of corse the princeable conversation on the road was about this new religon, And has I had been talking about this new doctrin I got on my Horse and rode around to the differant houses and invited my neighbours to come and hear for themselves what the Mormon preacher would say to them has he Mr Walker would preach at my house that evening.[9]

So a few of them came to hear a few of the things that they had heard through

[Page 355]

the papers. The discorse of Mr Walker was princeably on Baptisam and the Savour been Baptized by John in the river Jordon.

And also the multitude that was Baptized on the day of penticost. And of Philip Baptizing the Eunuch, and Mr Walker explained those passages of scripture to meain that it was intended for addult persons or persons who had come to the years of maturity for the forgivness or washing away of sins by emersion and also by one having authority from God and been ordained

[Page 356]

of the Lord to the office of the high priesthood and that Baptism of infants was not of Christs nor his disciples, such was the language of Mr Walker at

---

8. William Walker noted on February 23, 1855, "Mr Eli Wiggill had come from Queens Town & wished to see me. Saturday 24th of Feb. I spent my time in reading & singing & talking with mr Wiggill who seemed to be enquiring after the truth." The following day, Walker preached a Sunday sermon and wrote, "I spoke to the saints [and] mr Eli Wiggill said he thought that my instructions would of done credit to the Apostles of Old much pleesed." On February 27, 1855, Walker penned "mr Eli Wiggill took a Quantity of books home with him & told me when I came to Queens Town that I should have his House to preach in that he had made up his mind to be baptized." On May 7, 1855, Walker noted, "I wrote a letter to mr Eli Wiggill Queens Town," which is the last mention of Eli in his journal. Walker, *Missionary Journals of William Holmes Walker*, 160–61, 170. Although Wiggill told Walker he had decided to be baptized in February 1855, Wiggill was not baptized until three years later on March 1, 1858.

9. Unfortunately, William Walker's journal abruptly ends on Sunday, August 12, 1855, so later interactions between Walker and Wiggill are not available. Walker, *Missionary Journals of William Holmes Walker*, 182.

CHAPTER 23

this meeting. And any school Boy might read it for himself in the new testament and sprinkling is not found within the lids of the Testament for infants.

And when I heard Mr Walker explain things in the manner he did I could not help beleive the truth of it. The next morning after hearing this sermon one of my naighbours Mr Staples came to ~~see~~

[Page 357]

my house to see Mr Walker and asked him a great many questions on differant subjects so after talking some time Mr Staples said well it is the same old controvirsy that as been in the differant Churches for Centenarys past. That is the doctrin of Baptiziam I mean. After this my Brother and Mr Walker stayed with me two or three days, and of corse the time was princeably occupied in asking questions on the princeables of Mormonism. And all the questions that I asked was answerd Scriptural and sattisfacterly so that

[Page 358]

I could not gain say them Mr Walker also brought a Book of Mormon with him and left it with me to read and also several tracks.

And one of them astonished me more than the others it was called a warning to all People high and low rich and poor, to Kings and Queens and to the Clergy of all denomonations. And it further stated that they came with a message and authority from the God of heaven as revealed in these latter days through Joseph Smith the Prophet and Mr Walker could

[Page 359]

vouch for him been an honnest and upright man and sent by the God of Heaven. And the message which he (Joseph Smith) ~~brought~~ received, the nations of the Earth would be judged by it as much so as the antediluvians, was in the days of Noah.

It said that they did not come to Africa to quaril or rangle with any party or cect as quarling was no part of the religon of Christ, But that they had a message to deliver and they were detirmined to do it so that they might rid their garments of the blood of all men whom

[Page 360]

they came in contact with, such were some of the language which was embodyed in the track entitled a warning to all. Having read the Book of Mormon through which gave me great sattisfaction and also the tracks. And while my Brother was with and he been very well of in this Worlds goods and haveing plenty of money at his command all the time, I asked him to lone me some twenty or thirty Pounds to settle of a few Depts which I had contracked before the Kaffir War of 1851

[Page 361]

in the Town of Fort Beaufort. When I asked him he said that he did not know wether he could do it or not but said he would see. My Brother been a man that always took time to think well upon anything of the kind such as bargons or the Lone of money But when he had once given his word it could be depended on so a few weeks after he had left me and gone to his home I had a Dream and I dremed that I went to his house in the Winterberg and that he went with me to Fort Beaufort and settled the Depts that was troubling

[Page 362]

me, and as I got notice from the partys I was oweing they wanting to settle up their accounts so I rode down to my Brothers, And when I got there I found the Mormon Elder[10] there at my Brother's house and of corse our conversation was all on the princeables of Mormonism,

And after staying two or three days my Bro Mr Walker and myself started on Horseback and went to Fort Beaufort which was about twenty miles, And just has I had Dreamed my Brother fulfiled it to the very letter for he payed every

[Page 363]

penny that I owed in Fort Beaufort. So we stayed one night with Mr Thomas Parker. Iron Monger. whos house was Mr Walkers home when he was in Fort Beaufort,

That night I enjoyed myself that very much what with the singing of Mormon Hymns and the conversation which was very interesting and has Mr Walker had a great many Mormon Books and Pamphlets which he had for sale I think I bought one of each kind. For by this time I had become very much interested in reading their book and begun to investigate for myself. The Book of Mormon was the first, and

[Page 364]

then the Doctrine Covenants containing the Revelations that the Lord gave to the Prophet, Joseph Smith, concerning the latter day work upon the earth. And the latter day Saints Hymn book, and also a smal book entitled Spencers letters, and another smal book called the voice of warning to all people. And a serious Pamphelts entitled the devine authenticty of the Book of Mormon by Orson Pratt one of the twelve Apostles of said Church. And also Pamphlets entitled the Kingdom of God, and several others by the same Auther.[11] so when went home I thought

---

10. "Elder" is an ecclesiastical term for male Latter-day Saint missionaries; it is also used for male Church members who have been ordained to the office of elder in the Melchizedek Priesthood.

11. Pratt was "the most prolific and perhaps most influential early Mormon pamphleteer.... He authored over thirty works on both religious and scientific topics.

CHAPTER 23

[Page 365]

I would have a good time in reading and studing over this new doctrine. So the next morning we three started and went home to my Bro George's in the Winterberg and our conversation was Mormonism all the way and I stayed with them a day or two and while I was there Mr Walker was so convinced in his own mind that I beleived that he wanted to Baptize me right then, my Brother George and Wife and all his family who were old enough had been Baptize, and become members of this new religion which my Brother called the old

[Page 366]

religion revived again and as my Brother inlaw Francis. P. Bentley had accompanyed me from Queens Town [Queenstown] and was waiting my return from Beaufort at the house of a friend in the neighbourhood so I left so I left my Brother George to meet my Broinlaw according to appointment and returned home to Queenstown, and on the road home my mind was so full of light and knowlage of the scriptures and it seemed to me that I could see the meaining of every text in the Bible, so when I got home my Wife said she thought that I had got completely

[Page 367]

converted to Mormonism at this time I resided in Queenstown, so then all the leasure time that I had I read and investigated all the books that I had bought, And although some of them were written by differant authers, I could not see anywhere that they contridicted each other, They all bore the same testimony to each other that God had spoken once more from the Heavens, to the people on the earth after a long night of darkness and especly those written by Orson Pratt on the devine authenticity of the Book of Mormon.

[Page 368]

and the Kingdom of God. The truth of the apostasy of all the christian Churches his reasonsings was so forceable in every paragraph that I could not help seeing the truth of his remarks, and I also was led to see that the Bible had been through so many differant Translations that it had been very much corrupted and a great portion of the original scripture is lost and other portions rejected by the Popish Church and others which this Mr Pratt entitled the Mother of Harlots and the Abominations of the earth. And none of the churches at the preasant

[Page 369]

time beleives in any new revelations from the Heavens.

Influential during his own lifetime, he wielded even more influence after his death." David J. Whittaker, "Orson Pratt: Prolific Pamphleteer," 27. "Divine Authenticity of the Book of Mormon" was published via a series of six different issues or numbers and "The Kingdom of God" in four different issues or parts. Both pamphlet series were printed in Liverpool in 1851. Orson Pratt, "A Series of Pamphlets."

As an instance I coppy upwards of 250 Popes pretend to have successively filled the chair of St. Peter. All these Popes, we are told, have possessed the same authority and power as St. Peter whom they designate as the first Pope; if this really be the case, then each of these Popes must have been inspired of God, and the writings of each must be equally as sacred as the writings of Pope St. Peter. Why then has the Church showed such great partiality? Why has she placed Pope St. Peters

[Page 370]

writings in the sacred canon, and left all the writings of the other Popes out.

Mr Pratts remarks was so pointed in hundreds of his passages of the Apostasy from the origanal faith of Christanity that all his remarks appeared to me to be written by the pen of inspireation. So reading and investigateing all those books and Pamplets set me to thinking in earnest. I used to think that the Bible was the pure unadulterated word of God, such I have heard spoken from the Pulpits of them days. And also in what errers the Jewes may be in they

[Page 371]

could not be accuesed of fulcifing the Old Testament I was taught to beleive that the Bible was puer from their hands, But after investigateing those Pamplets of Mr Pratts and also the writings of other learned men I find that the Jewes are accuesed of corrupting and altering many texts and passages of the Bible, where it spoke so clear of the coming of Christ, they altered the meaning of the reading so that it should not appear that Jesus was the Christ, and what was more astonishing to me was from reading those Pamplets I found that the Church had apostised from

[Page 372]

the faith as taught by Christ and his Apostles and that it had not been taught on the Earth for seventeen centeryes only as taught by the Precepts of men, and all these things set me to thinking And about this time I had a great many arguments with religous people with whom I was surrounded and especially with my Wesleyan Breathren with whom I was conected and sometimes with the Preacher, one in peticlur who came to my house one evening and I brought up Mormonism to him telling him how clear and scripturel their arguments and doctrins

[Page 373]

were and his answer was to me that he would not spend five minits with me to talk about Mormonism but I kept him talking on Scriptural toptics for about half an hour, When he said realy I said I would not spend five minits with you when he first commenced to talk with me but this way going on I shall preach all my surmon away, has he had to preach that evening It seemed so easy for me to confute them in their idea, of scripture and the plan of

CHAPTER 23

Salvation, so I went about my work and buisness as usal and conversed with whom I came in contact with who would broach

[Page 374]

the subject to me for the more I read and investigated the more I was convinced of the truth of the new religon as it was called, so at the end of a few months I got the illwill of some of my own relations most all my religous friends and also my Wife who could not see has I did, it made her feel very bad when she seen all our old friends turn a cold shoulder on me, Well at this time seeing how things was working I put all my Books up on a very high shelf and thought that I would not bother with them, for at this time I was a member and a classleader of the Wesley

[Page 375]

an Church and local preacher and of corse attended all the meetings, Well I left the books on the shelf for a few weeks and thought over the matter a great deal in my own mind and I found that the truth had taken such deep root in my heart with what I had read, But I kept very quite and said but very little, and to use a scriptural phrase, I pondered it in my mind, But I thought this way, To convince a man against his will, He is of the same opinion still, so it was with me in regard to this new faith for I found when I had to preach and speake

[Page 376]

in public that scriptural topics would flow from me with such force and meaning has I had never experianced before that my Brethren thought that I had got a renewal of the spiret of the Methodists religon, but I advanced nothing new to them but that was scriptural and plane, They did not seem to know or consider that I had gained the knowlage from the books that I had read refered to above so things went on in this way for several months untill at last I pulled down my books again and began to investigat them the second time and found

[Page 375]

them to contain more truth than I had ever seen before in them. And about this time a traveling Elder came along whos name was John Wesley, he also had been a member of the Wesleyan Church,[12] and a local preacher and had joined this new faith and came from Cape Town to Grahamstown as a traveling companyon and preacher with Mr William Walker from him I received more light and also baught more books from this John Wesley but at this time I had not joined this new Church so in one way and another, about one year had past, so that

[Page 376]

---

12. To understand the Wesleyan Methodist Church influence on LDS converts, see Christopher C. Jones, "'We Latter-day Saints are Methodists': The Influence of Methodism on Early Mormon Religiosity."

the reader can see that I did not do anything hastly, but my mind was convinced of the truth of ~~Mo~~ the doctrines and faith (of what they called it the Church of the Latter Day Saints) There seemed to me somthing so grand about the words of Latter day Saints. The word Latter day seemed so appropriate that Christ church when he was on the earth was called the former day Saints and has we live in the Latter days I thought it very appropriate.

Book No. 3

[Page 377]

Chapter 24

To the best of my recollection I still lived in Queenstown South Africa, and working which was has I have said princeably Wheelwrighting and sometimes Carpentering, and many other kinds of wood work,

And at this time my mind was well convinced in regard to Mormonism for I still kept investigateing and reading my Books and Pamphlets and I also read and explaned the doctrins to my Friends and naighbours and many of them was convinced of the truth of the work, one man in peticular a Mr Robert Wall, which had read the Bible all his lifelong but he said that he had never understoad the bible before, that it apeared like a new book to him now

[Page 378]

and he wondred that he had not seen it before in the light that he now sees it, But the reason was he had not had the key which had not unlocked the truth has he now seen it, and wondred where they got the light and knowlage from to write and explain as they did on those topics of this Latter day work.

He said that he had read a great many book on the explaination of the Bible but these throwed them all into the shade or background so I used to spend two and three hours at a time reading and explaining from these books and pamphlets and the scriptures of the old and new Testament, They all tallyed so well with the Scriptures that he began to think there must be

[Page 379]

some truth in it, so the naighbours began to look upon him as a deluded fanatic as they did upon me I had known this Mr Wall for many years, so he read and explained to his naighbours and acquaintances has I had done, But to one man in peticular a Brotherinlaw of his, a Mr Henry Talbot,[1] who began to gather in the truth as we had done, and when he was convinced of the truth of this new

---

1. Henry Talbot was seven years old when his parents, John and Priscilla Talbot, and four of his siblings embarked on the ship *Aurora* for South Africa in 1820 as members of the Hezekiah Sephton Party. Nash, *The Settler Handbook*, 114–16. Henry was born in Pimico, London, on October 15, 1812. He married Ruth Sweetnam, February 4, 1817, and later worked as a mason with his brother John in Grahamstown. Talbot moved with his family to Winterberg, ca. 1843, to be nearer his in-laws. He worked on his "Wellington" farm in the Queenstown District and had 1,100 acres as a reward for the services he and his oldest son rendered in the Eighth Frontier War. In 1860 Talbot moved to Port Elizabeth and embarked for America in 1861 to be with the Latter-day Saints in Utah. He and Ruth had sixteen children. Henry died December 15, 1895, from pneumonia in Layton, Utah. Ruth passed away in Layton on May 21, 1903. Denis H. Patrick, "Settler of 1820: John Stuart Talbot and his wife Priscilla and their descendants in South Africa," 38.

religon it brought to the mind of his Wife of a dream that she had had some years before in regard to her Husband she said to him when talking about it that you will join them, for as I saw in my dream there would be a religon that was not in Africa at that time, but that it would be brought by some one at some time

[Page 380]

and that you joined it

Well at this time my eldest daughter was married whos name is Jemima was married to a Young Man whos name is George Elles a Carpenter by trade, so him and myself worked togather for a time, and often talked about Mormonism in the shop while at work, But he at that time he could not see the truth of Mormonism, and it used to be so offensiv to him to hear me reason on that subject, so he told me afterwards so we worked togather for a while untill he agreed to go on to a mission Station by the name of Lessenton [Lesseyton] Station[2] that belonged to the Wesleyan denomination so he engaged as master Carpenter to instruct the Kaffir Boys in House Carpentering, and they also emplo

[Page 381]

yed a Wheelwright at the same station, and I have no doubth but they would have given me the master Wheelwright situation only for me imbibeing the doctrins of Mormonism (which was in their eyes a dreadful delusion)

Has they had known me and my work for years before, that they would have taken me in prefferance to any other man in that naighbourhood, But as it was they did not ask me to go, and if they had I should not have gone knowing what I did at the time for I had all the work that I could attend to just then, so I beleive they hired a man as Wheelwright by the name of Helce,

While my Soninlaw was residing there they built a very large Mansion at

[Page 382]

the Government expence, it rested on a solled flat ironstone rock for its foundation, My Soninlaw worked there for over a year at monthly wageses and done very well.

And I myself contunied to work at my trade in Queens town [Queenstown], But so far I had not joined Latter day Saints, for one reason there was no one near having authority to do so, for I had learned enough from the books that I had read to know that to be Baptized by one not having authority would be of no avail to me eather in time or in eternity. So I came to the conclusion in the year February 1858 I made a Journey with my Wife

---

2. "Wesleyan Methodist Mission Station in the Eastern Cape Province was established in 1851 to train natives for the Ministry." Rosenthal, *Encyclopedia of Southern Africa*, s.v. "Lesseyton," 321. See also Taylor, *Christian Adventures in South Africa*, 215.

CHAPTER 24

and family in my Wagon which I fitted up on purpos to go to my Brother George in the Winterberg. Then after a day or two visit there, my Brother

[Page 383]

and myself went to a place called the Kat river settlement where an Elder of the Mormon Church lived, who having authority to Baptiz by the name of Mr. John Green,[3] he been the nearest in that vecinity, The head quarters of the Church at that time been in Algo [Algoa] Bay or Port Elizabath,[4] which was over a distance of a hundred miles.

So the following day this Elder Green came to my Brother's house at the Winterberg for the purpos of Baptizing myself my Wife and those of my family who was old enough that was willing to comply. So on the first of March 1858 myself, my Wife, and two Daughters Sarah Ann and Margaret were Baptized by Elder John Green. And he ordained me the same day to the Office of a Priest, in said Church.

[Page 384]

And that evening he preached at my Brothers house on the princeables of the doctrins of the Latter day Saints, So we stayed and visited around for about a week enjoying ourselves for just at that time the fruits of all kinds was ripe and the Children had a very good time,

Well after having a good visit we started on our Journey home again to Queenstown but as my Soninlaw George Elles was still living at Lessonton [Lesseyton] which was all in our road we caled to see them, and finely arrived at home I still contunied to follow my buisness, and talking and explaining and somtimes Preaching in my own house to my naighbours and to all who would come in to hear.

And at this time all my

[Page 385]

old Methodist friends after hearing that I had been Baptized, thought that I had been deluded and deceived by these Mormons that was going around the country, I had many a debate with many of them and sometimes came in contact with the Preachers but they were all prejudiced and blind that they would not see the truth of the gosbel, one of my old friends said that there

---

3. John Green's family voyaged on the *Weymouth* with the Menezes Party, arriving at Algoa Bay on May 15, 1820. The names included on the list are "GREEN, John 39. Laborer. W[wife] Ann 30. C [children] Hannah 9, May 7, John 6, James 5, Thomas 3, William 2, a baby born at sea." The John Green noted by Wiggill appears to be either the father or the son listed herein. Nash, *The Settler Handbook*, 91.

4. The original copy of the Port Elizabeth Branch Record (1858–1864), including records prior to these dates, are located at the Church History Library in Salt Lake City, Utah.

was no use in talking or arguing with me for it seemed to him that I knew the Bible from end to end off by heart and I thought that was better than not knowing it at all.

About that time I sold property in Queenstown consisting a House and a small plot of ground, and went to reside on my farm in

[Page 386]

the Bongolo where I had lived some time before, my two Sons John and Jeremiah who had stayed on the farm all the while that I lived in Queenstown and kept it under good cultivation, And now and then they would bring a load of firewood into the town for sale. And when I got back to ~~Queenstown~~ the Farm I contunied to make and repair Wagons as usal, for where ever I would go I always had as much work has I could do, And my Son Jeremiah attended to the farming with a little of my assistance, has my Son John was often away on the road with Wagons Freighting or as it is caled in Africa by the Dutch Carvaing, or Transport riding at this time my Soninlaw

[Page 387]

George Ellis was still at work at the Lessenton [Lesseyton] Station as ~~been~~ has been already mentioned. So myself and my Wife road over to see them after we had got settled on my farm I call it riding over because we had to go over a very high rugged mountain covered over with great ironstone bolders. We went that road for nearness but in going over this mountain we had to walk and lead our Horses, on acount of its rufness, and it made a differance of six or eight miles nearer, we genearly stayed one or two nights with them, and before I would leave I generaly went around among the differant work shops, and has at that time a Mr John. P. Bertrum, was govenor or Master of the institution and has he had known me for many years he used to like me to go through

[Page 388]

the Wagon shop to pass my opinion of the work which was on hand, has my opinion on Wagons and Wagonwork. Has my fame was known so well both far and near in regard to Wagon makeing that it could not be disputed by any one, And while staying there and in corse of conversation with my Soinlaw I found that he was dissatesfide with his situation.

In the first place his health was failing, and in the second place it was too confining. And in the third he had to overlook several K.affir Boys who who were apprentices to the Carpentering buisness which was very annoying to him. So I told him that if he did not like the place to quit and come to Bongolo to my Farm where I was then residing, so in a few weeks he notifide

[Page 389]

Mr Bertrem that he should leave which was rather sooner than I wished him to do.

CHAPTER 24

So he came and brought his family to my house. then I assisted him to put up a smale house a little distance from mine, And when that was done and his family settled he worked at his trade around the naighbourhood.

It was at this time that he began to take an intrest in reading and investegating the books and Pamphlets that I Loned him especley the Book of Mormon, The book of Alma seemed to attract his attention more peticlar than any other part. And he began to investigate and beleive the statements of the books and of the preaching and as Elder Wesley was at my house at different times with others Elder he attended to with others to preaching services which was held in my house every Sunday, and when none of those Elders were not there it always fell on my lot to officiate.

[The text here suddenly jumps to page 400 with no pages listed from 390–399].]

[Page 400]

And as Elder Wesley was at my house at differant times with others Elders he attended to with others to the preaching service which was held in my house every Sunday, and when none of those Elders were not there it alway fell to my lot to officiate.

So in one way and another Ellis was convinced that Mormonism was true,

And it was about the year 1858 and on the first of June there was a call from Salt Lake City, That all the Branches of the Church scattered abroad that they members should renew their covenants by Baptism to the Lord, so at the above date Elder John Wesley was at my house and had been for several days so myself Eli Wiggill was Baptized and ordained an Elder in the Church of Jesus Christ of Latter day Saints,[5] And second

[Page 401]

my Wife Susannah Wiggill was Baptized. Second my Daugher Jemima Elles, and also her Husband George Elles, and at the same date my Daughter Sarah Ann Wiggill and also my Daughter Margaret. Alice. Wiggill and also my Daughter Roseannah. Marria. Wiggill. and also my Daughter Fanny Amelia Wiggill. and my youngest Son Joseph. Elijah. Wiggill. been under age was not Baptized. And all confirmed as members in the Church the same day.

So I contunied on to work at my trade and attend to my farm, and Preach on Sundays to my naighbours who would come in to listen and also to my family, And it was about this time that Mr Henry Talbot and fam-

---

5. During this reformation period, Latter-day Saint Church leaders requested that members worldwide be re-baptised as a demonstration of their willingness to renew their covenants. Wiggill, his family, and other Church members of the Queenstown Branch complied. Paul H. Peterson, "The Mormon Reformation of 1856–1857: The Rhetoric and the Reality," 45–63.

Henry Talbot (1812–1895) and his wife Ruth Sweetnam (1815–1903), friends of Eli Wiggill, ca 1870. Courtesy Russell and Diana Lindeman.

ily of which consisted seventeen souls. And in November 13th 1859 in the Bongolo near Queenstown was Baptized the following persons by Elder

[Page 402]

Henry. James. Talbot jun.[6]

first Jeremiah. Francis. Wiggill. born at the village of Bathurst. South Africa. May 12th 1839. Second Robert. William. Wilson. Wall. third. William Henry. Watson.

And at the Queenstown Branch Baptized by me Eli Wiggill. in the Bongolo. Charles Fancott, and his Wife Catharine Fancott, third Lavinia, Ann. Talbot. and confirmed the same day by myself and other Elders.

Now I must say somthing more about this Mr Robert Wall who I have mentioned before has I mentioned before as haveing written a letter to me on some of the doctrines of the Church in a faultfinding spirit so that I did not visit him at the time the letter referies too, So in a few months after this letter referies too he moved into

---

6. Henry James Talbot noted how he traveled to church meetings in Queenstown: "I had a novel way of giting to the Church. We went in a wagon with seven yoak of oxen . . . because I was a Mormon. But that was all right we went in our own rig to the church, and no thanks to anyone." "Short Sketch of the Life of Henry James Talbot," 11.

CHAPTER 24

[Page 403]

the Bongolo on to a Farm joining mine where I then seen him occassionly at my house on buisness affairs and at this time he was visited by a Mr Green, who was a Preacher of the Church of England, and in the mean time he had this Preacher confirm two of his unmarried Daughters into the Church of England and on that account I discontunied my visits to him.

And soon after this he was taken sick and confined to his bed so that the Doctor who visited him had not much hopes of his recovery so one day I went over to see him and read some portions of the Scripture to him and prayed for him and asked the Lord to bless and restore him to health and life. So on one of those visits I asked

[Page 404]

him if I should administer to him or anoint him with oil has the Apostle James said in the 5 Chapter and 14th and 15 virses which reads as follows, "Is any sick among you, let him call for the Elders of the church; and let them pray over him, anointing him with oil in the name of the Lord:

And the prayer of faith shall save the sick, and the Lord shall raise him up and if he have committed sins, they shall be forgiven him.

And has I asked him if I should anoint him he answered yes I would like you to do so, so I complyed with his wish,

When he had been anointed he seemed so much better and became so cheerfull and talkative to what he was before so after this I visited him

[Page 405]

several times and convirsed with him on differant subjects mostly on the scriptures. And on one of my visits he told me that he beleived the doctrins of Mormonism has I had explained it to him. And also said that he had a great desire to be Baptized and wished me to Baptize him has he fully beleived the doctrine.

And in the mean time while I was visiting him this Mr Green the Church of England Preacher called on him several times, and on one of those visits Mr Wall told him not to trouble himself about coming to see him for he did not wish him to do so, for my naighbour who lived on the next farm visited me regluer and with his reading and talking to me I am perfectly sattisfied.

So has he had made up his mind to be Baptized

[Page 406]

sick has he was I sent for his Brotherinlaw and his Son Henry. J. Talbot who were Elders in the Church so when they arrived having to travil some fifty or sixty miles, we made preprations to Baptize him near the house has he had to be caried in an armed Chair from the bed to the water, so on the 6th of November 1858, I Baptized him and he was confirmed the same day by four Elders first myself Eli Wiggill, second Henry Talbot sen. third Henry Talbot jun. fourth George Elles. Elders in the Church of Jesus Christ of Latter day Saints.

After the Baptism and confirmation Mr Wall seemed perfectly happy and resinged and often said that the administeration with the oil which he had taken inwardly

[Page 407]

had kept him alive so long. He lived sixteen days after his Baptisim, he told me just before he died that he wanted me to attend to his funeral and bury him in the Bongolo has he told me that he did not want to be taken to Queenstown to be buryed, for this reason they had their concerated Churches and also their concerated burying grounds and concerated Parsons and that he did not want anything to do with any of them. So he left it all to me and I buryed him on my Farm.

Mr. Robert Wall was fifty four years and nine months and twenty one days when he died on the twenty second day of November 1858. He was born in England on the first of Feb in the year of our Lord 1804.[7]

[Page 409]

So this Mr Green and others after Mr Wall's Death,)

Made a great talk about me for takeing a sick man out of his bed to Baptize him, by puting him in cold water, as much as to say that I was the cause of his death but in a few weeks it all passed away like other storms dose.

As I have refered to a letter that Mr Wall wrote to me some months before he was taken sick I will now copy it as it will show the state of his mind at that time,

Queens Town [Queenstown] 1856

November 18

Most Respected Friend.

With painfull regret, I have to observe that indifferance, and reserve shew themselves, in consiquence of the indifferance of Opinion over which sinfull man would have no control.

[Page 410]

You may beleive me, that I am struck with astonishment, was it upon worldy matters, of buisness were loss, and injury were sustained or liable their might be reason assigned.

I would entreat of you to examine the case, within your own concionce, and then point out to me where and by what I have wounded your feelings to cause such reservedness.

---

7. Robert Wall was born February 1, 1803, in London, England, and he passed away November 22, 1858, in Bongola, District of Queenstown. See FamilySearch.

CHAPTER 24

Men in this age of the world are noted for learning and we are even informed, that the day will arrive that they will deceive the very elect, and as we very well know that even the Angles in Heaven are not to know our makers secret will, it behoves us therefore to be carefull and watchfull not being led too and fro by every whirlwind.

[Page 411]

We do acknowledg our Church to be a fallen Church, full of error and traditions of men, We know we support a hireling Priesthood and that we are far from the true and ancient Church,

But we also beleive that Almighty, and all powerfull God, still exist, who in his own good time, will call to account all nations of the Earth.

And untill then we may expect to see the conning craft of men in all its shapes and forms, now in refferance to that sect called Mormons I beg to acknowledge, that I have found great pleasure in reading their Books insomuch so that it has often caused edification to the reader.

I therefore after a carefull examination of their Books pronounced

[Page 412]

them good, so far as being a true copy of the Ancient Church, and now having read their Books I have a great desire to see their works also, before I dare come to any conclusion which if not true would be denieing my maker.

N. B. Orson Pratt says that Joseph Smith was ordained an Apostle by Peter, James, and John, He Joseph Smith having testified that Peter, James, and John being ministring Angels.

See Devine Authority[8]

4th page

Robert Wall

[Page 413]

---

8. This is referring to Orson Pratt's pamphlet, *Divine Authenticity of the Book of Mormon*, noted previously.

Chapter 25

Just about this time I was caled upon to attend a Conferance at my Brother Georges House in the Winterburg. And just has I was ready to start a man came to the Bongolo a Brotherinlaw of Mr Walls, by the name of George Hayward[1] from over the Orange river on his way to another Brotherinlaw of his a Mr Talbot who lived on a farm caled Thorn river which was from forty to fifty miles from Bongolo, and our conversation was the topice of Mormonsim and he seemed to fall in with some of the ideas especley with Baptisiam for the remission of sins so when we got to Mr Talbots, he, preached to him as it was the first time he Mr Talbot had seen him since he had

[Page 414]

joined the Church.

Mr Hayward and myself stayed about two days at Mr Talbots house, then we all three started for the Winterburg to attend the Confirance, The road leading over the top of a beautifull flat undulating Mountainous country, known by the name of the Buntiback [Bontebok][2] flat[s][3] which was between twenty and thirty miles across the country showing the districte of Queenstown all the way which was very beautifull and Picturesque, and this large track of mountain country was unoccupied government Land, It is a very cold place in the Winter but splendid for Cattle in the Summer almost destitute of wood but plenty of water so after riding this distance we came to the top of the Katburg known as the top

[Page 415]

of the old Katburg road a hill that is from eight to ten miles long, and part of that through a Forest Well has we were riding along we observed clouds rising which denoted a Thunder storm, but we thought they would go another direction and would not fall in our path but just has we got on the top of this heigh hill they gathered right over our heads and began to power down their rains upon us in torrents a perfect delluge of Water a regular African thunder

---

1. Laborer George Hayward, age 21, and his wife, May, age 17, arrived in the Eastern Cape via Algoa Bay aboard the ship *Weymouth* on May 15, 1820, as members of the Menezes's Party. Nash, *The Settler Handbook*, 91.

2. Bontebok are medium-sized antelope found in South Africa, Lesotho, and Namibia. Bontebok antelope also live in the Bontebok reserve near Swellendam. Rosenthal, *Encyclopedia of Southern Africa*, s.v. "Bontebok," 69.

3. The Bontebok flats contain well-watered grassland conducive for grazing livestock. General Sir Arthur Augustus Thurlow Cunynghame, G. C. B., *My Command in South Africa 1874–1878*, 58.

CHAPTER 25

Storm, so that we had to lead our Horses for it was not safe to ride them But fortunitly for me I had a good Waterproof coat with me which kept me dry but my two companyons were just as wet as if they had been plunged in the

[Page 416]

river, But when we arrived at the foot of the hill we came to an accommodation house where we stayed for the night and got dryed and was made comfortable.

So the next morning we started riding through a part of the Kat river settlement, to where a Mr. John Green lived who was an Elder in the Mormon Church so we three stayed a day with him, and the next morning, Mr Talbot, and myself started for the Winterburg to my Brother George's and Mr Hayward started on his way to Grahams town [Grahamstown] on his own buisness, and that was the last time I ever saw him.

Well we arrived at my Brother's house all safe and there I found a Mr Joseph Ralph who had come from the distrect

[Page 417]

of Queenstown to attend the Confirance, He being the presiding Elder,

When we were all gathered togather there was five Elders of us namely Joseph Ralph, and John Green, George Wiggill, Henry Talbot, and myself,

We held a two days meeting and settled up all the buisness that was to be done and had a very good time for the Spirit of the Lord was with us.

Well after the Conferance was over we stayed a day with my Brother, and then we four left for our homes, but on our way we stopted at the house of Mr John Green and while there we Baptized a young girl who was living in the family a Daughter of Mr George Prince and the next day we Mr Henry Talbot and myself started on

[Page 418]

our homeward journey and over the same Mountainous road again to the Thorn river farm, Mr Talbots home.

I stayed with him one night and has an old friend of mine was living on the joining farm to Mr Talbot's I went to his house and stayed with him one night, has I had known this man for over twenty years and of late him and me had talked about mormonism several times so I thought I would see him again. And when I got there I found him and his Daughter Mary Jane at home, his Wife was not at home, so after Supper he asked me to tell him a little about Mormonism, But before I commenced I asked him to bring me a bible. He told me that he did not know wheather there was one in the house, for

[Page 419]

he had lately been burnt out, so I told him to never mind that I could do without one But it was for his sattisfaction that I wanted it, so I explained the doctrin of Mormonism to him from memory, and I spoke and reasoned with him for about an hour I dont think that I ever had such a flow of Language, and the passages of Scripture came to my mind with such force, He asked me very few questions but just sat and listened to me.

This same William Morris and myself had been local Preachers in the Wesleyan Church togather for years and we were very peticular friends, and in the last two Kaffir Wars him and myself had been hemed up in a Military Post for over one year, That night he told there was a great

[Page 420]

talk in Queenstown about me and that I was liable to be taken up for takeing Mr Wall, a sick man out of bed and Baptizing him and he seemed to put great stress upon his words has he spoke about it, and I told him that what I did it was done at the request of himself and his family so the next morning I saddled up my Horse and bid him good by and started for my home in the Bongolo which I reached after a ride of about fifty miles, safe and in good health,

After geting home I went to my work and finished some Wagons that I had on hand and also attending to the Harvisting my Crops, after my Wheat was cut and shocked, Myself and Wife had to go to Queenstown on buisness

[Page 421]

and could not get home that night on account of a tremendious Thunder Storm which detained us. it was so fearfull that it caused the river to flood and brought down drift wood and sheaves of Wheat to a great amount.

So the next morning we started for home and I found when I got home that the bulk of the water had fell on my own farm the upper part of the farm from the bursting of a Cloud, which swept right through my Wheate field and took my Wheate down the river which I seen when I was in QueensTown but did not think that it was mine untill I arrived at home and found it to be so, It tore up Trees which I suppose was hundred years old

[Page 422]

and it moved stones from their resting places of a ton whight, My Son Jeremiah was at home with the Children and was dreadfully frightend. He told me that the Water came down the glen back of the House like a Tidal Wave, and when opposit the house it spread to the wedth of, I should suppose some six or eight hundred yards wide which was a broad flowing stream. But by the time we got home it had run off and left my farm in a fearfull condicion, it washed the soil away as deep as a Plow would go so I never plowed it afterwards,

It began to be well known to me after joining the Church of Jesus Christ of Latter day Saints that I could not stay here long

[Page 423]

CHAPTER 25

that I must pull up stakes and begin to get ready for the place of gathring,

And has Mr Talbot had sold his farm at the Thorn river, and that the Flood had made such Havoc with mine I began to think that it was time I was selling mine, so I soon found a customer to buy mine who was a Dutch man whos name was Covaus Boato,[4] I sold my farm for one thousand and twenty Pounds, at Bills payable at so many months after dated holding the house for so many months untill I was ready to leave, and in the mean time the Dutchman lived in a small house that was on the farm untill I moved away.

I have mentioned already that Mr Talbot as sold his

[Page 424]

Farm and went to reside in the district of Queenstown to arraing his buisness affars, And while he were there we regulated the meetings, somtimes he would come up to the Bongolo and Preach, and at other times I would go down to Queens Town [Queenstown] and Preach to the people at his House.

At one time when I was preaching in Queenstown the Rev Mr R. Giddy. came in to hear and to ask questions, but he did not ask many questions but sat still and listened, to what I had to say.

I refered him to a great many passages of Scripture which he knew was there and I asked him if he did not beleive them. I told him that I knew he believed what I had said, and some of those who had come in to hear, said that they thought

[Page 425]

he beleive, I think I reasoned and talked for about an hour, and at the conclusion Mr Giddy asked me for some books and Tracks that I had so I gave him all that I could spare,

Mr Giddy was the residant minister in the village of Colesberg, at the time I was talking to him he had come to Queenstown to attend a Wesleyan Conferance Mr Giddy and myself had been old friends and Brothers for a great many years in the Wesleyan Ministery and I always looked on him as a good natured honest man.

About this time Mr Talbot left Queenstown for Algo [Algoa] Bay, or Port Elizabeth and also his Son Henry who at this time was married to a Daughter of Mr R. Wall who has been mentioned. And as I had sold my farm, I also went to Algo [Algoa]

[Page 426]

Bay from Queens town [Queenstown] takeing my family it being the begining of April, but called at my Brother George's on my way and left my Soninlaw there to work, and I proceded on my journey with two Wagons and my Son Jeremiah driving one of them, Passing through Fort Beaufort and

---

4. This may refer to Kobus (Jakobus) Botha.

Grahams Town [Grahamstown] on our way, And when in the naighbourhood of Sundays river our oxen got asstray and went into a dence Bush and was lost for two days so there we had to stay.

Well after a good deal of hunting we managed to find them all, which was twenty four in number, and caled two Span in Africa, so we arrived in Port Elizabeth in May 14th 1860 where I was appointed Conferance president of the Church and Mr Talbot President of the Branch of the Church [5]

[Page 428]

of Jesus Christ of Latter day Saints.

Well after I got settled in this place I took charge of the Branch which consisted of about from thirty to forty members more or less, so we held meeting in Mr Talbot's House, twice on Sunday and once through the week, and by paying strict attention to our duty by acting has Teacher and visiting the sick, and also attending to my daley labour it kept me well employed,

After holding our meeting in Mr Talbot's house for a while we hired a place on purpose and fitted it up very comfortable, and then we got the people more united than they had been for some time I must say that before I came to this place there had been a Mr John

[Page 428 (repeated page number)]

Stock presiding, And while presiding himself and some others baught a smal vessel a Brig caled the Unity,

This Brig was baught with a vew of bringing the Saints from Africa to America, This vessel took the first Saints who started for the place of gathering and had to go by the way of England, and arrived there all safe And while in England they hired a man as Captain who belonged to the Church by the name of Rich, whom we used to call Captain Rich, and he also brought his Wife and two Children with him back to Port Elizabeth, And when after coming back this vessel was put to work as a coaster from Cape Town to Natal and other places, And on one of those occasions she took in her

[Page 429]

---

5. The month before on April 5, 1860, seventy Saints disembarked from Port Elizabeth on the barque *Alacrity*, which reduced the number of members in the Port Elizabeth Branch and in the conference region. In April 4, 1860, an issue of the *Cape and Natal News* noted that in the Eastern Province, "some sixty or seventy Mormons, it is reported, are about to leave this town in the barque *Alacrity*, for Boston, en route to 'Salt Lake,' Utah. On her last voyage to Boston, the *Alacrity* took a large number of the believers in the 'doctrines' of Brigham Young from this port, also for the Salt Lake." To view the *Alacrity* passenger list, see Fred E. Woods, *Saints by Sea*, Port Elizabeth to Boston, April 5, 1860, to June 18, 1860.

CHAPTER 25

Cargo at Table Bay for Algo [Algoa] Bay, and as she was never heard of afterwards it was supposed that she was foundered at Sea, and all that was ever seen of her afterwards was a few fragments that was found washed asshore with marks on them that was recognozed as belonged to the Brig Unity, And it was also supposed that all on board were lost for they were never heard of afterwards,

I mention this sircumstance to show that part of the disturbance that existed when I came to preside at the Bay, Captain Rich was still Captain of the Brig when she was lost and on monthly pay and has his Wife and her two Children was living in the Bay she natterely

looked for her Husband's wages besides privet money which her husband had used in fitting up the Brig for her return voige from England, and has this John Stock was the one of princeable owners she made appleycations to him several times for a Settlement but without any sattisfaction which caused a bitter feeling in her mind against John Stock,

And has John Stock was a great buisness man in Algo [Algoa] Bay, for one thing he carried on a large Tannery, and as a partner a Mr Slaughter who belonged to the Church, so the time came that John Stock left Africa for America and leaving the Widow; Slaughter and others in dept to them and nothing settled up sattisfactery which caused the trouble among the member of the Church.

But after Mr Talbot and myself arrived at the Bay and took charge of the Branch we soon got a good feeling amongest the people by talking and giving good councel and we also administered the Sacrament, and by so doing we got the people all feeling pritty well except the Widow of the Captain, This Mr Stock, it must be understood was not a bad man, not by no means, for he had kept the Branch togather for a long time and was very good to the poor and in fact to everybody untill just before he left the Bay, He seemed to get carless and left (as the saying is) he let things go at lose ends, In fact the Branch had grown up under his care from the time it was organized by L. [Leonard] I. Smith and J. [Jesse] Haven up to the time of his leaving and me takeing charges,

About this time George Ellis my Soninlaw and his family left the Winterberg and came down to the Bay to join me and my family before leaving for Utah.

Some months before this he had a very singular Dream while residing in Bongolo Queens town [Queenstown] district and after he had become a member of the Church of the Latter day Saints, He dreamed that some one had a sum of money for him to pay his Emigration to Utah, he did not see the money but he was told it was for that purpose and a truere dream could not possiabley have come to pass than it turned out to be, Well, it was me who had the money, and I furnished him and his family with everything they needed from Africa to Utah

[Page 433]

But while we were yet staying in Algo [Algoa] Bay he got a pritty good job of work at his trade,

After I had resided some time in the Bay, it was on the ninth of August 1860 that I sent my first letter to the Liverpool Office, to Mr N. V. [Nathaniel Vary] Jones giving an account of the state of the Branch in Port Elizabeth and other Branches of the Church of Jesus Christ of Latter day Saints in the Eastren Provinces,

And about this time Mr Talbot's Son Thomas sold his Wagons and Oxen in the Bongolo and came to the Bay to meet his Father who was geting ready to megrate, and he brought me the money for my farm which as already being mentioned ~~unfortaun~~ unfortunately the money was all Queens Town [Queenstown] Banknotes and of

[Page 434]

no use to me to pay my Passage to America neither could I get them discounted in the Bay without a great sacrifice has I would have to get gold for them Thomas Talbot also brought word to me that my Son Jeremiah did not intend to come down to go with me to America, at this time but said that he would come at another time which made his mother feel very bad has she was then leaveing her eldest Son and her second Daughter So my Wife proposed to go to Queenstown to get the money changed so I baught a Horse and Mr Talbot had a light Cart so Thomas Talbot (I had one horse at the time when I bought the other one) offered his service to go with my Wife. And after they got started a few days on their

[Page 435]

Journery the Horse that I baught did not prove to be a good one for he soon gave out and cause quite a bit of trouble on the road, I would have gone on that buisness myself but I had some work on hand that I wanted to finish before I left the Bay,

My Wife went to the Bank and got the money changed into gold but she had quite a time about it for the folks at the Bank hated to give the gold out to be taken to Salt Lake but they could not help themselves for it was their own Bills they were changing, And while my Wife was on this buisness she was close in the neighbourhood of her Father Brother and Sisters, so she thought she would like to see them all again and went to them

[Page 436]

CHAPTER 25   157

her father at that time was about 80 years old she spent a few days with them, and persuaded my Son Jeremiah to come back with her to the Bay to say goodby again,

My Wife also brought a little girl back with her one whom she had promised to take care of, She being a relation of my Wife's.

My Wife told me after she came back that it was not particulary the changeing of the money that she was so ancious to go for but it was to try to get her Son to come and go to Utah with her which she did by a little persuading; And while she absent I engaged our passages and also payed a part of the passage money, It was an American vessel which belonged to Boston whos name was the Race Horse,[6] Captain John Searles,

[Page 437]

so when my Son Jeremiah came to the Bay by the persuasion of myself his mother and others friends he made up his mind to go with us, but the difficulty was then, he had left his property unsold in the Bongolo which consisted of two Wagons and from thirty to forty Oxen which he had left in charge of his Brother John, It happened that my Brother, his Uncle Aaron was in the Bay and he knowing the Cattle well so he baught them but he could not pay for them then but gave him a note of hand payable in eight months, And turned over his Wagons to his Uncle Francis Bentley and his Brother John to sell them and to pay what few depts he was owing, He sold the Cattle to his Uncle for

[Page 438]

about one hundred and fifty Pounds as near as I can remember, had his uncle been in Grahams Town [Grahamstown] he could have got the money for the Cattle and given it to him but being a stranger in the Bay he could not get it,

I proposed to my Son to get the Bill discounted in the Bay in preferance to leaveing it with an agent. But he thought that he would lose too much by doing so, so I sent him the money for his passage to America, There was a man in the Bay by the name of William Swift whom we were well acquainted with and my Son had great confidance in, and he left him to colect the money and to send it to America after him, But my advice was to him that if it was me I would rather get the

[Page 439]

half of it than to lose the hole perhaps, not at that time I did not think that Mr Swift would do anything wrong to my Son in regard to the money, But I thought that my Son would need some money after arriveing in America,

---

6. The *Race Horse* was an American cargo vessel that sailed out of Boston. This explains why there were only thirty-seven passengers on board, consisting primarily of the Wiggill and Talbot families. Woods, *Saints by Sea*, Port Elizabeth to Boston, February 20, 1861, to April 19, 1861.

The Bill became due and my Brother hated to put it into the hands of this colector for he had no confidance in him For he had heard of some of his doings and did not like him so my Brother held the money some time after it was due, thinking my Son might make some other arraingment has he had heard that John Talbot was coming from Utah to Africa on a mission and that my Son might give him the power to colect it, but receiving no word from him, and the bill over due, Swift threatened to sew my Brother

[Page 440]

for it, so he had to pay him and that was the last of it for my Son never got one farthing and I must say that if ever a man wanted a little money after he got to Utah he did.

Well after staying in Algo [Algoa] Bay from ten to eleven months and attending to all the Church dutys that was involving upon me, and also doing all the work that I could get to do at my trade, and I must say that I never felt more comfortable and happy than I did while I stayed there. It was a beautiffull place just where I lived it was close to the Harbor and I could overlook the Sea for miles and with my Spyglass I could see the Ships going out and coming in on one Sunday there was a Southeast wind which had being blowing for two

[Page 441]

days and when it blows in this way it lashes the Sea to fuery and causes the waves to roll mountain high, and in this gale there was an American Whaler belonging to Nantucket which was riding at low ancher, and had come there to discharge her chargo of oil to another American Ship, I suppose her cables was not very strong or at any rate they were not profe against that gale for they both brok and let her lose and she tryed to get out to Sea but failed so the Captain put her before the wind to run her ashore she just picthed and rolled about like a cockelshel and finely she embeded herself in the sand and became a perfect rack.

And afterward they dove down and fished up her

[Page 442]

Anchers, The name of this Ship was the Hero and the Captain's name Hussey.

And while I was staying in the Bay I had the pleasur of seeing one of the members of the Royel family, Prince Alfred who was then serving before the Mast on board her Magisty Ship Urilass [*Euryalus*][7] which made a great time in the Bay there were several Triumphal Arches for him to pass under, and from the Ship for a half mile the Jettay was carpeted for him to walk on from the Landing to the Carrage which took him to his

---

7. Urilass is a misspelling of *Euryalus*. Theodore Martin, *The Life of His Royal Highness the Prince Consort*, 5:195.

quarters, The Bay was also beautifully Eluminated on the occasion, and he stayed in the Bay about one week looking around and accompanyed by the Governor Sir George Grey, Then He and his Flete left the Bay

[Page 443]

and went through Grahams Town [Grahamstown], Fort Beaufort, Queens Town [Queenstown], and the Free States, to Port Natal and hunting by the way, And while the Prince was away on this visit his Ship lay at ancher in the Bay and visiters were aloude to go on board so I availed myself of the oppertunity so myself and Wife and a part of my family went on board to look at the vessel has I had never seen such an one, It was perfectly grand the Princes Cabbin was like a splendid Parlor, and the Band was playing and a great many was danceing, The Engineer was very accomodating and showed us all the Machinery which was very interesting to me, so after the Ship staying about a fortnight at Algo [Algoa] Bay she steamed

[Page 444]

away to Port Natal to receive the Prince on board the Princes visit to the Cape of good hope was in the month of July 1860.

Well having payed the ballance of my passage money and settled up all my buisness affairs, and still expecting two Elders from Utah to come and take charge of the Conferance when I left But before I started on my journey I heard that they was detained in England for the want of meains to carry them to Africa, so I could wait no longer for them so I left the Church in the hands of Elder E. Slaughter, which was the best I could do. But after I left those Elders soon came along first was Henry Dickson. [Dixon] Elder Zederland. [Zyderlaan] W. Fogingom. [Fotheringham] John Talbot. M. Atwood. and John Stock.[8]

[Page 445]

---

8. A March 15, 1862, issue of the *Cape and Natal News* noted "MORMON PREACHERS AT THE CAPE.—Four preachers had arrived from Utah, with a view of promulgating Mormon doctrines, and winning over converts to the Mormon faith. Two of them were natives of Graham's Town, who had been dwellers in Utah, and who had returned to convert the colonial-born. Their names were John TALBOT and Henry DICKSON. A Hollander named Martin ZYDERLAAN, also from the Lake, was to preach in Dutch, and convert the Dutch population. William FOTHERINGAM, a Scotchman born, but now, like the other three, a Mormon preacher and a citizen of the United States, and direct from Utah, was the leader."

Chapter 26

On the twentyeth day of Feb 1861 we bid farwell to the Branch of the Church where I had presided over for about eleven months and also to Algo [Algoa] Bay. And went on board the Bark Race Horse, commanded by Captain John Searles.[1] First myself Wife & five Children two Sons and three Daughters, My Soninlaw George Elles Wife and three Children, Mr Henry Talbot Wife and family. Mr Henry Talbot & Wife and one Child making in all thirty two souls.

It got to be quite late in the afternoon when we weighed ancher, so after we got out to Sea a little distance the wind arose and caused the sea to be quite rough, and has I had not been on the Sea for at least forty years

[Page 446]

and then I was quite a boy, I became very sick and giddy so that I could not help myself and was glad to lie down in the first place that I could find, and all the Company became so sick that night that one could not help another or look after the Children, But as luck would have it we had a very good and kind Steward who took charge of the little Children unroled the beds and arranged them and put them to bed, and for several days we were all so sick but some of the young men was the first to get over their sickness and they would help others. But for myself I was sick more or less all the voige [voyage] I could not bare the smell of the cooking and had no appitite to eat anything. The Captain had ten Sheep brought on

[Page 447]

board to kill on the voige and of corse brought a good supply of furage or Oat hay to feed them with and to sit and pick the grains from the Oats and eat them was the only thing that I rellished and tasted good to me and also now and then I could eat a few sour dryed apples, I think when people are going on a sea voige even as first class passingers, they aught to lay in a supply of little dellicacys for their own use independant of Cabbin fare, For when I was so sick I often wished that I had done so which I could have done as well as not for I had plenty to do with. I have already mentioned that thes young men soon got over been sick, Well one of them whos name was Thomas Talbot made

[Page 448]

---

1. Henry James Talbot recalled, "We had [been] waiting a year at Port Elizabeth for accomodations on a sailing vessel. But finally set sail February 28 [20], 1861 on a small sail ship called the <u>Race Horse</u>. The Captain of the ship was John Sirles [Searles] of Cambridge, Massachusetts. He was [a] fine little man." Talbot, "Short Sketch of the Life of Henry James Talbot," 12.

CHAPTER 26

himself very usefull, for he would get around amongest the young women and help them to go upon deck to get the frish are, and our Captain been a very clever and sociable man he gave him the title of Doc Talbot, and also a young man by the name of Robert Wall was very attentive to the girls which were six in number, and they also paid great attention to the married Women of which there were four,

Mr. Talbot sen brought along with him a little Kafir Boy who was between six and seven years old he was one of those starved and abandoned Children that as already been mentioned in this History. Mr Talbot got him at that time and kept him and the little fellow became so

[Page 449]

attacthed to his family and himself so that when Mr Talbot was leaveing Africa he would come along and his name was Gobo,[2] and the Captain gave him

---

2. The Henry Talbot family had cared for the Xhosa boy Gobo since the 1856–57 great famine resulting from the prophecy of a young Xhosa girl named Nongqawuse that required killing of all the Xhosa cattle. Talbot family history records that during the period of famine caused by "the Cattle Killing Delusion, [there were] starving natives by the thousand[s] . . . At this time a native woman with a babe in her arms, appeared at the Talbot home half-starved, and told them she had abandoned an older child back along the road. They rescued the child, Gobo Fango, and he became one of the family." Talbot, "Henry James Talbot and Descendants." Henry James Talbot wrote, "There was a little negro boy found by father [on] our Wellington farm about 1857 eating gum from a tree for food. He had been separated from his parents during the cattle 'killing delusion' by their chief. Efforts to find the childs parents were not successful, so father had been raising him, calling him by the name Gobo Fango. When father bought passage for his family to go to America, the authorities refused to give passage to Gobo. Just as they were about to sail, father saw the boy standing on the dock with tears streaming down his cheeks, this was more than he could stand. He rushed down the gang plank took the boy into the store room of the ship and rolled him in his bedding. When the Captain discovered him he was angry, but [we] were too far out to sea to turn back, so Gobo got to go to America with the Talbot family." Talbot, "Short Sketch of the Life of Henry James Talbot," 11–12. Fango is possibly a derivation of Fingo, referring to an Indigenous Bantu nation called the Fingo, Mfengu, and even Abambo. Rev. John Ayliff and Rev. Joseph Whiteside, *History of the Abambo Generally Known as Fingos*. For more information on Gobo Fango's life, his smuggling into America, and his tragic murder, see H. Dean Garrett, "The Controversial Death of Gobo Fango," 264–72; Amy Tanner Thiriot, *Slavery in Zion: A Documentary and Genealogical History of Black Lives and Black Servitude in Utah Territory, 1847–1862*, 30, 36, 137, 218–20. Concerning the cause of the famine and its repercussions, see J. B. Peires, *The Dead Will Arise: Nongqawuse and the Great Xhosa Cattle-Killing Movement of 1856–7*; Peires, "The Central Beliefs of the Xhosa Cattle-Killing," 43–63. For a treatment on Xhosa religious beliefs, see Janet Hodgson, *The God of the Xhosa: A Study of the Origins and Development of the Traditional Concepts of the Supreme Being*.

the Office of Sheep feeder while on the voige, some times the Captain would doupt him whether he had fed the sheep, and used to call him gumbo and would call him to him and tell him to let him look at his hand and that would prove whether he had fed them or not, The Captain told him that he could tell by cirtain vains in his hand when he was telling a story. On one occasion the Captain asked him if he had his dinner and the boy said no sir but the Captain had seen him eating with the Sailors and so he the Captain proved it by his hand.

[Page 450]

Well after our company got right well over their seasickness things went on all right and we enjoyed ourselves, especily the young folks The Captain's Son, John Searles Jun, was a very nice young man, his father wanted him to stay at home and go to School but he did not want to do that, but felt a great desire to go to Sea, so his father told me that he was so determined to go to Sea that he thought that he had better take him under his own charge, so he held the Office of second Mate, and made himself very agreable with the young folks of the passingers and our evenings used to be spent in danceing singing and playing music which made the time pass very agreable, and very often the Captain would prevail on the

[Page 451]

girls to sing for him.

In addission to our company we had the Captain and two seamen of the Wrecked Whaleing vessel Hero who was very agreable company.[3] Well on the first of April the Boys wanted a bit of fun, and of them hollowed out a Whale ahead which made Captain Hussey jump and run to see, but there were no whale there and the Boys told him that it was the first of April which created a great laugh among them, But now and then we would in reallity see a Whale and flying fish in abundance as we drew near the Line, and when near the Line it was the hotest weather that I ever felt it was unbareable, and sometimes we would have what is caled a contrary wind or a calm and then the

[Page 452]

Captain would feel discouraged and say that we were going streight to England, But when the Ship would be rushing before a good strong wind then he would feel all right. The Race Horse was a Clipper built vessel and

---

3. Henry James Talbot recorded, "We also had the Captain of the ship Hero, that was wrecked in Algoa Bay. The ship was a whaler, it came into port to unload Whale Oil he had on board. We shipped it to America. He had put off three-hundred barralls of the Whale Oil he had on board of the ship when the storm came and wrecked his ship. So he returned home with us to Boston. His name was Husey, from the state of Kentucky. He was quite a good man." Talbot, "Short Sketch of the Life of Henry James Talbot," 12.

CHAPTER 26

was a very quick sailor, On one day we seen the wrecked Brig Benguela of Stockton dismasted full of Water and abandoned in the neighborhood of the Island Bermooda, Well all went well with us untill within about two weeks of arriving at Boston we encountred what I considered a very sevear storm[4] which lasted two days and nights and the waves roled mountains high and broke over the vessel in one mass of fome and all the sails were reefed close, and without any sails we were drove before the wind at the rate

[Page 453]

of ten or twelve nots an hour and the Ship roled and picthed fearfully so that I thought to be sure it would founder and that we would all be lost, The Captain had two smal Cannons on board which he said he carried for orniment, an well in this storm one of them broke lose from its fastings and roled about for some time breaking everything it strock it was just like a battering ram, untill finely it gamed itself fast and the sailors lashed it fast so that it had to stay there untill the storm was over, and the weather was intencely cold while the Storm lasted, This storm has near has I can remember was in the gulf stream known as the gulf of Mexico by sea fareing men Sailors always know when they are in the

[Page 454]

this stream especely the Cooks who dip so much water because it is so much warmer, and also by the abondance of sea weeds that floats on the surface of the Water which comes from the Gulf of Mexico and runs across the ocean to the England coast.

Well after this we got along first rate for the rest of the way and finely the Pilot came on board and brought papers and also the news that the War had broke out in the United States between the North and the South,[5] it did not surprise the Captain much for he was expecting to hear of it The battle of Bullrun had already been fought.[6]

---

4. Henry James Talbot noted, "We were on the ocean fifty-one days during which time a terrible storm came up which nearly capsized the boat. It was on its side for sometime before righting it-self and the people abroad were afraid they were lost, the Captain locked them down in their berths. But the ship came out of it alright. But it was an awful looking sight the next morning. The benches, tables, dishes and nearly everything being dashed about and broken. It was such a terrible storm, and the Captain could not understand why the ship was saved unless it was because it had Mormons aboard." Talbot, "Short Sketch of the Life of Henry James Talbot," 12.

5. The company aboard the *Race Horse* arrived at Boston on April 19, 1861, their voyage lasting about two months. The Civil War had begun one week before they landed, when Confederate forces in South Carolina attacked Fort Sumter.

6. Eli, who wrote his account decades after his embarkation, was mistaken on the date, since the first Battle of Bull Run at Manassas Junction, Virginia, occurred several months later on July 21, 1861.

At this instance the Pilot took charge of the vessel as it is their custom and run her into Boston harbor which was in the night and about four Oclock in

[Page 455]

six miles outside of Boston Light, the Race Horse lost her bowsprit the head of her foremast, and all above by contact with schoner Fenmore which sustained but little damage, so we had to remain there untill a steam Tug came and towed us in and also another vessel at the same time a Bark as large as the Race Horse the Captain said that, that was the second time the same accident had happened to him and the same vessel in Boston Harbor after the Pilot took charge.

Well we arrived in the Dock about the twentyeth of April 1861, and the Captain was very kind and allowed us to remain on board untill we could find quarters, so we stayed on board about one week and still eat of the ships

[Page 456]

provisions there was a very fine Pig killed on board a few days before coming into Harbor, and it was just about this time that my appetite had come to me and that Pork tasted better than anything that I had eat all the voige.

Well after arriving all right in Boston, we looked around and found a Branch of the Church in East Boston, and the members hearing of our arrival the Presidant and some of the members came on board to see us and make our acquaintance, And also a great many strangers hearing that we had come from Africa thought to besure we were black for they thought it imposable that white people could come from Africa, so when they seen us and talked to us they said why these people are like ourselves and we said why not we

[Page 457]

came from England just the same as many of you have done, Then the Preasident of the Branch Telegraphed to New York to Elder N. V. Jones to know what to do about us, so Elder Jones Telegraphed back word that we must stay in Boston and make ourselves as comfortable as we could untill an Emigrant ship arrived, which was expected from England, so I hired a large house which answered for the several familys in East Boston, But as there were no fireplaces in the house we had to buy Stoves to do our cooking by, But there was plenty of good water in every room in the house and as provisions were very plentyful and cheape we lived and made ourselves contented for a month with in a few days, and as the

[Page 458]

wheather was very fine we went around a great deal and seen a great many things that was new to us, such as railroads Machines Shops and Dock yard and bars on the rails all such things we had not seen for there were no such things in Africa But I had read a great deal about all those things but had not seen them untill I came to Boston, We also visited Bunker Hill, When I said there was no railroads in Africa it was a mistake in me for there were a railroad in Cape Town and also in Natal, but I had never seen them for they were several hundreds of miles from where I lived. So while we were there it was all comotion with the Bands of Music Fife and drum and recruting parties and Flags flying in every direction

[Page 459]

it being the comencement of the War of 1861 between the North and the South,[7]

Well after staying in Boston nearly a month we received word that we must go to New York has the Ship had arrived that was expected, so we packed up all our goods and chattles and took the Cars and bid good by to Boston and all our friends that we made while staying there, so when we arrived in New York the company we waited in Boston for had started on their journey to Florance [Florence, Nebraska] so we had to take a house in Jersey City and wait the arrival of another Ship which kept us about one week longer,[8] There was a family in the house we engaged who was very kind has all our cooking utentials were all packed up they let us

[Page 460]

do our cooking on their stove so we got along very well and there we had a chance for a few days to look around New York and there we got our English money changed into American money, Through the assistance of N. V. Jones, Well at the end of a week we took Cars again for the great outfitting place Florance as it was then caled takeing the rought through Hannable [Hannibal] and Chicago, while waiting at Chicago for a change of Cars and as the War had commenced about Slavory and Mr Talbot having the little Kafir Boy who has been already mentioned, some Collard men happened to spy the little fellow in the Car made an attemped and was determined to take him away they accuseing us of takeing him away into Slavoury and they thought to liberate

[Page 461]

---

7. The American Civil War era was a tumultuous time for immigrating Latter-day Saints who crossed the Atlantic and disembarked on the East Coast. Fred E. Woods, "East to West through North and South: Mormon Immigration during the Civil War," 7–29.

8. Talbot recalled, "We landed in East Boston April 20, 1861, and had to rent houses and stay there for three weeks before enough emigrants were ready to make up a company. We were sent to New Jersey where we had to stay another three weeks and rent houses making the trip very expensive." Talbot, "Short Sketch of the Life of Henry James Talbot," 12.

him and caused great disturbance but they did not get him for a Lady of the Company hid him under her Crinoline and they surched through the Cars but could not find him, so after that he was kept concealed as much as posable and put girls Cloaths on him,[9] Well after leaveing Chicago we got along all right untill we arrived at St. Joes which I beleive was the Terminus at that time.

Well after staying at St. Joes a few hours we went on board the Steam Boat Omaha, and steamed up the Missouri river to Florance [Florence], But I must say one or two words about the mate we had on board He was a greate passy fussy fellow. And the greatest swearer that I ever heard especely when we

[Page 462]

stopt at the differant Landings to take in fuel or goods, I could not help thinking when I was on board of that Boat that I was just has near <u>Hell</u> has I wanted to be, and I made the remarke at the time to a friend of mine, Their were from eight to nine hundred souls on board, and we were huddled together so close which made us very uncomfortable, But I took Cabben passage for my Wife for I could not stand to see her in such confusion for she was not very well at the time for she was getting very tired of her journey, and I took charge of my three Daughters near to the Boiler,

We were between two and three days on the river we were on sandbars

[Page 463]

two or three times which detained us longer, I was much pleased with the scenery along the banks of the river, and when we Landed at Florance I beleive it must have rained for we could not find a dry spot to put our Luggage down it was almost like puting our boxes down in the river every place was so wet, and after we had got all landed our girls were invited on board the Boat again but was not told that the Boat would start away soon, well they had not been on board long when the signal was given to start which made the girls have to run as it where for life to get on shore again.

[Page 464]

---

9. Gobo lived twenty-five years after arriving in Utah Territory, herding sheep in Utah and Idaho. He was killed at age 32 on February 10, 1886, by cattleman Frank Bedke during a range war. Although a murder trial was held, no conviction resulted, likely due to Gobo's ethnicity. While there is no record of him being baptized into The Church of Jesus Christ of Latter-day Saints, his will stipulated that after designating money for his friends, the remainder of his assets were to be given "to help build the temple in Salt Lake City Utah." His will is located at the Cassia County Records Office in Burley, Idaho. An entry from the journal of Helen Louisa Hunter indicates a proxy baptism was performed in the Salt Lake Temple for Gobo on September 20, 1930. The editors thank Suzanne Hannah for providing a copy of this record. Garrett, "The Controversial Death of Gobo Fango," 264–72; Thiriot, *Slavery in Zion*, 137, 218–20.

Chapter 27

Well after landing at Florance we hired Wagons to take our luggage up into the settlement, And just at or about this time a great many of the houses had been taken down and moved away to Omaha to build up that place, so we had to take our luggage into a very large Barn, and we all stayed there which made it very unpleasent to be so croweded, well I only stayed there about two nights then I looked around and found a small house and moved my family to it which made my family more comfortable while we stayed there, I think we, I mean the Company, had to stay at this place about three weeks waiting for our Wagons to be fitted

[Page 465]

up for us, And while this was all being done myself and Mr Talbot went to the stores at differant times and baught a great many things such as provissions for the Plains besides a great many usefull articals for the journey, and tools of differant kinds I liked Florance very much to my fancy it is a pritty park like undulateing Country well wooded and plenty of Water and an abundance of grass, and I beleive it to be a very good agricultural country But some of the people told me that it was a very cold place in the Winter.

And while I stayed at Florance two of my Children were married my Son Jeremiah married one of Mr Talbots Daughters, and my Daughter Margaret

[Page 466]

was married to Mr Talbots Son Thomas the one that Captain Surles gave the title of Doc Talbot,[1] Well when got my new Wagon into my hands which I payed 80 Dollars for I fitted it with side boxes and covered it with two covers and a Carpet and made it very comfortable for the long journey that was before me of a thousand miles, I had six Oxen two Cows and one Calf which I baught at Florance, so when we were all ready we were organized into a Company of about fifty Wagons and Homer Donkin [Duncan] was chosen to be our Captain[2] who was just returning home from of a mission from

---

1. Henry James Talbot recalled, "At florence, Nebraska we got out outfit together for crossing the plains and we bought some of our provisions for the trip. We traveled in the Homer Duncan Co. My brother Thomas B Talbot was married to Margaret Wiggill . . . and my sister Precilla married Jeremiah Francis Wiggill as soon as they arrived in Salt Lake City September 28, 1861." Talbot, "Short Sketch of the Life of Henry James Talbot," 12.

2. The Duncan company consisted of 264 individuals in forty-seven wagons. They departed on June 25, arriving in Salt Lake City on September 13, 1861. "Homer Duncan Company (1861)," Church History Biographical Database.

England on account of poor health, eight of those Wagons belonged to my company who came from

[Page 467]

Africa, Well after we were organized the Train left Florance and went about one mile, and Camped, and I beleive we stayed there two days, so I went into a small Bush, or Forest, and has I had been so used to going into the Forest when in Africa I thought that as it was so near the Camp that I would amuse myself by rambling about awhile but I found it to be very much like the African Forest, so tangled with underbrush that it was almost imposable to get through it, However I cut a small Hickory stick to take along with me in case of any breakeage,

And while Camping there Mr Henry Talbot Sen, was chosen Chaplen by the Captain, And about the last of June 1861 we left that Camp and made a

[Page 468]

grand starte to cross the Plains, and for many days we traveled over a beautiful rolling Country where there was plenty of good grass and water but very little wood, and it contunied so for miles and miles, untill we came to wood river center, which to my mind is a very beautifull Country well wooded and watered and the creeks seems to come from so many directions, we could trace them by the growth of the splendid ash timber which lines their banks, and between those Streams was nice level farms and the grass I am sure was two feet high then waveing beautifull, and here at this Station caled wood river Center, and in the Company there was a man whos name was Charles Dean who

[Page 469]

had baught an old Wagon to start on such a journey and at this place one of the wheels gave out, and the Captain knowing that I was a Wheelwright by trade, He asked me to repair the Wheel, I told him there was a Wagon Shop here at the Station to get it mended there but he made me no reply but commenced to work at it himself, so when I seen Captain Donkin [Duncan] at work I took it in hand and repaired the Wheel and put the Tire on, or has they say in America setting the Tire, Well we moved on from this Camp and when we Camped the next night myself with two or three others was caled on to go out to gard the Cattle which was to me a very disagreable

[Page 470]

job for the night was very dark so that we could not see the cattle when they moved a little distance off, and the grass was up to our knees and has wet as it could be with the Dew.

Well we contunued on our journey through a Country undulated rolling and in many places well wooded. We also passed several very nice farm houses, which I beleive were mostly tradeing stations who kept quite a veriety

CHAPTER 27

of goods and Buffalo robes one of which I baught and found it very usefull and warm, So we journeyed on untill we came to Loopfork Ferry passing a village caled Columbia, and at this ferry there was a middling sized Boat and every Wagon being fifty in number had to be taken over one at a time

[Page 471]

which took very near all the day, and after Landing the Dean Wagon had to undergo more repairs, so I went to work at it, It was a beautifull place on the Bank of this river adorned with cotton wood and some other kinds of trees so it was very shady where we Camped and pleasent to work,

And I think it was some where in this vecinity that we meet a train of Wagons from Utah going down to Florence for Emegrants and goods, In company with those wagons were two missionerys on their way to South Africa,

One of those men was the son of Mr Henry Talbot, Sen, who had Emegrated out to Utah about one year before whos name was John Talbot, and the

[Page 472]

other was William Fothengom [Fotheringham], John Talbot stayed and Camped with his father and mother one night, while the other man Camped with the other Train,

So that night John gave his father and mother a detailed account of the manners and customs of Utah, so next morning John bid goodby to his folks again, and he started East and our Company to the West, And as the Wagons kept breaking every day or two it kept me pritty buissy mending, so the Captain thought that I ought to be exempt from the Cattle guard been has I had so much work to do at the Wagons which sutted me much better,

So we contunied on our journey day after day untill we came to the

[Page 473]

Platte river where we contunied off and on its banks for two or three weeks, the road been very level and smoth and in some places not a stone to be seen, and in others not any wood, and it was then we had to gather what is caled in Utah Buffalo Chips, But what we call in Africa, Cowdung, to burn And but very little game except Hares, But on one occation one of the Boys killed an Antilope which was devided in the Camp for frish meat, This river abounded all along its banks with wild grapes and Curents, We Campted one night on this river in a place caled Ashhollow and there we were visited by quite a number of Indians who came beging so the Captain came around

[Page 475]

the Camp and colected a little from differant ones and gave it to them and they went away very civel, This Camp was very scarce of fuel.

Then after traviling for some days we came to some dreadfull heavy Sandridges where we could not get along at all without doubleing ~~and~~ and helping each other along Those ridges contunued up and down for at least ten miles, It took us all one day to go that distance, and when we left the Platte river in the morning we made a perfect Horseshoe shape to get to the river in the evening to Camp

And all along this sandy road there lay such lots of broken Wagons and one stove and so many lose Tires that the Boys just rolled them down into river for pass times a person could gather

[Page 476]

Wagon loads of real good materials of differant kinds on those Plains at the time we past in 1861,

Well we traveled on and on, till we came to what is caled Chimney Rock, a place of note that has been mentioned in History but in reality it is not rock, none of those romantic looking mounds although they are called rock and looks like rock at a distance, But I have been close up and examined for myself and found them to consist of hard muraly clay which to my mind and understanding of things generly I think that most of the Plains has been the bed of the Sea, And by some mighty convultions of the earth the Water as been run off with great force which has caused those mounds to stand

[Page 477]

in some places, and those great and heavy Sandridges to be gathered in others by the washing of the current of Water from the higher Country, There are very great mountains which can be seen at a distance, with which appeares to be dotted here and there with Pine Timber, and passing on the next place of note that we came to is a place caled the Divels gate, And the great Independence Rock which is of hard ironstone granet and many a traveler pasing that way left their name up on its sides, well we passed this rock a little distance and crossed the river caled the sweetwater (which is a beautifull stream) and then Camped, and here I had to mend a broken axle.

And right in this

[Page 478]

naighbourhood is the Diviles gate, that has been so much talked about, Well it is a very narrow glen whos sides rises up some hundreds of feet perpendicular, and in between the two rocks the beautifull sweetwater river runs, and there is some trees and shrubery grows along the margen of the stream, I did not go through the gate myself but some of my children did, and meet the Wagons on the opposite side of the glen.

After Camping at this place one night we travled on and on untill we came to a very beautifull river caled green river which we crossed, or forded, and at

CHAPTER 27

a rough guess is about two hundreds yards wide, and it is a very rapped stream and the water ~~is as green~~ as very green apperance and its banks is beautifully

[Page 479]

wooded with Cottonwood and Birch. Well after getting across this stream we drove on about a mile and then Camped in a grove of Cotton wood trees so that we had plenty of fuel and we had some of the biggest camp fires and enjoyed ourselves well, and for better protection for the Cattle that night Captain Donkin [Duncan] had them drove across the river to an Island just oppesiet the Camp, for on the side of the river where we was it was nothing but sand and sagebrush, My Son Jeremiah was out on guard that night with two or three others and they amused themselves by telling storys, One of them told a yarn about the jumping Ranters or Methodist which made great fun for them one of them was an old

[Page 480]

woman who had a wooden leg and she unscrued it and used it to beat on the flore with and make all the noise she could and hollow glory Hallelujah, and hold him fast meaning to get hold of Jesus, and some of them trying to climb up the walls for the same purpose, so that night the guard enjoyed themselves firstrate.

Well from this place we rolled out and the next Camp we made that I can remember that was of any note was at a place caled Fort Bridger which is a village and was at that time a Military Post, This place took it name from an old mountaineer who used to live there years before there was much, or any travel that way, by the name of Bridger, It is a very pritty place

[Page 481]

and well suplyed with several beautifull streams of water runing through it, and the mountains around seemed to be very well wooded, and the soil in and around the villiage was very nice and loamy, and has far as I could see it had every capability of makeing a very good Town. This place is about one hundred and fifty miles from Salt Lake City.

And from there we traveled for days and seemed to be assending all the time but when we got on the level it was very pleasent and we was surrounded with shrubery and Sagebrush, and then again we traveled on ridges and there were vallies on each side of the road and here we had to go a long distance for good water

[Page 482]

And the next place of note we came to was the Bear river, which is a very beautifull stream just as clear as posable, a person might count every boulder and pebble stone in its bottom, and the banks are well wooded princably with the Cottonwood tree,

And the next place which attracted my attention was going through what is caled Echo Canyon, which is the most romantic scenery that I ever saw, up each side is the most conglomerated mass of rocks and pebbles all cemented togather in the most fantastic shapes imaginable, and some of them on account of their curious shapes has been caled the witches rocks in one place there is three collums of such rocks standing nearly in a row and they

[Page 483]

are caled the three witches,

This Cluff or Canyon has got its name from the wonderfull hollow sound on echo from the crack of a whip or people talking, and through it runs a creek of nice clear water which we had to cross a great many times, and some times the road run close to such fearfull preceptious rocks, and the sides or banks of this creek is lined with willows and other kinds of brush wood and just at the time that we pased through the Hops were ready for picking and some of the people gathered great bundles of them. This Canyon is about twenty miles long from one mouth to the other, or from one end to the other, It leads right to what is caled the Weber

[Page 484]

river which we crossed and here we found the first Mormon settlement along the side of this river which is caled Heniferville. This Weber river is also a very beautifull stream and well supplyed with plenty of wood on its banks. This settlement is about forty miles from Salt Lake City.

Well after leaveing this Settlement we traveled some five or six miles up in the mountains and Camped that night, and the next morning Mr Talbot and my self left the Camp and started for the City, with his Horses and Wagon but we did not make the City that day, But we camped between the Big and Little Mountains with another company who was ahead of Captain Donkins [Duncan's] Company a day or two, But

[Page 485]

the next day we arrived in the City. And found an old acquaintance from Africa by the name of Charles Roper, who lived in the Seventh Ward, he resided in the Winterberg when he broke up his home to come out to Utah. He was a naighbour to my Brother George. Well we found him very comfortable and he was very glad to see us and invited us to stay at his house untill our Company came into the City who came in the next day and we campted on the Emigration Square in the eighth Ward that night and the next morning Captain Donkin [Duncan] came to me and invited me and my family to come to his house and make ourselves comfortable untill we could look around to see what would be best for us to

[Page 486]

CHAPTER 27

do, so we went and stayed three or four days with him, And in this time Mr William Walker ~~cam~~ who had been out to Africa heard that I had arrived came to see me and spent one day in takeing me around to try to get me a house but we did not succeed, so I finely got a small House in the seventeenth ward.

[Page 487]

Chapter 28

Well after staying at Captain Donkins [Duncan's] place about a week I moved on or about the 14 of September 1861 into the house in the seventeenth ward, and remained there untill after Conferance.

But while Conferance was being held there was a Mr Paul who owned and lived in the fifteenth Ward had a House and half a lot which is a ~~little over~~ half an acre, and as this Mr Paul had friends who had gathered to Salt Lake City some time before this from Africa, and they living some hundred or more miles ~~be~~ South of the City, and was in the City to attend the Conferance, They prevailed on Mr Paul to sell out his home in the City and move to Fillmore so they made up

[Page 488]

their minds to do so, and Mr Paul hearing that I wanted such a place, He found out by some means where I was staying and came to see me about buying it, and has I had just such kind of pay as he wanted which was my new Wagon and two Yoke of Oxen, so we made a bargon right away, which gave him an oppertunity to move right away with his friend, And of corse I took posesion of the House and moved into it, It was quite conveniant with four rooms and there was a nice Apple Orchard in the Lot,

And he had also a good stack of Hay which I got into the Bargon which came in very good to feed my Cow which I had brought across the Plains, so I stayed there

[Page 489]

that winter and worked at my trade and at what ever I could get to do, and then take for my pay, Bacon, Potatoes, flour, and Squash and what ever I could get in the shape of provisions For money was out of the question, for at that time there were none in the Country.

So when the spring opened I filed the Land I had baught with vegetables and Sugercane directly after I had got my garden made my two Soninlaws George Elles and Thomas Talbot went out north of the City about 25 miles to a place caled Kaysville[1] one to live on a Farm he had baught and the other

---

1. Kaysville had a population of three-hundred Latter-day Saint settlers in 1851. Doneta MaGonigle Gatherum, "Kaysville," *Utah History Encyclopedia*, 298. One of the first settlers was William Kay, the first bishop whom the local ecclesiastical ward and town was named after. Settlers either lived in their wagon boxes or in dugouts during the first decade of settlement. A number of British settlers, including Kay and his counselors in the first Kaysville Ward bishopric, had formerly belonged to the United Brethren congregation, a break-off group from the Wesleyan Methodists. By

CHAPTER 28

(Elles) to work at his trade who was a Carpenter, Well after a while I went out to pay them a visit so I stayed a few days to look around. Well I did not like the place very well it seemed

[Page 490]

so scatered and the houses so far apart except the little villige which had lately been settled, so I returned to the City with my mind made up to settle in the City. Well I had not been at home long when my Soninlaw George Elles and others of my Children came to me and gave such glowing accounts of Kaysville, and they knew that I could make a good living there. Well the place I had baught in the City as I said it was in the West end of the City near the Jordon river and was very damp especily in the spring and my Wife complained a good deal and felt that her health was failing. so I made up my mind to go to Kaysvile[2] and let my Son Jeremiah go into my house, which saved him paying rent for a season, and he also had the

---

the end of the 1850s, settlers commenced building adobe homes. This would have been the setting when Eli and Susannah moved into this small farming community to join with other family members in 1861. Carol Ivins Collett, *Kaysville – Our Town: A History*, 9–15.

2. Eli and Susannah's home was west of Salt Lake City near the Jordan River, and their property was quite damp in the spring. Since Susannah's health was failing, they decided to move to Kaysville to be nearer to two of their daughters who lived there with their families. The Wiggills let their son Jeremiah and his family move into their Salt Lake City home. The Wiggills "tryed for three days to rent a house in Kaysville, but did not succeed. In the meantime, there was a place for sale, which they bought for $400.00. It was a small farm of thirty acres . . . and was right in the neighborhood where their children were living. There was a three room house on it, so they took possession of the farm, paying the first payment by giving a wagon one yoke of oxen and some furniture. The rest was to be payed in wheat, at so much a bushel. But they lost their wheat crop that year. However, they managed that winter by great grandfather [Eli] working his trade of wheel right and he also did some carpenter work." Eli and Susannah ran into financial problems because of a poor wheat harvest and had to sell their house in Salt Lake City and trade some items including silver plates, all worth a total of $150.00, to help with their Kaysville property debt. "After living in Kaysville on the farm for about three years, in the spring of 1864 they rented the farm to their son-in-law Thomas Talbot for one year on shares, and they went back to Salt Lake City to live. They intended to go back to the farm the next spring but Susannah didn't want to go, so they rent the farm to their son Jeremiah . . . for the next year and stayed in the city. Eli worked at carpentering for Joseph Woodmance [Woodmansee] who kept a store. . . . They deceded [decided] to stay in the city for good, and the[ir] son Jeremiah now living on the farm, wanted to buy it, so they sold it to him for $400.00. With the money they bought a 1/2 lot (1/2 acre) for $400.00. Their was no house on it. . . . In the they had a house built by Mr. whiting, and they moved in. Eli dug the garden and planted it. . . . In Aug. 1869 Susannah was taken

Wiggill home in Kaysville, Utah. Courtesy Michael T. Lowe.

[Page 491]

good of my garden that I had planted, And has He had a Wagon and Team I engaged him to move me to Kaysville not knowing at the time where I was going to live I tryed for two or three days to hire a House but did not succeed, so in the meane time there was a place offered for sail that I thought I would like so I succeeded in buying it from the Person for 400 Dollars it was a small Farm of thirty acres all fenced with what is caled a Brush fence, and also a Log House on it, with three rooms and situated right in the neighborhood where my Children were living. So before my Son Jeremiah returned to the City, I took possession of the Farm paying the first instalment by giving a Wagon and one

[Page 492]

yoke of Oxen and some furniture, and the rest to be payed in Wheat at so much per Bushell. But I lost the Crop that season, for when I baught it it was all sawed and planted. So I managed the first year to work at my trade which is Wheelwright and also done a good deal of Carpenter work, so the next year I plowed and planted but it was such a dry season and such a scaricity of Water that instead of reaping one hundred bushels I only gathered twenty, and when the time came to pay the ballance on my farm I had no Wheat to settle the dept, so I sold my place in the City, or almost gave it away, for all that for it was an old half worn out wagon and a yoke of oxen. My son Jeremiah took the Wagon and I worked the Oxen a while and then I gave

---

sick and died after one week of illness of dysentary. She died August 29, 1869, age 56 years." Zelda Jane Wall Shipley (great granddaughter), "History of Susannah Bentley Wiggill Pioneer," typescript, 5–7.

CHAPTER 28

[Page 493]

them in part payment on the Farm, and by bowring some wheat of some of my kind neighbors untill the next harvest with some that I got in pay for my work I settled for the farm, which left me entirely without eather Wagon or Team to work the farm with.

Having crippled myself by parting with my Team and very often wanting to go to the City to get things that was not to be got in the Settlement, and then to have to depend on our neighbors to ride in their Wagon become very disagrable both to myself and Wife, so she was determined to have a Team of our own, and there was a man close by who had a Span of Mules and we had a good Stove that he wanted so my Wife let it go with some silver plate and some other things which altogather amoun

[Page 494]

ted to one hundred and fifty Dollars, and when we had got them they were so slow and good for nothing that before it was time to Plow I had to make another change which I did for a good yoke of oxen and got a Plow with them, Then I was built up again for when the spring came I was ready to go to work to Plow and sow, and when harvest came around I had a middling good Crop of wheat and a very good Crop of suger cane, and we had a good Cow which kept us in plenty of Milk and Butter, And with what work I got to do at my trade we lived very comfortable by puting my House in good repair and adding a nother room to it, and the Farm all settled for and then I replaced my Stove again by selling and tradeing mollasses,

[Page 495]

So after living in Kaysville on this farm about three years, which made it the year 1864, I hired my farm to my Soninlaw Thomas Talbot for one year on shares, And I came to the City to work at my Trade which I got plenty to do that Summer but got little or no money but got orders on differant Stores which answered the same purpose,

And when the fall of the year came around I intended going back to my farm, But my Wife did not feel to want to go back to it again, one thing I had parted with my Team and Wagon so if I had gone I had to work and depend on my trade so she thought that we might just as well stay in the City, so I came to that concluseion and rented my farm to my Son Jeremiah for the next year, and I fell into a good job of work for

[Page 495 [repeated number]]

that winter at Carpentering for Joseph Woodmancie [Woodmansee][3] who kept a store, so that I had no trouble in geting my Pay,

---

3. Joseph Woodmansee was a Salt Lake merchant. Polly Aird, "'You Nasty Apostates, Clear Out': Reasons for Disaffection in the Late 1850s," 203.

Then when the spring opened I went to work at the Wagon makeing for the Nailors [Naylors] Brothers[4] at 4 Dollars per day, then I got both money and store orders, Then the following Summer I worked for one Mr White, who had come to Salt Lake City and started a large buisness in the Wagon makeing and Blacksmithing, and at this place I got nearly all money for my pay at 4 Dollars per day.

About this time it was 1866 that I concluded to stay in the City and as my Son Jeremiah was living on my farm and wanted to buy it I concluded to let him have it in prefferance to a stranger for about the same amount that I gave for it which was about 4 hundred dollars

[Page 496]

And he was to pay me in instalments just has He could make them, so the first was in 1867 which amount was 2 hundred and ninety dollars and with that and some money which came to me from my Fathers estate in South Africa who Died at Uitenhage February 21st 1863 aged 73 years, my father Isaac Wiggill was one of the settlers who came to the Colony, Cape of Good Hope, in the year 1820.[5]

So with this money I baught what is caled in Salt Lake City, a half Lot, for 4 hundred and fifty dollars, having no House on it, but it was planted with some nice young Trees such as Apples Peaches Apricots and Plums.

And at this time I had a Span of Horses and light Wagon and my Son Joseph been at home with me I had him haul the materials for building

[Page 497]

such as rock Bricks sand and clay, and when the materials was on the ground, I engaged a man to build for me, but he disapointed me that year, But in the mean time my Son Jeremiah came to the City and built the foundation for me for one

---

4. British converts Thomas, William, and George Naylor immigrated to Utah Territory in 1852, where they manufactured carriages and wagons in Salt Lake City on First East Street. One local Salt Lake City newspaper mentioned Naylor & Bro.'s Blacksmith Shop. "Hopper of a Malt Mill," *Deseret News*, August 26, 1868, 8. Another undated newspaper clipping advertised, "NAYLOR BROS., Carriage and Wagon Makers, First East Street, Salt Lake City, U.T."

5. "DIED at Uitenhage on the morning of the 21st February 1863, after an illness of 14 days, Mr. Isaac WIGGILL, in the 73rd year of his age. Deceased was one of the Settlers who came to the Colony in 1820. Friends and relatives will please accept of this notice." *Grahamstown Journal*, February 24, 1863. Isaac Wiggill wrote his last will and testament on August 2, 1856. Among other things it states that all his household belongings go to his then-second wife, Mary Ann Wiggill, which included "six hundred pounds sterling," and upon her death, he wrote, his household goods were to be sold "and the proceeds be equally divided among my children." The original resides in the Western Cape Archives.

CHAPTER 28

room a little over twenty by twelve feet in the clear He also layed the joistes for me and so it had to lay untill the next Spring for the Winter came on so severe that I had to postpone building untill the next Spring, and cover all my materials up from the weather so when the Spring opened I soon had my House built by a Mr Whiteing the same man who disapointed me in the fall before and I very soon had it finished and moved into it to save paying a heavy rent And I dug my garden and planted it, But when the things grew up the grasshopers

The Death of my Wife [Page 498]

came and eat everything up and also distroyed several of my fruite trees, And as we were a little cramped for room I built at spare times when I was not very buissy at my trade, another room, which made it more comfortable,

And the next year I plowed and sowed and gained nothing for my trouble for the grasshoppers were just has bad and eat everything up. But the next year was better. I raised quite a good Crop of both fruit and Barly in my Lot also a good quantity of vegetables, which was the year 1869, Things went on with me well that year untill the month of August when my Wife was taken sick, and died after one weeks illness of dysentry on the 29th of August aged 56 years, after a union of 42 years, She died in the full Faith of the

[Page 499 Death of my Wife]

Gospel as taught by the latter day Saints, She wished to go and had no dissire to live any longer, She was surrounded at the time by four Daughters and her Son Jeremiah, and also three soninlaws, my youngest Son Joseph been away from home at the time to Bear Lake Valley with my Soninlaw William Lowe to make a home there, When I knew that my Wife was dieing I asked her what I should say to Joseph (Her baby boy) She said give him my love, I also asked her at the same time if she was going to her Sister she said yes and to my mother, whom had been dead for many years, and then she passed away in that quite way has as been discribed above, Leaving me and our Children to mourn the loss of a faithfull Wife and loving mother,

Death of my Wife [Page 500]

just a little while before she died I asked her if I should take her to Kaysville to be buried she did not answer me for some time then when I was not thinking about it I think it was the next day. She told me she wanted to be taken to Kaysward, so accordingly I took her there which is about 25 miles and layed her by the side of her grandson, She was born in Yorkshire September 1812, She was the Daughter of Francis. Parrot. Bentley and her mother's maiden name was Harriot Kitchen, She Emigrated with her Parents to South Africa Cape of Good Hope, in the year 1820, When about five Thousand souls were sent out by the British government to settle a large tract of Land which the Kaffirs had been driven from by the government some two or three years before.

[Page 501]

Has I mentioned about my Son Joseph being away from home when his mother died. It happened in this way, That about three years before my Daughter Fannie [Frances Amelia], (My youngest girl) was married to a Blacksmith whos name is William Ju. Lowe. He being caled to some time the latter part of the Spring with others to go to Bear Lake Valley, and it was just about a month before my Wife took sick that he fitted himself out with a good Wagon and Team and all his Tools, and took my Son Joseph with him leaving his Wife at home.

He went with the intention of Building a home and a buisness out in Bear Lake Valley, and he baught a place for 4,00 Dollars and with a House on it, and while he was there himself with the help of my Boy he partly

[Page 502]

built a Shop to go to work in, Then he came back to the City intending to move his family right back, But when they arrived at Kaysville where my other Children lived, It was then they heard of the Sickness and Death of their mother which caused a great change in his arrangements, So he came to the City to see his family, and his Wife thought she would not like to go to that far off lonely Country to live so he started my Son with him again and to Bear Lake payed for his place and left it in care of the man he baught of whos name is Johnson, Then he gathered up his Tools, leaving all the rest of his load there and came back to the City and went to work at his trade never going back to Bear Lake again, Well, when I returned to the City after

[Page 503]

the Funeral of my Wife I been left alone I went and stayed with my Daughter Mrs Lowe seeing that she was alone, her Husband away to Bear Lake, Well I still stayed with them after his return for two or three months, and in that time I made up my mind to marry again, and there being a person living here whom I had known for years both in Africa and also in Salt Lake City as a Widdow for seven years so I proposed to her and She excepted and we were married the latter end of October, and broughter her Home to my own house, which was all furnished as my Wife had left it, my Wife had also known this person for meny years before she died,

I had been married about two months when my Soninlaw William Lowe[6]

[Page 504]

---

6. Eli, a wagonmaker, met William Lowe, a blacksmith, in Salt Lake City during their employment at Naylor Brothers, a blacksmith and wagon-making business. William soon met Eli and Susannah's daughter Frances Amelia, who either "helped convert William or refused to marry him until he joined the new religion." Love prevailed and William Lowe, age 25, was baptized in Salt Lake City in 1863, and on

CHAPTER 28

Home of William and Amelia Lowe who remained in the Eastern Cape for several years after Eli Wiggill returned from the trip they took together to South Africa. Courtesy Michael T. Lowe.

took it into his head to go to Africa. He owned a nice property besides his Wagon and Team, Tools, and many other valuables which he sold to good advantage, and his family being small, but one Child. Himself and Wife. he invited me to go with him. and that he would pay my way there on condisions that I would pay him again after we arrived there,

So after reflecting and thinking, and it been in the Winter and nothing doing at my Trade and consulting the thoughts and feelings of my Wife who did not have any peticluar objections to my going, but thought a voige accross the Sea might do me good, and she also said she thought with the help of her Sons who were four that was able to work that she could get along, So I made up my mind to go, Has I

[Page 505]

perhaps another such an oppertunity might never offer again for me to go to see my Friends.

My own Children did not feel very willing for me to go they felt bad and thought it hard because they had so recently lost their mother, and then for me to go so far away thinking that I might never return to them again. But however I made up my mind to go,

So we Telegraphed to Kaysville to my Son Jeremiah to come to the City with his Team and Wagon and take our baggage back to the Kaysville Depot.

November 5, 1866, he married Amelia Wiggill, age 18, in the Endowment House. Michael T. Lowe, *African Eden II: The Lowes of South Africa*, 29, 240.

(For in them day the Cars had not reached the City) so after makeing all arrangments for Starting we left the City on Sunday Dec. the 12th 1869, and went to Kaysville and stayed there Monday 13 to visit with my Children

[Page 506]

Chapter 29

And on Tuesday 14th we took the Cars at Kaysvill for Ogden after biding my Children and friends goodby, arrived at Ogden the same day, Then we took the Cars for the East and passed Omaha and changed Cars by having to crossing the Missouri river on a ferry Boat and arrived at Chicago on the 17th Dec, and crossed the Niagara Bridge near the falls, and going out of our way for what cause I dont know, but we halted there about a hour, and in the mean time I took a walk and went down and looked at the ~~under~~ Bridge at one end, It is a very extencive Wire Bridge, but it was so cold that I could not stay long It looked to me to be about one hundred feet above the foming restless water below. Then ~~I~~ we took the Cars again and

[Page 507]

recrossed the Bridge and came to the City of Toronto on Saturday evening the 19 and stayed there over Sunday it seemed to be a fine Town having some old fashoned Churches and other building and beautifull shrubbery in front of genteelmens Houses,

Leaving Toronto on the 20th and arrived in the City of Otawa [Ottawa] in Cannada [Canada] the same afternoon, and went to the House of Mr James Lowe, Brother of William Lowe, and we stayed there over Christmas and New Year and spent a very pleasant time in eating and drinking and enjoying ourselves emencely for two weeks.

I went around the City some but it was so dreadfull cold, But I notested some very handsome buildings and also the Court House which

[Page 508]

stood on an Eminance over looking the City and the Otawa [Ottawa] river, also the Country around for many miles which is well wooded, And I never saw so much Lumber in one place as there was there. I beleive there was acers of it packed up ten and twelve feet high.

On the 3rd of Jan 1870 we left Otawa [Ottawa] for New York, and on the 4th ~~and~~ we came to a villige caled Peston on the St Lawrance river and on the Cannada [Canada] side, and when we arrived there the river was so rough and boisterous and rageing like the Oacion [ocean] that we could not cross that night and take Lodgeings at an Hotell. I never would have thought that a fresh water river could have been so boisterous. On the morning of the 5th the river had become so calme that we crossed

[Page 509]

without any trouble or danger to a villege caled Ogdenburg where we took the Cars. and passing through many villeges and beautiful Park like Country dotted here and there with comfortable looking farm Houses shrubery and a veriety of beautiful Trees of various kinds.

We contunied on our Journy and traveled along a stream which I considered a Tributary to the Hudson river. And I notest the Margen on both sides were lined with great blocks of ice which had been broken up by a freshet and has we came down the Hudson river I though it was the grandest seenery that I ever beheld, and its broad waters was alive with Crafts of all discriptions, and islands with

[Page 510]

beautiful mansions and gentleman's privet dwelings which made it look like a Paradise. And in the distance I could see villiges with there Churches and Spires looming up which made it look very Picturesquest, and the Cars run just above the level of the water of the river an and as we neared New York the mountains on each side of the river was considerably elevated with Bluffs runing to the Waters edges which were Tuneled and between the Bluffs was filled in with rocks to lay the rails on. so that every now and then we passed through a Tunel which was quite a few and they were all arched in with Bricks, and on the cragey mountains sides were adorned with beautiful Trees such as Cypress and

[Page 511]

differant species of Fures trees which line the Perseptous mountains sids to the sumets. and the beautiful islands contunied all the way down the river with beautiful Cottages built on them.

And has we neared New York we passed many Iron Founderis and extensive Brickyards, and many other buisness places. And arrived in New York on the 5th of Jan 1870.

On arriving in New York we took a Carrage (Those Carrages are kept in waiting at the differant Stations been imployed by the differant Proprietors of Hotell) and went to an Hotell and stayed one night. But it being so far away from the Docks William thought we had better move nearer to be handy to look out for a vessel, so William and I

[Page 512]

walked around to look for another and cheaper place to stay not knowing how long we would have to wait for a Ship. So in our wanderings we found a place which William thought would do, so we went in to enquire, The first place we went into was a store where the people sold groceries and many other things.

Well he engaged a room and board for so much per day. And not takeing perticular notice of the room that we were to occupy we moved our baggage there.

CHAPTER 29

And when came time to retire for the night, there was a sensation came over my Daughter that she could not account for seeing two or three illlooking and suspicious men in the place we thought that we had got into a den of

[Page 513]

Theves so thinking of our surroundings we did not sleep much that night.

The man was very inquisitive wanting to know where we were from and where we were going, and when we told him that we was going to the Cape of Good Hope He said what do you want to go thear for to spend your money, why dont you stay here and spend it in New York.

(For my part I beleive he was one of the Finnians [Fenians][1] which was so much talked about at that time)

So when morning came William payed for our nights Lodgings, and when we left the woman was so angrey at us leaving she banged the door after us. Then William took Lodgings at the Centurial[2] Hotell near to Castle Garden[3] which was close

[Page 514]

to the Dock where we stayed for one week and was very comfortable. And in the meain time in looking over the paper William found a vessel takeing in fright for Capetown and Port Natal so we went to see the Agent and we went on board the Ship and there seen the Captain. And found everything nice and agreable on the Bark Deadorous [barque *Deodarus*][4] who belonged to Dundee Schotland. Captain and Commander, William Amos [Ames].[5] And first Mate Mr McCloud who was a real good man The Captain and Crew was all Scotchmen.

---

1. "The Irish Republican Brotherhood, or as it was known in America the Fenian Brotherhood, was founded by James Stephens in Dublin in March 1858. . . . Fenianism gave expression to the militant and violent aspect of nineteenth-century Irish nationalism. Convinced as they were that Britain would never freely relinquish its interests in Ireland, the Fenians set about planning the overthrow of British administration." Oliver Rafferty, "Fenianism in North America in the 1860s: The Problems for Church and State," 257.

2. This appears to be the Centennial Hotel as noted in Wiggill, "Eli Wiggill History."

3. Castle Garden was America's first immigration depot located at the Battery, at the tip of Manhattan, New York. It opened in 1855, later burned, and then closed down in 1890, being replaced by the Ellis Island immigration station in 1892. For a detailed study of Castle Garden, see George J. Svejda, *Castle Garden as an Immigrant Depot, 1855–1890*.

4. The ship *Deodarus* was a Scottish vessel built in 1868. "Deodarus," *Scottish Built Ships*.

5. The master of the barque vessel *Deodarus* was named Ames. *Aberdeen Built Ships*.

So we engaged our passages at I think about 125 Dollars per head. And on the 19th of Jan we were towed out by a steam tug past Sandy Hook. And as we was the only passingers on

[Page 515]

Board we were made very comfortable in the Cabin.

The Cook John Smith said when he was fixing up the Stove on in the Cabin that it was cold in New York. But we shall soon Sail out of it and get into warmer weather the further we get away on our voyage. And so we found it, for in about two weeks time we did not need the stove the weather had become so pleasent and warm. And when we had farely got out to sea, we, my Daughter her Husband and myself got fearly seasick which lasted a few days, but my Daughter and myself got well over it But every time that we had ~~ruff~~ rough weather and the Ship would roll a little more than usal

[Page 516]

then William would get sick and so he was all the way over the sea.

There was nothing very particular transpired only now and then we would see a Sail at a distance and catch a few fishes untill we came to the Line. Then Old Neptune came on board and told the Captain that he would be on board tomorrow to attend to any subject that might have never crossed the Line.

The Captain told him alright to come. So he came the next day according to promis, to adopt those into his Kingdom which had never been that way before the Captain the Carpenter and my Soninlaw three in all who had to be adopted by the usal way of been Shaved. But the Captain he dodged it by

[Page 517]

shuting himself in the Cabin. But finely got a bucket of water thrown over him. The other two tryed to fight against been Shaved, but by a good deal of persuasion they finely consented and were Shaved which made quite a good bit of fun. Has for myself I had crossed the Line twice before so that I was not interfeared with.

While crossing the Line the heat is intence for we are under a vertical Sun, and it was so hot and sultery in the Cabin, it was almost imposable to stay in it. So we used to get up on deck in the Shade of the Sails or under the Awning to try to catch a little air Well the heat was so great that the Captain had

[Page 518]

the deck strewed with fine sand, which was brought on purpos to keep us from sticking fast to the Tar, which the Sun would draw out of the joints of the Deck.

Well after passing the line we had a very good passage with the exception of about a week puting it all together that we were becalmed, which is very disagreeable to a Sea Captain.

CHAPTER 29

Well we saw the top of Table Mountain for a long time perhaps a day before we would see any low Land, and the night before the Sailors seen the flashes of the Light House. The Captain went a little out of his corse having never been there before so we could not land that night but

[Page 519]

layed too untill morning when He found that we had nearly gone ashore.

So the next morning we had to Tack Ship several times before we could enter the Harbor of Table Bay, after a voyage of 64 days which we entered and Anchored on the 24th day of March 1870.

The Pilot that came on board and showed us where to Anchor seeing that I was a passinger got into a conversation with me by asking me where I came from, I told him that I had just come from America, where I had been and for the last ten years, and that I was the Son of one of the British Settlers of 1820. Then he told me that I had just come in time to attend a great Jubilee which was going to be held in Graham

[Page 520]

Town [Grahamstown], in memory of the first fifty years of their Settler life in South Africa.

As we came into Table Bay early in the morning, the Captain felt ancious to go ashore, to see the Partyes he had part Cargo for, so has he was going ashore, myself my Daughter and her Husband with their little Child, went ashore with Him, and as the day was very fine we thought we would take a ramble about the City of Cape Town. Although I had lived in Africa a little over forty years I had heard a great deal about Cape Town from a Boy, but had never seen it, so has the day was very fine we rambled about the streets, and finely came to the Botanical Garden, which is also caled the Government Garden, and while looking in at

[Page 521]

the gate a Colored Man came to us and we asked him if there was any admitance. He told us that the Garden was open for the Inhabitants of the City, two days in the week,

However we told him that we were strangers and had just landed, and was from America, so he told us that he had orders to let strangers in, so we went in and found it a very beautifully layed out Garden with gravel walks in every direction, and planted with flowers and Shrubbery of every discription. And also young Trees of many differant kinds, Timber that I had been used to work the greater part of my life into Wagons. I pointed them out to my Soninlaw and caled them by name and there were very large Oaks and Blue Gums along some of the walks as shade

[Page 522]

Trees, And in the Garden was a Large building which was the Library and museum the Library it is said to contain forty Thousand volumes, besides the valuable colection presented by the Governor of most rare manuscripts scarce aditions and works chiefly in dead languages,

This Governor named above was Sir George Gray. K. C. B. then Govenor of Cape Colony. 1861.

And a few yards from the Library Building is a beautiful Statue of Sir George Gray represented in full dress the Pedestal and Statue was about ten feet high,

After walking and looking around untill we were tyred, we went to a restaurant or Boarding house and got our dinners it was the first dinner

[Page 523]

we had, had on shore for so long a time that we enjoyed it emencely,

And after looking around a little more we returned to the Ship with the Captain in the evening.

The next morning I, and my Soninlaw went as ashore in search of some People whos adress we had we started to go to a villige some distance out of town 3 miles, (Mowbray)[6] and as we were on the road we were overtaken by a Dutchman with a Wagon, and we enquired of him if he could tell us where Mr George Rook lived, he said he could show us the House, so we got up in his Wagon and rode into the village. There the man had buisness to attend to at a Store and left the Wagon stand but he had not pointed out the house

[Page 524]

to us yet, so seeing a Blacksmith and Wheelwright Shop near by and we both being of them Trades we thought we would go in to have a look around while the Wagon was standing on the street, and while there and in conversation we told the workmen where we were from America,

And while we were talking there was a Boy had been listeing to us, and he went out quitely home to his mother and told her that there were two men in the Shop who had come from America, so directly he came back and told us that his mother would like to see us which made us wonder as we were total strangers there, we went with the Boy to see his mother, so when we got to the House the secret of it was this Woman was

---

6. The Mowbray Branch in the Wynberg District, Cape Division, was the first ecclesiastical unit of The Church of Jesus Christ of Latter-day Saints established in South Africa. Officially organized on August 16, 1853, at the home of Nicholas Paul, thirteen of the fifteen branch members were in attendance when Elder William Walker gave "an interesting discourse on the organization of the Church of Jesus Christ of Latter-day Saints, and the order of the Priesthood." Mowbray Branch Record (1853–1869), 1.

CHAPTER 29

[Page 525]

a member of the Church of Jesus Christ of Latter Day Saints, and almost the first question she asked if we were Elders in said Church, of corse we told her we was, Then I asked her if she could tell us where Mr Rook lived, she said yes. I will send my Boy with you to the House, This family name is Penfold,[7] and from there we had to go about a mile through Avenues of beautiful Pine Trees which lead to Mr Rooks farm, and when Mr Rook seeing us coming and knowing the Boy, he judged that we were Elders and where we were from, He was real glad to see us and made us very welcome to his house.

After staying with him awhile, and haveing a good talk togather, we made

[Page 526]

arraingments with him to come to the jetty or Landing with his Cart to take and take our Luggage to his house, for we understode that we could not leave Cape Town for a week to come, on account of the Steamer been detained over her time from England and the Coasting steamer had just left Cape Town the night before we got there or Landed,

So having made arraingments with Mr Rook to fetch us the next morning we left him and went to the railway Station at Ronderbush [Rondebosch], and has we had one mile to walk we arrived there a few minuts too late for the Train had just started, and consequently we had to wait for the next Train so that threw us a little late.

But it just happened that the Captain was late in leaving the City to go to the Ship so we were

[Page 527]

just in time to go with his Boat. Well next morning Mr Rook was at the Dock in good time to take us with his Cart to his house where we spent the week visiting one place and another and looking around and also visiting the few members of the Church who were in the vinicity.

And one day Mr Rook took us up into one of the wooded reveins which runs up the Table mountain some two miles, and the seceanry was most romantic with Trees and Shrubbery and after we got a cirtain hight we turned and crossed over a rockey ridge still covered with trees mostly Pine and coming down into the other Cluff clime over and through Brambles of two or three kinds such as Blackberys Roseber

[Page 528]

rys and Cape Gooseberryes also the wild grapes that runs up very large trees like large cable ropes then spreads over the tops of the trees forming network where they bear their fruite and when the frute is ripe it is jet black and about

---

7. William, 32, and Mary Ann Penfold, 26, joined the Church on June 21, 1856, and attended the Mowbray Branch. Mowbray Branch Record (1853–1869).

the sise of a small walnut and very sour, But when preserved they are very nice and of a beautiful color.

And when I saw them it put me in mind of the time when I was a Boy and used to ramble about the Forests near Grahams Town [Grahamstown], and used to climb the Trees and creep over the tops on the network and gather and eat the fruit. So we waded on through this romantic Cluff till we came to a fountain of beautiful spring water which had in former years been lead out into

[Page 529]

a water Dich or as the Dutch stiles it a waterfurrow.

We followed this furrow for a considerable way through the Forrest, and sometimes on our hands and knees or as some would say on all fours, untill we came to a good sized cemented Tank in ovel shape about thirty feet long and about twelve feet wide and about three feet deep, But quite dry, which had trees growing in it from 20 to 30 feet high, and a little below that we came to the ruines of a Mansion, the blue coloring was still visiable on the walls and as it stood on the hillside the grounds around it had been Terraced and planted for there were remnants of of differant kinds of

[Page 530]

Trees such as Chesnuts and Walnuts trees.

Mr Rook was very well acquainted with the place but he never said one word about the ruined mansion till we were right on to it,

Then I asked him if he knew the history of it. He told me he did, and at the time the Dutch held the Cape of Good Hope that it was Built and beautified by one of the Dutch Governors for his country residence, so on leaving this place we went about one mile down a good Carrage road through a Forrest of trees which is now used for bringing firewood down to take to Cape Town, and at that time this place was owned by a Widow Lady and her family whos name was

[Page 531]

Kreewogon,[8] We finely came out of this mountainous place to the out skirts of the village of Ronderbush [Rondebosch] and by the time we arrived at Mr Rooks we were very tired,

Rondebosch, is one long succession of jentlemens seats; and in the beauty of its scenery, and comfortable appearances of its homes, is perhaps unsurpassed by any suburbs in any part of the world. With a railway runing through it to Wynberg the third town in size and importance in the Cape division. it is beautifuly situated at the east base of Table Mountain range, about eight miles distant from Cape Town;

---

8. Kreewogon may refer to Cruywagen. Antonia Malan, "Households of the Cape, 1750 to 1850: Inventories and the Archaeological Record," 283.

CHAPTER 29

Well, I and William went once or twice in to Cape Town through the week to see when the Coast

[Page 532]

Steamer would be going again to Algo [Algoa] Bay, For it was there we wanted to go.

And has we had to stay at Mr Rooks house over Sunday, He invited several of his neighbors, and also the few members of the Church of Jesus Christ of Latter day Saints to come to his house on Sunday, That there were Elders from Salt Lake City that would Preach to them, so we held two meetings, afternoon, and evening which was well attended. I explained a great deal to them about the afares in Utah and our religion, the City and its surroundings, which of corse was very interesting to them who had never been in Utah,

Well staying the week out the Steamer Bismarck named after the

[Page 533]

Prince, She was a German Craft the Captain and all the hands were German people the Captain's name was Mr States [Staats].[9]

So Mr Rook brought us down to the jetty with his Cart. Then William hired a Boat which took us to the Ship Deadorous [Deodarus] where we got the remainder of our Luggage and bid the Captain and the mate good by who had been very kind to us all through the voyeg,

So we were soon on board the Steamer on our way to Algo [Algoa] Bay or as it is often caled Port Elizabath [Elizabeth]. It I think we was about 4 days on this Steamer, and there were very high mountains in sight all the way, and when we were about half way we put in to a port caled Massel [Mossel] Bay, and discharged Cargo and took in quite

[Page 534]

a large amount of Brandy and other goods. I could see the village in the distance but did not go on shore, The Mountains just back of the village cut off the view from seeing very far inland. But from what I could see and understand it was a great fruit growing place, and where they made a great deal of Brandy and Wines, and also dryed a great deal of fruits.

Then we started on again still keeping the Land in sight but the Mountains were not so high and rugged as they was near the Cape we could also see small patches of Forrests dotted here and there over the Landscape. So we landed in Port Elizabath [Elizabeth] on Sunday the 3rd of April 1870. Then I went and found an Old acquaintance whos name

[Page 535]

---

9. German commander Captain Staats "bore a magnificent beard." Commander W. Caius Crutchley, *My Life at Sea*, 136.

was Charles Grubb, and Stevedore by buisness.

I thought we would stay a few days with him till we could see a way to go on to our friends. But he said he could not accomadate us, on account of some old friends of his at house, a Sea Captain and his Wife.

But he was kind enough to harness up his Horses and took us to a Ladys house who I was well acquainted with whos name was Mrs Rich. She was real glad to see me and enquire about her Son who was in Utah.

And she knew of a room that we could get for a few days, of an acquaintance whos name was Mr Hyman, Then William Hired a Cart to fetch our Luggage from the jetty to the room we had hired

[Page 536]

which was at Mr. E Slaughters old Tannery, who Emegrated to Utah some years ago.

This Mrs Rich lived on a Public St so she could see all the Wagons coming and going from differant parts of the country, and she knowing that we were wanting a convayance to take us to our friends in the Queenstown District, and the Wagons generaly having the owners name and where they are from on their Wagons

So on the Monday after Landing on Sunday she happened to see Wagons passing by with the name. Wiggill. on them they were loaded with Bales of Wool, and at that time William and I were out in search of a convayance and looking around the Town and happened to call at Mrs Riches, and she told us that the Wagons had passed

[Page 537]

so we went to hunt them up and found them after a while unloading the Wool at a Merchants Store. And of corse we knew the Wagon by the name, and I enquired of the colored servant or Leader of one of the Wagons where his master was, and he pointed me to where the two men was sitting watching the Wool been wheighed so I went up to them and asked them a few questions who they were and where they were from and they answered me according to my wishes so I was sattisfied who they were.

so I found one to be my Brother's Son Henry and the other a Man who was in my Brother's employ whos name was Abraham Wild,[10] whos Grandfather I had known in earlyer days I then asked Henry where his Brother Francis was

[Page 538]

He told me that he was somewhere in the Bay with the other Wagons, so we soon found him, and he expecting me, through a letter which I had sent to my Brother George, so he recognized me directly knowing that I was coming.

---

10. Abraham Wild, born in 1790 in Oldham, Lancashire. British 1820 Settlers to South Africa.

CHAPTER 29

We thought ourselves very luckey to find such a good oppertunity to go to our friends with out having to hier, for by this time our money was geting short, So Francis had one of the Wagons fitted up very comfortable for us and also had a light Ladder made for our convenience to get in and out of the Wagon.

After seeing my Nephues and makeing all things right with them in regard to our pasage, and as we had a days leasure William and I went up on what is caled the Hill. an Emeniance two or three hundred feet

[Page 539]

above the village, where there are a great many Gentlmans residence's built. I found it greatly improved, built up and streets layed out and also a beautiful Botanical Garden made since I was there ten years before, from that hill we had a splendid vewe of the village or buisness part of Port Elizabeth and also the harbor and Shiping, and the Sea for miles. Up on this elevated spot is a beautiful level stretch of Land doted over with evergreen trees, and lawn grass which is nice and green all the year round being no frost to check it in the winter,

And on this level spot there are hundreds of pritty Cottages built and also a large Hospital.

And on the next day which was the seventh of April I stayed at home and

[Page 540]

wrote letters to my Children back to Utah. While my Daughter and her Husband took a walk on the Beach, and went some two or three miles, which left me quite and alone to my writing.

I would ~~have~~ liked to have enjoyed the walk with them but I wanted to get my letters wrote to let my Children know that I had arrived safe in Africa, and on Saturday the ninth my nephue had three of the Wagons ready, and we started from the Bay, and went about seven or eight miles to what is caled Zwartkop's river.[11] and campted there over Sunday.

Buisness detained Francis at the Bay untill Monday.

The Zwartkops is not a very big river it takes its rise from the mountains in the vicinity of the Town of Uitenhage about twenty miles distent from where we were Campt.

[Page 541]

Where we Camped, the High or Spring Tides ebbs and flows up to the crossing which I supose is some four or five miles, The mouth of this river is a large Bay a beautiful sheet of water which would make a nice Harbor for Shiping but like all the African rivers are obstructed by Sandbars, and about one mile from the mouth of this river there is a Bridge called the Zwartkop's Bridge

---

11. "Uitenhage," South African History Online.

which is built on Pile's which is several hundreds yards in length, we should have crossed this Bridge but it was not safe for Wagons to cross it been out of repair and consequently we had to take the old road which was traviled by the Settlers of 1820. and in whos company my own Father and Mother traviled, who had long since pasted away with many others.

Zwartkops [Page 542]

Chapter 30

Well, we are still at the Ford where we arrived on Saturday and now it is Monday the 11th and as it rained very hard on Sunday night it detained us untill late in geting started for the Hill that we had to travil up was so wet and slippy. But we got the Oxen up and started out with the greatest difficulty. After several hours hard pulling for the Wagons was very heavy loaded.

Now then that we have got fairly up the Hill I want to take the reader back to where we started from. in the place there is a level flat about a quarter of a mile before we come to the hill which is dotted thickly over with a variety of thorney evergreen trees and many of them bearing berryes. My Son in law remarked that nearly every tree he saw had thorns on them.

This hill must have got its name from the early Dutch Settlers on account of its been black with one mass of differant kinds of underbrush or dwarfe forrest trees, And on the top of this hill is one long range of Conical shaped mounds, covered with a dence growth of trees which it is imposable to penetrate.

And those hills ranges for a great many miles from the Sea to Uitenhage some twenty miles. And as this Bush is of such a dark green, boardering on black at a distance it looks black the word Swarts which in English means black and kopes means those Conical hill which as been refered to on the range of the hill from which it as got its name swartkopes and the river runing in a parallel line with the mountain got its name Swartkopes river from the early Dutch Settlers.

This bush is intermixed with Aloes and a veriety of runing vines, and also plants caled the milkey Ufobia [Euphorbia][1] which grows from twenty to thirty feet heigh with leaves three squair and about two feet in length and gives a small flower up the three angles.

This Aloes is the well known bitter Aloes which is sold by the Druggists for Medicen it is extracted from the leafe, and abounds in many parts of South Africa, and whos branched scarlet blossoms looks very handsom and stands like Solders on the mountain sides and growing from two to five and ten feet high although it is such a bitter plant it is strange to say the flower contains sweet Honey,

---

1. "Euphorbia L.," Plants of the World Online.

been once more on the Top of this mountain, Abr[a]ham Wild turned off to go to the Salt Pans, Although his Wagon had a heavy load on, he went and load up as much Salt as would have loaded an ordinary Wagon, or what the Dutch would have considered forty years ago a Load for their Wagons.

So we went on some five or six miles till we came to a Farm House and Outspaned, (Or as it is caled in America Unyoked) the Cattle and Camped there untill Mr Wild returned with his salt. while there we had hard work to get any thing Cooked for the wind blowed such a gail that

[Page 546]

we could not keep any fire burning till we went under a bank then we managed very well and got up a good dinner,

And by the time the dinner was ready to my surprise Mr Wild came back with his load of salt, After we had dinner we inspaned again and left the heigh Land and got down in to a lower part of the Country where it was more mild and mostly through a dence Bush, The road went through the bush, and now and then we came to a Farm House, which was altogather a new Country to me and lead on to the Sundays river Pont which we had to cross, and this brough us to the mane road leading to Grahams Town [Grahamstown], We had to take this rout on account of the Swartkops Bridge been

[Page 547]

out of repair. This Pont or Ferry Boat is long enough to take on board a large Wagon and twelve Oxen, and is worked by ropes spaned across the river, and got over all safe and outspaned for the night. And during the night my nepheu Francis Wiggill came up and joyned us, and at this place there were several wagons Camped haveing wild Beasts in them on there way to England, such as Zebra's, Lions, and other kinds of animals of which I dont remember,

On the next morning we traviled through a park like Country where we had a commanding vew of the lower Country and the Sea at a distance,

Here I found living and keeping a wayside accomodation house for man and Beasts, by the

[Page 548]

of Charles Fan Cot [Fancutt],[2] so myself my Daughter and her Husband were invited to take dinner with them, He was trying to rise Cotton, after we had dinner I asked him what there was to pay and he said nothing to old friends and has his Fatherinlaw lived some ten or twelve miles off the road whos name is Charles Talbot and he also been an old friend of mine, and Brother to Mr Henry Talbot who as is mentioned in this work, He having to go to this place on an erand after a Child he proposed takeing me along with him

---

2. Charles Fancutt (1835–1917), whose family came with the Clarks Party. Nash, *The Settler Handbook*, 59–60.

CHAPTER 30

in his Buggy, and when I got there they were very much surprised for they thought that I was in America and never expected to see me again, so I had to sit up till after midnight

[Page 549]

and give them a History of Utah and the Church, and Mr Fan Cot [Fancutt] hurryed me away so early the next morning before I could get a cup of Coffee which my friends wanted me to have before starting, But we got some at a place called Dassy [Dassie] klip,[3] which is in English Rabbit Rock, and from there he took me to join the Wagons again and was there in time to take Breakfast with my people.

After taking breakfast we inspaned and started on our jorney, some times travling through beautiful Parklike Country, But nothing of note happened in the four days which it took before we arrived at Grahms Town [Grahamstown], only that we passed some very good farm houses and Hotells on the

[Page 550]

road,

A few miles before we arrived at Grahamstown we passed through a place known as Howesenport [Howison's Poort][4] so named after a Mr Howeson [Howison], a man whom I knew well when I was a Boy, It was a long narrow Gorge between two very heigh mountains but here and there space enough to make small farms The road through it as been made by Government with Convict labour, and at the top part of the Port or Canon, as it is caled in America was a large Wool washing Establishment where the merchants of Grahams town [Grahamstown] sends their Wool to be washed, before Shiping it to England.

The distance from this place to Grahamstown seemed so short to me, to what it used when I was younger so we soon arrived in

[Page 551]

Grahamstown and went through the main St which is caled high street, and from entering on this street at the one end and out at the other is not less than two to two and a half miles

And while passing through the Town I recognized many of the Buildings which I knew when I were a Boy that had undergone no change. But in between those Houses on spaces that was, there had been some spacious buildings put up for stores, in fact Grahams Town [Grahamstown] and the vicinity

---

3. "Dassie Klip Farm," mentioned in Boyd Richardson, *Alfred Robinson's Record of His Service with British Forces in the Second Boer War February 1900–December 1901*.
4. "Prehistory of the Port Elizabeth Area," South African History Online.

is the place where I spent my Boyhood days, and also where I got married and entered into buisness.

And wher my dear mother and a Sister lays burryed which causes me to remember it, But when I passed

[Page 552]

through this Town I felt like a stranger for I had not lived there for the last twenty or thirty years so that a great many of my old acquaintances had passed away and strangers come in their places, and the that was living I had not time to hunt them up,

Well we arrived at the out skirts of the Town on to what is known as the Cricket ground, and there we outspaned and stayed there the greater part of the day has my nepheu Francis Wiggill had buisness to attend too,

While staying there myself and Soninlaw started out to deliver a letter and also a parcel to from Henry Dixson [Dixon] of Utah to his aged Father John. Henry. Dixon of Grahamstown, whom we

[Page 553]

found very feeble and infirm so much so that he was not able to open the letter, and from thereWilliam and I went upon a hill over looking the Town, and also the Cluff where my father lived and had his water mill which was caled Wiggill's Cluff in the early times, I would liked to have gone down to the old spot once more but I had not time on account of the Wagons been ready to start again.

It was late in the afternoon when we started and left the burying and Cricket ground, where we had been staying all the fore part of the day.

First crossing what is caled the Grahamstown racecorse flat. and then going over Boauters [Botha's] Hill, Then we

[Page 554]

went down in the night what is caled the Queens Road which is from seven to eight miles as near has I can judg. It was excavated out of the Decliv[i]tous sides of the hills or mountains and those mountains are one mass of impenetrable under Brush, in fact it is a part of the great Fishriver Jungle, and full of what the great hunter Gordon Coming [Cumming] calls waitabit [wait-a-bit] thornes.

And the seenery down this road is so romantic and grand that it cant be surpassed, and finely at the bottom of the deep hollow to what is caled Brack [Brak] river,[5] Then we had to assend a hill two or three miles long, and when at the top we came to a beautiful park like Country all dotted with Bushs a

---

5. Brak River (Afrikaans word meaning "brackish") is a tributary that enters the Orange River about twenty kilometers northeast of Priesks. Raper, *Dictionary of Southern African Place Names*, 71.

CHAPTER 30

[Page 555]

level flat beautifuly decerated with a great veriety of vines and flowers, This flat was some five or six miles over which brought us to Fort Brown on the Great Fishriver [Fish River], where there is a splendid Bridge built by the government, which we crossed in the night and outspaned on the opposit side of the river, After traveling from Grahamstown a distance of eighteen or twenty miles without outspaning.

Here we stayed till it was midday, to rest and for the Oxen to feed, And as the Fishriver [Fish River] is known to abound with what is caled the Prickely Pear, And as the fruit were just ripe my nephew sent the Hottentot servants to gather two or three buckets full which we

[Page 556]

enjoyed, but my nephew seemed to eat emencely of them, but for myself I felt afraid to eat too much,

Starting from there we crossed the Konapriver [Konap River] over a splendid Bridge, Then we assended a hill caled the Konapridge [Konap Ridge] through a dence Bush and arriving on the top of this hill we came on to another parklike Country where we outspaned and rested quite a while.

Then going goin from there which we traviled in the night, and left Fort Beaufort on the right which is 46 miles from Grahamstown, still going on till we came to Kat river where we outspaned, and stayed most of the day there after traveling the greater part of the night.

[Page 557]

From this place we traveled to the commencement of the New Katberg road, where the Convict village, from this place we begin to go up the Katberg hill which took us nearly half a day to get to the top. The road was cut through a Timber forest and excavated out of the sollid rock in many places, and other places built up by masion work some hundreds of feet at the heads of Chasms or heads of Clufs, just at the top of this hill there were a great veriety of beautiful Shrubery, but the hill contunied in many places very steep.

After arriving on the top of this hill, we had to desend quite a number of long bare grassey ridges mostly excavated on the steep sides of those ridges,

[Page 558]

Till we came down to the level, to what is caled Ox Kraal, there we spaned out to get some refreshments, which was late in the day, Here I found living an Old acquaintance whos name was John Armstrong, with his Wife and family, who were real glad to see me. They came down to where the Wagons was and we had a long chatt about things of younger days, This place now goes by the name of Busby Park, as well as Ox Kraal The propritor of the farm is named Busby James, and there is an accomadation House kept by his Brotherinlaw a Mr Langfield.

From this place we traviled the most of the night till we came to a village caled Whittle sea, and it

[Page 559]

rained half the night and the next day which detained us at Whittlesea half a day in this time it stoped for a little while and we started on again, and we arrived at Swartkay [Zwart Kei] river there we outspaned and was detained quite a while on account of the rain, The rain still contunied in showers, but we started on again and came to Classmits [Klaas Smits] river. which we had to cross and which we was able to Ford.

And from this place one of the Hottentots servants went on a head from the Wagons to where my Brother Elijah and my Son John was living to inform them that I was on the road,

So the next day my Son came to meet us in his Buggy we were about half way between Classmits [Klaas Smits] river and Queenstown when he met us

[Page 560]

on the Queenstown flat after been absent from each other for ten years,

Then he took myself my Daughter (His Sister) her Husband and Child away from the Wagons in his Buggy and we went through Queenstown, But stoped there and got some refreshments, and then went on to the Bongolo which was about eigh miles, Where we was received with great joy especily by my Brother Elijah who never expected to see me again,

Then my Son John asked his Uncle Elijah what he should do with us wheather he should take us home with him or wheather we should stay with my Brother so it was desided that we should stay with my Brother for the preasent.

[Page 561]

Chapter 31

Well, has I have said in the former chapter. I stayed with my Brother Elijah, But I had another Brother, James Wiggill[1] whom I had to visit besides many other relations whom I visited who were all real glad to see me.

And has for my Brother Elijah he thought that I had come back to Africa to stay with them, He never gave it a thought that I had only come on a visit and with the intention to go back again to Utah. It was a general question with all my friends, you are not going back to America again I told them all from the first yes if I live I intend to go back some day that I had never seen anything in America to hurt or frighten me. That I was perfectly sattisfied with the doctrin

[Page 562]

of the Latter day Saints which caused me to leave my home and friends.

Had it not been for that I would have lived and died at home with my friends in Africa.

So the next day after arriving in Bongolo my Son John had buisness to attend to in Queenstown, and having many friends and also a Sister living there I went down with my son in his Buggy, my Sister was married one John Watson[2] He also been the Son of one of the Settlers of 1820. She was my youngest Sister and I had not seen her for years before I left Africa on account of her living in a distant part of the Country, She was very glad to see me once more has I was to see her. And I found many of my old

[Page 563]

friends making ready to go to attend the great Jubilee of the Settlers of 1820. And amongst the rest I found the Rev. Henry H. Dugmore a person whom I had been acquainted with for many years, He was the principal Lecturer at the meeting or Jubilee He been one of the Settlers Sons and having traviled

---

1. The *Queenstown Free Press*, September 27, 1892, noted the death of Eli's brother James: "OBITUARY. We regret to announce the death of the late Mr James WIGGILL. He was for some time resident in Queenstown, previously a farmer in the district. The deceased was one of the brothers WIGGILL amongst the pioneer farmers who came here at the close of the 1850 war, and was one of the original grantees. He saw many ups and downs in the early struggles with the kafirs, but his sturdy persevering character overcame them all and when he settled down in this division success was secured to him. He was enabled to retire from farming and settled in Queenstown, where he has been living a quiet retired life for some time. We tender our heartfelt sympathy to his large family in their sad loss."

2. John Watson. British 1820 Settlers to South Africa.

and seen a great deal of the early life of the Settlers, and been a man of keen observation he had many anecdotes stored up in his mind which he resited to as many of the Old Settlers as could be got togather, And their Sons and Daughters which were many hundreds if not thousands.

I did not go myself to this Jubilee has none of my relations were going, and I having just come off such a long journey I did feel like

[Page 564]

traviling a hundred miles just then and to be a stranger among them and in a strange place, This Jubilee was held in Grahams Town [Grahamstown] in the year 1870 (May)

Then having rested a day or two myself and my Soninlaw went up the Country to see my Brother Joseph and also a Brotherinlaw Francis. P. Bentley who were both living on the same farm, we found them and their familys all well and they were all glad to see me once more we stayed with them two or three days, then I wanted to go and see my Brother George in the Winterberg which was some eighty or ninety miles, so Mr Bentley lent us each a Horse for our journey, Then in a day or two I feeling ancious to see my Brother George William

[Page 565]

and I, started on our journey to the Winterberg, and on that day we went as far as the Swartkia [Zwart Kei] river where a friend of mine was living whos name is Joseph Ralph a member of the Church of Jesus Christ of Latter day Saints, And has he had not heard of my coming or my arrival, so when he seen me he was struck with amasement and could hardly beleive that it was me, but was very glad to see me, and we stayed with them that night, and the next day we left Mr Ralph and traviled about twenty or thirty miles when we came to the residence of Mr Edward Goddard who reseived us kindly and made us very welcome both him and his good Lady, They live on a Farm near the big Winterberg a place caled Bottle Koot [Bottelgat], where he keeps

[Page 566]

a large flock of Wool Sheep the farm is so destetute of wood for fuel that they have to depend on the Sheep Dung which they dig out of the Kraal in large squairs and when it is dry it makes a very hot fier, not only Mr Goddards farm is so destetute but many others in that neighborhood.

Leaving Mr Goddards we took a bridle path leading across the spers of the big Winterberg Mountain, from Mr Goddard's farm untill we came to the main road on the upper part of the Tarka river which is from fifteen to twenty miles, By going this rout we saved ourselves some six or seven miles. This road was well known to me has I had traviled it many years before,

When we had reached the main road we had about

[Page 567]

CHAPTER 31

two hours ride mostly up hill along the princable sorce of the Tarka river, which takes its rise from the Winterberg mountain, and a part of Country which is destitute of wood and few people residing thear it is a succession of long grassey ridges, spurs of the big Winterberg, till we came to a Plateau overlooking the valley of the Konap river which also takes its rise from the big Winterberg and from this elevated spot we had a magnificent view which is parklike and dotted here and there with Farm Houses, From this hight it took us about an hour to ride to my Brothers House which was down hill and which is caled the big Winterberg Wagon road, and arrived at my Brother George's house all safe, who

[Page 568]

I had not seen for ten years, He was very glad to see me has I was to see him, and has he was of the same faith and religion has myself we had a long talk about Salt Lake and Utah affares and after spending two or days with him we rode over to a place caled Kall hook [Kaal Hoek] where I once resided and still had a sister living, so we stayed at her place one night and visited some other friends in that Locality and, then returned to my Brothers the next day, William seemed uneasy and ancious to get back to his family whom he left in the Bongolo so he started alone on a differant road to what we had come, and arrived quite late at night at Mr Armstrong's residing at Busby Park where we

[Page 569]

had caled on our way up and hearing by accident that he had a Cousen living in the neighborhood he caled on him and found him engaged as a Sheepfarmer and well, and gave William quite a history of his relations whom he himself had left in England, And arrived in the Bongolo all safe,

And has I had not seen my Brother for such a long time I stayed a few days longer with him and Preached at his house on the Sunday, And when I was ready to leave him got his Soninlaw to returln with me to the Bongolo, as he had never seen that part of the Country, His name is H. Holles. And we return back on the same rout that William Lowe had gone and caled on an old friend by the

[Page 570]

name of James sweetnam which was about 8 miles from my Brother's place and has he pressed us to stay with him the night we concluded to do so and he made us very welcome and the next day we started on and arrived at Mr Armstrong's and stayed with him that night, and the next day we arrived in Bongolo.

And when I arrived in Bongolo I found William very buisey repairing and papering a Cottage at my Son John's place for his family to live in and of corse I had to turn too and help him, and made two new doors and a dineing Table towards his going to housekeeping, and has he my soninlaw William was a Blacksmith, my Brother Elijah took quite a likeing to him and built a Shop

[Page 571]

for him in Queenstown to start buisness in for himself, and for this Shop I also made door and window frames for it, and after geting moved and fixed in this house, a Brother of mine Aaron Wiggill who was passing through Bongolo and in company with a Mr Wooley a well known trader with the Dutch, calned[3] had been for many years, And has my Brother was going down to Britshkafferarer [British Kaffraria] to see his Farm so he said to me you had better go along with us, it will be such a good chance for you to see the Country we have two Wagons and plenty of room, So I concluded to go with him and the next day we started and I enjoyed myself very much, my Brother was very kind to me, and I saw a Country which I had never seen before and also King william's Town I had heard a great deal about it

[Page 572]

so after traveling three or four days we arrived at King williams Town, and as my Brother had some buisness to attend too we stayed there one night.

It is a very pritty Town built a nice dry rolling ridges's the Town been built on two or three of those ridges and on the head of the Buffalo river whos Waters empty themselves some twenty into the Sea, at the Port of East London, The seenery in and around East London King william Town is beautiful and Parklike, and as it as been the military headquarters for many years, and an one of the rises there is built by the British Government one of the finest Hospitals in South Africa. The grounds around it is beautifuly layed out with walks and planted with all kinds of Trees and Shrubery. Leaving this

[Page 573]

place we traviled some ten or fifteen miles, and stopted at the place of Mr Nathaniel Brown[4] Fatherinlaw to my Brother a man whom I had known for many years, and stayed over Sunday with him and attended the place of Public Worship with him to which place was two or three miles and we went on Horseback

and while there I met two or three very old acquaintance who was very glad to see me and invited us to go home with him and take dinner which invitation we excepted. and after dinner we went back to Mrs Brown's, and on Monday morning we bid him good by and started on our way home my Brothers farm which was has neigh has I can recolect was five or six miles it was occupied by a man whos name was Mr Danieles a Blacksmith by trade and

[Page 574]

---

3. This word is undecipherable.
4. Nathaniel Brown, an 1820 British settler. British 1820 Settlers to South Africa.

CHAPTER 31

who I was well acquainted with has he had once lived in Queenstown where I got acquainted with him.

And has my Brother had a little buisness to transact with Mr Danieles, so I stayed about two days and my Brother showed me the ruens of the House that our Father used to live in and also the garden of corse I was interested.

It is a pritty rolling country and the Kloofs or reviens are threaded with usefull Timber of differant kinds, and the surrounding hights are dotted with the moimosa or what is caled thorntrees with an abundance of grass.

The house which now stands is built of Stone it is very large and unfinished a story and a half high and covered in with a galvanized Iron roof, such iron is used mostly all over

[Page 575]

the country for roofing especially for farm houses as it is considered the safest from fire. On the third day my Brother and Mr Wooley left the farm and went on a visit to the seaport of East London, a place which I have not seen myself, I would have gone with them, But having a Daughter living in the neighborhood which I had not seen since my return from America, so Mr Danials was kind enrough to let his son go with me, to show me the way to my Daughter's has I was a stranger in that part of the Country, so we started on Horseback and rode from ten to fifteen miles through a beautiful Parklike country passing several comfortable looking Farmhouses, and arriving at my Daughter's in the latter part of the day, I wanted the Boy to stay with us that night, But he perfered going home and

[Page 576]

started that evening, Well I was very happy to see my Daughter and found her quite well and glad to see me, for I came quite unexpected on her has she did not know that I were in that part of the country, She is married to a Mr William James, Well it was arranged that I should stay with her untill my Brother and Mr Wooley returned and they would call for me, which gave me two or three days with my Daughter and to look around the country where she lived, which is a beautiful roling country dotted here and there with the mamosia, and in the British Kafferia district on the Gonubie river, There were some of my Old acquaintences living in the neighborhood who I would liked to have seen but it was too far to walk and my Soninlaw

[Page 577]

was too buisey twith his Sheep so I did not ask him to go and contented myself in talking to my Daughter giving her a history of America, and also of her Brothers and Sisters whom I left in Utah, Then after staying a few days with her my Brother caled according to promis, and I bid my Daughter goodby and left at once as we had to meet the Wagons some ten miles distance at a place caled the Bush Hotell where the Wagons had to pass, and when we arrived Mr Nickelson said they had not passed, and my Brother could not account for it of there not passing and thinking that some accident must have happened He rode back for several miles to where he knew they had passed and was gone all night.

[Page 578]

I was very glad that we did not have to go any further that night, for I was so very tired and also sick. and so I had a good nights rest and in the morning I felt better. But soon after my Brother had started to go back to look after the Wagons Mr Nickelson Son came home and told us that the Wagons had passed that afternoon so my Brother had his ride for nothing But while on the road he met with an old acquaintance of both his and mine whos name is James Gibbins [Gibbens][5] who I was very glad to see when they came up the next morning, Then we started on and found the Wagons outspaned some five or six miles ahead and in due time we got back to Bongolo

[Page 579]

all safe after traviling from fifty to sixty miles and on arriving at Queens Town [Queenstown] I found some of my friends there and leaving the my Brother and his Wagons I went with them home to the Bongolo,

    This was in the month of June 1870

    Isaac Wiggill died 26 Feb. 1863 he died at Uitenhage South Africa.

[The manuscript jumps from [Page 579 to 600 here, with no other page numbers listed]

[Page 600]

Book 4

---

5. James Gibbens, son of George and Margaret Gibbens. British 1820 Settlers to South Africa.

Chapter 32

When I arrived at my Brother's I found him and his Son Francis and my Soninlaw William J Lowe and William Maythem [Maytham][1] with others who had formed themselves into a company to go the Vaal river to hunt and dig for Dimonds, as the hole country was on the move at that time going to the newly discovered Dimond fields which was from five to six hundred miles from Queenstown.[2] There had been such great reports about the finding of Dimonds that it set everybody in motion to go to the fields that could posibley make it sute to leave home.

A rush somthing like it was to Callifornia at the time gold was found

[Page 601]

there.[3] Before giving a detailed account of the Vaal river Diamond fields I thought I would give a short history about how they were discovered. In 1868 a Child of a Dutch farmer named Jacobs who was living in the banks of the Vaal river, would amuse itself by picking up the pritty Peblles and picked up one which attracked its Mothers attention, so that she showed it to one Schalck Van Niecark [Schalk van Niekerk][4] who was curious in such matters, He was puzzled about its nature, and offered to buy it. But Mrs Jacobs

---

1. William Mathem was three years old when he came with his family to South Africa as a member of the Dyason Party. At age 57 he formed a partnership to mine diamonds with William Lowe. Nash, *The Settler Handbook*, 69–70.

2. A diamond discovery near Kimberley started a diamond rush in 1870. Eli went with his son-in-law William Lowe, his brother Elijah, his nephew Francis, and a few others who had formed a company to mine in the Vaal/Harts River area. Anthony Trollope, *South Africa*, 2:160–205; Oswald Doughty, *Early Diamond Days: The Opening of the Diamond Fields of South Africa*, 97–135; Percy Albert Wagner, *The Diamond Fields of Southern Africa*.

3. James Shigley, "Historical Reading List: The Diamond Fields of South Africa: Part I (1868–1893)."

4. In March 1869, a Griqua shepherd discovered a large stone on the banks of the Orange River, which was then brought to Schalk Van Niekerk. Van Niekerk immediately purchased the valuable 83-carat Star of South Africa from the Griqua man for a horse, ten oxen, and five hundred sheep. Van Niekerk sold the diamond to a Hopetown merchant for £11,200 who, in turn, later sold it in London to the Countess of Dudley for £25,000. This Dudley Diamond sparked a diamond rush along an eighty-mile length of the river near Kimberley. Martin Meredith, *Diamonds, Gold, and War: The British, the Boers, and the Making of South Africa*, 16–17. See also Frederick Boyle, *To the Cape for Diamonds: A Story of Digging Experiences in South Africa*; Stefan Kanfer, *The Last Empire: De Beers, Diamonds, and the World*.

laughed at his offer and gave him the pebble, which afterwards passed carelessly through two intervening pairs of hands befre it reached a gummed envelope

[Page 602]

and unregistered to Dr Atherstone of Grahamstown, an exceilent mineralogist. This gentliemen having examined its physicl character and tested its degree of hardness and density, and its behaviour when subjected to optical tests by means of polarized light pronounced it to be a Diamond. This is the stone which was examined by scientific men of Europan nations, during the Paris Exhibition of 1867, and purchased at the close of it by Sir Phillip Wodehouse for five hundred pounds. In 1870 Mr Streeter's Diamond expedition party weare exploring the Transvaal far and wide and ascertaing facts which complete our knowledge of the new wonder of the

[Page 603 The Diamonds]

world. As the Diamond diggings on the Vaal river and De beers or the new rush as it was caled, and also Du Toits Pan.[5]

At Du Toits Pans a Dutch Farmer named Van Wyk[6] who occupied a farm house in this Locality 20 miles south east of Pniel was surpised to find Diamonds imbeded in the walls of his house, which had been built of mud from a naighboring pond, This led to an examination of the soil which was soon found to contain Diamonds, on continuing to dig lower and lower Diamonds were still bought to light, nor did they cease when the bed of rock was at length reached. It was but natural that the discovery of Diamonds at the Cape should

[Page 604]

excite only moderate enthusiasm in Briazil, The Briazilan Diamonds had supplyed the market in ɟ Amsterdam and other countrys where the Briazil Diamonds had been in demand, But when the Cape Diamonds were brought to market in such quanties by Diamond holders and so fascinated the Amsterdam Lapidaries that for a long time they would cut no other, The Briazilian market went down and down, and has never recovered itself, the Cape yield of large stones enhanced the difficulties of influencing the Amsterdam lapidaries, they finding a superabundance refused to cut small ones, that came from Briazil, so the Briazil went down in price and the

[Page 605]

---

5. "Original name of Beaconsfield. Named after Abraham Paulus du Toit, owner of the farm Dorstfontein on which it was laid out in 1870, and a pan near the old farmhouse." Raper, *Dictionary of Southern African Place Names*, s.v. "Du Toit's Pan," 130.

6. Dutch farmer Adriaan van Wyk owned six thousand acres on a farm named Dorstfontein, but the farm was generally called Du Toit's Pan after Abraham du Toit, the previous owner. Meredith, *Diamonds, Gold, and War*, 17.

CHAPTER 32

Cape Diamonds went up in price, not because they were better but because the Cape Diamonds were larger, To show the earley state of the Diamond diggers on the Vaal river I will coppy a few lines from a news paper caled the Friend, which says that the news from the Diamond field is more encouraging. Looking down the reports given in that paper we find that they mention 46 diamonds as having been found lately. Amongst these are one of 30 carats, one of 26 1/2 carats, two of 26 each, one of 18 carats, one of 16 carats one of 11 carats, one of 10 1/2 carats three of 5 carats, one of 3 carats and the remainder of weights not stated. The Friend says that of the discoveries not one tenth

[Page 606]

part is mentioned; but if the parties keep their secret we do not see how this proportion is arrived at. It is, however, reasonable to suppose that every success is not blazed abroad. The diamond mentioned above as weighing 26 1/2 carats is the one found by Mr Rickets, and was reported by us last week. He is now said to have refused £2.200 for it. The 30 carat diamond is of inferior quality. The Friend says in a postscript that there were non the day of issue £5.000 worth of diamonds in Bloemfontein. The Pniel mission station appears to be gradually falling into the hand of the diggers. The missionary cannot prevent it, nor do we see that the Free state will be able to

[Page 607]

assist Mr Kallenberg, although the station is said to be in that territory.

The papers by last evening's post chronicle the movements of several parties. Lady Gray Philippolis and Rouxville are mentioned as contributing their twos and threes to the crowd. Port Elizabeth has started two more companies from Na the Natal papers received by the Saxon we learn that, when one of the maritzburg volunteer companies was called out for drill, twenty members were absent. having left for the diamond fields. This was in 1870.

The diamond news could be made very sensational; but it is

[Page 608]

better to say little than too much. No doubt large numbers of diamonds have been found and discoveries are being made every day. About 600 men are at the Fields. The Every day witnesses the departure of parties for the diamond fields. At Hopetown on the great Orange river the people are going mad. And the place is being deserted; so says one of the local correspondents. Parties swarms along the roads.

A brief but most interesting letter in the (Friend) of the Free State of the 23rd of June gives a fair estimate of the success of the diggers over at least a portion of the field. Whether the writer be an overseer or not, we are not informed; but it seems to be his buisness

[Page 609 Diamond]

to "take a round through the tents," to ascertain what parties have been successful during the day; and, if we may judge from the letter, he has no objection to tell the world the result of his visits. Such a gentleman is just the man the newspapers and the news reading public are in search of; and as his letter seems singularly destitute of anything like exaggeration. or even enthusiasm. we may. we beleive. rely upon its statements. It is within the certain knowledg of this gentleman that thirty diamonds had been discovered in the diggings on the four days previous to the date of his writing (the 7th of June). A "number he remarks, "which consid

[Page 610]

ering there are about fiver hundred men digging, is not so very great after all." He makes a brief reference to the luck of several parties. "Some of the Bloemfontain [Bloemfontein] parties," he tells us, "have been successful. Slock and Van Venrooi[7] have three or four diamonds; Green's party, I beleive, two; but the most fortunate company is Messrs. Shaw. Jollie, and Deneys. The very first day they washed, out of two loads of earth a diamond of thirteen carats was found, valued at £320 to £350. They have not found anything since. On the other hand, we hear of dozens of people who have been digging from a month to six weeks, and have got nothing." Some of the Boers, disheartened at their want of success, talk of leaving the fields, while new ones comers are still

[Page 611 Diamonds]

pressing on to try their luck.

The Tyd [De Tijd][8] (Free state paper) says: - "The diamond mania is raging among our officials. The government Secretary has gone and left a man in his place who a few weeks ago knew nothing of the duties of the office.

The Postmaster General, who had been pertinaciously importuning the Volks raad [Volksraad][9] for assistance, has gone too as fast as he could to the El Dorado, and left his office to anybody to discharge. The President is very indulgent to all applicants for leave to go; in short, nobody is refused, so that there is reason to beleive that one of these days His Honor will have to discharge the duties of all the Government offices himself."

[Page 612]

All the foregoing was in the early stage of the diggings in the year 1870 on the Banks of the far famed Vaal river, which devieds two Dutch republican governments, one caled the Orange Free state, represented by President Brand, and the other is represented as the Trans Vaal [Transvaal] governed by H.

---

7. Eli Wiggill Autobiography, 109, contains alternate spellings of these names.

8. *De Tijd* means *The Time* in Afrikaans, and it was the name of a newspaper published in the Oranje-Vrystaat (Orange Free State) Province.

9. Volksraad means "the House of Assembly" in Afrikaans.

CHAPTER 32

Potorus [M. Pretorius],[10] but the land was owned by a native Chief whos name was Waterbore [Waterboer].[11] He was a Chief of eather the griquas or Korannas [Koranas] or both togather, And in his country was where the diamonds was first discovered at a mission station caled Penal [Pniël].[12] and at a crossing of the river caled Klipe Drift [Klipdrift], or in english it is Stoney Fords [Stony-ford][13] And as the diamonds were found near his Station he demanded a cirtain

[Page 613]

portion of what the diggers found for a time while the diggers was under the superintendence of a man by the name of Parker also a digger.[14]

At this time both these Presidents of the two states wanted to clame the territory where the diamonds were found, and Waterbore the Chief owner of the land gave his clame over to the British government and to put down all disputes the British government sent a responsible man to take charge of it, and licensed the diggers so much for a diamond clame to the great annoyence of Preisent Brand and the Dutch republic which caused a paper War for over one year, which was

Gold [Page 614]

eventualy settled by Brand going to England and it was settled thare by the home authoritys which they did by giving the free state several thousand Pounds to be expended on the railway works.

---

10. Marthinus Wessel Pretorius was the "first president of the South African Republic [elected in 1857].... He was "re-elected President in 1868, [but] he resigned in 1871.... He died in Potchefstroom, during the South African War, on May 19, 1901." Rosenthal, *Encyclopedia of Southern African*, s.v. "Pretorius, Marthinus Wessel."

11. On September 17, 1896, "Nicholaas (Nicolaas) Waterboer, Griqua chief of Griquatown and eldest son of Andries Waterboer and his wife Gertruida Pienaar, dies in Griquatown. He was born in 1819." *South African History Online*.

12. Pniël was a "Dutch Reformed mission station between Stellenbosch and Groot Drakenstein, established in 1843. The name is of biblical origin (Gen. 32:20), referring to the place where Jacob wrestled with God; it means 'face of God.' The name was also given to a station of the Berlin Missionary Society founded on the Vaal River near Barkly West in 1849." It is the mission station at Barkly which Wiggill is referring to, as Rosenthal, *Encyclopedia of Southern Africa*, s.v. "Pniel," 436, notes. Pniel was a "mission station and diamond digging centre near Barkly West." Raper, *Dictionary of Southern African Place Names*, s.v. "Pniël," 445.

13. Reference to diamonds first being found in the region of the Vaal River at "places called Phiel and Klip-drift, or Stoney-ford." See "Stoney-ford," 374.

14. Stafford Parker, an adventurous digger selected as president of "another free and independent Republic on the Vaal" after President Pretorius had given exclusive rights to three people to mine this wealthy region. Gardner Fred Williams, *The Diamond Mines of South Africa*, 1:159–60.

A little before this time of the diamond discovery, there was a rumor of the existence of vast and rich fields of gold in the interior, North of the Vaal river, attracting numbers of prospectors but as yet without any positive result.

With regard to these gold fields they appeared to have been worked by some party or nations some centurys back as large pits or holes were found where gold had evidently been taken out, and there were

[Page 615]

fragments of hewn stone lying about in differant places, and near the gold pits, But when or who the people were is unknown at this preasent time.

The reader may wonder how it was that a mission Station was in that locality for forty or fifty years passed and never discovered Diamonds, as many lay on the surface of the ground I can only account for it in this way, has many parts of Africa is strwn with bright crystles like transparent glass, especily on the Orange river and also on the banks of the Caledon and Vaal river, and many other streams, so I expect the missionerys and travelers must have looked on the diamonds as not

[Page 616]

hing more than crystals.

I will now leave the diamond field for a little while I may speake of it again by and by.

Well after returning from King Williamstown and British Kaffraria has mentioned before, to Bongolo were my Son John resided and stayed with him for about two years and went to work at my trade and made some 8 Wagons such as they use for Freighting or Transporting goods from the seaports to the interer towns and villiags, and for bringing Wool and other produce to the differant seaports.

Those Wagons are twenty feet in length and about four feet in width, and made of the very best of materials both of wood

[Page 617 Cape Wagon]

Iron, The axels are made in England, from a model or pattern sent home for the purpose, and are sent out to Africa in differant sizes for both light and heavy Wagons, The African or Cape wagon are very different in the make from eather English or Amiracan Wagons.

Being a model from the Origenal Dutch Wagons which sutes the country much better than the English or the American Wagons would do, as the wheels of those Wagons are spoked too stright or in other words not dished enough to hold heavy loads, as a general the roads are eather very rough or very sideling It is a very common thing to see these

[Page 618]

CHAPTER 32

Wagons drawn by twelve and sixteen well trained oxen, and two persons to conduct them which is the Leader and the Driver and to protect the goods from the weather when Loaded they have a cover caled the Tarpolen that they draw over the length and breadth of the Wagon when the weather is bad but at other times it is foulded up and carried on the top of the load,

And for the conveience of carring passingers they have what is caled a tent in the back part of the Wagon about 8 feet in length, and to get in and out of the Wagon they generaly have a light a Ladder some 6 or 8 feet long which makes it very conveniant for Ladys

[Page 619]

traveling, And besides that there is also place caled a trap for the purpus of carring the Cooking Utensils, But in English it is caled a step. This Trap is framed and mortised togather with bares and hangs under the back part of the Wagon forming the step.

After discribing the carriers heavy Wagon which is comonly caled in the Cape the Buck Wagon, I thought I would discribe the Dutch farmers traveling Wagon such as they have had in use for over a hundred years in Cape Colony, There is no people I suppose in the world who is more peticular about their Wagons than a Cape Dutchman,

[Page 620]

nor is there any people that is a better judge of a good Wagon than they are. When they go to examine a Wagon they take hold of the Wheel and give it a shake to see if it is likely to run well, Then they will knock the fellies[15] with their nuckels to see if the wheel is tite and will ring well,

Then they will take a knife and get under the Wagon and chip bits of where it wont be seen to see what kind of wood it is made of, has they are exelant judges of all the wood that Wagons are generaly made of.

Then he will ask the Wagonmaker if he can warrant that Wagon to be made of dry and well seasoned wood, Has

[Page 621 Cape Wagon]

a Dutchman would generaly have his wood drying six or sevan years before he would have it built in a Wagon. And there is but very few Wheelwright that can please them especely an English Wheelright that had lately come over from England, But has I learned my trade in the Cape Colony it came easey for me to make such Wagons as would sute their taste. Now I will try and discribe the Dutch traveling wagon.

---

15. Fellies, or felloes, are segments or whole rims of a wooden wheel to which the spokes are attached, and onto which metal tires are usually shrunk. The Free Dictionary, s.v. "felloe."

In the first place the after Wheels are from four feet ten inches to five feet, and the front Wheels are three feet six inches high, with the felles [felloes] measure in depth four and a quarter inches with a neat Moulden

[Page 622]

all around each Wheel and every spoke with a neat quarter bead up the center of each spoke leaving a square on the spoke at the Hub, or nave of the Wheel, The length of the Wagon is about 14 feet, And the width three and a half to four feet that is to say between the sids,

The sides are framed togather having thirteen flat bars mortised, and the top rail being bent about a foot makeing the side about three feet high at the back part of the Wagon, While the front part of the side is about twenty two inches heigh, And the bottom of the Wagon is made of two inch plank firmly scrwed or riveted togather. riveted with

[Page 623]

crossbars back and front and two in the center projecting about a foot on which rests two side boxes one on each side about three feet in length and about a foot deep, which is compleatly waterproof, And in them they pack their Provisions and drinking cups, and in fact every little conveinance that is used on the road when traveling is put into those Boxes and all locked up, and then there is the front Chest which the driver sits on and also the Leader when he is not in front of the Oxen, there is very often a Chest at the back of the Wagon and if not a neat tailboard,

[Page 624]

Then, for the convenience of sleeping they have what swong in the Wagon what is caled in the Cape a Cartle with head and footboard, and on each side of the Wagon, inside they have canvas pockets which they fill with cloaths and anything they may need when traveling.

Now I will discribe the top of the Wagon in the first place there is six bars to each sides being twelve in all about four feet in length riveted or scrwed to the sides, on the top of those bars comes the Bows, bent to the shape and riveted to the up right bars, and then comes about twenty bars which is caled the rids

[Page 625 Cape Wagon]

which is neately beaded This tent does not come to the front of the Wagon not by three feet so as to give the driver room to use his Whip, which will reach over ten Oxen when he is siting on the Chest. And to make the Wagon more comfortable there is a plank on each side. (inside) resting on the top rail, and screwed or riveted to the upright bars that as been already mentioned which supportes the tent, so the smallest artical can not lose out of the Wagon.

CHAPTER 32

On the top of those side boards there is a rail on each side notched and riveted to the upright bars that supports the tent on the top of the Wagon,

[Page 626]

and is the length of the inside of the Wagon, And to these rails on the out side is tacked a lining of green Baze [baize][16] generaly. And over that again is tacked a covering of canvas which is well painted on the outside. And over this again comes the top sail of made of good canvas which covers in the hole, both back front and the sides comeing about 18 inches below where the under saile is tacked on, The back and front is left so that they can be roled up in the day, and closely fastened down with brass buttons at night, and the sides is also secured with brass buttons driven into these uprights. The buttonholes are made very nearly in the canvas generaly with

[Page 627]

a soft bit of Leather for a foundation and cut in the shape of a heart. and altogather makes the Wagon perfectly warn and Water proof, so that the heavyest storms can not penetrate and with such Wagons it is a pleasure to travel with a family, But of corse they have a trap at the back of the Wagon like the one discribed on the freight or carrier, Wagon, and for the conveinence of the Dutch Ladys who often weighs as much as three hundred pounds and over,

They have leighter ons which they call Horse Wagons fitted up in the same manner and is drawn by six or eight strong Horses. Those Wagons which has been

[Page 628]

discribed costs from 70 80 and to a hundred pounds sterling.

---

16. Baize, green wool or cotton fabric resembling felt, covered tented or half-tented wagons in southern Africa. Baize is commonly used on the tops of billiard tables. Hendrick A. Brouwer, ed., *Practical Hints to Scientific Travellers*, 1:31.

Chapter 33

After discribing the African Wagons I now settle down with my son John on his farm 8 miles from Queens Town [Queenstown], To make a few of these Wagons for some of my relations at their particular request, as they were all glad to see me back amongst them once more from America, The Wagons I am about to make is of the discription of the ~~discript~~ first one discribed which is the fright Wagon which at that time my friends were all engaged in. The first one that I made was for my Brother Elijah, And

[Page 629]

he was very glad to think there was another chance to get another Wagon of my make, Has I had made him one ten years before, before I left Africa to come to America, And that same Wagon he had in his possession when I went back to Africa. But accedently he had broke one of the front Wheels and strang to say instead of geting that one repaired he had a new Wheel made and after I got to work I repaired it for him

Nothing would have induced my Brother to have parted with that Wagon if I had not gone back to Africa a gain to make him another one.

For he was keeping it in rememberence of me and my work,

[Page 630]

But has I was there to make him another Wagon he sold that Wagon for sixty pounds after useing it for ten years, in heavy work, so I made him two Wagons one for a keepsake which had a good of fancy work on it in the way of Carving. And which he kept in Lew of the one that he sold, and the other one he put on the road to hard work,

The next one was for my Son John. And the next one was for my Soninlaw William Lowe

And the fifth one was for a nephew of mine by the name of James Merphy, and the sixth one was for my Brotherinlaw Francis. P. Bently [Bentley].

And the seventh one was for my Brother

[Page 631]

Moses Wiggill, and the eight one was for Francis Wiggill my Brother's Son.

For all those Wagons the parties found their own material that is the Timber. And to these Wagons I neither made sides nor Buck or rack as the Americans call it.

And for makeing those Wagons I received thirty pounds for each one for my labour, which makes £240, and if I could have stayed longer I could have made as many more and all for my relations, They would often come

CHAPTER 33

to see me and want to know when I was going to make them a Wagon, so I had to tell them that I could not make Wagons for them all for my time was

[Page 632]

too short to stay with them I found it very hard work having to work such very hard wood, I think it was the hardest Timber that I ever worked.

And at that time Wagon Timber was very scarce on account of it been baught up to make Wagons and Carts to go to the Diamond fields for the demand was greater than could be supplyed, and where there was wood to be got it was imposable just then to get a Wagon to go after it where it was to be Sold for they were all going to the Diamond field so most of the parties that I made the Wagons for had to pay almost dubble for the Timber But they did not care

[Page 633]

so long has they could get it, so that I could make the Wagons while I was there with them.

While working at those Wagons I took my time and worked at my leasure has I was not bound to time. So now and then I would take two and three days or a week to visit amongst my relations and friends for a change sometimes I would go with my Son John for two or three on buisness with his Wagon.

One time I will mention on the 16th of September 1870 I left the Bongolo with my Son John for to go to the Bush for to get three Loads of Timber into Krelis[1] Old Country a distance of 60 miles, The first day we got to St Marks Mission Station,[2] the station belonged

[Page 634]

to the Church of England and the Minester name was Rev. Cannon [Canon] Waters.[3] stayed there on Sunday, and on Monday 18 we left for the Bush

---

1. Kreli, a Xhosa chief born around 1818 to his father Hintsa. Kreli rose to prominence in 1854 when he defeated Tembu warriors. He displayed remarkable diplomatic skills during negotiations with the British. Kreli died in February 1893. Rosenthal, *Encyclopedia of Southern Africa*, s.v. "Kreli," 305.

2. St. Mark's Mission Station was established by the Scottish Episcopal Church to proselyte among Bantu peoples of the Eastern Cape. By 1873, St. Mark's was "a prosperous Mission village with trades of many kinds flourishing around it—'the centre of Christianity and civilization' for some 500 Europeans and 95,000 natives." C. F. Pascoe, *Two Hundred Years of the S. P. G.: An Historical Account of the Society for the Propagation of the Gospel in Foreign Parts, 1701-1900 (Based on a Digest of the Society's Records.)*, 313. See also Henry Bredekamp and Robert Ross, eds., *Missions and Christianity in South African History*; Elizabeth Isichei, *A History of Christianity in Africa: From Antiquity to the Present*, 98–127; Bengt Sundkler and Christopher Steed, *A History of the Church in Africa*.

3. Rev. H. T. Waters served at the St. Mark's Mission Station rather than Rev. Canon Waters, but Canon may have been a nickname. Pascoe, *Two Hundred Years of the S. P. G.*

which was 20 miles from the Station and arrived there at sundown and at night it came on a drizling rain which made it very disagreable and on the next day we went to Mr Winters who kept a small tradeing store and baught Timber from the sawers who worked in a neighboring Forest. And on tuesday 20th we loaded up three Wagons with Timber. And on the 21 left Mr Winters on our return home, with the wind blowing a perfect gale while assending a long ridge several miles in length which made it

[Page 635]

very disagreable to travil and on the 22 we got to a trading station which was kept by a German where we stayed all night and found them very agreable people, and I had quite a chat with them untill a late hour all about America He haveing relations there, in the City of Baltimore.

And on the 23rd got back to St Marks Station on our way home. And on the 24th arrived in the Bongolo at my Son's house in good health. And haveing seen a part of the Country that I had never seen before, and I was very much pleased with the appearance of it, It was mostly inhabited by Kaffers belonging to Krelis with here and

[Page 636]

there a White man staying on farms and living under the Kaffer Law and such was Mr Winters where we loaded up the Timber.

I was very comfortable when at home with my Son John. And most of the time my Daughter was right there with me who went out to Africa with me which still made it more pleasant But in the mean time she was twice away to the Diamond field with her Husband, and at times my Son would be away to the Diamond fields for a month at a time, with his Wagons, But his Wife was always at home and made me very comfortable, so the time passed along quite agreable has I had other relations in

[Page 637]

the neighborhood that I often went to visit with, and sometimes I would go on Horseback as far has Queenstown and to visit friends living there has I once resided there myself, And also had relations living there.

On another occation I made a visit to the Winterberg to see my Brother George Wiggill, has I wished to see him on peticular buisness concirning a long journey which he was going to take into the Trans Vaal Country which lays behyond the great Orange and Vaal rivers where he had buisness to attend to, And has I had never seen that Country and he having invited me to accompany him I thought I would go, So on the 16th of Nov

[Page 638]

ember 1870 I left Bongolo on my way to the Winterberg on Horseback which was some 60 or 70 miles from Bongolo and I went the over a very ru-

CHAPTER 33

ged rough mountain on a road which is caled a Bridle path. being a spoor of the well known Hunglip [Hangklip]4 mountain in the Queenstown district. This rough path saved me four or five miles other wise I would have had to go right through Queenstown. This brought me to the ~~mission~~ Wesleyan mission Station at Lesenton [Lesseyton] which is a very pritty place which as been alread discribed and from there I crossed the Classmits [Klaas Smits] river coming to an old friend of mine Joseph Ralph5 living on the Swart Kie [Zwart Kei] river where I stayed for the night. And the next morning after

[Page 639]

traveling three or four miles I came to Mr Westerber's [Mathew Roudman Westerbar]6 farm who was a distant relation of mine and I found him in a very poor state of health, But very comfortabley fixed as far as worldly goods is concerned living a Batchlers life with his Son, and there I had to stay two nights on account of stormy weather, and we talked over a great many things of by gone days, And from there I went across the Country takeing a short cut which my friends directed me which I found without any trouble. and caled on a Mr Padden [Paddon]7 who had married a young Lady whom I knew and has I had a message fror her from her friends in America I wanted to see

[Page 640]

her. She been a Daughter of an old friend of mine by the name of Wall.

Her husband was at that time a School Teacher to a Mr George Whightheade [Whitehead]8 Children. She recognized me at once and was

---

4. Hangklip mountain rises some "15 km north-north-west of Queenstown, on the border between the districts of Glen Grey and Queenstown. *Hangklip* is Afrikaans for 'hanging rock,' presumably referring to the precipitousness of the cliffs. The Xhosa name for this mountain is Emfabantu, said to mean 'death of the people,'" presumably from an incident where rocks fell and killed Xhosas. Raper, *Dictionary of Southern African Place Names*, s.v. "Hangklip Mountain," 198.

5. Wiggill would have been acquainted with Joseph Ralph for about fifty years. Ralph was twenty-seven years old when he embarked with the Ford party onboard the *Weymouth* from Portsmouth on January 7, 1820. He is listed as a "labourer and naval pensioner." He came to the Cape with his wife Elizabeth, 28, son Joseph, 3, and daughter Mary who perished at sea. Nash, *The Settler Handbook*, 72.

6. Mr. Westerbar served as superintendent of Isaac Wiggill's water mill. *Grahamstown Journal*, February 10, 1848. See Ancestry's record for Lydia Sayers (sister of Mary Sayers, wife of Isaac Wiggill) and her husband Mathew Roudman Westerbar, likely the gentleman Wiggill is referring to.

7. Mr. Padden appears to be either William Edwin Paddon or Edward William Paddon. British 1820 Settlers to South Africa.

8. Farmer George Whitehead, age 25, joined the Wainwright Party (no. 38 on the Colonial Department list) that was led by Jonathan Wainwright from Leeds,

very glad to see me, The weather being very bad and made traveling unpleasent I stayed with them two nights. This ~~pl~~ farm was just at the foot of the two noted Table Mountains in the Tarka district. The morning I left there the clouds was very heavy and I expected I should get a ~~thor~~ thorough weting but it kept cloudy all the day and made it pleasent to travil. And in the evening I arrived at my Brothers House in the Winterberg all right

[Page 641]

but found him very poorly in health, and I told him that I had come to go with him on that Journey but he had given up the idea of going after giving me all that trouble of riding all them miles on purpose. Well has he had given up going I stayed with him about five weeks and visited my sister Elizabeth who lived about six or seven miles away at a place caled Calehook [Kaal Hoek] where she as resied [resided] for many years and brought up her family been a widow for many years,

And from there I visited a friend name George Sumner[9] Father in law to my Brother George, and also other friends who lived in the neighborhood.

[Page 642]

And while staying at my Brothers I intened to visit Post Reteif [Retief] to see some of my old friends who was living there but the Knoap [Konap/Koonap] river being so swollen through the late rains that I did not consider it safe to cross it, so I did not get to see them at all.

So at the end of five weeks and on the 14 of Dec I ~~got~~ left ~~to~~ my Brothers House on my way back to the Bongolo, And when I left the morning was very fine and not a cloud to be seen

But when I got to the top of the Winterberg on the Wagon road which crosses over. I could see heavy Clouds luming up at a distance, which I knew well to be thunder clouds, being accustumed to seeing them

[Page 643]

that I almost made up my mind that I would get a good soaking before I got to any shelter, has I had about 15 or 20 miles to ride over the spoor's or ridges of the big Winterberg on the Turka side which was a very lonely road, and I was alone and the clouds kept geting more dence and heavy over my head, untill I got within a mile of the first House on the road, when the thunder began to roar and the Lightning began to flash and the rain began to pour down in torents ~~s~~which I was expecting from the appearance of the clouds, and in about five minuts I was wet through haveing no waterproof

---

Yorkshire. Nash, *The Settler Handbook*, 131.

9. George Sumner was born in 1851, and he died on February 5, 1941. He was buried in the Queenstown Cemetery. His wife Susan Augusta, born in 1861, bore him a child, Issac Sydney Bruce Sumner. British 1820 Settlers to South Africa.

CHAPTER 33

[Page 644]

with me, But when I arrived at the house which was the first on the road and those people were relations of Mr Edrd Goddard where I intended to stay that night, so I took shelter at this place untill the storm abated siting in my wet cloaths, But they were kind enough to make me a cup of coffee which was very exceptable

So when the storm abated I was about to saddle up and start and just then Mr Goddard just happened to drop in and through his kind invitation I went with him and was made very comfortable for the night and their kindness I shall forget for myself and my Horse, and on the next day I found

[Page 645]

myself feeling very poorly from takeing a bad cold through geting so wet has I was still 30 miles from my home, I left Mr Goddards the next morning and traviled untill I came to my old friend Mr Ralphs who resided on a Farm on the Swart Kia [Zwart Kei] river and it was very luckey that I crossed the river that night, for in the night and from the same storm that caught me the day before came down and flooded the river so that I would not have been able to cross it for a day or two,

And while I stayed at Mr Ralphs I felt very poorly and wished myself at home, so I started the next morning, and

[Page 646]

when I came to the Klaas smits river I found that flowing pritty rappid but I got across all safe

Then striking a crossing the country leaving Lessenton [Lesseyton] on the left about a half mile, and caling at an acquaintence of mine William Staples[10] has he was about on the Line of road that I was on, and when I reached the house I found that both Him and his Wife was away on a visit to Queenstown, But their Daughter was at home and was very thoughtful and made me a very nice cup of Tea which refrished me has I felt so poorly and in the mean time I rested while my Horse feed, and while there the clouds

[Page 647]

lumed up as they did the day before and gathered blackness al around especly in the direction which I was about to ride, As the weather looked so thretning, the girl wanted me to stay all night and see her Father and Mother said she knew that they would be glad to see me and that they would be at home soon. But being so near home and having that rough and rugged mountain to cross I thought I would start although it looked very suspicious and I

---

10. Although there are several William Staples listed on the 1820 settler's list, the one most likely referred to here is William Mosyer Staples, born in the Albany District on June 24, 1825. He passed away December 15, 1907, in Queenstown.

thought that I would get another weting but luckely it held up untill I arrived in the Bongolo and stoped at my Brother Elijah house then it just poured

[Page 648]

down rain with thunder and Lightening like it did the day I got so wet.

That part of Cape Colony is very frequently visited with such Storms in the Summer time as I have just discribed.

So I got home to my Son John's where I made my home on the 16 of December and when I got there I found my Daughter Fannie had come home, who had been away for several months visiting her Sister Sarah Ann who lived in the district of King William's Town on a Farm. Her sister and Husband Mr W. James[11] brought her home to where I was staying, But it happened that they had left to return to their home before I arrived for which I was very sorry, For I would liked to have seen them.

[Page 649]

So after I got settled down I made no more long visits for a year for I had so much work before me at makeing those Wagons.

So I contunied on to work, and about June or July has near has I can remember 1871 a letter came to my Brother Elijah saying that my Brother George was dangerously ill and wished Elijah to come down to see him as quick as posable that he wanted to see him,

So Elijah and myself got ready and went with out delay, and when we got there we found him very sick appearently in the last stage of Consumption, and the Doctor of Fort Baufort [Beaufort] so in attendance examined him and found that

[Page 650]

his Lungs were about gone and gave him but very slite hopes of his recovery

So my Brother and myself stayed with him about a week, The most principal thing that he wanted to see Elijah for was to make him his Executor in cace of his Death has he seemed to know of no other whom he could trust as well has his Brother Elijah, Elijah would rather he would have chosen someone els, but as it was his Brothers particular request he did not like to refuse him and told him that he would do the best he could according to his ability, so during the week he conversed a good deal on differant subjects but mostly on reg

[Page 651]

religion has he had studied the Bible a good deal of late years and had for more than ten years before had embraced the doctrin and faith of the Latter day Saints which I fully beleived in.

---

11. There are many males with the surname James and a first initial beginning with W. See possibilities for W. James at British 1820 Settlers to South Africa.

CHAPTER 33

So after sattisfing my Brother in buisness matters we left him and returned home, But before we left, Brother Elijah asked him if he would like to take a Journey as far has Queens Town [Queenstown] thinking a change might do him good and there being a good Doctor in Queenstown whos name was Doctor Krance [Krantz],[12] He thought that he would venture if Elijah would come and assist him in the Journey, which Elijah

The Death of George [Page 652]

promised to do.

So after we had got home Elijah started in a few days back to Winterberg to make arraingments to bring my Brother to the Bongolo if he was not too weak, so having a good comfortable traveling Wagon he thought he could stand the Journey, so he started in company with his Wife and his two little girls and also a Daughter of fifteen by a former Wife,

They traveled through the Kat river and up the new Kat Berg [Katberg] road so as to avoid rough roads, and when they arrived on the top of the Katberg Mountain Elijah told me that he breathed better and more free and easey than he had for some time which was oweing to the frish air on the mountain

[Page 653]

But when they arrived in the Bongolo which was in the evening, and in the morning of the same day I left to go two or three days with my Son in law William Low and his family on their way to the Diamond field

And on the next day my Son John over took us, He also going to the Diamond field, and it was then that I heard of the arrival of my Brother George in the Bongolo, so I accompanyed them as far as the village of Dordreht [Dordrecht][13] on the top of Stormberg Mountain so after I had bid them good by and seen them started, I stayed and spent a day there with a friend whos name

---

12. The *Queenstown Free Press,* January 16, 1894, noted, "German papers to hand by last mail give very interesting particulars of the life and work of the late Dr KRANTZ, whose name is household to the older inhabitants of Queenstown, Cathcart and Tarkastad. We quote from the '*Rheinischer Kurier,*' Wiesbaden, dated Dec. 2nd, 1893: On Wednesday last the remains of the late Dr KRANTZ were taken to their last rest. Dr KRANTZ was a gentleman who enjoyed very wide spread esteem and love in our town, where for the last fifteen years he has been a very successful practitioner."

13. Dordrecht, a town built on the northern slopes of the Stromberg, located "some 76 km north-north-east of Queenstown and 88 km southwest of Barkly East. It was established in 1856 on the farm Boschrand and became a municipality in 1867. It was named after Dordrecht in Holland, in memory of an historic synod of Reformed churches held there in 1618–1619." Raper, *Dictionary of Southern African Place Names,* s.v. "Dordrecht," 125.

[Page 654]

is T. Harden,[14] And leaving there the next day I caled on my Brother Joseph and stayed one night with him, and the next day I went to my Brother in Law Francis Bentleys who lives on the same farm and I found when I got there that he had also gone to the Diamond fields, so I stayed and spend a day or two with his family, I think it was about the third day I saddled up and had started from the House when I seen a Kaffir man going to the house, But as such people are often seen I took no notice of him and when I had got about a few hundred yards from the house I heard my Sister calling after me so I rode back to see what

[Page 655]

was wanting and when I got to her she told me that the man had a letter which aught to have been there the day before But the man lost his way

Well the letter contained the news of the Death of my Brother George,[15] so when I had heard the news I started again and had about 30 miles to travil alone, and reflecting on his Death and the many differant seens and changes that we had gone through for we had played and worked a great deal togather, in our time, so when got home the family and friends was just returning from Queens Town [Queenstown] from the funiral of my Brother, and soon after I got home

[Page 656]

my Brother Joseph came to attend the funeral but like myself was too late

My Brother just lived one week after coming to the Bongolo.

So after seeing him at his own home when my Brother Elijah and I went on the last visit, and when I left him then I thought in my mind and said so to Elijah that I never would see him again, and so it happened For as it has been stated they were just coming from the funeral when I got home, He being

---

14. There was a Timothy Roland Harding in Dordrecht, Eastern Cape, South Africa, at this time. This might possibly be the same person. Ancestry.

15. The *Grahamstown Journal*, June 2, 1871, noted, "DIED at Aloe Grove, Bongolo, near Queenstown, the residence of his brother Elijah WIGGILL, on the 29th inst, George WIGGILL of Bram Bush, Winterberg; aged 55 years. Friends at a distance will be good enough to accept this notice. Queenstown 30th May 1871." Several months later, this notice was published, culling from the *Fort Beaufort Advocate*: "The sale held by Mr. J.H. PARKER of the late Mr. Geo. WIGGILL's property was very successful. The farm "Brandbosch Spruit", 1,500 morgen, fetched £2,000, the BOTHAs being the purchasers. Another farm, "Thornhill", fetched £1,600. Oxen fetched £10 each; and a second-hand wagon and span of oxen together realised £205. Cows sold for £6, £7 and £8; hamels 8s9d; ewes and lambs, all to count, 6s6d. Many who had gone to the sale in the expectation of getting stock cheap were disappointed." *Grahamstown Journal*, November 13, 1871.

about 58 years old,[16] He was born in Glostershier [Gloucestershire] England in the year 1813.

He was what is caled a selfmade man for anything that he ever saw eather in machinery. Wagons and a great

[Page 657]

Millwright which was his favourite buisness in fact he has invented machinery that he had never seen such as grape crushing machinery and also a machine to run by the same Water pour to trach [thrash]Wheat.[17]

And the last time our Father seen him he said well George I dont know where you have got all your knowledge to make all these things that I see here around, You surpass me in makeing machinery altogather.

Well he was very ingenious in everything from a Boy

He by his hard work and industry he acculat accumulated a great deal of Wealth. As my Brother had a great deal of trouble with what is caled the Orphan Chamber, a kind of

<u>Cape Orphan Chamber</u> 658

Bank which takes care of money for Orphan Children, has I am writing in America I thought I would explain or give a short account of the Cape Orphon Chamber.

In the first place it was established by the Dutch Government many years ago, and when the English Government took it this Orphan Chamber remained as it was and contunies so up to this date,

And I suppose the reason why is because the greatest part of the community were Dutch, and I expect they thought it a good Law to protect their Orphan Children

All marriages that was entered into in the Cape Colony came under the Orphan Chamber Law and that was in

[Page 659]

case of the Death of eather one of the parties, they had to send a statement and that very correct one of all they possess eather Landed on money property or any other effects and after the account has been investigated by the Master

---

16. "It is our melancholy duty to record the death of Mr Elijah WIGGILL, which sad event took place at Bongolo on Friday last, the 21st inst. Mr WIGGILL was one of the original grantees of this district, taking possession of his farm in the Bongolo immediately it was allotted, and working it up to the day of his death. He was a fine specimen of the Colonial farmer and his farm was well worth a visit, where all were hospitably entertained. He passed quietly away on Friday at the ripe old age of 72. The funeral took place in Queenstown on Saturday and well attended. We tender our sympathy to the bereaved ones in their sad loss." *Queenstown Free Press*, July 25, 1893.

17. Wiggill is likely referring to a wheat-threshing machine.

as he is so caled He appoints a day of Sale, And accordenly everything is put up at auction, But the surviveing party as the prvlidge of buying in to half the value of the Estate,

And the other half is at the disposial of the master of the Orphan Chamber which as to be sent to him for the minor Children,

But if not sent they have to furnish good security Then money then lies in the Orphan

[Page 660]

Chamber Bank on intrest untill the Children become of age or get married,

But the intrest can be drawn for the Education and Cloathing of the Children untill they become of age,

But if there be any Children of age at the time they receive their portion at the time of Settlement But the surviveing partie is not allowed to get married again according to this Law till all is settled up satisfactorily, And any Clergyman marrying such parties before the Estate is settled is liable to a fine. But parties geting married in the Cape Colony by which is caled the ante nuptial contract as the generalty of marriages of late years have entered into this contract to avoid the

[Page 661]

Orphan Chamber's interfearence with their properity.

This ante-nuptial Law has far as I can understand is for each of the parties before been married to get a document drawn up by a component Lawyer and signed by Witnesses and tested before a magistrate so that each party can will their property to whom they like.

So to exempt the settlers of 1820 who were married in England from this Dutch Law that was in force in the Cape Lord Charles Somerset which was at that time Govenor of Cape Colony issued a proclamation exempting the settlers from this said Dutch Law.

[Page 662]

The following is his proclamation.

It shall be considered lawful and of full force to all residents and settlers in the Colony of the Cape of Good Hope, being natural born subjects of the Kingdom of Great Britain and Ireland, to enjoy the same rights of devising their property both in real and personal, as they would be entitled to exercise under the laws and customs of England; provided, however that in case any such natural born subjects shall enter into the marriage state within the Settlement without making a previous marriage settlement, (ante nuptial contract) his property shall be administered according to the Colonial Law."

Grave doubts of the legal force of this proc

[Page 663]

lamation have been maintained by two of the Cape Attorneys General, and the consequence has been that several of the settlers after accumulating large wealth, have removed to England to enjoy their birthright; and capitalists thus deterred from settling or remaining in the Colony, the creation of a permanently resident monied aristocracy has been prevented, or at least postponed.

[Page 664]

Chapter 34

So after the Death of my Brother I felt ancious to get those Wagons finished that I had on hand, for by this time I had been away from my Home in Utah about two years. And begining to feel ancious to return home I finished the Wagons, eight in all, and made several fancey Boxes as keepsakes for my friends

And feeling more ancious to leave the Bongolo I wanted to spend a month or six weeks in Cape town with a Friend whom I had coresponded with from the time of putting in at Cape Town on my way out from America. My friend's name is Mr George Ruck.[1] And settleing all my little affairs and biding my

[Page 665]

relations and friends farwell has I expect never to see them anymore in this life.

And as my Son John and others where about to start with several Wagons loaded with Merchandise for the Diamonds fields.

(Three of those Wagons were of my own make)

And has I had arrainged to go to the Diamond field with this company, I left the Bongolo on the ~~tweel~~ twelfth of December 1872 after staying with my Son about 2 years and a half, which He, and others of my friends done everything they could to make me comfortable while I stayed with them,

And there in the

[Page 666]

Bongolo I left my Daughter Fannie with two little Children who went out with me from America. Her husband having started for the Diamond fields some time before,

So when we got on the way two days from the Bongolo it brought us to my Brother in Laws farm Francis Bentley where we stayed one day has he was sending two Wagons also loaded with merchandise for the fields

Having wished his family farewell, we traveled on till the 15 of December when we came to a Village caled Willow Park,[2] to have some repairs done to one of the Wagons This village contains a Blacksmith Shop, and Wheel ~~shop~~ wright shop and also a very large

[Page 667]

---

1. George Ruck may have been born in 1781 and later married Ann Collyer on April 30, 1815. FamilySearch.

2. Willow Park is about fifteen miles from Dordrecht. Rev. G. Weaver, "SOUTH AFRICA: A Trip with the Chairman through the Northern Part of the Queenstown District," 283.

CHAPTER 34

veriety store and an Inn an accommodation for travelers, And on the 16 of the month we left Willow Park, and soon arrived on the top of the Storemberg Mountain range being a high and elevated country laying between the Queenstown district and the Orange river, or the district of Albert[3] or Aliwal North.[4]

This elevated Country is inhabited by Dutch farmers. But I remember well when it was only inhabited by Game of vairous kinds and Wild Beasts such as Lions Tigers and Wolves.

It took us from three to four days to travil over this high country. In the winter it is very cold for Africa. But in the Summer when I crossed it, it was

[Page 668]

very pleasent.

And about the 20th of December 1872 we reached Aliwal North on the Great Orange river, there we were detained on account of the river being very high, and so many Wagons been there ahead of us which had to be Ferryed over on the Pont or ferryboat, and we had to wait our turn which kept us waiting two days, This river is several hundreds yards wide, and the Pont which is used takes one Wagon and twelve Oxen at a time, there were two Ponts going and coming all the time carring Wagons over at one pound each and strange to say in the two years that I was out there the river was in flood so that it was not fordable, And the Wagons

[Page 669 Orange]

had to be taken over on the Pont.

So we got over all safe, which was 8 in number to the company that I was with and all being my relations except one man.

We had an addition to our company of two young Ladys who wished to go to the Diamond field one of them was a Miss Saddler whos Parents was at the fields and the other one was a school companion of hers whos parents lived at Port Elizabeth.

---

3. The Albert "region [is] between the Stromberg and the Orange River embracing approximately the present districts of Albert, Wodehouse and Aliwal North. Named after the consort of Queen Victoria." Raper, *Dictionary of Southern African Place Names*, s.v. "Albert," 25.

4. Aliwal North, a town along the Orange River is "some 195 km from Bloemfontein, on the road to East London. It was founded in 1849 and named by the Governor of the Cape Colony, Sir Harry Smith (1847–1852), to commemorate his decisive victory over the Sikhs under Runjeet Singh at Aliwal in India on 28 January 1846. Municipal status was achieved in 1882." Raper, *Dictionary of Southern African Place Names*, s.v. "Aliwal North," 28.

So from there we traviled on till we came to the Caledon which detained us one day before we could cross on the Pont, I beleive our company was about the first to cross on that Pont it been just started, and

Free State [Page 670]

they charged one pound for every Wagon.

We was then in what is caled the Free State or what is caled the Dutch republican Orange Free State governed by President Brand. which is thickly inhabited by Dutch and English farmers But I knew it when it was inhabited mostly with wild game such as Quaggas Zebras Hartebeest and Blesbaks [Blesboks],[5] Weldebeast and Springboks by thousands and little troups of Ostrich's and where all this game abounded there were no scarcity of the Lordly Lion who preyed and lived on those animals, He would hide himself in bushes's on the river side and when the game would come to drink he would spring out upon them, And

[Page 671]

now and then might be seen a small villege of Bushmen who also lives on the game mentioned.

And at times the Dutch farmers catches their Children and makes servants of them.

I have seen some of those Children after been taken they are taken care of and get plenty to eat, and are better cared for than when romeing about the country, For the Bushman never cultivates the soil, and if he ever raises anything it is only a little Tobacco,

Their food consists generaly of wild game which they kill by pitfall or poisoned arrows and also bulbous roots of different kinds which they know well where to look for, and also Ostrich eggs which they often find from ten to fifteen in the nest away in the Desert prairie

Bushmen [Page 672]

And after useing the meat out of those eggs they use the shells for Water vessels, and fix them togather with cords and then hang them around their bodys, and if they are out on a long Journey they bury a number of those shells of water in the sand so has to save them on their return as water is a very scarice on these prairie deserts,

And also amongest their articals of food is the African Locusts and white Ants which they dig out of the earth and which resemble rice, in fact they are caled rice Ants.

---

5. Blesbok, a South African antelope, stands about one meter in height and runs very fast. It is now a protected species owing to excessive hunting. "The name 'bles' signifies a white patch, a characteristic feature of its markings." Rosenthal, *Encyclopedia of Southern Africa*, s.v. "Blesbok," 64.

CHAPTER 34

And some times they get a little wild Honey to mix with their Locusts and Ants They also make an intoxicateing drink from the honey and young Bees, mixing the combe with and leting it foment but wheather they

[Page 673 Bushmen]

add any herbs of any kind to help make their Beer or not I do not know.

Their homes are generaly in caves in the mountains you can generaly know their original caves by the paintings which they leave behind them in the caves painted in red ochre some resembling their own persons. But they produced images the most ridiculous that are more like apes than human beings

And in those caves are drawings of Lions Tigars and many other kinds of animals and in one cave in which I myself were in I saw a drawing of a company of Solders, Whatever they use to make their collors I dont know, But they keep brilliant I should say for fifty or a hundred years.

Many of the caves that

In the Orange Free State [Page 674]

I was in there is no knowing how long the figures had been painted that I saw and looked quite fresh.

If all the exploits and the adventures with Bushmen and Hottentots by the earley Dutch settlers of the Cape Colony were numerated would fill a volume

But as the Bushmans nation is so little known to the civilized world, I have been induced to write this short account of them, Having both seen and conversed with them.

Having said so much I will return to my friend again on the banks of the Caledon. Well we had several days travil before us over extencive plains but not destute of mountains we traviled between them leaveing one big flat to begin another and now

[Page 675]

and then crossing or fording a small river, Those flats were well covered with grass but rather destitute of wood only on the mountain sides where would be a few scraggy trees, The flats had quite a sprinkling of game on them such as springbok Blesbok and quaggs or Wild Ass,s and now and then an Ostrich as the Dutch farms was from 20 to 30 miles apart those animals had plenty of room to range, But in the vicinity of the farms they were hunted down pritty well, for we could hear their guns any hour in the daytime,

And the flats were litterly covered with bleached bones of animals that had been killed in former years,

At this time of the

[Page 676]

year which was near the last of December the sun shone so hot that we had to lay by in the day, and travil in the night, The roads were very good and the drivers knew it so well that it was no trouble to them For they had often traviled the road before, and thunder storms was every days accourence if it did not come upon us we would see them at a distance,

And as my Son often traviled this road he was well acquainted with the Farmers and sometimes they would get him to attend to some little buisness for them and at other times he would call and see them through friendship for they were always glad to see him.

[Page 677 Orange]

While on the road we passed a small village at a distance but I forget the name of it,

Some of the company went to it and baught a few articles which was needed, And at another time we passed a Moravian Missionary Station caled Betheny [Bethany][6], it is like a little village thickly planted with Weeping Willows and Locust trees and also having a beautifull Dam of Water and the people who are taught there are a part of a tribe of Koranna Hottentots and Bushmen.

And passing along we came to a very peticular friend of my Sons, named Fenter [Venter],[7] where my Son leaves his tired Oxen and gets fresh ones that th[8] has been resting for

Free State [Page 678]

a month or two.

And at this place brought in the New Year of 73 having had Christmas while near the Caledon river, and at the next farm where Mr Fneter's Brother lived, Mr James Murphy baught a Span of twelve Oxen I think at about ten pounds each they where all fat and in good order, and while they were bargaing for the Oxen I went into Mr Fenter's garden and had a good feast of mulberys which was of the large kind some of them as large as pigon eggs, and also enjoyed the shade of the Tree, as it was a very hot day, Those Mr Fenters were of a religous sect caled Doopers [Doppers][9] and will sing no other Hymns in their meetings but the

---

6. "[Bethany] Station of the Berlin Mission Society established in 1834 by Gebel and Kraul to serve the Korana. Hebrew for 'house of misery.'" Raper, *Dictionary of Southern African Place Names*, s.v. "Bethany," 52.

7. Venter, not Fenter, appears several times as a place name in the settlers' list. British 1820 Settlers to South Africa.

8. Wiggill began writing a word and then stopped; it is unclear what is meant here.

9. "Popular name for the Gereformeerde Kerk van Zuid Afrika, a section of the older Dutch Reformed Church (Nederduits Gereforemeerde Kerk), which seceded

CHAPTER 34

[Page 679]

Psalms of David, and seldom marry outside their own sect.

On leaving Fenters we past over simmerler plains and many farms and on each side has we traviled there were droves of springboks, and could see lots of Game at the distance and swarms of Locusts,

And as my Brother Joseph had gone to the Diamond field a few months before we found him living on a farm on the Banks of what is caled the Fatt river,[10] It took this name from its greasy appearance for when it is in flood it washes down the mud which looks like grease He was staying at this place for the convenience of his Cattle, for there was plenty of grass, We stayed

[Page 680]

with him one night.

This place is an open flat country with mountains in the distance, destute of wood only on the margan of the river, There is also plenty of good eating fish, this river with its tributary emptys itself into the Great Orange river,

On leaveing this place we did not pass many Houses on account of the country been short of good Water, we had several heavy sand ridges to get over before we came to the Diamond field and as some of our Wagons were heavely loaded they had a difficult job to get over them, The one that I myself was rideing in was several hours before it got over, But as it was in the night I did not trouble myself to get out of the Wagon has

[Page 681]

my assistance was not needed

And by this time we were drawing near to the field and the surrounding hills were dotted trees in the shape of umberellas caled the Camelthorn which is very hard and durable of the Mohogany color, we now came to a part of country where there were clumps of Mimosa and other shrub trees of small growth, so I think that we arrived at the field about the 4th of January, 1873 after being ten or twelve days from Queenstown.

Diamond Field [Page 682]

---

from the latter in 1859. It was begun by the Rev. Dirk Postma (q.v.) and follows the Presbyterian usage laid down in 1618–1619 by the Synod of Dordt, as revised in 1913 and 1924. The word 'Dopper' is believed to be a corruption of 'Dompter'—one who damps down—in allusion to their Calvinistic principles, even stricter than those of the older Church." Rosenthal, *Encyclopedia of Southern Africa*, s.v. "Doppers," 160.

10. Vet River [Vetriver] (Afrikaans for "fat"; Khoikhoi for Gy Koub: "large fat") is a tributary of the Vaal. Raper, *Dictionary of Southern African Place Names*, s.v. "Vet River," 567.

Chapter 35

As I am now at the Diamond field which has made such a stir in South Africa and also in Europe especially in England, But seems to be very little known in America although a great many people went from America to the African diamond feilds and worked themselves and found diamonds and also baught diamonds off the diggers.

And one Jentleman wrote a short History of the feilds which I heard was a very truthfull account, But I did not see it myself,

I have already given an account of the Vaal river diggins in its early state, But that dose not embrace the one which I will now discribe,

[Page 683 New Rush]

This one in the begining was caled the new rush, a Dutchman had a farm by the name of De Beer it was said that he found diamonds and kept it a secrete for a while, for he did not want the hundreds of diggers that was at the Vaal river to over run His farm Has a Dutchman dose not like to be crowded, But with all his endevers the secrete leaked out, and the concequence was that hundreds of diggers made one grand rush and took it by Storm to the grate annoyance of the Dutchman and his Wife who was very angery about it especely the wife when they had to leave their farm for they could not keep their Stock there any more for it was soon overrun

Diamond diggings [Page 684]

by thousands of both men and women from all parts of the Colony, so the Dutchman soon sold his farm to a merchant whos name was D. Ebden[1] of Port Elizabath.

And then the diggers had to pay a License for their clames to this Mr Ebden, for a very small bit of ground it might be 20 feet long by 6 or 7 feet wide on the surface, so that one man could only get one clame,

The way the men done at the first onset after geting a clame for themselves if they had Sons or Nephews they would send them to take up clames, and the advantage of those clames was after they had worked and made hundreds and thousands of Pounds out of them, Moneyed men

[Page 685 New Rush]

was contunily arriving at the feild, and wished to speculate in diamonds digging, and would give five hundred or a thousand Pounds for a half or a quarter of a clame.

---

1. Probably Alfred Ebden. Anneke Higgs, "The Historical Development of Diamond Mining Legislation in Griqualand West during the Period 1871 to 1880," 18–56.

CHAPTER 35

Now I want to give a discription of the field has it was when I was there myself in Jenury 1873, In the first place there is three places about two miles apart lying in a tryangle passion First, the first one mentioned as the new rush or Colesberg Coppy [Kopje][2] so named from a partie of diggers from the village of Colesberg, And the second is what is caled Old De Beers diamond digging, Then the third is caled De Toites pan so named after a Dutchman

Diamond diggings [Page 686]

by the name of De Toite and pan is a shallow sheet of water which covers two or three Acars of Land in rainy seasons. These diamonds villages as they may now be caled lays about 20 miles from the Vaal river or what is caled Clipt drift [Klipdrif][3] diamond digging which is also a village,

Now I will discribe the first diggings that I visited caled De Toites pan and where we unloaded the merchandise which we took up.

A good deale of it consisted of Brandy and Gin in fact all kinds of Liquor are taken to the fields.

Well I found De Toites pan reguarly layed out in streets with large Stores Hotells Resterants and everything for the conveiniance of Man and

[Page 687]

Beasts, To the best of my reclecleclection there was a hundred good Houses and several of the Stores were kept by Jews. And also Depots for the Overland passinger Coaches which was coming in two or three times a week from Cape Town Grahams Town [Grahamstown] and Port Elizabeth, and from all the Villages in the Colony, and besides the stage Coaches there were vehicles of all kinds runing from all the Towns and Villages in the Colony

And besides these there was an American Company had American made Coaches such as Wells Fargo & Co used across the Contenant in America before the railroad was built.

Now I must say

[Page 688]

somthing about the diggings where the people had excavated seeking for and and finding diamonds in the clay and gravel to the depth of some sixty or eighty feet untill they came to good frish water which was a great benifet to the people

---

2. Colesbert Kopje. Higgs, "The Historical Development of Diamond Mining," 18–56.

3. Klip Drift or Klipdrif (Afrikaans for "stony ford" or a shallow stream crossing) is a town on the Vaal River, some 36 km north-west of Kimberley that began as an alluvial diamond diggers camp in 1869 and was also called Parkerton after Stafford Parker. In 1870 it was renamed Barkly West after Governor Sir Henry Barkly. Raper, *Dictionary of Southern African Place Names*, s.v. "Barkly West," 70..

And also releived them from useing the water from the Horse pond which as been discribed.

From this place I went to what is caled the new Rush where my relations were staying, which was about two miles from De Toites pan.

This new rush is the princeable diamond diggings, I hardly know how to discribe it, in fact I feel almost like the Queen of Shaba when she visited Soloman

[Page 689]

I had heard a great deal about the place from my relations who had being traveling backwards and forwards for two years,

But when I seen it myself I could hardly realize that there had been so much done in such a short time, and there seemed to be as much buisness and bustle has one could emagion would be in London,

And to say how many Tents and Houses were there would be imposable but I judge they covered an hundred Acres scattered up and down,

And in every direction there were heaps of gravel which the diggers had hauled home to their tents to sive and surch for diamonds which[4]

[Page 700]

is caled dry diggings some of this gravel is hauled as much.as a mile away from the pit where it was taken out to be sived and surched when it is sived it is put on a Table and spreade very thin, with a ledg on the table so that it cant fall of only at a cirtain place where it is pushed of after being examined, Hence so many heaps of gravil for there is thousands of diggers and a heape of gravil to almost every house or tent.

I remember well when I was there in wl walking out one day to look around and going down to the clame, and on returning to go to where I was staying with my Sister Mrs Watson, and has I was on my way back I saw some

[Page 701 Colesberg Kopye [Kopje]]

thing that looked like Coal and thought I would have a look at it, and when I came to it I found it to be black rock where they had been diging a Well the Well was an ovel shape ten feet one way and six feet the other and I think some forty or fifty feet deep, and starting from there in the direction of the tent has I thought where I wanted to go it was then that I lost my way among the gravel hills, and had to retrace my steps to where I started in then I knew where I was, For that was in the vicinity of the store, then I knew where I was then I soon got home.

I think I will

[Page 702 or New Rush]

---

4. Wiggill jumped ahead for unknown reasons, counting to page 700 instead of what should have been pages 690–699.

CHAPTER 35

try to discribe the locality of the clames where the gravil came out, Has I was there and seen the place and was down in the clame which was about one hundred feet deep, and I had a drink of very good fresh water out of a broken bottel which William Lowe my Son in law gave me, He also owned parts of two or three clames and was showing me the differant clames, at that time he had let his clames out on shares to be worked.[5]

It happened to be on Sunday when I was down in those clames had it been on a week day I could not have had the chance for the men were there like Bees both White and Black men, But

[Page 703 Colesberg Kopye]

on another occasion, on a week day I was there looking around and down into the clames, all those numerous clames would cover the space of Ten Acers has nigh has I can judge and at first they left roads in between the clames so as to go in between with their Carts to haul the gravil away till they worked down so deep untill they began to cave in and became dangerous so that they had to abandon them and worked the gravil out by other means, which was addapted by means of small wire ropes on which the Bucket run on small pullies wheels those buckets were set in motion by windlass power by a small rope

Or new Rush [Page 704]

These windless's are on the margen of the diamond clame on all four sides,

And not being room for all the diggers on the ground they had to build up scaffold work to make platforms over the heads of other men to work their buckets,

And I have heard it remarked that it could not be compaired to anything but a spiderweb on a dwey morning,

And all around the clames was quite large ridges or mountains of gravil which had been taken out at the early stage of the digging,

And on the top of these gravil heaps the windless machinery was receted which as already been mentioned above and one ridge which

[Page 705 Colesberg Kopye]

was considerabley higher than the other they named it Mount Ararat.

And on one side there was a steam engine drawing the gravil out of the clames with little Trucks runing on rails layed down for the purpose and to work all this machinery there were hundreds of natives from the inter interior

---

5. William J. Lowe became wealthy through the diamond industry. "My father told me that while William indeed struck it rich working the claims, he was a man of enterprise and saw quickly that the serious money was being made not in the mining of the diamonds, but in the buying and selling of them. So, with no experience, except what the fields provided him, William became a diamond merchant and apparently acquired great wealth doing it." Lowe, *American Eden II*, 35.

I may say thousands employed by the clame owners to work the clames for them and mostly feed on flesh and rice, and that of the best quality,

And their pay was eather Fierarms or Silver or Gold coin, When one set had got their pay they would quit and go home and another set would come and work for the same like pay, and

Or New Rush [Page 706]

when asked what they was going to do with the firearms they would answer that they was going to shoot the Dutch farmers.

This diamond field that is to say this new rush that I have been trying to discribe, at some age of the world has been a volcano is very eveident, For down in the clame was found a kind of Lavia which had the appearance of volcanic action, and at other times while digging would come down on to layers of soft ashes, and at others it would be like hard Chalk and at other times they would come to differand collors of clay so it was not only gravil that was excovated out of the clames. These differant

[Page 707 Colesberg Kopye]

kinds of clay when exposed to the sun and air would slack like Lime, and diamonds would be found in all these differant kinds of clay and gravil, and strange to say that diggers out side of this clame dug holes to try to find diamonds but none was found out side that I ever heard of that is to say in the immeidate viscinity of the New rush although one part of the hill looked as likely as the other which was a long grassey ridge and had no appearance of a volcano, and after I was there I heard that they had to use pumps to get the water out of the clames after going down

or new Rush [Page 708]

another hundred feet and finding diamonds all the way. A person vewing it from the top it had the appearance of old ruins, For the clames was worked to various depths makeing it appear like the ruins of an Old Castle, and everything was covered with a white chalk or Whitening which was very injurious to the health of the diggers especely to them who sived the gravil so that several of the Natives died from effects of the accumalation of dust settleing on their Lungs.

Well having discribed the machinery and Tackel by which they draw the gravil from the clames and many other Items, I will try

[Page 709]

and discribe the appearence and traffic and buisness of the place, In walking around the place, I saw scores of Liquer saloons, some of them was kept in large Markie [marquee] Tents[6] and others in Cottages, But while I am speak-

---

6. Marquee tents are large canopy tents.

CHAPTER 35

ing of Liquer saloons I will give a short account of one which was kept in a firstclass stile, by a man named Parker who was mentioned in the first part of the diamond digging at the Vaal river and also at the new rush, Having made a great deal of money by buying and selling diamonds he went to England and ordered a Large Hotell fittings and fixings of every discription with the

[Page 710]

Counter and in fact everything of the best that could be got for fitting up a firstclass Hotell.

And also brought out several young Women experienced waiters to attend in the Hotell but I heard that he did not keep all of them long for some of them soon left him and got married I heard Their excuse was that they had two much to do in waiting on the people that it keept them buisy from morning till late in the night. This Hotell was opened just about the time that I arrived at the field,

And I had the honor of been on the field when the first govenor arrived sent there by the British Governer-

[Page 711]

ment to take charge of the diamond fields,

Whos name was Mr Southy [Southey],[7] and who was the son of one of the British settlers of 1820 and crossed the ocean in the same Ship with myself, and he has been in office for many years such He held the office of secretary in Cape Town for Government, so when he arrived on the field they gave him a grand reception and also a grand Ball in the evening, and in the vecinity of the Hotell was illuminated with Fireworks which looked very grand, So much for Saloons and Hotells.

And while looking around I saw

[Page 712]

a great many little wooden houses with signs up saying diamonds baught and sold here, and in the Streets and Alleys there were lots of Boys (I took them to be Jwes) with their Satchel buying all the diamonds they could off the diggers, so these Boys was trusted both with money and diamonds and in fact every store and Saloon keeper was a dealer in diamonds, and if a digger wanted anything at the Store he would take his diamonds and get anything he wanted just the same as if he took Gold Silver or Bank notes

And in fact there was no scarceity of money while I was there for every steamer that came

---

7. Mr. Southey refers to one of Richard Southey's sons who traveled with the Wiggills on the *Kennersley Castle*. Richard Southey led the Southey party, and the names and ages of his sons who voyaged with him to the Cape were William (13), Richard (11), George (9), Henry (4), and Canon (1). Nash, *The Settler Handbook*, 123.

View of Kimberley Diamond Mine workings, 1874. Courtesy Western Cape Archives.

[Page 713]

from England to Cape Town brought thousand of Pounds for to buy diamonds with,

There was two Lines of Steamers by two separate companys going too and from England every week which would make the voyage in about thirty days, They came loaded with passingers merchandice and money mostly for the diamond field

That traffic increased from 1870 up to the preasent time and as the steamers run so regular and made such quick passages that many of the Old settlers and their Sons took the advantage and went to see their Mother Country Old England. Many of them were born there but brought away when very young

[Page 714]

and a great many went who was born in Africa to see their relations and friends and also to transact buisness.

Takeing with them vallueable lots of Diamonds both for themselves and others,

I was on board of one of those Steamers just after comeing into the Dock, She was fitted up very ellegantly with numbers 1st, 2nd and 3rd class saloons,

At the time I was at the field there were hundreds of Frame buildings that had been framed and fitteted togather in Queenstown and other places, and built mostly of American wood and covered with Galvanized Iron and then

CHAPTER 35

loaded up and carried to the diamond field. Besides those there were large Stores built all of Galvanized iron both sides and roof.

[Page 715]

There were also Churches of all denominations built mostly of the same material even the Catholic's rushed out to see what they could do and also the Photographers so that there was hardly one left in the towns, and also the Doctors and Lawyers went, in fact all classes of people even Jews from Germany Holland and every other place rushed to the diamond field,[8] Such is only a faint outline of the Farefaimed diamond field of South Eastran Africa where a great many men made their fortunes and saved themselvs from Bankruptcy, Th

At this date this diamond field is was caled Kimberley has I imagian from a London missionary who resided in that

[Page 716]

vecinity many years back by the name of Kimble,[9]

And at the preasent date there is Telegraphic comunication from all parts of the Colony to the Diamond Field.

---

8. Wagons pulled by eight horses transported German Jews and others across South Africa to the diamond fields. "The transport waggon is a gigantic van, with low wooden sides and a flat roof of canvas supported on iron stanchions. . . . Under these, now rolled up, big pouches are suspended, by the four corners, full of bottles, flasks, meat-tins, and other objects. They oscillate and bang your miserable head to bits should you crouch up too snugly in the angle." Frederick Boyle, *To the Cape for Diamonds*, 44–78, passim 55.

9. Wiggill is mistaken on the origin of the name. Kimberley was named after the British Colonial Secretary, the Earl of Kimberley, and represents the foremost diamond center of South Africa. The diamond fields were annexed in 1871 and incorporated into the Cape Colony in 1880. Christopher Saunders and Nicholas Southey, *Historical Dictionary of South Africa*, 145–46.

Chapter 36

After a stay of about one week with my frinds at the diamond field, I should have looked around more than I did but the Sun shone down so Hot that it was sufficating and very disagreable to be from under shade, in fact it was the hotest part of South Africa that I was ever in, I had all along heard from my friends that it was so hot But when I were there I realized it to be so.

A day or two before

[Page 717]

I left the field I went to see the Agent of one of the Stage Companys to engage my passage for Cape Town, which cost me twelve Pounds for my passage and eight for my Luggage which consisted of two very large chests which was to be convayed by another train which would take from three weeks to a month in going eight hundred miles,

So on takeing leave of my friends at the New Rush, and on the 12th of Janurey 1873 my Son John and William Lowe my Son in law came to the Agent and also to see that I was comfortablely fixed and the Agent told them that he had aloted me the back seat which he thought was the most comfortable

[Page 718]

My Son told me that the agent had told him that there was a Lady passinger ~~was~~ going to Cape Town and that she was going to occupy part of the back seat with me,

So when they had seen me comfortabley seated in the Stage, They took their final leave of me by the shake of the hand,

They would have left the field before I did but the Herds man had gone to sleep and let a span of twelve or sixteen Oxen stray away which detained them them three or four days, But that day they had conclueded to leave without them, But after I arrived in Cape Town my Son in law wrote to me from Queenstown and told me that he

[Page 719]

had found his Cattle after a fatigueing search on a Dutchmans farm in the Naighborhood of the diamond field.

So when I left Du Toits pan it was on Satuaday about noon the stage been pritty well filled with passingers, with the one Lady and a little girl about two years old, The Stage was drawn by eight Horses So after we had started I found it pleasent traviling for the roads was good and the Country all around looked very beautifull, dotted here and there with the Mimosa thorn trees, We travilled on that day and also all night till daylight when we came to the great Orange river which was Sunday morning, and there we had

CHAPTER 36

[Page 720]

had to wait for an hour for the Ferry men had been on a drunken Spree the night before, and could not be aroused and got togather which kept us waiting and then they were not sober but how ever we soon got the stage and Horses on to the Pont or Ferry Boat, none of the passengers had occation to leave their seats while crossing the river, They puled the Ferryboat several hundred yards up the stream some of the men walking on the bank of the towing the ropes while others men on the Boat were stearing to keep her a scirtain distance from the Bank or Shore, and when they had towed it as

[Page 721]

far as necessary those on board took their ors and rowed her to the opposet side of the stream and we landed all safe the river being several hundred yards wide with steep banks on both sides.

At this crossing there is an English village caled Hope Town [Hopetown],[1] I but as we did not make any stop there I cant say anything about it, it been Sunday we contunied to travil through a beautiful roling grassey country l on eather hand there were beautiful trees between the mimosa and the Camelthorn such has I had never seen they were full of beautifull yellow blossoms such as I have seen on the Mimosa in the lower coun

[Page 722]

try, and the next day we came to a wilder country mostly covered with a shrub caled Karoo, and as we traviled along we could see where the thunder storms had fallen which would be beautiful and green, and perhaps a mile or two everything farther on every shrub and the grass would be dry and parched

and on this line we passed Dutch farmhouses and at one of them we stopt and changed Horses and has we traviled day and night I expect we passed many Houses and farms that I did not see, and sometimes we changed Horses in the night and for the conveinance of the passengers at those places they would have Coffee ready weather

[Page 723]

it was day or night,

I have not forgot how refreshing it was to get a cup of coffee after traviling all day or night or a cup of Tea as it might be with a nice bisket.

The second day from the Orange river we encountered a dreadful thunder storm such as one as comes to sudden in Africa The thunder was fearful and the Lightening played around the Wheels of the Stage, and the rain came

---

1. Hopetown, named after Major William Hope, auditor general and acting secretary of the Cape, and located "133 km north-east of Britstown and 134 km south-west of Kimberley." It was the location of the first diamond discovery. Raper, *Dictionary of Southern African Place Names*, s.v. "Hopetown," 217–18.

down in Torants so that we had to come to a standstill till the heavyest of it passed away, It filled the rivers and creeks in a few minuts, but we got through them all without any trouble

When this Storm

[Page 724]

overtook us we were within a mile orf two of Beaufort West,[2] which is cheafely a Dutch village and according to reports it contains 7248 inhabitants, so when we came to this place we found that the Storm had been very heavy the river which run through the village was flooded so that it overrun its banks, we did not stop there but passed on till we came to a place caled the Swart ruins, or black ridges[3] which appeared like old ruined walls and in some places they were eight or ten feet high, and in other places so low that the stage could go over them quite easey, They appeared to be from three to four feet thick and about a hundred

[Page 725]

yards between of nice level road,

I should think there was between twenty and thirty of those ridges and they were all just as black as coal and has stright as a line But how far they extended through the country I could not say, My opinion is that they have been forsed up by Earthquake or Volcanic action at a very earley period,

In passing along we travilled through a part of country that was thickly wooded with Mimoso and other trees crossing many creeks or rivelet and now and then a farm house Then the country became more mountainous and good water was very

[Page 726]

scarce through all this track of country and what little there was it was brackish and not pleasant to drink.

The following day after passing Beaufort West, having changed Horses at a Dutch Farm, These horses was kept at farmhouses at about from twenty to thirty miles apart and men or there drivers to take care of them,

---

2. Beaufort West is a town "573 km from Cape Town, established in 1818 on the farm of Hooyvlakte. Named by Lord Charles Somerset, Governor of the Cape, 1814–1826, after his father, the fifth Duke of Beaufort." Raper, *Dictionary of Southern African Place Names*, s.v. "Beaufort West," 46.

3. Swartruggens (Afrikaans for "black ridges" or hills known as *Zwartruggens*) is "56 km west of Rustenberg and 34 km north-west of Koster. It was founded in 1875 on the farm Brakfontein." Raper, *Dictionary of Southern African Place Names*, s.v. "Swartruggens," 523.

CHAPTER 36

This was done all along the road from the diamond field to Cape Town. We passed a good many farm houses but stopted at none of them only where we changed Horses.

I think we was about half way from the fields to Cape Town when we changed for an unusely smart and frish horses for they started off at

[Page 727]

pritty good speed, When we had gone about two miles and the road being very ruf and stoany and just before geting those frish horses we took up two extry passingers, and they been large enough to make three or four common people, so when we was going along at pritty good speed all of a suddon the iron axel of the stage broake and let the Wheel of which brought us to a full stop,

But having an extra axel in the Coach we thought or rather the conducter thought that the breach could soon be repaired, so the Conducter and passingers went to work and put the axel in, When done and got on the

[Page 728]

road a mile or two we found that it did not act right for there was too much friction, and the Box began to ware away and became so hot that every few miles we had to stop and throw water on it to keep it from takeing fier,

Well we travilied has well as we could for some time in that condition when we met two Mail Carts which was on the way from the Cape to the fields so the Conducter with a little persuation got them to take what passingers they could to the next station where we changed horses and I happened to be one who was taken the distance was some six

[Page 729]

or seven miles, and the broken Coach was brought along afterwards with the rest of the passingers,

I found that when I arrived at the Station that I knew the place for I was there in the year 1823 when a Boy travling as the reader will remember with Edward King, and what is more remarkabl it was the very place that Mr Kitson [Kidson] took me from this King and home to my parents, I have never seen Edward King from that time,[4]

When at this Station the Conducter had to make arrangements to get the passengers to their destination, which was soon effected the Dutchman who

[Page 730]

happened to be there having a Wagon that answered the purpose so the Conducter went to work and arranged the seats and transfered the Treasure

---

4. Edward King, born October 11, 1801, in Gloucestershire, England, and died March 30, 1843, in Swellendam, Western Cape, South Africa at age 42. No children were recorded in his death notice. British 1820 Settlers to South Africa.

Box from the Stage to the Wagon, and while all this was going on I had quite a rest,

Having got all things ready and it geting late in the afternoon we started again, and soon entered a Gorge in the Swartberg Mountains or in other words Black Mountain range, a range of mountains which reaches from the Cape district to the Eastern Province, and when you once enter those mountains you keep traviling between mountains for several

[Page 731]

days.

After all the passingers got into the borrowed Wagon we were dreadfully crowed and cramped, We had not room eather to sit stand or lean with any conveinence I found it very uncomfortable while in the Stage to sit day and night where there was more room. And this Wagon was without Springs which made it still more uncomfortable, And in changeing from the Stage to the Wagon I lost my back seate and when I spoke to the Conducter about it He answered me very short and said you are not at the diamond field now.

But I expect it was his nature for he was an Irishman named Dunn.

[Page 732]

And what made it worse for me I was jamed in along side of two very disagreable passingers, who at this part of the journy they was full of Brandy and at every stoping place the would recrute their bottles, which made them disagreable to all the Company, and sometimes would quarel with the Conducter.

Well we contunied through those mountains the roads being pritty good till we came to a small village situated on the Hex river[5] jambed in between two very high mountains, Here we halted to change Horses, while staying there I managed to get out of the wagon but when I got on to the ground I was so cramped and stiff that I could

[Page 733 On the road from]

---

5. "Tributary of the Breede River, rising north-east of De Doorns and flowing southwest between the Hex River Mountains and Kwadouwsberg to enter the Breede River south of Worcester. Dutch for 'witch river', the name is variously stated to refer to the ghostly atmosphere of the deep ravine through which the river flows, or to a legend of a lover who plummeted to his death while picking a rare disa for Eliza Meiring, who subsequently became deranged and acted like a witch. Other explanations link the name with Afrikaans hek, 'gate,' or with x's, referring to the numerous times the road crosses the river. Actually the name appears to be a translation of Khoekhoen *Cobeeb*, referring to a witchdoctor or magician, a powerful and influential figure in Khoekhoen society. The Afrikaans form Hexrivier is preferred for official purposes." Raper, *Dictionary of Southern African Place Names*, s.v. "Hex River," 211.

CHAPTER 36 247

scarcely walk, however I managed to get down to the river side which was a beautifull stream the water was so clear, Well I while they were changeing the Horses I took some wine and some other refrishments down to this stream washed my hands and face and eat and drank of what I had which refrished me very much and I felt better.

In the vecinity of this village there were a few very handsome Mimosa trees and if I remember right they were in full bloom And on the margen of the river there were some very large sycamores Trees But just before we came to this

The Diamond field [Page 734]

village we came down a very long Hill which had been escavated on the side of a high mountain two or three miles long at a great labour and expence I think it is caled Sir Lowry [Lowry's] Pass.[6] Why I allude to this place it is so beautiful with shubery on both sides of the road, There growed a Cactus from six to C eigh feet in hight and fluted all around like that I have seen columns from four to five inchs thick both milkey and prickely and what is so strange abat them they give a small yellow flower all up the angles.

On leaving this village we came on to a more open Country, and seeing romantic looking mountains in the distance

[Page 735]

thrown up in all the most fantastical shapes immagniable and every now and then passing beautifull streams coming out from this mountain range, and between those mountains the flats are covered with a kind of shubery caled Karoo[7] or heath[8] and grass in between.

And our next halting place was at a town caled Worcester,[9] Here we changed horses, and I got a good dinner, and stoped about two hours and in

---

6. Sir Lowry's Pass is a "mountain pass across the Hottentots Holland Mountains, between Grabouw and Somerset West. At first known as Gantouw, Khoekhoen for 'eland's path,' and then as Hottentots Holland Kloof or *Onderkloof*, it was rebuilt and renamed in 1830 after Sir Galbraith Lowry Cole (1772–1842), Governor of the Cape from 1828 to 1833." Raper, *Dictionary of Southern African Place Names*, s.v. "Sir Lowry's Pass," 501–02.

7. Karoo is "applied to several species of fodder-shrublets, especially the *Pentzia virgata* and *P. globosa*, both much valued." Marloth, "*The Flora of South Africa*," 47.

8. Heath refers to "nearly 500 species of *Erica* in South Africa, many of them with showy flowers." Marloth, "*The Flora of South Africa*," s.v. "HEATHS," 39.

9. "Town in the Breede River Valley, 121 km east-north-east of Cape Town and 52 km north-west of Robertson. . . . Named by Lord Charles Somerset, then Governor of the Cape, after his brother, the Marquis of Worcester." Raper, *Dictionary of Southern African Place Names*, s.v. "Worcester," 594.

the meantime I walked around the Town to stretch my limbs which done me a great deal of good.

Worcester is in the Cape devicion Cape Colony and contains according to re-

[Page 736]

ports 20,000 square miles and contains about 10,000 inhabitants

Well after leaveing this village, towards evening of the same day we came to a Station caled Darling Bridge[10] not that it was a over a large river but it appeared to me that it was a Bridge being built over a Swampy boggy place for a railroad Bridge,

Been so named for a Lieut govenor Darling who was Lieut govenor of Grahms Town [Grahamstown], When we arrived at this Station I felt my self compleately worn out and tired and I went to the Hotell and got a Cup of Coffee and somthing to Eat which done me a great deal of good,

And after partakeing of these refrishments

[Page 737]

I thought I would take a walk to strecth my Limbs and have a look at the Bridge already mentioned, and while I was there it began to get dusk and I thought I had better make my way back to the Station before it was quite dark and that I might miss my way and be left,

When I got back to the Station it was then quite dark and the Wagon was ready to start and the Conducter told me He had fixed me a seat in the back of the Wagon and that I had better get in and seated,

I took his advice and I had not been long seated when to my surprize those two men who had been so annoying on the

[Page 738]

road to the Company I found was seated along side of me, and in irons Handcufted togather and has I learnd from the conversation by the passingers that it was for an Assault on the Lady passinger,

We very soon got started on the road, But I little thought what kind of a road or what a night I would have to pass through, soon after we started I found that we were in a terrible mountain pass, which I beleive is caled Bains Pass in Honor of Andrew Geddes Bain,[11] the one who Superintended cutting

---

10. Darling lies "75 km southwest of Cape Town, named after Sir Charles Henry Darling, Lieutenant-Governor of the Cape from 1851–54." Raper, *Dictionary of Southern African Place Names*, s.v. "Darling," 112.

11. "Mountain pass over the Drakenstein range 29 km west-north-west of Worcester, between the Breede River Valley and Wellington. Started in 1849 and opened in September 1853. Named after its builder, Andrew Geddes Bain . . . road

CHAPTER 36

this stupendous mountain Pass caled the Berg river mountains in the Western District connecting Cape Town with the interior and

[Page 739]

the diamond field.

I would very much liked to have seen this Pass in daylight for it must have been a very dangerous road as the Conducter had a Lamp under the Wagon to see to guide the Horses,

Thy also had a Lamp in the Wagon and between the two lights or the reflection of the lights, they threw the most hideous figgers and Shaddows on to the rocks that I ever saw which put me in mind of Devils and the Infurnal regions, it must be a very romantic place if I could have seen it by daylight for I heard water rushing in Chasms ap by the sound it appeared to be an hundred

[Page 740]

or two feet below the level of the road that we were on, and in the turns and cornors the rocks were pilled up like Cordwood out of the way it had been quaried out of this new road it was a hard granit rock,

This pass must be three or four miles long for I thought we would never get to the end of it, It been dark they had to drive very slow I noticed in one or two openings a Cottage where people seemed to be living

I have often heard of the Roman Catholic Purgatory and I thought I was in it and jambed up by those two hand cuffed men I was compleatly forsed off my seat by them and got

[Page 741 On the road]

out of the Wagon and thought that I could walk for I was in such misery that I did not know what to do with myself, I thought that the next Station was near by and I could walk to it but the Conducter told me to get into the Wagon again that I could not walk there that it was too far away, so I had to get into Purggatory again

I think in about half an hour we reached the Station a place caled Wellington in the night which we travíled through that fearful pass.

Comeing into this village we drove up to a house what I supposed to be a magistrate's office but being in the night

To Cape Town [Page 742]

we found no admitance so one of those men in Irons told the driver to drive to another place which he discribed, so the Wagon was drove to the place and halted and found an Officer there so all the company driver and the

---

engineer, explorer and geologist." Raper, *Dictionary of Southern African Place Names*, s.v. "Bain's Kloof Pass," 40.

Conducter went in to the Office and left me to myself in the Wagon for which I was very glad of for I got a little sleep after being six days and nights confined in the Wagon, and to my surprize when daylight came I seen those two men freed from their handcuffs and asleep on the Porch of the Office, But how the buisness was settled or how they got free I never heard but I expect money baught them free so they never troubled me afterwards

[Page 743]

 This village of Wellington is about 80 miles from Cape Town and at that time was one of the Turminous's of the railroad line leading to the great interior of the western division But since I was there I understand that the railway line runs over Bains [Bain's] Pass and to the village of Worcester.

 So that same morning we quit that awfull Wagon and went on board of the Cars which was the greatest relief from mysery to ease that I ever experianced in all my life we passed several farmhouses on each side of the road has we went along, Then we passed a beautifull village caled stellenbosch[12] a place known far and wide it was laid out many years ago by the

[Page 744]

Dutch govenor whos name was Van der Stell [van der Stel], and was named for him. And I arrived in Cape Town on the 20th of Jenuary 1873 where my friend Mr Ruck met me at the Depot with his Cart and took me home to his House where he resided in the village of Roundebosch. After being on the road eight days and nights in the Wagon and Cars makeing a Journey of eight hundred miles.

 Has Mr Ruck and I had been corsponding for over two years of corse I wrote to him to let him know when to meet me at the Depot which he did very punctual almost before I expected, Well I stayed with Mr Ruck and his family about a month or six weeks makeing

[Page 745]

his house my home, and visiting around at differant villages and friends I feel sorry that I did not visit many other places has I had plenty time on my hands such as Simons Bay and the village of Wineberg, But now and then I would take the Cars and go to Cape Town and look around the City and also the Dock Yard where they had a powerful Steam Engine to draw up Ships which wanted repairing, and also one in Simon Bay similar which will draw up full riged Ships on to the Slip,

---

 12. Stellenbosch, named in 1679 by Simon van der Stel after himself and "the *Wilde Bosch* [wild forest], along the Eerste [first] River Valley, forty-eight kilometers east of Cape Town." Raper, *Dictionary of Southern African Place Names*, s.v. "Stellenbosch," 515.

Well while I stayed there I enjoyed myself for it was just in the time of friut there were grapes in abundance and Peaches

[Page 746]

apples and all kinds of Tropical friuts, and the Brandy was only one shilling per bottle, and very good Wine for sixpence per bottle

So after staying the time already mentioned I found a Brig being fitted out for Boston, The Captain and Commanders name was Mr John Bynon. [F. Bynam] Commander of the Brig Piccadilly.[13] And the owner was a Mr Muerson [Murison][14] merchant of Cape Town, This Brig traded regular between Cape Town and Boston she was put on in place of one that was wrecked on the American Coast near Boston.

Having discribed Cape Town and its surroundings in the fore part of this book or History I dont think it necesary

[Page 747]

to go into detailes in this part of the book.

---

13. F. Bynam is evidenced as the commander of the *Piccadilly*. "Massachusetts, U.S., Arriving Passenger and Crew Lists, 1820–1963 for George Ruck," on Ancestry.

14. Lloyd's Register of Shipping shows the *Piccadilly*, owned by A. Murison in 1873–74. *Lloyd's Register 1873–74*, PIIE, on Internet Archive.

Chapter 37

having payed my passage and also that of George Ruck Son of my friend Mr Ruck. So on the 12th of March 1873, I left Cape Town on Wedensday. There were two other passingers besides myself in the Cabin one a Mr Jones and the other a Miss Thompson going to a place caled St Johns in Canada to visit her Brother who was a Merchant, and from there she was going to England.[1]

The Steamer towed the Brig out of the Dock

[Page 748]

into the Table Bay where we dropped Anchor for a few hours while the Captain went ashore to make final arrangements before starting.

So towards evening we sat sail for the Sea and passed close to what is caled Robings Iland [Robben Island] so close that could see the houses, and the next morning we were entirely out sight of land with a midling rough sea.

When the Captain left Table Bay he did know whether he would put in at St Helena but when we were drawing near to it he thought he would to take in more water and some provicions having a pleasent run that far, with the exception of the weather being very warm.

We arrived at the island in the morning part of the day so the Captain and

[Page 749]

his Wife and Miss Thompson and also Mr Jones went ashore but I remained on board the vessel, having or feeling no desire to go ashore.

Mr. Jones visited the Tomb of Napoleon and he said that there was a gard of French Solders around the place, while Napoleon was living his Residence was caled Longwood Old House.

I shant attempt to discribe the island myself as it has already been described by other writers especially by Captain Cook in his voyages around the world

But from the vessel it looked to be a very romantic place I could not see the Town being hiden by a bluf point of the mountain, I could see a few Batterys which was situated on the rocks

[Page 750]

almost over hanging the sea and the surf dashing and breaking up against them. while the Brig lay at anchor there were several Women came on board to

---

1. The passenger list for the *Brig Piccadilly*, master F. Bynam, notes that Eli Wiggill, age 61; George Ruck, age 21; Jane Thompson, age 40; and Herbert Jones, age 20, sailed on this vessel together. Ruck was listed in steerage and the other three were listed as cabin passengers. "Massachusetts, U.S., Arriving Passenger and Crew Lists, 1820–1963 for George Ruck," on Ancestry.

CHAPTER 37

sell fruit and some curiositys. And in the mean time a beautifide mail Steamer caled the Africa stoped at the island on her way from England to Cape Town. so about sunset the steamer left for Cape Town. and we left for Boston.

The weather contuned fine and we traviled on at good speed and nothing of much intrest transpired only now and then we would see Ships at a distance and sometimes one so near that the Captain would speak to them when we came to the

[Page 751]

Line. when we found it very warm, and in the evening Old Neptune came on board in his strange dress and long beard, and wanted to know of the Captain if he had any subjects on board to be adopted into his Kingdom The Captain told him yes there was two on board who had never crossed the Line Mr Jones and George Ruck, so Neptune told him that he would be on board tomorrow and attend to them speaking in a very rough manner. So the next day he came according to promis and George Ruck had to go through the opperation of been shaved while Mr Jones baught himself

[Page 752]

off by buying a bottle of Brandy of the Captain and treated the company the bottle was soon emtyed corked up and thrown overboard. This makes the fourth time that I have crossed the Line.

To give the reader an idea of the distance from Capetown to the Line is about twenty one days sail in a packet Ship and I think it is about the same distance from New York to the Line.

To the best of my recolection after leaving the Line we came to what is generaly known by seafareing men as the Gulf stream it is a stream which takes its rise in the Gulf of Mexeco. Captains of vessels whom I have sailed with say that it is a

[Page 753]

stream which runs across the Ocean towards England. There are two tokens by which it can be known when a vessel is in this stream. First, the water is warmer than the other part of the Ocean the Ship's cook soon finds that out by haveing to draw so much water for his use, And secondly it is known by masses of weeds floating on the surface of the water which is said to come out of the Gulf of Mexeco.

I have heard the sailors say that they seldom get through that stream without having a storm

Well on leaving this stream we came to a very romantic looking island similar to the island of St Helana [St. Helena]

[Page 754]

caled Fonnando De Hermanha [Fernando de Noronha] and belonged to Brazil. We were alongside of this island April the ninth 1873. On leaving this place we had a change of weather which was cold and stormey, and about this time a vessel passed us by the name of George Anderson who left the Cape a few days before we she was so near us that with the glass we could see her name on the stern as she passed, and the Captain wondered at her being so quick on her return and then said he guessed that she had only taken in a Cargo of Brooms.

But we heard afterwards that she had not been to Boston yet, that she was beating out to Sea to escape showls of sand

[Page 755]

which was in that part of the sea. So then we contuined on till we came near to Cape Cod when we were enveloped in a heavy Fog, and had to lay too for two days and nights keeping the fog horn blowing all the time and having no Pilot on board. The sea was strewn with the wreck of a Brig which must have been loaded with Lath as the Lath and her spars were floating alaround us.

Has soon as the fog abated we soon had a Pilot on board which soon took us into Boston or in other words to the Pier or Dock which was on the 11th of May 1873 after about 60 days from Cape Town.

[Page 756]

The same afternoon after coming into the Dock there came up a terable Thunder Storm and rain and wet the sails and everything on deck, and the Captain fearing to have his sails stolen he had them wet as they were folded up and put into my Bunk where I had slept all the voyage so I had to do the best that I could for everything was in confusion as it generaly is on arriving in to port so I had to make my bed on the wet sails. But the next night I done better for I slept in the first mates Berth and all the time while I remained on board.

so after staying a few days in Boston looking around and buying a few things for myself and some things for

[Page 757]

George Ruck[2] the young man that I brought over and made arraingments for him to go to the State of Main to his Sister I payed his passage and seen him on board the Cars.

And also payed my own passage 65 Dollars to go to Utah from Boston from Boston I went to New York part of the way by Cars and part by Steam Boat arriving in New York on the 16 of May 173.

And leaving the same afternoon on the Cars enrout for Utah on what is called the pan handle Line, and came to Pitsberg where we stayed over

---

2. A sixty-four-year-old white male named George Ruck lived in Knox Township, Maine, in 1920. The 1920 US Census, Maine, Enumeration District No. 84, Sheet 7A.

CHAPTER 37

Sunday Then on Monday morning we started and continued on the Journey and on or about the 24th of May

[Page 758]

I arrived in Ogdon which was in the night and the Conducter told the passingers they could stay in the Cars till morning for which I was glad to hear for I was a stranger there. So the next morning after leaving the Cars, I met Mr John Taylor and W Woodruff two of the twelve Apostles of the Latter day Saints

And they knowing that I had just come from off a mission told me that I should have come all the way for half Fare but I did not know it at the time I payed my fare in Boston but they seen that I only payed half fare from Ogdon to Salt Lake City which was the 25th of May being away from my home a little over three years.

[Page 759]

So having arrived in the City the next day from Ogden I would liked to have caled at Kaysville when on the way from Ogden, but having my Luggage on board the Cars I thought I had better go right through to attend to that and see my Children afterwards.

So when I arrived in at the Depot I was surprized to see what changes had been made while I was away so I hired a job Wagon to bring my Luggage home to where I lived in the tenth Ward, and all the way I could see large new Stores had been built in places where there was nothing when I left, and such gaudy painted signs over the doors and windows well I hardly knew the place to be the same, and in fact I hardly

[Page 760]

knew my own place when I came to it. But I expect what made it look strang about my home, there had been a large Cottonwood Tree which stood at the corner of the Block which used to be my guide had been cut down, But I soon found the House and had my Luggage unloaded and discharged the man with his wagon

~~This is as far as my this history was written by my~~

This is as far as the history of his life was written by my Grand Father Eli Wiggill in the year 1883. Soon after this he took ill and ~~so~~ the history was never completed. So I take great

[Page 761]

pleasure in writing a short sketch of the last years of his life.[3] Soon after his return his wife joined the Josephite or Reorganised Church and did not try to

---

3. These additional six pages following Wiggill's 760-page autobiography were written by Eli's granddaughter Susannah "Susie" Margaret Lowe Dodge. The daughter of William Lowe and Frances Amelia Wiggill, Susie was a child when she and her parents left for Cape Town in December 1869 with Eli. "The remainder of this book

make him comfortable or happy. So they agreed to separate. He then closed his home and made his home with his son Jerimiah in Kaysville where he was happy, as his son and daughter-in-law were very good and kind ~~in~~ to him. I 1874 He married a very worthy and good woman. a Mrs Hammer. After living a few

[Page 762]

months in Kaysville. they decided to move to the City. on to his own property. which was on 7th East. between 2nd and 3rd South. There they lived in peace and happiness. He attending his garden, and doing odd jobs of Carpentering ~~a~~ during Summer-time. and in the Winter reading, writing or studying. Sometimes his Grand-daughter from Kaysville would stay with them. He was present at the opening and dedication Services of the Assembly Hall.

[Page 763]

They both enjoyed the Old-Folks Day in Liberty Park in the year. His Son Joseph was married to Miss Mary Whitesides of Kaysville in 1~~880~~78. In the Summer of 1881, Joseph was kicked by a horse, which knocked his front teeth out and injured him severely. In 1882, Grand. Pa was taken ill. he recovered somewhat from the first Attack but was never quite well. In November 1883 His Son-in-law William Lowe and family arrived in Utah from South Africa.[4]

[Page 764]

---

was written by Mrs. Susie Dodge, granddaughter of Eli Wiggill, and the baby whom he mentions as going to Africa with them in 1869–1870." Wiggill, "Eli Wiggill History 1810–1884," MS 23753, Church History Library, Salt Lake City, 82. This history was taken from a transcript produced by Leda Dawson McCurdy in 1975, based on the handwritten account of the Eli Wiggill autobiography, edited by Reva Marchant in 2000. It contains useful information but also factual errors, which the editors have corrected in this transcription of the original Wiggill autobiography manuscript.

4. William and his wife Frances Amelia (Eli's daughter), now wealthy from the diamond rush, returned to Kaysville, Utah, where their son William Francis was born in 1884. The family returned to South Africa, and twin girls Frances and Marjory were born in Queenstown in October 1886. They had three additional male children born in Queenstown: "Cecil in 1886, Reginald in 1891, and Eric in 1894." Lowe, *African Eden II*, 30. Unfortunately, Lowe adds that although William and Frances Amelia were faithful to their Latter-day Saint beliefs, they "kept their faith from their children . . . because they feared for their lives and could not trust their small children to keep their new faith to themselves. They were regular attenders and 'kept a pew' in the Anglican Church in East London, South Africa. . . . The Lowes were very prosperous, owning a beautiful home, a large farm, [and] businesses. . . . Not until the family immigrated in 1908 was the gospel taught openly." On May 1, 1900, William died, leaving his wife a widow with a large family. It appears her faith brought her back to Utah eight years later. Upon returning, no disclosure was made with regards to the amount of money William had made through diamonds, as Frances Amelia wanted to blend into the Utah culture without any ripples. Lowe, *African Eden II*, 31, 35–36.

CHAPTER 37

He was then ill in bed. but so glad to see them all. After they came he seemed to feel better. At Christmas-time was able to sit up in his chair. On 9th January 1884, being my birthday he presented me with a book and gave me a blessing. He felt he would not live another year. He took to his bed again in March. His wife and many kind friends and neighbours gave him good Care and nursing. but he grew weaker. and passed away on the

[Page 765]

13th day of April. being 72 years. deeply regretted by his family and friends. He was a true and faithful Latter-Day Saint and died in hope of a sure Resurrection.[5] His Casket was of polished ~~Calz~~ Red Wood made by Thomas James a neighbor, according to the directions he gave a few weeks before his death. At his request his body was brought to Kaysville and laid in the Cemetery beside his wife Susannah. The funeral Services in the Meeting House were largely attended. Several speakers testified

[Page 766]

to his life and Character. Brother Talbot speaking of their friendship, began as boys in the far away land of Sunny South Africa. where they both heard and accepted the Gospel. travelling from there to Utah in the same Company.[6] At the time of his death he was a High Preist.[7]

---

5. In a letter written by Eli's wife, Ann Hammer Wiggill, to Henry Talbot, less than a month after Eli passed away on April 13, 1884, Ann explained to Eli's dear friend Henry, "He [Eli] had a longing desire to live and do the work in the Temple, for his dead friends . . . [but] that someone else would have to do that work for him, for he always felt he never would recover." Ann H. Wiggill to Henry Talbot, May 6, 1884, inserted with the autobiography of Eli Wiggill, MS 8344, Church History Library, Salt Lake City. Latter-day Saints do proxy ordinance work in temples for their loved ones who are deceased. This doctrine was taught by the apostle Paul in 1 Corinthians 15:29.

6. According to Henry James Talbot, son of Henry Talbot, his father was told in his patriarchal blessing, "the eye of the lord has been upon you, and with outstretched arm has led you to the [Salt Lake] valley." H. J. Talbot added, "with all our troubles and hardships the lord has truly watched over the Talbot family as every one of us was preserved to come to Zion and be with the saints. The Gospel means more to us than all the land and possessions that we left in South Africa." Talbot, "Short Sketch of the Life of Henry James Talbot," 12.

7. An ecclesiastical office in the Melchizedek Priesthood within The Church of Jesus Christ of Latter-day Saints.

Bibliography

Aberdeen Built Ships. http://www.aberdeenships.com/single.asp?offset=730&index=99601.

Aird, Poly. "'You Nasty Apostates, Clear Out'": Reasons for Disaffection in the late 1850s." *Journal of Mormon History* 30, no. 2 (Fall 2004): 129–207.

Albany Settlers. http://www.albany1820.com/.

Alexander, James Edward. *Narrative of a Voyage of Observation Among the Colonies of Western Africa in the Flag-ship Thalia; and of a Campaign in Kaffir-Land, on the Staff of the Commander-in-Chief in 1835.* 2 vols. London: Henry Colburn Publisher, 1837.

Anderson, Gerald H., ed. *Biographical Dictionary of Christian Missions*. New York: Simon & Schuster, 1998.

Archer, Robert H. "Euphorbia L." South African National Biodiversity Institute. 2005.

Ayliff, Rev. John. *The Journal of "Harry Hastings" Albany Settler*, edited by Rev. Dr. L. A. Hewson and Rev. F. G. van der Reit. Grahamstown: Grocott & Sherry, 1963.

———. *The Journal of John Ayliff*, edited by Peter Hinchliff. Cape Town: Rhodes University, 1971.

Ayliff, Rev. John, and Rev. Joseph Whiteside. *History of the Abambo, Generally Known as Fingos*. 1912. Reprint, Cape Town: C. Struik, Africana Specialist and Publisher, 1962.

"Backhouse & Walker—Quaker Missionaries." Port Phillip Pioneers Group. https://portphillippioneersgroup.org.au/pppg5gt.htm. Accessed July 30, 2019.

"Backhouse, James (1794–1869)." Dictionary of Australian Biography. http://gutenberg.net.au/ebooks15/1500721h/0-dict-biogBa.html#backhouse1. Accessed July 30, 2019.

Backhouse, James. *A Narrative to the Mauritius and South Africa.* London: Hamilton, Adams and Co., 1844.

Basutoland Records: Copies of Official Documents of Various Kinds. Vol. 1, 1833–52. Cape Town: W. A. Richards & Sons, Government Printers, 1883.

Bateman, C. H., ed. *The Children's Missionary Newspaper*. [*Children's Monthly Missionary Newspaper*] 16, no. 8 (August 1859): 57.

"Bathurst." South Africa History Online. Accessed July 30, 2023. https://www.sahistory.org.za/.

Beck, Roger B. *The History of South Africa*. 2nd ed. Oxford: Greenwood, 2014.

Belich, James. *Replenishing the Earth: The Settler Revolution and the Rise of the Anglo World, 1783–1939*. Oxford: Oxford University Press, 2011.

Bird, William Wilberforce. *State of the Cape of Good Hope, in 1822*. London: John Murray, 1823.

Bowker, John Mitford. *Speeches, Letters, and Selections from Important Papers of the Late John Mitford Bowker, Some Years Resident and Diplomatic Agent with*

Certain Kafir and Fingo Tribes, compiled by his widow. Grahamstown: Godlonton and Richards, 1864.

Boyce, W. B. *Memoir of the Rev. William Shaw*. London: n.p., 1874.

Boyle, Frederick. *To the Cape for Diamonds. A Story of Digging Experiences in South Africa. With Comments and Criticisms, Political, Social, and Miscellaneous, Upon the Present State and Future Prospects of the Diamond Fields*. London: Chapman and Hall, 1873.

Braun, Lindsay Frederick. *Colonial Survey and Native Landscapes in Rural South Africa, 1850– 1913*. Leiden/Boston: Brill, 2015.

Bredekamp, Henry and Robert Ross, eds. *Missions and Christianity in South Africa*. Johannesburg: Witwatersrand University Press, 1995.

British 1820 Settlers to South Africa. http://www.1820settlers.com/.

———. "Bezuidenhout."

———. "Bradshaw."

———. "Isaac Wiggall letter." https://www.1820settlers.com/documents/settlerletters/W/WIGGALL_Isaac.htm.

Bredekamp, Henry and Robert Ross, eds. *Missions and Christianity in South Africa*. Johannesburg: Witwatersrand University Press, 1995.

Brouwer, H. A., ed. *Practical Hints to Scientific Travellers*. Leyden: E. J. Brill LTD Publishers, 1922.

Buckley, Jay H. "'Good News' at the Cape of Good Hope: Early LDS Missionary Activities in South Africa." In *Go Ye into All the World: The Growth & Development of Mormon Missionary Work*, edited by Reid L. Neilson and Fred E. Woods, 471–502. Provo: Religious Studies Center and Deseret Book, 2012.

Buckley, Jay H., and Joshua Rust. "Eli and Susannah Wiggill: South African Saints." *Journal of Mormon History* 49, no. 2 (April 2023): 129–42.

Butler, Guy, ed. *When Boys were Men*. Cape Town: Oxford University Press, 1969.

Calderwood, Rev. H. *Caffres and Caffre Missions: With Preliminary Chapters on the Cape Colony as a Field for Emigration, and Basis of Missionary Operation*. 1858. Reprint, London: James Nisbett and Co., 1997.

Cannon, Jeffrey G. "Mormonism's Jesse Haven and the Early Focus on Proselytizing the Afrikaner at the Cape of Good Hope, 1853–1855." *Dutch Reformed Theological Journal* 48, nos. 3/4 (September/December 2007): 446–56.

Carter, Kate B. *Treasures of Pioneer History*. Vol. 6. Salt Lake City: Daughters of Utah Pioneers, 1957.

———, comp. "Eli Wiggill." In *An Enduring Legacy*, 8:169–212. Salt Lake City: Daughters of the Utah Pioneers, 1985.

Cathcart, Sir George. *Correspondence of Lieut.-General the Hon. Sir George Cathcart, K.C.B., Relative to his Military Operations in Kaffraria, Until the Termination of the Kafir War, and to His Measures for the Future Maintenance of Peace on that Frontier, and the Protection and Welfare of the People of South Africa*. New York: Negro Universities Press, a Division of Greenwood Publishing, 1969.

"Chalumna River." Wikipedia. Accessed July 30, 2019. https://en.wikipedia.org/wiki/Chalumna_River.

BIBLIOGRAPHY

Church History Biographical Database. Accessed January 1, 2024. https://history.churchofjesuschrist.org/chd/landing.

Collett, Carol Ivins. *Kaysville – Our Town: A History*. Salt Lake City: Moench Letter Service, 1976.

Colley, Linda. *Britons: Forging the Nation 1707–1837*. New Haven: Yale University Press, 1992.

Cory, G. E. *The Rise of South Africa: A History of the Origin of South African Colonization and of its Development towards the East from the Earliest Times to 1857*. 4 vols. London: Longmans, Green, and Co., 1913.

Couzens, Tim. *Battles of South Africa*. South Africa: David Phillips Publishers, 2004.

Crutchley, Commander W. Caius. *My Life at Sea*. London: Chapman and Hall, 1912.

Cunningham, General Sir Arthur Augustus Thurlow, G .C. B. *My Command in South Africa*. London: Macmillan and Co., 1879.

Currey, John B. "The Diamond Fields of Griqualand and their Probable Influence on the Native Races of South Africa." *Journal of the Society of Arts* 24, no. 1217 (March 17, 1876): 372–81.

Currie, Marion Rose. "The History of Theopolis Mission, 1814–1851." Master's thesis, Rhodes University, 1983.

Cutten, Theo E. G. *A History of the Press in South Africa*. Cape Town: National Union of South African Students, 1935.

"Daggaboersnek (N10)." *Cyber Drive: Mountain Passes South Africa*. Assessed September 11, 2022. https://www.mountainpassessouthafrica.co.za/find-a-pass/eastern-cape/item/173- daggaboers-nek-pass-n10.html.

"Deodarus." Scottish Built Ships: The History of Shipbuilding in Scotland. Accessed January 5, 2024. http://clydeships.co.uk/view.php?ref=53662&vessel=DEODARUS

Destination Albany 1820. Assessed September 11, 2022. http://www.albany1820.com.

Doughty, Oswald. *Early Diamond Days: The Opening of the Diamond Fields of South Africa*. London: Longmans, Green and Co. Ltd., 1963.

Douglass, Arthur. *Ostrich Farming in South Africa: Being an Account of its Origin and Rise*. New York: Cassell, Petter, Galpin & Co., 1881.

"Drostdy House." RoomsForAfrica. Accessed September 11, 2022. https://www.roomsforafrica.com/attraction.do?id=130.

Du Plessis, J. *A History of Christian Missions in South Africa*. New York: Longmans, Green & Co., 1911.

Dugmore, Rev. Henry Hare. *The Reminiscences of an Albany Settler by Rev. Henry Hare Dugmore, Together with his Recollections of the Kaffir War of 1835*, edited by F. G. Van Der Reit and Rev. L. A. Hewson. Grahamstown: Grocott & Sherry, 1958.

Dugmore, Rev. Henry Hare. "Past and Present." *A Treasury of South African Poetry and Verse*. Collected from various sources and arranged by Edward Heath Crouch, 2nd enlarged ed. London: A. C. Fifield, 1909.

"The Dutch Settlement." South African History Online. Assessed September 11, 2022. https://www.sahistory.org.za/article/dutch-settlement.

Edwards, Rev. John. *Reminiscences of the Early Life and Missionary Labours of the Rev. John Edwards, Fifty Years a Wesleyan Missionary in South Africa.* 2nd ed. Edited by W. M. Clifford. London: T. Woolmer, 1886.

Eldredge, Elizabeth A., and Fred Morton, eds. *Slavery in South Africa: Captive Labor on the Dutch Frontier.* Boulder: Westview Press, Inc., 1994.

Encyclopedia Britannica or Dictionary. 8th ed. Vol. 8. Edinburgh: Adam and Charles Black, 1857.

Erasmus, P. "The 'Lost' South African Tribe: Rebirth of the Koranna in the Free State." *New Contree*, no. 50 (November 2005): 77–91.

"Euphorbia L." Plants of the World Online. Accessed March 6, 2024. https://powo.science.kew.org/taxon/urn:lsid:ipni.org:names:327729-2

Fast, Hildegarde H. "'In at One Ear and out at the Other': African Response to the Wesleyan Message in Xhosaland, 1825–35." *Journal of Religion in Africa* 23, no. 2 (May 1993): 147–74.

———, ed. *The Journal and Selected Letters of Rev. William J. Shrewsbury 1826–1835.* Grahamstown: Witwatersrand University Press, 1994.

"Felloe." The Free Dictionary. Accessed January 1, 2024.https://www.thefreedictionary.com/felloe.

Findlay, G. G., and W. W. Holdsworth, *The History of the Wesleyan Methodist Missionary Society.* 5 vols. London: Epworth Press, 1921–24.

"Fort Wiltshire." South African History Online. http://www.sahistory.org.za/places/.

The Free Dictionary. https://www.thefreedictionary.com/.

Garrett, H. D. "The Controversial Death of Gobo Fango." *Utah Historical Quarterly* 57, no. 3 (Summer 1989): 264–72.

Gatherum, Doneta MaGonigle. "Kaysville." *Utah History Encyclopedia*, edited by Allan Kent Powell. Salt Lake City: University of Utah Press, 1994.

"George Sumner." British 1820 Settlers to South Africa. https://www.1820settlers.com/genealogy/.

Goldswain, Jeremiah. *The Chronicles of Jeremiah Goldswain, Albany Settler of 1820.* Edited by Una Long. 1949. Reprint, Cape Town: The Van Riebeeck Society, 2014.

Grahamstown Journal. Various dates, including February 24, 1863; June 2, 1871.

Hammond-Tooke, W. D., ed. *The Journal of William Shaw.* Cape Town: A. A. Balkema, 1972.

Hewson, L. A. *An Introduction to South African Methodist.* Cape Town: Standard Press, 1952.

Higgs, Anneke. "The Historical Development of Diamond Mining Legislation in Griqualand West During the Period 1871 to 1880." *Fundamina* (Pretoria) 24, no. 1 (2018): 18–56.

"History of Slavery and Early Colonization in South Africa." South African History Online. https://www.sahistory.org.za/article/history-slavery-and-early-colonisation-south-africa.

Hodgson, Janet. *The God of the Xhosa: A Study of the Origins and Development of the Traditional Concepts of the Supreme Being.* Cape Town: Oxford University Press, 1982.

BIBLIOGRAPHY

Holden, Rev. William C. *History of the Colony of Natal South Africa.* London: Alexander Heylin, 1855.

"Homer Duncan Company of 1861." Overland Travel Pioneer Database. Accessed June 1, 2018. https://history.churchofjesuschrist.org/overlandtravel/companies/43/homer-duncan- company.

"Howieson's Poort Shelter." Wikipedia. Accessed June 1, 2018. https://en.wikipedia.org/wiki/Howieson%27s_Poort_Shelter.

Hromnik, Cyril A. *Indo-Africa: Towards a New Understanding of the History of Sub-Saharan Africa.* Cape Town: Juta and Company Limited, 1981.

Isichei, Elizabeth. *A History of Christianity in Africa from Antiquity to the Present.* London: Society for Promoting Christian Knowledge, 1995.

Jaff, Fay. *They Came to South Africa.* https://archive.org/stream/TheyCameToSouthAfrica/TheyCameToSouthAfrica_djvu.txt.

"James, W." British 1820 Settlers to South Africa. Accessed February 27, 2024. https://www.1820settlers.com/genealogy/getperson.php?personID=I102283.

Jones, Christopher C. "Methodism, Slavery, and Freedom in the Revolutionary Atlantic, 1770–1820." PhD diss., College of William and Mary, 2016.

———. "'We Latter-day Saints are Methodists': The Influence of Methodisim on Early Mormon Religiosity." Master's thesis, Brigham Young University History Department, 2009.

"Kaal Hoek." Getamap. http://www.getamap.net/maps/south_africa/eastern_cape/_kaalhoek/.

"Kaffir: Racial Slur Used in Africa to Describe Indigenous African People." OriginalPeople.org. Accessed May 31, 2018. http://originalpeople.org/kaffir-racial-slur-used-in-africa-to- describe-indigenous-african-people/.

Kanfer, Stefan. *The Last Empire: De Beers, Diamonds, and the World.* New York: Farrar Status Giroux, 1993.

"King, Edward." British 1820 Settlers to South Africa. Accessed May 31, 2019. https://www.1820settlers.com/genealogy/getperson.php?personID=I137545.

Kotzé, D. J., ed. *Letters of the American Missionaries, 1835–1838.* Van Riebeeck Society, 1950.

Krüger, D. W., et. al, eds. *Dictionary of South African Biography.* 3 vols. Cape Town: Tafelbrg-Uitgewers Ltd., 1972.

Legassick, Martin Chatfield. *The Politics of a South African Frontier: The Grinqua, the Sotho-Tswana, and the Missionaries, 1780–1840.* Switzerland: Basler Afrika Bibliographien, 2010.

Lindenfeld, David and Miles Richardson, eds. *Beyond Conversion and Syncretism: Indigenous Encounters with Missionary Christianity, 1800–2000.* New York: Berghahn Books, 2012.

Lowe, Michael T. *African Eden II: The Lowes of South Africa.* Salt Lake City: Michael T. Lowe, 2007.

Lubke, Roy and Irene de Moor, eds. *Field Guide to the Eastern and Southern Cape Coasts*, 2nd ed. Rondebosch: University of Cape Town Press, 1998.

Lye, William F. "The Difaqane: The Mfecane in the Southern Sotho Area, 1822–1824." *The Journal of African History* 8, no. 1 (1967): 107–31.

Maingard, L. F. "The 'Lost' South African Tribe: Rebirth of the Koranna in the Free State." *New Contree* 50 (November 2005), 82.

Malan, Antonia. "Households of the Cape, 1750 to 1850: Inventories and the Archaeological Record." PhD diss., University of Cape Town, 1993.

Marloth, Rudolf. *The Flora of South Africa: Dictionary of the Common Names of Plants with List of Foreign Plants Cultivated in the Open.* Cape Town: Specialty Press of South Africa, 1917.

Marquard, Leo. *The Peoples and Policies of South Africa.* London: Oxford University Press, 1952.

Marshall, Richard. "A Social and Cultural History of Grahamstown, 1812–c1845." Master's thesis, Rhodes University, 2008.

Martin, Theodore. *The Life of His Royal Highness the Prince Consort.* 5 vols. New York: D. Appleton and Co., 1880.

"Massachusetts Passenger and Crew List, 1820 – 1963." Ancestry.com. Accessed July 31, 2019. https://www.ancestry.com/interactive/8745/MAM277_84-0845 (site requires an account to view).

McClellan, Grant S., ed. "South Africa." *The Reference Shelf* 34, no. 2. New York: H. W. Wilson Company, 1962.

Meredith, Martin. *Diamonds, Gold, and War: The British, the Boers, and the Making of South Africa.* New York: Public Affairs, 2007.

"Methodist Missionaries [Pamphlets] No. 4," in BP 4, vol. 43, Western Cape Archives and Records Service.

Missionary Register for 1842. London: L. and G. Seeley, 1842.

Moffett, Rodney. *A Biographical Dictionary of Contributors to the Natural History of the Free State and Lesotho.* Bloemfontein: Sun Media, 2014.

Monson, F. R. "History of the South African Mission of The Church of Jesus Christ of Latter-day Saints." Master's thesis, Brigham Young University, 1971.

Montgomery, John. *The Reminiscences of John Montgomery.* Edited by A. Giffard. Cape Town: A. A. Balkema, 1981.

"Mormon Preachers at the Cape." *Cape and Natal News.* March 15, 1862.

Mostert, Noël. *Frontiers: The Epic of South Africa's Creation and the Tragedy of the Xhosa People.* New York: Alfred A. Knopf, 1992.

"Motivation for the Excavation of Platberg Mission Station in the Eastern Free State." https://www.sahra.org.za/sahris/sites/default/files/additionaldocs/Platberg.motivation.pdf.

"Mowbray Branch Record, 1853–1869, 1886–1890." *Church History Catalog* 1, (1853–1859, 1864). Accessed August 2, 2019. https://catalog.churchofjesuschrist.org/assets?id=fc56569c-05bb-4a77-a9dd-7a9f66ce543c&crate=0&index=6.

Muller, C. F. J., ed. *Five Hundred Years: A History of South Africa.* 3rd rev. ed. Cape Town: Academica, 1981.

Murray, Colin. "Land, Power, and Class in the Thaba 'Nchu District, Orange Free State, 1884– 1983." *Review of African Political Economy* 11, no. 29 (July 1984): 30–48.

Nash, M. D. *The Settler Handbook: A New List of the 1820 Settlers*. Cape Town: Chameleon Press, 1987.

Nielson, Reid L. and R. Mark Melville, eds. *The Saints Abroad: Missionaries Who Answered Brigham Young's 1852 Call to the Nations of the World*. Salt Lake City: Deseret Book, 2019.

"Paddon." British 1820 Settlers to South Africa. https://www.1820settlers.com/genealogy/search.php?myfirstname=&mylastname=Paddo n&mybool=AND.

Pascoe, C. F. *Two Hundred Years of the S. P. G.: An Historical Account of the Society for the Propagation of the Gospel in Foreign Parts, 1701–1900 (Based on a Digest of the Society's Records.)*. London: Published by the Society's Office, 1901.

Pama, C. *British Families in South Africa: Their Surnames and Origins*. Cape Town and Johannesburg: Human & Rousseau, 1992.

Patrick, Denis H. Patrick, comp. "Settler of 1820: John Stuart Talbot and his wife Priscilla and their descendants in South Africa." SMG 203 (1), Talbot file, Albany Museum, Grahamstown, 38.

Peires, J. B. "The Central Beliefs of the Xhosa Cattle-Killing." *Journal of African History* 28 (1987): 43–63.

———. *The Dead Will Arise: Nongqawuse and the Great Xhosa Cattle-Killing Movement of 1856–7*. Johannesburg: Ravan Press, 1989.

———. *The House of Phalo: A History of the Xhosa People in the Days of Their Independence*. Berkeley: University of California Press, 1982.

Peterson, Paul H. "The Mormon Reformation of 1856–1857: The Rhetoric and the Reality." *Journal of Mormon History* 15 (1989): 45–63.

Phillips, Thomas. *Phillips, 1820 Settler: His Letters*. Edited by Arthur Keppel-Jones and E. K. Heathcote. Pietermaritzburg: Shuter and Shooter, 1960.

Plummer, Hakeem. "South African Shield and Assegai Spear." Cazenovia Public Library. https://www.cazenoviapubliclibrary.org/wp-content/uploads/2016/04/South-African- Shield- and-Assegai-Spear.pdf.

Port Elizabeth Branch, South Africa Mission. "Port Elizabeth Branch Record, 1858–1864." Church History Catalog. https://catalog.churchofjesuschrist.org/record?id=d4e3815a-e726-4272-8488-9360a6dbdabf&view=browse&subView=arrangement.

"Port Elizabeth to Boston, 20 Feb 1861–19 Apr 1861." Saints by Sea: Later-Day Saint Immigration to America. Accessed June 1, 2018. https://saintsbysea.lib.byu.edu/mii/voyage/318.

Port Phillipp Pioneer Group. https://portphillippioneersgroup.org.au/.

"Prehistory of the Port Elizabeth Area." South African History Online. https://www.sahistory.org.za/article/prehistory-port-elizabeth-area.

"Pretorius, Andries Wilhelmus Jacobus." South African History Online. https://www.sahistory.org.za/people/andries-wilhelmus-jacobus-pretorius-0.

"*Ptaeroxylon obliquum* (Thunb.) Radlk." South African National Biodiversity Institute. Accessed July 30, 2019. http://pza.sanbi.org/ptaeroxylon-obliquum.

Pratt, Orson. "A Series of Pamphets." Digital copy at Harold B. Lee Library, Brigham Young University, Provo, Utah.

Queenstown Free Press. Various dates, September 27, 1892; July 25, 1893; January 16, 1894.

Rafferty, Oliver. "Fenianism in North America in the 1860s: The Problems for Church and State." *History* 84, no. 274 (April 1999): 257–77.

Raper, Peter E. *Dictionary of Southern African Place Names*. 2nd ed. Johannesburg: Jonathan Ball Publishers, 1989.

Returns from Inspectors of Native Locations Under Acts Nos. 6 of 1876 and 8 of 1878, Detailing the Number of Huts, Natives, Stock, &c of the Several Locations up to the 30th April 1880. Cape Town: Saul, Solomon & Co. Steam Printing Office, 1880.

"Rev. Henry Hare Dugmore." British 1820 Settlers to South Africa. https://www.1820settlers.com/genealogy/getperson.php?personID=I3004&tree=master.

Richardson, Boyd. "Alfred Robinson's record of his service with British forces in the Second Boer War February 1900-December 1901." South African Military History Society. http://samilitaryhistory.org/diaries/alfred.html.

"The Right Hon. Nicholas Vansittart." *Memoirs of Eminent English Statesmen, Being a Complete Biographical Sketch of all the Public Characters of the Present Age*, 554–56. London: Thomas Tegg, 1807.

Robson, Linda, and Mark Oranje. "Strategic Military Colonization: The Cape Eastern Frontier 1806–1872." *South African Journal of Military Studies* 40, no. 2 (2012): 46–71.

Rosenthal, Eric, ed. *Encyclopedia of Southern Africa*. 6th ed. London and New York: Frederick Wayne & Co. LTD, 1973.

Ross, Andrew C. *John Philip, 1775–1851: Missions, Race, and Politics in South Africa*. Aberdeen: Aberdeen University Press, 1986.

Ross, Robert. *The Borders of Race in Colonial South Africa: The Kat River Settlement, 1829–1856*. New York: Cambridge University Press, 2014.

Sales, Jane. *Mission Stations and the Coloured Communities of the Eastern Cape 1800–1852*. Cape Town: A. A. Balkeman, 1975.

Saunders, Christopher, and Nicholas Southey. *Historical Dictionary of South Africa*. 2d ed. Lanham, MD: Scarecrow Press, 2000.

Shaw, William. *The Journal of William Shaw*. Edited by W. D. Hammond-Tooke. Cape Town: A. A. Balkema, 1972.

Shearing, David, and Katryn van Heerden. *Karoo: South African Wild Flower Guide 6*. Kirstenbosch: Botanical Society of South Africa in Association with National Botanical Institution, 1994.

Shigley, James. "Historical Reading List: The Diamond Fields of South Africa. Part I (1868–1893)." Accessed March 18, 2023. https://www.gia.edu/gia-news-research/historical-reading-diamond-fields-south-africa-1868-1893.

Shillington, Kevin. *History of Africa*. 3rd ed. London: Palgrave Macmillan, 2012.

Shingley, Dr. James. "Historical Reading List: The Diamond Fields of South Africa: Part 1 (1868–1893)." Gemological Institute of America.

Shipley, Zelda Jane Wall. "History of Susannah Bentley Wiggill Pioneer of 1861." Typescript.

Smith, Kenneth Wyndham. *From Frontier to Midlands: A History of the Graaff-Reinet District 1786–1910.* Grahamstown: Institute of Social and Economic Research, Rhodes University, 1976.
Soga, John Henderson. *The Ama-Xosa: Life and Customs.* London: Kegan Paul, Trench, Trubner & Co., Ltd., 1931.
———. *The South-Eastern Bantu (Abe-Nguni, Aba-Mbo, Ama-Lala).* Johannesburg: Witwatersrand University Press, 1930.
South African History Online. https://www.sahistory.org.za/
South African Heritage Resources Information System online. https://www.sahra.org.za/sahris/sites/default/files/additionaldocs/Platberg.motivation.pdf.
South Africa Mission Manuscript History and Historical Reports, 1853–1977. LR 8452 2. Church History Library, Salt Lake City, Utah.
South African Settlers. "Isaac Wiggill." http://www.southafricansettlers.com/?p=2030.
Speeches, Letters, & Selections from Important Papers of the late John Mitford Bowker, Some Years Resident and Diplomatic Agent with Certain Kafir and Fingo Tribes. 1864. Reprint. Cape Town: C. Struik, 1962.
"Staples, William Mosyer." British 1820 Settlers to South Africa. https://www.1820settlers.com/genealogy/getperson.php?personID=I22523&tree=master.
"Stockenström, Sir Andries." British 1820 Settlers to South Africa. https://www.1820settlers.com/genealogy/getperson.php?personID=I61794&tree=master.
"Stoney-ford." *The Journal of the Society of Arts* 24, no. 1,217 (March 17, 1876): 374.
Stow, George W. *The Native Races of South Africa.* London: Swan Sonnenschein & Co. Ltd, 1905.
Stubbs, Thomas. *The Reminiscences of Thomas Stubbs including Men I Have Known.* Edited by W. A. Maxwell and R. T. McGeogh. Cape Town: Rhodes University, 1978.
Sundkler, Bengt, and Christopher Steed. *A History of the Church in Africa.* Cambridge: Cambridge University Press, 2000.
Svejda, George J. *Castle Garden as an Immigrant Depot, 1855–1890.* Washington DC: National Parks Service, U.S. Department of the Interior, 1968.
"Sweetnam, James." British 1820 Settlers to South Africa. https://www.1820settlers.com/genealogy/getperson.php?personID=I21718&tree=master.
Talbot, Henry James. "Henry James Talbot and Descendants." Typescript in possession of authors, courtesy of Diana and Russell Lindeman.
———. "Short Sketch of the Life of Henry James Talbot in South Africa." Typescript in possession of authors, courtesy of Diana and Russell Lindeman.
Taylor, Rev. William. *Christian Adventures in South Africa.* New York: Nelson & Phillips, 1879.
Theal, George McCall. *History of South Africa Before 1795: The Portuguese in South Africa from 1505 to 1795.* Vol. 2 in *History of South Africa.* Cape Town: C. Struik, 1964.
———. *History of South Africa Before 1795: Foundation of the Cape Colony by the Dutch.* Vol. 3 of *History of South Africa.* Cape Town: C. Struik, 1964.
———. *History of South Africa Before 1795: The Cape Colony to 1795, The Koranas, Bantu & Portuguese in South Africa to 1800,* Vol. 4 of *History of South Africa.* Cape Town: C. Struik, 1964.

———. *History of South Africa Since September 1795: The Cape Colony from 1795 to 1828, the Zulu Wars of Devastation and the Formation of New Bantu Communities*. Vol. 5 of *History of South Africa*. Cape Town: C. Struik, 1964.

———. *History of South Africa Since 1795: The Cape Colony from 1828 to 1846, Natal from 1824 to 1845 and Proceedings of the Emigrant Farmers from 1836 to 1847*. Vol. 6 of *History of South Africa*. Cape Town: C. Struik, 1964.

———. *History of South Africa Since 1795: The Cape Colony from 1846 to 1860, Natal from 1845 to 1857, British Kaffraria from 1847 to 1860, The Orange River Sovereignty & the Transvaal Republic 1847 to 1858*. Vol. 7 of *History of South Africa*. Cape Town: C. Struik, 1964.

———. *History of South Africa Since 1795: The Cape Colony From 1860 to 1872, Natal from 1857 to 1872, Orange Free State from 1859 to 1871, S. A. Republic From 1858 to 1870*. Vol. 8 of *History of South Africa*. Cape Town: C. Struik, 1964.

———. *History of South Africa Since 1795: The South African Republic from 1870 to 1872 Synoptical Index*, Vol. 9 of *History of South Africa*. Cape Town: C. Struik, 1964.

———. *History of South Africa 1873 to 1884: Events in the Cape Colony from 1873 to 1877*. Vol. 10 of *History of South Africa*. Cape Town: C. Struik, 1964.

———. *History to South Africa 1873 to 1884: Twelve Eventful Years From 1873 to 1884*. Vol. 11 of *History of South Africa*. Cape Town: C. Struik, 1964.

———. *Records of the Cape Colony from January 1820 to June 1828*, vol. 13 of *The Records of the Cape*. Cape Town: Printed for the Government of the Cape Colony, 1902.

———. *South Africa: The Cape Colony, Natal, Orange Free State, South African Republic, Rhodesia, and All Other Territories South of the Zambesi*. New York: Negro Universities Press, a division of Greenwood Publishing Corp., 1969.

Thiriot, Amy Tanner. *Slavery in Zion: A Documentary & Genealogical History of Black Lives & Black Servitude in Utah Territory, 1847–1862*. Salt Lake City: University of Utah Press, 2022.

"Thomas Holden Bowker." Wikipedia. https://af.wikipedia.org/wiki/Thomas_Holden_Bowker, accessed 9 August 2019.

Thompson, Leonard. *A History of South Africa*. New Haven: Yale University Press, 2001.

Tilby, A. Wyatt. *The English People Overseas. Vol. 6, South Africa, 1486–1913*. London: Constable and Company, 1914.

Trollope, Anthony. *South Africa*. 2 vols. London: Dawsons of Pall Mall, 1968.

Turpin, Eric W. *Grahamstown: Hub of the Eastern Cape*. Grahamstown: Grocott and Sherry, 1967.

"Typescript History of Eli Wiggill." Church History Catalog. Accessed September 12, 2022, https://catalog.churchofjesuschrist.org/assets/78e69525-f991-4ea7-971a-2db927a299ff/0/0.

"Uitenhage." South African History Online. https://www.sahistory.org.za/place/uitenhage.

U.S. Census. "1920 US Census for Maine, Knox Township." FamilySearch. Accessed July 31, 2019. https://www.familysearch.org/ark:/61903/3:1:33S7-9R6L-Q5Y?i=12&cc=1488411.

Van der Hoogt, C. W. *The Story of the Boers Narrated by Their Own Leaders: Prepared Under the Authority of the South African Republics.* New York: Harper & Brothers, 1900.
Van Heerden, Gary Paul. "The Work of the Reverend James Cameron of the Wesley Methodist Missionary Society, 1829 to 1835." Master's thesis, Rhodes University, 1993.
Van Schalkwyk, Helena. *Afrikaans.* Birmingham: Southern Book Publishers, 1988.
Verwey, E. J., ed. *New Dictionary of South African Biography.* Pretoria: HSRC Publishers, 1995.
Voigt, J. C. *Fifty Years of the History of the Republic in South Africa (1795–1845).* 2 vols. New York: Negro Universities Press, a division of Greenwood Publishing Corp., 1969.
Voss, Megan. "Urbanizing the North-eastern Frontier: The Frontier Intelligentsia and the Making of the Colonial Queenstown, c. 1859–1877." Master's thesis, University of Cape Town, 2012.
Wagenaar, Elise J. C. "A History of the Thembu and Their Relationship with the Cape, 1850– 1900." PhD diss., Rhodes University, 1988.
Wagner, Percy Albert. *The Diamond Fields of Southern Africa.* Cape Town: C. Struik, Ltd., 1971.
Walker, Eric A. *A History of South Africa.* Toronto: Longmans, Green, and Co., 1947.
Walker, William Holmes. *Missionary Journals of William Holmes Walker: Cape of Good Hope South Africa, 1852–1855.* Transcribed by Ellen Dee Walker Leavitt. Provo: Ellen Dee Walker & the John Walker Family Organisation, 2003.
Watson, R. L. "Missionary Influence at Thaba Nchu, 1833–1854: A Reassessment." *The International Journal of Africa Historical Studies* 10, no. 3 (1977): 394–407.
Weaver, Rev. G. "SOUTH AFRICA: A Trip with the Chairman through the Northern Part of the Queenstown District." *Wesleyan Methodist Magazine*, Missionary Notices (December 1886), 283.
Wesleyan-Methodist Magazine for 1852. Fourth series. Vol. 8. London: John Mason, 1852.
The Wesleyan Missionary Notices Relating Principally to the Foreign Missions . . . The Methodist Conference vol. 7 for the year 1849. London: Wesleyan Mission House, 1849.
Western Cape Archives. MOK vol. 59 1/1/62, no. 6132.
Whiteside, J. *History of the Wesleyan Methodist Church of South Africa.* London/Capetown: Elliot Stock/Juta & Co, 1906.
Whittaker, David J. "Orson Pratt: Prolific Pamphleteer." *Dialogue: A Journal of Mormon Thought* 15, no. 3 (Autumn 1982): 27–41.
Wiggill, Ann H. "Ann H. Wiggill to Henry Talbot, May 6, 1884." Church History Library, Salt Lake City, Utah.
Wiggill, Douwina. Letter to Ms. Sandra Fold, October 25, 1986. MSS 18 378. Cory Library, Rhodes University, Eastern Cape, South Africa.
Wiggill, Eli. "Eli Wiggill Autobiography." Church History Catalog. Accessed September 12, 2022. https://catalog.churchofjesuschrist.org/assets/c77ff79e-114e-495a-82be-73f1429e3088/0/0.
———. "Eli Wiggill Autobiography." MSS 9137, L. Tom Perry Special Collections, Harold B. Lee Library, Brigham Young University, Provo, Utah.

―――. "Eli Wiggill History." British 1820 Settlers to South Africa. Accessed September 12, 2022. https://www.1820settlers.com/genealogy/Media/documents/Eli%20Wiggill%20History.p df.

Wiggill, Isaac. "Last Will and Testament, August 2, 1856." MOOC 7/1/266, no. 86. Western Cape Archives.

―――. "Letter of Isaac Wiggill to William Hayward, 25 August 1824." Book 8541, Western Cape Archives.

Wiggill, Theo N. *The Cotswolds to the Cape: Isaac Wiggill, 1820 Settler*. Melbourne, Victoria: Monash University, 2012.

WikiTree, s. v., "Gerrit Victor." https://www.wikitree.com/genealogy/Victor-Family-Tree-214.

"Wild, Abraham." British 1820 Settlers to South Africa. https://www.1820settlers.com/genealogy/getperson.php?personID=I50383&tree=master.

Williams, Gardner Fred. *The Diamond Mines of South Africa*. Vol. 1. New York: B. F. Buck & Co., 1905.

Wilmot, Alexander. *History of the Colony of the Cape of Good Hope. From its Discovery to the Year 1819 by A. Wilmot from 1820 to 1868 by the Honorable John C. Chase*. Cape Town: J. C. Juta, 1869.

Wilson, M. "Co-Operation and Conflict: The Eastern Cape Frontier." In *A History of South Africa to 1870*, ed. M. Wilson and L. Thompson, 233–71. Boulder: Westview Press, 1983.

Wilson, Monica, and Leonard Thompson, eds. *The Oxford History of South Africa*. 2 Vols. Oxford: Oxford University Press, 1971.

"Winterberg (Eastern Cape)." Wikipedia. Accessed June 1, 2018 https://en.wikipedia.org/wiki/Winterberg_(Eastern_Cape).

"The Work in Hindostan: Extracts of Letters from Elders William Willes and Joseph Richards." *Latter-day Saint Millennial Star* 14, no. 34 (1852): 541–42.

Woods, Fred E. "East to West through North and South: Mormon Immigration to and through America during the Civil War." *BYU Studies* 39, no. 1 (2000): 7–29.

―――. "From South Africa to Salt Lake City: Eli Wiggill, the Latter-day Saints, and the World of Religion," *Historia* 64, no. 1 (May 2019): 1–22.

―――. *Saints by Sea: Latter-day Saint Immigration to America*. Harold B. Lee Library, Brigham Young University, Provo, Utah. https://saintsbysea.lib.byu.edu/.

Worsfold, W. Basil. *South Africa: A Study in Colonial Administration and Development*. New York: Negro Universities Press, 1969.

Wright, E. P. *A History of the South African Mission, 1852–1970*. 3 vols (1977–1986).

"Xhosa Royalty of Southern Africa." Geni. https://www.geni.com/projects/Xhosa-Royalty-of-Southern-Africa/14436.

Yale Center for British Art Collections Online. https://collections.britishart.yale.edu/.

Zarwan, John. "The Xhosa Cattle Killings, 1856–57." *Cahiers d'Études Africaines* 16, nos. 63/64 (1976): 519–39.

Index

A

Alacrity (ship), 154n5
Albert district, 229
Alfred, Prince, 158–59
Algoa Bay (Port Elizabeth), South Africa, 4, 5n11, 60n1, 85, 14n1, 143n4, 153–58, 160n1, 193, 209, 229, 235
Algoa Bay branch, x
Aliwal North, South Africa, 82–83, 229
Allison, Joseph, 94, 108
aloes, 195–96
Ames, William, 185–87
antenuptial contract, 226
ants, white, 39
apostasy, 137–38
Archbell, James, 60n1, 91
Armstrong, John, 200, 203
Atwood, Miner C., 159
Ayliff, John, 83, 87, 89, 104, 161n2

B

Backhouse, James, 74–76
Bain, Andrew Geddes, 248
Bain's Pass, 248–50
Baker, Thomas, 6n15, 7
Balfore, South Africa, 116
bamboo, 77
baptisms, 7, 133n6, 134, 137, 142–48, 166n9
Barolong, 60n1, 67, 94
Bathurst, South Africa, viii, 13–15, 42n5, 56–58, 60–62, 73, 100–103, 146
Bear River, 171
Bear, Cloake, 100, 108
Bear, William, 24, 101
Beaufort West, 244
bedbugs, 69–70
Bell, James, 65
Benguela (ship), 162–63
Bennett, Samuel, 6n15, 7
Bentley, Francis Parratt
  became Eli's father-in-law, 46, 179
  got wagon made by Eli, 216
  land of, Eli built on, 104

Bentley, Francis Parratt, Jr., 109, 157
  bought Teodores Rant land from Eli, 103
  exchanged land with Eli, 123
  gone to diamond fields, 224
  traveled with Eli, 137
  visited by Eli, 202, 228
  during Xhosa war, 108–9
Bentley, George, 85, 91–92, 94
Bentley, Harriot Kitchen, 179
Bentley, John, 56–57
Bentley, Thomas, 84
Bertrum, John P., 144
Bethany Mission Station, 232
Bezuidenhout, Caspar Nicolaas, 82
Bingham, George, 76, 85, 94
Birt, Samuel, 6
Bismark (ship), 191
Black Mountain, 30, 35–36
Black Mountain Pass, 36, 41
Blinkwater, 85, 100
Blinkwater Pass, 61–62
Boato, Covaus (Botha, Kobus/Jakobus?), 153
Bongolo (Wiggill homestead), viii–x, 122, 134, 144–50, 152–57, 200–206, 212, 217–25, 228
Bontebok flats, 150
Bonvana, 121
Book of Mormon, 135–37, 145, 149n8
Botanical Garden, Cape Town, 187–88
Botha's Bush, 108
Bowker, Thomas Holden, 119
Bradshaw, Richard, 6
Bradshaw, Samuel, 5–6
Brak River, 198–99
Brand, President, 210–11, 230
Brent, Thomas, 6n15, 7
Brown, Nathaniel, 204
Bruce, Captain, 118
Buffalo River, 204
Buffels Valley, 81–82
Burns Hill, 101
Busby Park, South Africa, 200
Bushmen. *See* San peoples.
Bynam, F., 251, 252n1

C

Caledon River, 66, 80, 89
Cameron, James, 79, 94, 96
Cape of Good Hope, 3, 159, 178–79, 185, 190, 226
Cape Town, South Africa, 187–88, 190–91, 228, 235, 239–40, 242, 245, 249–55
cars. *See* railroad.
Carter, Richard, 6n15
Cathcart, George, 119, 124, 129
cattle, 8n18, 13, 16–17, 26–27, 31, 34–37, 41, 48–50, 55–57, 77, 82–83, 87, 92, 97, 101–2, 105–11, 114–18, 123–29, 157, 168–71, 196, 233, 242
cattle-killing movement, 125–29, 161n2
cave paintings, 231
Chalmers, Thomas, 50
Chalumna River, 56
Chimney Rock, 170
Chipperfield, John, 56–58
Civil War, American, x, 163, 165n7
Clark, George and Mrs., 131
Cock, William, 15
Colesberg Kopje, 235
Colesberg, South Africa, 98–99
Collins, Colonel, 81
Compassberg, 28
conference, 150
Cook, John, 6n15
Cornelious, 85
Cowderoy, Lieut., 81
Cox, Major, 56
crossing the Line, 186, 253
Cumming, Gordon, 198
Curtus, Mr., 114

D

Daggaboers Nek, 65
Dale, John, 25, 32–33
Daniels, Mr., 204–5
Darling Bridge, 248
Darling, Charles Henry, 248
Davies, Joshua, 7
Davis, William, 123
de Pree, Jacub, 105–6
De Tijd (newspaper), 210
de Wet, Petrus, 82
Dean, Charles, 168
Deneson, Mrs., 94

Deodarus (ship), 185–87
Devil's Gate, 170
diamonds, 207–12, 234–41
Dixon, Henry A., 159, 198
Dixon, John Henry, 198
Dodge, Susannah "Susie" Margaret Lowe, 255–56
Domhas (Dumas), Rev., 74–75
Donkin, Rufane Shaw, 14
Doppers (Gereformeerde Kerke in Suid-Afrika), 232–33
Dordrecht, South Africa, 223
dreams, 136, 142, 155–56
Du Toit, Peter, 27
Du Toit's Pan, South Africa, 208, 235
Duff, Thomas, 104
Dugmore, Henry Hare, 7n17, 18n5, 21, 52n17, 53, 201–2
Duncan, Homer, x, 167–68, 171–72
Dunn, Mr., 246
Dutch settlements, 26, 66, 83

E

Ebden, D. (Alfred?), 234
Echo Canyon, 172
Edwards, John, vii, 60–61, 70, 107
Edwards, Mrs., 105
Elephant's food (shrub), 19
elephants, 20
Ellis, George
  baptized, 145
  discussed Mormonism with Eli, 142
  dream of, 155–56
  helped baptize and confirm Robert Wall, 148
  investigated Mormonism, 145
  married, 124
  moved to Algoa Bay, 155–56
  moved to Kaysville, Utah, 174–75
  worked as carpenter, 142–44
Equator. *See* crossing the Line.
Erasmus, Stephanus, 82
euphorbia, 195
Eurylaus (ship), 158–59
Ever, Mr., 121

F

fair/market, 21–23
Faku, 125
Fancutt, Catharine, 146

INDEX

Fancutt, Charles, 146, 196–97
Fango, Gobo, 161–62, 165–66
Fenian Brotherhood, 185
Fenmore (ship), 164
Fenter (Venter?), Mr., 232
Fernando de Noronha (island), 254
Fingos, 105
Fish River, 24
floods, 17, 88–91, 152
Florence, Nebraska, 167
Ford, Surveyor, 82
Fort Armstrong, 115–17
Fort Beaufort, 24, 103, 107
Fort Bridger, 171
Fort Hare, 117
Fort Peddie, 102
Fort Wiltshire, 19, 21, 53
Fotheringham, William, 159, 169
Frontier Wars, 8n18, 29–30, 101–19
fruits, 9–10, 189–90, 250–51

G

Garner, H. H. (W. H.), 69, 73
George Anderson (ship), 254
Gibbens, James, 206
Gibbins, George, 107
Giddy, Richard, 67–68, 80, 91–92, 94, 153
Gittens, John, 7
Goddard, Edward, 202, 221
gold, 212
Goldon, Mr., 88
Graaff-Reinet, District of, 29–30
Grahamstown, South Africa, viii, xiii, 8n18, 15, 19–20, 23–28, 30, 35–36, 39–42, 47–53, 56–62, 76–79, 83–85, 101–2, 115, 126, 130–31, 139, 151, 154, 157, 159, 187, 190, 196–99, 202, 208, 235, 248
grasshoppers, 179
Gray, George, 188
Gray, H. G., 82
Great Fish River, 16, 20, 199
Great Fish River Jungle, 198
Great Kei (Nciba) River, 55, 83n4
Green River, 170–71
Green, George H., 61, 92
Green, John, ix, 143, 151
Green, Mr., 147–48
Griqua. *See* Khoikhoi.
Groenkloof, 68
Grubb, Charles, 192

H

Hangklip Mountain, 219
Hankey, South Africa, 98
Harden, T. (Harding, Timothy Roland), 224
Hartley, Jeremiah, 78, 92, 94
Haslope Hills Mission Station, 83, 87
Haven, Jesse, 130n1, 132, 155
Hayward, George, 150–51
Hayward, William, 42n5
Hermanus Matroos (chief), 106
Hermanus Kraal (Fort Brown), 20, 24, 107
Hero (ship), 158, 162
Hex River, 246–47
Holden, Mr., 88
Holden, William C., 101
Holles, H., 203
Holt, James, 107
homesteading, 12–13
Hopetown, South Africa, 243
horses, 21, 26, 29, 37, 39, 77, 79, 92, 94, 101, 104–5, 109, 116, 124, 144, 151, 170, 172, 178, 192, 215, 241n8, 242–49
hospitality, 32–33, 37–38, 75–76, 83, 99, 189, 202, 218, 221
Hoston, John, 103, 107
hotel, at diamond fields, 239
Hottentot. *See* Khoikhoi.
houses
 Barolong, 67
 Eli's, 74, 91, 103–4, 122–24, 174, 176, 178–79
 George's, 113–14
 governor's mansion, 190
 Isaac's, 12, 205
 John Edward's, 69–70
 Korana, 77
 photographs of, 57, 176, 181
 William Lowe's, 180–81
Howison's Poort, South Africa, 197
Hudson River, 184
Hussey, Captain, 158, 162
Hyman, Mr., 192

I

Independence Rock, 170

J

James, Busby, 200, 203
James, Thomas, 257

James, William, 205, 222
Jennings, James, 121
Jones, Herbert, 252–53
Jones, Nathaniel V., 156, 164
Jubilee, 201–2

K

Kaal Hoek, South Africa, 86, 203
Kaffir mellons, 33
Kaffirs. *See* Xhosa.
Karoo, 247n7
Kat River, 24, 50
Katberg Hill, 199
Kay, William, 174n1
Kaysville, Utah, 174n1
Keiskamma River, 21, 52, 93, 101
Kennedy, A., 127
Kennersley Castle (ship), 5–6
Khoikhoi, 31, 38, 50–51, 68n13, 70–80, 85n2, 94, 97, 105–18, 200, 207n4, 211, 231–32
  war with, 105–18
Kidson, William, 39–41, 245
Kimberly Diamond Mine, 240–41
King William's Town, South Africa, 204
King, Edward
  emigrated, 6n15
  had to let Eli go home, 41, 245
  took Eli as helper, 19, 25
  as trader, 19–41
King, Henry, 6n15, 7
King, Joseph, Sr., 6n15, 7, 62
King, Philip, 6n15, 7
King, Philip (son of Joseph Sr.), 62–63
Klaas Smits River, 83, 200
Knots, Geart (Knoetze, Gerrit or Gert?), 35
Konap River, 24, 86, 199, 203
Korana, 71, 73–74, 77. *See also* Khoikhoi.
Korana Mission Station, 72, 77
Kowie River, 13
Kowie, South Africa, 14–15
Kraai/Crow River, 81–82
Krantz, Dr., 223
Kreewogon (Cruywagen?), Mrs., 190
Kreli, 126, 217n1
Kurgon, John, 83
Kye River. *See* Great Kei (Nciba) River.

L

Langfield, Mr., 200

Lemon Valley, 11
Lemue, Jean Louis Prosper, 73
Lesseyton Mission Station, 142, 219
Letu (Xhosa chief), 53
Links, Peter, 94
lions, 66, 79
Lloyd, William and Mrs., 131
Lombard, Mr., 65
Loopfork Ferry, 169
Lowe, Cecil, 256n4
Lowe, Eric, 256n4
Lowe, Frances, 256n4
Lowe, James, 183
Lowe, Marjory, 256n4
Lowe, Reginald, 256n4
Lowe, William Francis, 256n4
Lowe, William J.
  arrived in Grahamstown, 198
  called to settle Bear Lake Valley, 180
  diamond claims of, 237
  fixed up house and shop in South Africa, 203–4
  found lodgings in New York, 184–85
  got wagon made by Eli, 216
  home of, in South Africa, 181
  moved back to Utah, 256
  traveled from Cape Town to Algoa Bay, 191–92
  traveled to South Africa, 185–87
  wanted to go to South Africa, 180–81
  went sightseeing in Algoa Bay, 193
  worked in diamond fields, 223

M

Manatees, 68, 74, 92, 94
map, xiv
Maphasa, 119
Maqoma, 53–54, 115n2
Maytham, William, 207
McCloud, Mr., 185
mills
  gristmill, 43, 59, 85, 123
  water mill, 78–79
  windmill, 41, 42nn4–5
Mirametsu Mission Station, 74
missionaries
  Latter-day Saint, 130–36
  Quaker, 74–76
  Wesleyan, 47n5, 60–79, 83n5, 87n7, 91–92, 94–96, 97, 102n6

INDEX

Wesleyan, photograph of, 92
Mitton, Ellen, 25
Mitton, John, 25, 32–33
Modder River, 96
Montgomery, Mr. and Mrs., 99
Moroka, 67, 94
Morris, Mary Jane, 151
Morris, William, 151–52
Moshesh, 125
Mossel Bay, 191
Mottle, William, 74
Mount Coke Mission Station, 53
Mowbray Branch, 188n6
Murison, A., 251
Murphy, James, 216, 232

N

Native Americans, 169
Naylor Brothers, 178
New York City, 184–85
Newth, William, 6n15, 7
Ngquika, 8n18, 111n5
Nickelson, Mr., 206
Nongqawuse, 126
Nonkosi, 126

O

Old Neptune, 186, 253
Omaha (steamboat), 166
Orange Free State, South Africa, 210, 230
Orange River, 66, 81, 88, 98, 229, 242–43
Orphan Chamber, 225–26
ostrich, 16, 230
ostrich feathers, 16, 39, 68
Ottawa, Canada, 183
oxen, x, 7–10, 19–20, 25, 27, 31–37, 49, 55–56, 65–68, 77, 80–81, 85, 88, 90, 96, 98, 100, 104, 108–9, 114–18, 121, 125, 128, 146n6, 154–57, 167, 174–77, 195–96, 199, 207n4, 213–14, 224, 229, 232, 242

P

Paddon, Mr., 219
Parker, Mr., 239
Parker, Stafford, 211
Parker, Thomas and Mrs., 131, 136
Paul, Mr., 174
Paxton, G., 94
Penfold, Mary Ann, 189

Penhoek Pass, 88
Pertouers, William, 96
Philip, John, 49, 97–98
Philippolis Mission Station, 97–98
Phillips, Thomas, 6n14
Piccadilly (ship), 252–54
Pieter Tetief Bush, 43–44
Pinket Vail, South Africa, 86
Pienaar, John, 71, 75
Platberg Mission Station, 78, 91n9
Platte River, 169–70
Pniël Mission Station, 209, 211
poetry, 16–17, 52, 59
Port Elizabeth. *See* Algoa Bay (Port Elizabeth).
Port Elizabeth Branch, ix
Post Retief, South Africa, 101, 105, 108–9, 118
Pote, Harriet, 85
Pratt, Orson, 136–37, 149
Pretorius, Marthinus Wessel, 210–11
prickly pear, 20, 199
Prince, George, daughter of, 151
Pringle, Mr., 110

Q

Quakers, 75–76
Queenstown, South Africa, viii–ix, xi, 119–24, 133, 137, 141–56, 159, 192, 200–201, 204–7, 216–25, 229, 233, 240, 242, 256n4
Quivt, Spellman, 110

R

Race Horse (ship), 157, 160–64
railroad, 164–65, 183–84, 250, 254–55
Ralph, Joseph, 151, 202, 219, 221
rations, from government, 5, 12–13
rice ants, 39, 230
Rich, Captain, 154–55
Rich, Mrs., 154–55, 192
Richards, Joseph, 92, 130n1
Ridgway, Mr., 121
Robison, Mr., 121–24
Rondebosch, South Africa, 190
Rook, George, 188–91
Roorke, Mr., 103
Roper, Charles, 114, 172
Rowland, Mr., 66
Ruck, George, 228, 250
Ruck, George, Jr., 252–54

S

Sacuekanyale, 92
Saddler, Miss, 229
Salt, Mrs., 103
San peoples, 28–29, 81, 97, 230–32
Sand River, 73–74
Sandilli, 111
Searles, John, Capt., 157, 160, 162
Searles, John, Jr., 162
Shaw, Barnabas, 60nn1–2, 77–78
Shaw, William, 47, 131n2
sheep, 13, 17, 26–27, 29, 41, 44, 49, 83, 86–89, 101, 107, 111, 124, 160–61, 166, 202–3, 205, 207n4
Shepstone, Wm., 92, 119, 122
Shone, Thomas, 56–57
Sir Lowry's Pass, 247
Slaughter, Edward, x, 155, 159, 192
slaves, 5n12, 34n2, 63–64
Smith, Colonel, 52
Smith, G. (John?), 102
Smith, Harry, 119, 229n4
Smith, John, 186
Smith, Joseph, Jr., 135, 149
Smith, Leonard I., 130n1, 132, 155
Smiths Camp, 109–12
Soga, Tausi, 92
soldiers, 98–99
Somerset, Charles, 14–15, 226
Somerset, Henry, 115–16
Southey, Mr., 239
Spekbloom, 19
Spitskop, 28
St. Helena (island), 252
St. Mark's Mission Station, 217
Staats, Captain, 191
Stanton, Mr., 104–5
Staples, Mr., 135
Staples, John, 121
Staples, William, 221
Stellenbosch, South Africa, 250
Stock, John, 154–55, 159
Stockenstrom, Andries, 65, 81
Stormberg Spruit, 66
Straidam (Strydom or Strijdom?), Daniel, 38
Sulpher Springs, 81–82
Sumner, George, 220
Swartberg, 30, 35–36, 246
Swartberg Port, 41
Swartruggens, 244
Sweetnam, James, 109, 118, 203
Sweetnam, Ruth. *See* Ruth Sweetnam Talbot.
Sweetwater River, 170
Swellendam, South Africa, 35
Swift, William, 157–58

T

Taaibosch, Gert, 78
Taaibosch, Isica, 73–74, 78
Taaibosch, John, 78–79
Table Bay, 187
Table Mountain, 6n14, 87n6, 187, 189
Tafelberg's Neck, 87
Talbot, Charles, 196–97
Talbot, Henry James
    adopted Xhosa boy, 161
    appointed president of branch, 154
    arrived at Salt Lake City, 172
    attended conference, 150–51
    chosen as chaplain for wagon company, 168
    converted to Mormonism, 141–42
    described country where emigrated to, 5n11
    described Xhosa mode of attack, 49n10
    family of, 145–46
    helped baptize and confirm Robert Wall, 147–48
    moved to Port Elizabeth, ix, 153
    photograph of, 146
    proselytized, ix
    on Rev. William Shaw, 48n5
    sailed for Boston, 160
    spoke at Eli's funeral, 257
Talbot, Henry James, Jr., 148, 153
Talbot, John, x–xi, 159, 169
Talbot, Lavinia Ann, 146
Talbot, Ruth Sweetnam, ix, 141n1, 146
Talbot, Thomas B., x, 156, 160–61, 167, 177
    moved to Kaysville, Utah, 174–75
Tambookie (Thembu), 119, 121, 125
Tarka River, 86, 203
Taylor, John, 255
Teodores Rant, 103
Thaba 'Nchu Mission Station, viii, 60n1, 67, 73, 80, 90–91, 94, 96
The Friend (newspaper), 209
Theophilus Mission Station, 50
Thompson, Jane, 252
thunderstorms, 25, 90, 150–52, 221–22
timber, 41, 43, 45, 58, 187–88

INDEX

Toronto, Canada, 183
Transvaal, South Africa, 210–11
Trollip, Stephen, 121
Tyali (Xhosa chief), 49, 53

U

Uitenhage (Kariega), South Africa, 30, 49, 178, 193, 195, 206
Umlangeni, 125, 128
Umpukani (Umpukane) Mission Station, viii, 60n1, 68–70, 73, 92, 94
Unity (ship), 154–55
Upper Blinkwater, South Africa, 106

V

Vaal River, 27
van der Stel, Simon, 250
van Dyk, Joseph, 26
van Niekerk, Schalk, 207
van Wyk, Adriaan, 208
Vansittart, Nicholas, 3
vegetables, 12, 117
Vet River, 233
Victor, Gerrit, 26
Victoria, South Africa, 101

W

Waay Plaats, 57
wagons, 106, 212–15, 241n8
　painting of, 14
　photograph of, 7
Walker, George Washington, 74–76
Walker, William Holmes, vii–viii, 130n1, 131n2–4, 132–39, 173, 188n6
Wall, Robert, 141, 146–49, 153
Wall, Robert (young man), 161
Wall, William Wilson, 146
War of the Axe, 101–3
Warner, Joseph Cox, 121
Waterboer, Nicholaas (Griqua chief), 211
Waters, Canon, 217
Watson, John, 201
Watson, William Henry, 146
Weber River, 172
Weir, James, 51
Wellington, South Africa, 249–50
Wesley, John, 131n2, 139, 145
Wesleyville, South Africa, 55
Westerbar, Mathew Roudman, 219

White, Mr., 178
Whitehead, George, 219
Whiteing, Mr., 178–79
Whittlesea, South Africa, 119, 200
Wiggill, Aaron, 46, 157, 204–6
Wiggill, Ann Hammer, 256, 257n5
Wiggill, Eli, vii
　administered to Robert Wall, 147
　appointed conference president, 154
　appointed to build water mill at Platberg Station, 78
　appointed to Korana Mission Station, 72
　arrived at Boston, x, 254
　arrived at Cape Town, 187–88
　arrived at Salt Lake City, xi, 172–73, 255
　arrived at Umpukani Mission Station, 69
　attended conference, 150–51
　autobiography of, description of, vii, xi–xii, 255n3
　baptized, ix, 143
　became assistant to Rev. John Edwards, 61–62
　blind, temporarily, 41
　born, vii, 1
　in Boston, 164–65
　bought land in Queenstown, 122
　bought land in Salt Lake City, 178
　bought land in Teodores Rant, 103
　built home at Winterberg, 104
　as conference president in Port Elizabeth, ix, 154
　crossed the plains, 167–72
　cut timber, 41, 43, 45, 92
　decided to visit South Africa, 181
　at diamond fields, 234–42
　died, xi, 257
　emigrated to South Africa, viii, 3–8
　farm of, viii–x, 122–24, 134, 144–57, 200–206, 212, 217–25, 228
　head injury of, 100–1
　helped/traveled with Edward King, 19–41
　injured leg of, 10
　investigated Mormonism, viii–ix, 133–43
　as itinerant preacher to Koranas, 71–72
　lost wallet, 62–63
　married, viii, 46, 180, 256
　as missionary in South Africa, xi
　moved to Algoa Bay, 153–54
　moved to Bathurst, 58
　moved to home in Fifteenth Ward, 174
　moved to Kaysville, Utah, 175–77

moved to Queenstown District, 121–24
moved to Salt Lake City, 177–78, 256
moved to Winterberg, 59
nearly caught in water wheel, 43
ordained a priest, 143
ordained an elder, 145
as part of Homer Duncan Company, x–xi, 167–72
photograph of, 2
preached first sermon in Dutch, 70
rebaptized, 145
remarried, 180, 256
rode train to New York City, 183–84
sailed to Boston, 160–64, 252–54
sailed to Cape Town, 185–87
seasick, 160
separated from second wife, 256
sick, 256–57
sold Bongolo farm, 153
sold property in Queenstown, 124, 144
at Thaba 'Nchu Mission Station, 91–96
took steamer to Algoa Bay, 191
traveled by railroad to Utah, 254–55
traveled by stagecoach to Cape Town, 242–50
traveled to diamond fields, 228–33
traveled to Florence, Nebraska, 165–66
traveled to Queenstown to visit, 193–200
trip of, to Grahamstown for mill parts, 80–91
visited family and friends during South Africa trip, 188–206, 218–24
as wagon maker, 45, 47, 100, 103–4, 118, 123, 142, 144, 168–69, 178, 212–17
as Wesleyan Methodist minister, viii, 60–79, 91–96
Wiggill, Elijah
born, viii, 12
brought George to live with him, 222–23
built shop for William Lowe, 204
farm granted to, 122
got wagon made by Eli, 216
visited by Eli, 200–1
Wiggill, Elizabeth (sister), viii, 1, 220
Wiggill, Elizabeth Grimes (mother), vii–viii, 1, 41, 43
Wiggill, Frances (Fannie) Amelia (Lowe)
arrived in Cape Town, 187
baptized, 145
born, 104
lived in South Africa, 218, 222, 228
married, 180

moved to South Africa, 181
returned to Utah, 256n4
saw suspicious men near lodgings, 185
seasick, 186
Wiggill, Francis, 192–93, 196, 198, 216
Wiggill, George, 1
attended conference, 151
baptized, viii
camp of, 102, 113–14
died, 224
eulogy for, 224–25
homestead of, 113–14
investigated Mormonism, 133–37
led oxen, 10
married, 59
poor health of, 220–23
traveled with Eli, 61–62
visited by Eli, 203
as wagon maker and blacksmith, 85, 59–63
worked with Eli, 59
Wiggill, Henry, 192
Wiggill, Isaac
accompanied Eli to see Orange River, 85–89
built grist mill, 43
decided to emigrate to Africa, 3
detained in Winterberg because of war, 102
died, 178, 206
in England, vii–viii, 1
farm of, at Kaal Hoek, 86
mill of, burned down, 41–42
moved to Grahamstown, 42
remarried, 46
repaired water wheel, 99
settled in New Gloucester, Lemon Valley, South Africa, 6–8, 11–12
tried to give Bathurst farm to Eli, 103
Wiggill, Jacob, viii
Wiggill, James, 46, 201
Wiggill, Jane (Watson), viii, 201, 236
Wiggill, Jemima Rosetta (Ellis)
baptized, 145
eagle stole bone from hand of, 68
lived with grandfather Isaac, 103
married, 124, 142
moved to Bechuana Country, 65
sick, 94
Wiggill, Jeremiah Francis
baptized, 146
born, 73
decided to emigrate, x, 157

INDEX

did not plan to emigrate, 156
on guard duty, 171
helped build house in Salt Lake City, 178–79
married, x, 167
money of, from sale of cattle, 157–58
moves into Eli's home, 175–76
moved to Queenstown, 121
sick, 94
worked farm, 123, 144, 152, 177–78
Wiggill, John Wesley
born, 47
drove Eli, 201, 217
Eli stayed with, 212
as freight/transport driver, 144
got wagon made by Eli, 216
joined attack on Fort Armstrong, 116–17
log injured leg of, 100
moved to Bechuana Country, 65
moved to Queenstown, 121
picked up Eli's party on Queenstown flat, 200
saw Eli off from diamond fields, 242
soldiering of, 106–12
stayed with George, 85–86
taken prisoner, 109–12
worked farm, 123
worked in diamond fields, 223, 228
Wiggill, Joseph (brother), 1
accompanied Eli to Fort Beaufort, 65
emigrated to South Africa, viii
Francis Bentley stayed with, 103
married, 256
moved cattle near diamond fields, 233
sent oxen to Eli, 85
tried to attend George's funeral, 224
visited by Eli, 202, 224
Wiggill, Joseph Elijah (son), 119, 145, 178–80
Wiggill, Margret Alice (Talbot), x, 101, 143, 145, 167
Wiggill, Mary Ann (sister), viii
Wiggill, Mary Ann (wife of George), viii
Wiggill, Mary Sayers, 46
Wiggill, Mary Whitesides, 256
Wiggill, Moses, 46, 216
Wiggill, Priscilla Talbot, x, 167n1
Wiggill, Roseanna Maria, 102, 145
Wiggill, Sarah Ann, 48, 59, 143, 145
Wiggill, Sarah Ann Susannah (James), 94, 205, 222

Wiggill, Susannah Bentley, x
baptized, ix, 143
died, xi, 179
gave birth, 47–48, 73, 94, 102, 104, 119
married, viii, 46
not convinced about Mormonism, 139
as part of Homer Duncan Company, x–xi
photographs of, 46
rebaptized, 145
retrieved prisoners, 110
returned to Bathurst, 73
returned to Marimetsu, 76
sick, 99, 175
trip to convince Jeremiah to emigrate, 156–57
wanted to stay in Salt Lake City, 177
Wilcocks, John, 6n15
Wild, Abraham, 192, 196
wildlife, African, 9, 20, 27, 31, 66, 68, 196, 230–31
Wilkie, Mr., 63
Willow Park, South Africa, 228–29
Winterberg, 59, 84, 86, 100, 104, 203
Winterberg Mountains, 86
Winters, Mr., 218
Wittle, William, 114
Woodmansee, Joseph, 177
Woodruff, Wilford, 255
Wooley, Mr., 204–5
Worcester, South Africa, 247–48

X

Xhosa
cattle raiding by, 16–17, 107, 118
cattle-killing movement by, 125–29, 161n2
drawing of village of, 8
foods of, 127–28
history of, 11n1, 93, 217
hunting expedition of, 68
paintings of, 54–55, 115
trade with, 21–23
war with, xi, 8n18, 23n10, 48–58, 101–19, 217n1

Z

Zulu, 74
Zwart Kei River, 200
Zwartskops River, 193–95
Zyderlaan, Martin, 159

Also available from
GREG KOFFORD BOOKS

The Annals of the Southern Mission: A Record of the History of the Settlement of Southern Utah

James Godson Bleak
Edited by Aaron McArthur and Reid L. Neilson

Hardcover, ISBN: 978-1-58958-652-9

James G. Bleak's *Annals of the Southern Mission* (1900–1907) number 2,266 loose and lined pages and represent the finest early history of Southern Utah stretching from its initial Mormon settlement in 1849 into the early years of the twentieth century.

Bleak submitted the first portion of the history, numbering over 500 pages, to the Church Historian's Office in April 1903. He submitted additional increments of the manuscript when he visited Salt Lake City, usually for general conferences. He delivered the final installment of his Annals to the Historian's Office in October 1907. The complete holograph manuscript has been in the continuous custody of the Church History Department (formerly the Church Historian's Office) ever since.

Carefully transcribed and annotated by Aaron McArthur and Reid L. Neilson, this important work provides a detailed historical, ecclesiastical, agricultural, governmental, and cultural record of Southern Utah in the latter half of the nineteenth century.

Praise for *The Annals of the Southern Mission*:

"Professional historians and lay readers will be inspired by this vivid account of the pioneer experiences mostly before statehood or modernization. Developing water systems, establishing schools, creating courts and laws, constructing civic and commercial building and homes, raising food and animals promoting the arts, and generating faith and community harmony in some forty villages in Southern Utah and nearby Nevada and Arizona are all captured by James G.. Bleak. We will all be indebted to Brandon Metcalf for the fine Introduction and to Aaron McArthur and Reid Nielson for their brilliant editing of this important and extensive document." —Douglas Alder, Professor Emeritus and Former President of Dixie College

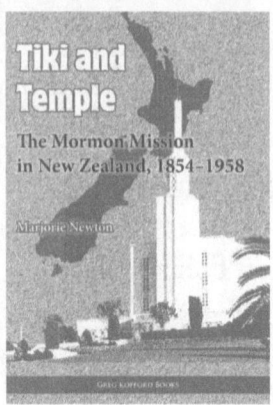

Tiki and Temple: The Mormon Mission in New Zealand, 1854–1958

Marjorie Newton

Paperback, ISBN: 978-1-58958-121-0

**2013 Best International Book Award,
Mormon History Association**

From the arrival of the first Mormon missionaries in New Zealand in 1854 until stakehood and the dedication of the Hamilton New Zealand Temple in 1958, Tiki and Temple tells the enthralling story of Mormonism's encounter with the genuinely different but surprisingly harmonious Maori culture.

Mormon interest in the Maori can be documented to 1832, soon after Joseph Smith organized the Church of Jesus Christ of Latter-day Saints in America. Under his successor Brigham Young, Mormon missionaries arrived in New Zealand in 1854, but another three decades passed before they began sustained proselytising among the Maori people—living in Maori pa, eating eels and potatoes with their fingers from communal dishes, learning to speak the language, and establishing schools. They grew to love—and were loved by—their Maori converts, whose numbers mushroomed until by 1898, when the Australasian Mission was divided, the New Zealand Mission was ten times larger than the parent Australian Mission.

The New Zealand Mission of the Mormon Church was virtually two missions—one to the English-speaking immigrants and their descendants, and one to the tangata whenua—"people of the land." The difficulties this dichotomy caused, as both leaders and converts struggled with cultural differences and their isolation from Church headquarters, make a fascinating story. Drawing on hitherto untapped sources, including missionary journals and letters and government documents, this absorbing book is the fullest narrative available of Mormonism's flourishing in New Zealand.

Although written primarily for a Latter-day Saint audience, this book fills a gap for anyone interested in an accurate and coherent account of the growth of Mormonism in New Zealand.

Lot Smith: Mormon Pioneer and American Frontiersman

Carmen R. Smith and Talana S. Hooper

Paperback, ISBN: 978-1-58958-692-5
Hardcover, ISBN: 978-1-58958-720-5

Lot Smith: Mormon Pioneer and American Frontiersman is the comprehensive biography of Utah's 1857 war hero and one of Arizona's early settlement leaders. With over fifty years of combined research, mother and daughter co-authors Carmen R. Smith and Talana S. Hooper take on many of the myths and legends surrounding this lesser-known but significant historical figure within Mormonism.

Lot Smith recounts the Mormon frontiersman's adventures in the Mormon Battalion, the hazardous rescue of the Willie and Martin handcart companies, the Utah War, and the Mormon colonization of the Arizona Territory. True stories of tense relations with the Navajo and Hopi tribes, Mormon flight into Mexico during the US government's anti-polygamy crusades, narrow escapes from bandits and law enforcers, and even Western-style shoot-outs place *Lot Smith: Mormon Pioneer and American Frontiersman* into both Western Americana literature and Mormon biographical history.

Praise for *Textual Studies*:

"An excellent and effective example of a 'life-and-times' biography, this history of the legendary Lot Smith as an imposing figure in the Mormon settlement of the West provides a fresh and very interesting retelling of that story. In the hands of two family members, the treatment is understandably friendly but remarkably thorough and complete. We follow Smith not only through his remarkable role as leader of the guerrilla force that harassed and delayed the U.S. Army during the Utah War but also his involvement in such other adventures as the Mormon Battalion, the Handcart Rescue, service in the Union Army, extensive involvement in polygamy, and an ambitious sortie into Navajo country that led to his death. This is a fascinating book worthy of a truly fascinating nineteenth-century frontiersman." —Gene A. Sessions, professor of history at Weber State University and author of *Mormon Thunder: A Documentary History of Jedediah Morgan Grant*

For the Cause of Righteousness: A Global History of Blacks and Mormonism, 1830-2013

Russell W. Stevenson

Paperback, ISBN: 978-1-58958-529-4

**2015 Best Book Award,
Mormon History Association**

"In Russell Stevenson's *For the Cause of Righteousness: A Global History of Blacks and Mormonism*, he extends the story of Mormonism's long-standing priesthood ban to the broader history of the Church's interaction with blacks. In so doing he introduces both relevant atmospherics and important new context. These should inform all future discussions of this surprisingly enduring subject."
 — Lester E. Bush, author of "Mormonism's Negro Doctrine: An Historical Overview"

"Russell Stevenson has produced a terrific compilation. Invaluable as a historical resource, and as a troubling morality tale. The array of documents compellingly reveals the tragedy and inconsistency of racial attitudes, policies, and doctrines in the LDS tradition, and the need for eternal vigilance in negotiating a faith that must never be unmoored from humaneness."
 — Terryl L. Givens, author of *Parley P. Pratt: The Apostle Paul of Mormonism* and *By the Hand of Mormon: The American Scripture that Launched a New World Religion*

"You might wonder what a White man could possibly say to two Black women about Black Mormon history. Surprisingly a whole lot! As people who consider ourselves well informed in African-American Mormon History, we found a wealth of new information in *For the Cause of Righteousness*. Russell Stevenson's well-researched exploration of Blacks and Mormonism is an informative read, not just for those interested in Black history, but American history as well."
 — Tamu Smith and Zandra Vranes (a.k.a. Sistas in Zion), authors, *Diary of Two Mad Black Mormons*

The Trek East: Mormonism Meets Japan, 1901–1968

Shinji Takagi

Paperback, ISBN: 978-1-58958-560-7
Hardcover, ISBN: 978-1-58958-561-4

**2017 Best International Book Award,
Mormon History Association**

Praise for *The Trek East*:

"In *The Trek East*, Dr. Shinji Takagi has produced a masterful treatment of Mormonism's foundation in Japan. Takagi takes an approach that informs us of Mormonism in Japan in a manner that focuses on inputs and results, environmental conditions in Japan and cultural biases of a Mormonism informed by western assumptions."
— Meg Stout, *The Millennial Star*

"This is a wonderful book, full of historical knowledge on a lesser-known subject in LDS history. The author, who is Japanese, LDS and lives in Virginia, is deeply invested in the subject and carefully includes all sides of the history."
— Mike Whitmer, *Deseret News*

"A monumental work of scholarship.... I can't imagine that any future study of this period could hope to provide a more thorough and engrossing analytical study of the origins and growth of the Church in Japan. This remarkable contribution is unlikely ever to be supplanted."
— Van C. Gessel, *Journal of Mormon History*

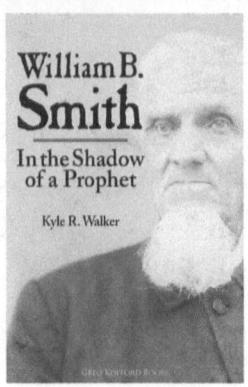

William B. Smith: In the Shadow of a Prophet

Kyle R. Walker

Paperback, ISBN: 978-1-58958-503-4

Younger brother of Joseph Smith, a member of the Quorum of the Twelve Apostles, and Church Patriarch for a time, William Smith had tumultuous yet devoted relationships with Joseph, his fellow members of the Twelve, and the LDS and RLDS (Community of Christ) churches. Walker's imposing biography examines not only William's complex life in detail, but also sheds additional light on the family dynamics of Joseph and Lucy Mack Smith, as well as the turbulent intersections between the LDS and RLDS churches. *William B. Smith: In the Shadow of a Prophet* is a vital contribution to Mormon history in both the LDS and RLDS traditions.

Praise for *William B. Smith*:

"Bullseye! Kyle Walker's biography of Joseph Smith Jr.'s lesser known younger brother William is right on target. It weaves a narrative that is searching, balanced, and comprehensive. Walker puts this former Mormon apostle solidly within a Smith family setting, and he hits the mark for anyone interested in Joseph Smith and his family. Walker's biography will become essential reading on leadership dynamics within Mormonism after Joseph Smith's death." — Mark Staker, author *Hearken, O Ye People: The Historical Setting of Joseph Smith's Ohio Revelations*

"This perceptive biography on William, the last remaining Smith brother, provides a thorough timeline of his life's journey and elucidates how his insatiable discontent eventually tempered the once irascible young man into a seasoned patriarch loved by those who knew him." — Erin B. Metcalfe, president (2014–15) John Whitmer Historical Association

"I suspect that this comprehensive treatment will serve as the definitive biography for years to come; it will certainly be difficult to improve upon." — Joe Steve Swick III, Association for Mormon Letters

www.ingramcontent.com/pod-product-compliance
Lightning Source LLC
Chambersburg PA
CBHW031328230426
43670CB00006B/277